Personal Investment Planning and Advice

Adrianne Johnson
Rachel Hirst
Lesley Cook
Wendy Telfer

BANKERS BOOKS LIMITED
c/o The Chartered Institute of Bankers
90 Bishopsgate
London EC2N 4AS

CIB Publications are published by the Chartered Institute of Bankers, a non-profit making registered educational charity, and are distributed exclusively by Bankers Books Limited which is a wholly owned subsidiary of the Chartered Institute of Bankers.

ISBN 0-85297-399-3

Contents

Introduction

This module has been written for students studying Personal Investment Planning and Advice for the Professional Investment Certificate. The module aims to cover all the material contained in the syllabus, the major areas of which are:

- Taxes and trusts

- Background to investment

- Nature of investments

The text is divided into 21 units which each deal with a different topic of the main subject matter. It should be noted that as topic areas vary in size, and as knowledge tends not to fall into sections of the same size, some units in this module are unavoidably longer than others. (Of course, the optimist might say that some are shorter than others!)

Each of the units consists of study notes designed to focus on the key aspects of the subject matter. These notes are divided into convenient sections for study purposes with each paragraph numbered for easy reference. Following each small group of sections there is a 'student activity' session which is intended to encourage you to think about what you have studied in the preceding few sections and to consolidate your knowledge. In the main, these student activity sessions comprise a series of short questions and a reference to the precise part of text (i.e. the relevant paragraph numbers) where the answer can be found is given for each. You are strongly encouraged to use these student activity sessions in order to test your understanding of the material. You should also note your areas of weakness and re-read the relevant parts of the text.

At the end of the unit there is a summary which states what you should have achieved from the study of that unit and should be used as a checklist.

Following this there are a number of self-assessment questions which aim to consolidate your understanding of the topic. The answers to these questions are given in an appendix at the end of the module. You should not refer to the text to assist in answering the questions.

It is anticipated that it will take approximately 150 hours to study the complete module. This will include time taken to complete student activities and self-assessments as well as any additional reading around the subject.

Although the module is designed to stand alone, as with most topics, certain aspects of taxation and investments are constantly developing with changes in legislation and the introduction of new and revised investment products. It is of great importance that you should keep up with the key areas of the syllabus and read around any topics of particular interest or relevance. Reading articles in magazines such as *Money Management* and *Planned Savings*, and using reference books such as the *Tolley's Tax Guides* and the *Allied Dunbar Tax Handbook* and *Investment and Savings Handbook* as well as the quality newspapers will increase knowledge and understanding of these topic areas.

Note that the masculine pronoun 'he' has been used throughout this module to encompass both genders and to avoid the awkwardness of the constant repetition of 'he and/or she'.

Study Guide

With an estimated study time of around 150 hours it is sensible to plan study time to cover the different topics, and to ensure that they are covered in the order that they are presented in the module. Each unit will assume that you have acquired the knowledge covered in the previous units so that the subject can be developed.

The aims and objectives of the syllabus are given below, and each unit also contains a list of the main topics to be covered and a summary at the end. These enable you to structure your study to meet these aims and objectives. The summary helps you to realise what has been achieved by studying a particular unit.

Everybody has their own method of studying and much will depend on particular circumstances and preferences. However it may be useful to look briefly at some hints on how to achieve the best environment and procedure for study.

Working conditions

(a) Choose a well lit, properly ventilated study area which is neither too hot nor too cold. Keep disturbances to a minimum and use a desk or table.

(b) Try to keep relaxed and get plenty of sleep and exercise. Keeping healthy and relaxed improves concentration and helps you to keep a better perspective on the work load. It also aids retention.

(c) Organise your time. Leaving study to the last minute will lead to panic and an approach that does not aid confidence or understanding.

(d) Prepare each study time. Write down the tasks to be achieved and then get on with the studying.

(e) Introduce variety by breaking up spells of concentration with short breaks. The student activities have been placed to help vary the type of study i.e. read some text, then complete the questions, then revise.

(f) Review your progress at the end of each study period. Some topics are more complex than others and it may be useful at the end of a study period to make a note of topics to review at the next study period to check understanding.

(g) Make notes while reading as this helps concentration and provides a summary for future reference. When completing calculations make a note of each stage carried out to enable understanding of the process at a later date.

Revision Techniques

You should aim to have completed your study about a month before the examination date. This will leave time for revision and practice of example questions from previous examination papers.

Everyone has their own approach to revision but it is useful to take a structured approach as with studying and to set objectives for each period of revision. Practice calculations and a style of writing explanations in note form. Ensure that you look at topics across the units as well as within each one. For example, it may be useful to build up comparisons of the tax treatment and risk profile of each type of investment and then relate these to different types of investor. Make charts and diagrams to help retention and to aid last minute revision.

In the final week revision should involve jotting down main headings and practising recall of those topics. It should not be necessary to refer to the text. This will aid recall in the examination itself where key words will trigger memory. Many students find the use of mnemonics very helpful.

Finally, remember that the examination is not just aiming to test knowledge but to test application skills, therefore it is vital to practice this aspect. If sample questions have been exhausted you can create a number of 'what if' scenarios of your own or use personal circumstances to test whether you can apply your knowledge. Use colleagues and fellow students to discuss any problem areas.

The Examination Paper

You are required to sit a three-hour examination which is divided into two parts. Part One consists of five questions, each worth five marks, broadly testing knowledge. Part Two consists of four case studies, of which you are expected to answer three, worth 25 marks each.

You are allowed to use non-programmable calculators in the examination so long as they are silent. You are also advised to note that individual questions may draw on knowledge from more than one topic in the syllabus

Examination Techniques

Once you are in the examination room it is important to remember the basic principles of examination technique. These can be summarised as follows:

(a) First read through the paper quickly looking for familiar words and phrases. This allows you to identify questions which cover the areas you have revised in detail and feel confident about. As there are two parts to the paper you may wish to tackle the first part before moving on to the second.

(b) Next read the questions in Part Two slowly deciding which ones to answer. Choose the questions carefully to ensure that you have interpreted them correctly. It is easy to see a topic and assume the question is aiming for a particular answer when in fact it is not. Remember that you have to choose three out of four questions to answer and you may change your mind on the one to reject on a closer look.

(c) Having chosen a question make sure you know what the examiner wants. As you read through the paper again underline the key words. Consider how you would go about answering the question.

(d) Choose the question you are going to answer first. Most candidates choose the easiest one first to give themselves confidence. Others may prefer to tackle the harder ones first and then come back to the easiest one when they are settled into the exam. You may want to answer the questions in Part One before moving on to Part Two to give yourself time to settle into answering more detailed topics.

(e) Once you have decided which questions you are going to answer, and in which order, work out the time you have to spend on each. The total marks for all five questions in Part One equal the marks for each one of the questions in Part Two so divide your time into four. Just to pass you have to score 13 marks in each question so if you only manage to complete two questions you will not pass. If you only answer three you will need at least 17 marks on each question to pass so it is best to ensure that you make a reasonable attempt at each question to ensure a pass mark.

Other points

Make sure your writing is legible and neat. The examiner must be able to read the answers! Make sure you follow the instructions for completing the answer book and where to write the question number etc. You can write your answers in note form unless the question states otherwise and this will save you time so do not start writing lengthy essays that are not required. Any calculations made should include full explanation of how you reached your answer. Even if you get the wrong answer you may be given marks for using the right method.

Finally, if you find you are running out of time make a plan of your intended answer as this may gain a few marks if it is clearly structured and self-explanatory.

The Syllabus

Aims and Objectives

On completion of this course, you should:

1.   Understand and be able to explain the practice of investment, the intrinsic nature of investments and their uses, risks, rewards and applications.

2.   Compare analytically and contrast different investments in the context of giving proper advice.

3.   Understand and be able to explain tax and trust law relevant to personal financial planning and take account of the influence and effect on investment considerations.

4.   Apply all of the above in advising clients and, in particularly, devising investment strategies and designing investment portfolios.

Content

The division of the syllabus into three main sections helps focus attention on individual subject areas and provides you with an appreciation of the balance of the subject matter. You should not regard the sections as being self-contained, it is in the nature of the subject that a full understanding of some areas of the syllabus demands knowledge of other areas. The questions set will reflect this.

1. Taxes and Trusts:

Personal taxes. Income tax: Liability to income tax; types of income; Schedules and cases; assessable and non-assessable income; allowances and reliefs; exemptions; deductions; employment/PAYE; self-employment - sole traders and partnerships; family circumstances - marriage and children; returns and payment timings; maintenance payments; covenants and other giving schemes; pension schemes; Miras; mitigation; rates of tax; anti-avoidance law; self-assessment. National Insurance.

Capital gains tax: What CGT is; liability; indexation; chargeable assets; exemptions; losses; rates; transfer of assets; rollover and holdover relief; bed and breakfasting; assets passing on death; payment; mitigation; self-assessment.

Inheritance tax: What IHT is; the taxable estate; exempt and potentially exempt transfers; gifts with reservation; chargeable transfers; spouses - special considerations; rates; payment; business property relief; mitigation; lifetime gifts; use of life assurance and annuities; equalisation of estates; use of settlements and trusts; use of a will; disposal of increasing value assets.

Stamp duty. Franked and unfranked income. Advanced corporation tax. Dividends. Trusts: Principles; types and uses; legislation.

2. Background to Investment:

Stock exchange (main market). Alternative Investment Market. Gilts market. New issues market. Options and futures market. Investment terminology. Investment theory and analysis. Sources of information. Risk: Market risk; product risk; degrees of risk within different products of the same type; provider risk; tax risk; offshore risk; clients' attitude towards risk. Rewards: Income; capital growth; combination of income and capital growth; security; protection; diversification; tax advantages/shelter; short, medium and long-term needs; relationships between foregoing. Inflation/deflation. The market economy. Interest rates. Exchange rates.

3. Nature of investments:

Deposit: Banks; building societies, National Savings Bank; finance houses; local authorities; money market.

National Savings: National Savings certificates; income bonds; pensioner's guaranteed income bonds; FIRST option bonds; capital bonds; children's bonus bonds; premium bonds.

Friendly society products.

Gilt-edged government and local authority stocks: Corporation and county stocks; local authority negotiable bonds.

Loan capital; corporate issues generally; debentures; unsecured loan stocks; convertible unsecured loan stocks; PIBS.

Share capital and equities: Ordinary shares; preference shares; zero dividend preference shares; convertible shares; warrants; scrip issues; rights issues; new issues; share options for directors and employees; securities.

Venture capital trusts; enterprise investment schemes; options and futures; traded options.

Collective investments: Investment trusts; unit trusts; split capital trusts; Peps.

Offshore deposits and investments: Types and sources, jurisdictions; OEICS.

Insurance bonds: managed bonds; guaranteed income bonds; growth bonds; property bonds; regular and single premium arrangements.

Annuities (non-pension).

Business expansion scheme.

Property: Real and personal; purchase (including mortgages); sale and letting.

Equity release schemes.

Currencies and hedging.

Protection products: Life assurance: Term assurance; whole life; endowment; FSAVC term assurance; personal pension term assurance; second-hand market.

Permanent health; medical expenses; critical illness. Long-term care.

Unit 1

Personal Taxes

Objectives

Students are required to study the following topics:

- **The personal tax system and how it works**

- **The formation of a Budget**

- **The legislative framework**

- **Residence and domicile**

- **Double taxation agreements**

---

1 Introduction

1.1 There are only two certainties in life according to Benjamin Franklin; death and taxes. Taxation affects every person in the United Kingdom regardless of their age or employment status. It is levied on earnings from employment, investment income and gains in the form of income tax and capital gains tax. It is also levied on the goods and services we buy in the form of value added tax, our residential property in the form of council tax and even when we die in the form of inheritance tax. In addition, we pay National Insurance to pay for state benefits. Some of these taxes are imposed directly on the individual while others are paid indirectly as part of a price paid for goods and services.

1.2 As the British tax system has developed it has become more complex. Exemptions and allowances have been made which are now accepted as standard, and tax rates and limits have tended to increase mostly on an annual basis. Employers have systems to deduct tax from employees' pay and the self-employed have to compile tax returns and give supporting evidence when making their tax payments.

1.3 The Inland Revenue is now trying to simplify the way in which income tax and capital gains are collected with the introduction of self-assessment and the use of current year basis. This has heightened public awareness of the British tax system, although their general level of understanding is probably low.

1.4 The information given in this module aims to give those involved in the personal investment market a basic understanding of the three main taxes, namely income, capital gains and inheritance tax, together with National Insurance, and apply them to personal financial planning situations. You will be able to make basic calculations and give general advice in particular circumstances. However, it is important to remember that taxation is a complex area and individuals should be advised to seek professional advice if necessary.

2 The Annual Budget

2.1 The annual Budget statement made by the Chancellor of the Exchequer is presented in November each year. Until 1993 the Budget was presented in the Spring and the Finance Act passed in the following July. However, since then it has moved to November to allow the Finance Act to be passed by the following March and so be implemented at the beginning of the new tax year.

2.2 In putting together his Budget the Chancellor will spend the previous months taking advice from his staff in the Treasury as well as his economic advisory group made up of heads of industry and eminent people from seats of learning. His purpose is to balance the government's estimated spending with likely income over the next year and he will set out specific aims at the start of his speech. This might include the aim of reducing inflation or maintaining a steady growth of the economy. Political influences cannot be avoided and different political parties have different aims, for example to be the party that cuts basic rate income tax to 20%. Of course the reality of keeping to a political party's vote winning declarations means that the books still have to be balanced and so the income lost by cutting income tax for example will have to be found elsewhere.

2.3 The Chancellor has to take account of inflation rates and the state of the economy, both in this country and also in Europe and worldwide. He will usually implement measures to close certain tax loopholes which have been brought to his attention as well as making changes to the welfare system.

3 Income Tax

3.1 Income tax was introduced in the UK in the 18th century by William Pitt to help pay for the Napoleonic wars. It lapsed in 1815 at the end of these wars but was revived in 1842 by Sir Robert Peel. It has remained a major UK tax ever since, raising more money for the government than any other source of funds.

3.2 Income tax is modified every year through the Finance Act which normally changes tax rates and allowances.

3.3 The other main legislation relevant to income tax is contained in the Income and Corporation Taxes Act 1988. The Inland Revenue also issues explanatory booklets and Statements of Practice which provide information on how the law should be interpreted.

4 Capital Gains Tax

4.1 Capital gains tax (CGT) was introduced with effect from 6 April 1965. The relevant legislation is found in the Taxation of Chargeable Gains Act 1992 although this has been amended since.

4.2 It is levied on the gains made from a variety of transactions, such as the sale of assets, and is payable annually at the same rates as income tax.

5 Inheritance Tax

5.1 Tax on estates and lifetime gifts has previously been known as estate duty and then capital transfer tax. Inheritance tax (IHT) was introduced by the Inheritance Tax Act 1984 and amended by subsequent Finance Acts. It is levied on certain lifetime gifts and on estates on death. It is also levied on certain transfers into and out of trusts.

5.2 Unlike income tax and CGT, it is a cumulative tax over a seven year period, with tax payable when the accumulated chargeable transfers exceed the nil rate band. There is only one tax rate, 40%, which has remained the same since 1988 although the thresholds have increased over that time.

6 National Insurance

6.1 The concept of National Insurance was introduced nearly 90 years ago, aiming to provide welfare benefits for everyone. The current relevant legislation is the Social Security Contributions and Benefits Act 1992 and the Social Security Administration Act 1992. National Insurance is the state's second or third largest source of income, with the 1996-97 tax year expected to yield over £41 thousand million.

6.2 Contributions are paid by employers and their employees, based on earned income. The self-employed also pay National Insurance. Contributions are accumulated to determine eligibility for certain state benefits. The rate of National Insurance contributions usually increases each year.

Student Activity 1

You should complete the student activity before reading the next section of the text. Answer the questions, then check your answers against the paragraph(s) indicated.

1. Make a list of the different taxes you have paid directly, or (1.1) indirectly, this month and how they were paid.

2. How does inheritance tax differ from income tax and capital (5.2) gains tax?

3. Who is liable to pay National Insurance contributions? (6.2)

If you are unable to answer any of the questions satisfactorily, you should read the relevant paragraphs again. Your understanding of the text will be further tested in the self-assessment section at the end of this unit.

7 Residence

7.1 An individual's liability to UK taxes will depend on his residence status. There are no hard and fast rules laid down in the relevant legislation about the definition of the various terms used but the notes that follow explain the terms commonly used following Inland Revenue practice. It should be noted that individuals may need to seek guidance on their particular circumstances and the Inland Revenue will need full details to make a decision on a person's residence status.

7.2   Generally speaking, the UK charges tax on:

(a) Income arising in the UK, whether the person to whom it belongs is resident in the UK or not.

(b) Income arising outside the UK which belongs to persons resident in the UK.

(c) Gains accruing on the disposal of assets anywhere in the world which belong to persons resident or ordinarily resident in the UK.

Residence

7.3   Residence relates to the status of an individual in a tax year and requires his physical presence in a country. A person will normally be regarded as resident for a full tax year if he spends at least six months, defined as 183 days, in the UK. The days of arrival and departure are normally disregarded. If a person spends less time than 6 months in the UK in a tax year he will be regarded as non-resident. There are, however, exceptions to this. Where a person visits for four consecutive years averaging more than three months a year (91 days) they will be treated as resident from the fifth year.

7.4   If an individual comes to the UK temporarily and spends more than six months here he will be regarded as resident. This could include foreign students who come to the UK to attend university or college, and persons who come to work here on a temporary basis.

Ordinary residence

7.5   This normally implies habitual or regular residence i.e. a person who normally lives in the UK will be regarded as ordinarily resident. This status applies over a longer period whereas residence applies for a tax year. Therefore an individual who leaves the UK for nine months could be ordinarily resident but not resident for that particular tax year. Conversely, someone who normally lives outside the UK but spends over 183 days in the UK in a tax year will be resident but not ordinarily resident.

7.6   The deciding factor in whether someone is ordinarily resident will be the regularity with which they visit the UK. If someone spends several months in the UK in one year but then does not come back in later years they could be resident for that tax year but not ordinarily resident. An individual who goes to work abroad for a period which will cover a whole tax year is regarded as neither resident nor ordinarily resident, provided any visits to the UK during this time total less than 183 days in a tax year and average less than 91 days in a tax year over four years. If employment abroad is not for a full tax year or the other conditions are not met, then the individual is treated as resident and ordinarily resident.

7.7   If a person coming to the UK for educational purposes intends to stay on in the UK after completing his education then he will usually be regarded as ordinarily resident. If a student stays in the UK for more than four years he will be treated as ordinarily resident from the fifth year regardless of intention.

7.8   If a person goes abroad for any reason other than employment then he can be treated as not resident and not ordinarily resident if he can prove his intentions e.g. by selling his house in the UK and buying one abroad. If evidence is not available at the time of leaving a provisional status can be granted and confirmed after three years.

7.9 Certain concessions apply to the granting of residence status where individuals leave or come to the UK part way through a tax year. This is important as it determines liability for UK tax. For example, if an individual who is not ordinarily resident in the UK comes to work in the UK for at least two years, he will be treated as resident from the date of his arrival. Therefore, his earnings can be taxed under the PAYE system from the date he starts work and will save delays and complicated arrangements. Note, however, that this may differ if there is a double taxation agreement, as explained below.

Husband and wife

7.10 A husband and wife are treated separately for tax purposes and so their residence status must be determined separately. If one spouse is a UK resident and the other is not then they will be taxed as though separated and the married couple's allowance will not be applicable. It may be allowed however, if there are children.

Table 1.1: Summary of liability to income tax

Income source	Resident and ordinarily resident	Resident but not ordinarily resident	Not resident
Earned in the UK	Taxed in the UK	Taxed in the UK	Taxed in the UK
Earned abroad	Taxed in the UK unless qualifying absence (see para. 7.6). If not remitted to the UK, may also qualify for relief	Taxed if received in the UK	Not taxed in the UK
Investment income earned in the UK	Taxed in the UK	Taxed in the UK	Taxed in the UK
Investment income from abroad	Taxed in the UK	Taxed if received in the UK	Not taxed in the UK

Residence and capital gains tax

7.11 If a person leaves the UK and ceases to be resident and ordinarily resident, any gains made after the date of departure are not chargeable.

7.12 If a person becomes resident and ordinarily resident during a tax year, not having been so during the whole of the previous 36 months, he will only be charged on gains arising after the date of arrival.

8   Domicile

8.1   This differs from nationality and residence and relates to the country in which a person has his permanent home. Domicile of origin refers to the country of birth and is normally that of the father, but can be that of the mother for illegitimate children. When a person reaches age 16 he can change his domicile of origin to a domicile of choice. Before this status can be granted a person will have to prove his intentions. Proof of this will include changing residence and obtaining citizenship of the new country but persons can live in a country for a number of years without changing their domicile of origin.

8.2   Domicile may affect tax liability if a person is resident in the UK but not domiciled here.

Domicile and inheritance tax

8.3   Inheritance tax (IHT) applies to all property, whether held in the UK or abroad, to individuals who are domiciled in the UK.

8.4   However, the definition of domicile is extended for IHT purposes and a person will be treated as UK domiciled if:

- He was UK domiciled within the three years preceding the transfer, or

- He was resident in the UK in at least 17 of the 20 tax years up to and including the year of transfer

8.5   This means that someone who emigrates to another country and acquires a new domicile will still be liable for UK IHT for three years after the new domicile was acquired.

8.6   If a person has a domicile other than the UK, IHT will only apply to property situated in the UK.

8.7   If there is a double taxation agreement, the situation may differ and relief on UK tax may be available.

9   Double Taxation Agreements

9.1   If a person has income or gains from a source in one country and is resident in another country, he may be liable to pay tax in both countries depending on their tax laws. To avoid this double taxation, agreements are often negotiated between countries to set out the taxation reliefs available to individuals in this situation.

9.2   The UK has over 90 double taxation agreements with countries around the world which apply to income and gains made either by UK residents abroad or to non-residents with UK income and gains. The conditions which apply in particular cases will be detailed in the relevant treaty. Some treaties are comprehensive covering taxes on income, profits and capital gains while others are more limited. There may be several treaties with one country covering different taxes and these may be amended in subsequent years. Each year the Inland Revenue consult with the UK business community before they draw up their annual treaty negotiations programme and priority may be given to particular areas such as setting up treaties with newly developing markets for UK businesses.

9.3 The usual situation is that where a UK resident pays tax on foreign income or gains then, if there is an agreement, any tax liability to UK tax will take into account foreign tax already paid.

9.4 Where a non-UK resident makes income or gains in the UK and there is a double taxation agreement, these may be exempt or charged at a reduced rate e.g. interest payments taxed at 10%. Normally the individual must be liable for tax in his home country to be eligible for UK tax relief. Generally speaking the following types of income will benefit from tax relief for a non-UK resident: pensions (but not UK state pensions), royalties, dividends and interest. Some exemptions from CGT are also available. If a non-resident is working in the UK he may be eligible for an exemption from income tax if he is in the UK for no more than 183 days and his employer is also non-resident. Where a non-resident has self-employed earnings he must not operate from a fixed UK base to qualify for a tax exemption.

9.5 If a double taxation agreement does not exist a UK resident may still be able to claim tax relief if he has paid tax already in a foreign country depending on special provisions in the relevant tax legislation.

10 European Community Legislation

10.1 With the growth in legislation which is implemented in this country as a result of EC legislation it may be useful to establish the different abbreviations used and who the member states are. The European Community (EC) was established in 1957 following the Treaty of Rome and was renamed the European Union (EU) in 1993 following the Maastricht treaty. Any reference to the Community as the EC will apply if it has been unchanged since 1993. For example, the EC Third Life Directive was made in 1992 and so is referred to as EC legislation but has been implemented in British legislation over several years since then.

10.2 The member states of the EU are as follows: Belgium, France, Germany, Italy, Luxembourg, Netherlands (all founder members), UK, Denmark, Ireland, Greece, Portugal, Spain, Finland, Austria and Sweden.

10.3 The European Economic Area (EEA) came into force on 1 January 1994 and includes the member states of the EU plus Iceland, Norway and Liechtenstein.

10.4 The tax liability of an individual will vary depending on his residence status, but if he is living or working temporarily abroad it will also differ depending on whether the country concerned is a member of the EU and/or EEA. For example, an individual working in an EEA country will pay National Insurance contributions to that country whereas in other cases liability is usually to the UK.

10.5 Liability outside the EEA will depend on whether the country has a double taxation agreement with the UK to prevent persons paying tax or NI contributions to both the host country and the UK.

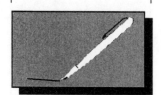

Student Activity 2

You should complete the student activity before attempting the self-assessment. Answer the questions, then check your answers against the paragraph(s) indicated.

Kim Tan is a Malaysian student who has just started a four year engineering course at Southampton University. He intends to return to Malaysia when he has completed his degree.

(a) What is his UK residency status while he is a student? (7.4)

(b) During his course, he works for a year with a UK civil engineering company. How are his earnings taxed during that time? (7.2)

(c) While a student, his parents send him regular lump sums which are paid into his UK bank account. Is he taxed on this? (7.2)

(d) At the end of the course, he changes his mind and decides to remain in the UK. This is mainly due to his marriage to an English girl and his new job with a UK firm. What is the domicile of origin of: (8.1)

- Kim?
- His wife?
- Any children they may have?

If you are unable to answer any of the questions satisfactorily, you should read the relevant paragraphs again. Your understanding of the text will be further tested in the following self-assessment.

Summary

Now that you have completed this unit, you should be able to:

☐ **Define the principal elements of the personal tax system**

☐ **Describe how a Budget is formed**

☐ **Understand how an individual's liability for income tax, capital gains tax and inheritance tax are affected by his residence status and domicile**

☐ **Know how double taxation agreements are used to reduce tax liability**

☐ **Know the member states of the EU and EEA**

If you can tick all the above boxes with confidence, you are ready to answer the questions which follow.

Self-Assessment Questions

1. What is the difference between direct and indirect taxation?

2. What are the four main personal taxes?

3. When does the annual Budget become enforced?

4. Briefly explain the definitions of the following:

   (a) Residence

   (b) Ordinary residence

   (c) Domicile

5. Why is it important to establish an individual's domicile or residence?

6. How is the residence status of a married woman determined?

7. Jane Brown was born in the UK and works for a British company. She owns a house in London and has a holiday cottage in France. What is the likely capital gains tax position if she sells her French cottage?

8. Which countries form the EEA?

9. Kevin Murphy is an American but has come to work in the UK for three years. He arrived in the UK in December. Will his earnings be liable for UK tax and if so, from what date?

10. Jenny's father emigrated to Australia two years before his death, changing his domicile at the same time. As his personal representative, will she have any liability to inheritance tax on his estate?

Unit 2

Income Tax

Objectives

Students are required to study the following topics:

- Types of income
- Liability to income tax
- Taxation of benefits in kind
- Tax schedules
- Allowable expenses
- Exemptions and deductions from income tax
- Taxation of married couples

1   What is Income Tax?

1.1   Income tax is an annual tax on income. It is levied on an individual's income from all sources and the rates increase for higher income levels.

1.2   There are certain exemptions and reliefs given to reduce tax liability, and different methods of collecting tax. For example, income from investments (known as unearned income) is often paid net of income tax and so collected by the investment provider e.g. building society. Employers are responsible for deducting tax from employee's pay while the self-employed are responsible for their own tax bill.

1.3   As income can arise from a variety of sources it is classified into schedules, some of which are further subdivided into cases, and reference is often made to a 'Schedule E taxpayer' or 'income arising under Schedule A' for example, to avoid having to make a full explanation every time.

1.4   Calculation of tax can be simple for those with few sources of income, or complex particularly for the self-employed.

1.5   The following three units explain the income tax regime, what is taxed, how it is taxed and how to calculate tax liability. Consideration will be made of different circumstances such as marriage and divorce, mortgage interest relief, convenants and tax mitigation. Units 2 and 3 cover employees, while Unit 4 looks at the differences for the self-employed and partners.

2   Who Pays Income Tax?

2.1   United Kingdom income tax is payable by all UK residents, on income arising in the UK and abroad, and by non-UK residents on income arising in the UK.

It is payable by trustees and personal representatives on trust and estate income. Companies pay corporation tax instead of income tax.

2.2　It is important to realise that the term 'all UK residents' includes children and that income tax applies to all income received by all residents.

2.3　The United Kingdom tax laws do not cover the Channel Islands and the Isle of Man, who have separate tax laws.

2.4　It should also be noted that there is an income tax liability on income from abroad, though in some cases double taxation agreements avoid the duplication of tax on income.

3　When is Income Tax Paid?

3.1　When income tax is paid depends on the type of income. For most people, income tax is normally paid when their income is paid. In other words, employees pay tax on their income from employment via the PAYE (Pay As You Earn) system. Tax is paid on a weekly or monthly basis, deducted from gross earnings to give an amount that is net of tax. This means it is a 'pay-as-you-go' tax.

3.2　For the self-employed, including sole traders and partners, income has been taxed on a 'preceding year' basis up to 1995-96, the tax being payable in equal instalments on 1 January in the tax year and 1 July following. Legislation was introduced in the Finance Act 1994 to abolish the 'preceding year' basis of taxation and replace it with a current year basis of assessment. New rules will apply from the 1997-98 tax year. 1996-97 is a transitional year, from the old to the new basis. Businesses that started up after 5 April 1994 were taxed from the outset on the new current year basis. This is covered more fully in Unit Four.

3.3　Tax on other income, for example from UK and foreign government stocks paid through a bank or other UK agent, may be deducted at source before the income is received.

3.4　The tax year runs from 6 April in the current year to 5 April of the following year and is normally referred to as the 'fiscal' year. This rather arbitrary date is due to a change in the UK calendar in the eighteenth century, but the reason for the dates is not as important as an awareness of the dates themselves.

4　Earned Income

4.1　Income classed as earned income for tax purposes includes wages and salary from employment, together with any bonuses and commission, plus 'benefits in kind', and statutory sick pay.

4.2　Earned income also includes income from a trade, profession or working in a partnership and any taxable amounts received on leaving employment, a trade or profession.

4.3　Certain pensions, for example from an employer's pension scheme, and income from furnished holiday lettings are also included in the category of earned income.

4.4   Certain state benefits are taxable as income. These are:

- Retirement pensions

- Widow's pension and widowed mother's allowance

- Invalidity allowance when paid with state retirement pension

- Statutory maternity pay

- Industrial death benefit paid as pension

- Job release allowance for periods beginning earlier than one year before state pension age

- Income support to unemployed (subject to special conditions)

- Income support to strikers

- Unemployment benefit (subject to special conditions)

- Invalid care allowance

5   Benefits In Kind

5.1   Benefits in kind include almost any form of indirect payment or advantage provided to an employee as part of the terms of his employment. Examples of typical benefits in kind are company cars and petrol, loans, living accommodation, vouchers and gifts.

5.2   Some benefits in kind are taxable on all employees, regardless of what they earn. Benefits in this category are the provision of living accommodation (with some exceptions, for example for caretakers) and vouchers such as child care or transport vouchers. Others are taxable only if earnings exceed £8,500 p.a.

5.3   Employees earning below £8,500 p.a. (under the 1991 Finance Act) will not normally be liable to any tax on other benefits in kind unless they can be turned into cash, in which case the assessable amount is the cash which could be obtained. This salary bracket of £8,500 includes the value of the benefits.

P11D employees

5.4   Persons earning over £8,500 a year are known as P11D employees after the tax return which employers have to complete on benefits in kind. Most directors are also included in this category, even if they earn less than £8,500. However, a director earning less than £8,500 a year, who works full time and controls 5% or less of the ordinary share capital of the company together with any associates, may not be liable to tax on benefits in kind.

5.5   For P11D employees, benefits in kind are taxable, usually at the cash value of the benefit. Certain special rules apply to company cars and petrol where a scale of charges applies, and on mobile phones supplied by employers, which are subject to a fixed benefits charge of £200 p.a.

5.6   The main taxable benefits in kind are outlined below:

- Company cars and fuel

- BUPA or similar health care

- Vouchers, gifts, holidays

- Transport vouchers

- Living accommodation

- Loans (with an exemption for small loans)

- Christmas parties (if more than £50 per head)

- Mobile phones, charged at £200 per phone, where the full cost of private calls is not reimbursed by the employee

- Use of employers' credit cards

5.7 The main current exclusions are:

- Child care supplied direct by employer

- First 15p per day of luncheon vouchers

- Meals in staff canteens

- In house sports and recreational facilities

- Counselling services to redundant employees

- Employer's contributions to an approved occupational or personal pension scheme

- Free car-parking facilities

- Payments to meet employees' personal incidental expenses when staying away from home overnight on business - up to £5 per night in UK and £10 per night abroad

Company cars

5.8 The main taxable benefit in kind which applies to a large number of employees is a company car. This will apply if the car is available for the private use of the employee or a member of his family. The value of the benefit is based on the list price of the car and a charge is also made for any fuel provided for private use.

5.9 The list price of a car is the manufacturer's published price including VAT and any delivery charges or extras. It excludes any discounts given by the dealer at the time of purchase. Also included are accessories worth over £100 that are added later (excluding mobile phones which are charged separately).

5.10 The maximum benefit that is taxable is shown in the table below.

Table 2.1: Car benefit scale charges 1996-97

Annual Business Mileage	Percentage of List Price
0-2,499 and second cars	35%
2,500 - 17,999	$23\frac{1}{3}$%
18,000 and over	$11\frac{2}{3}$%

5.11 A further reduction of one-third applies if the car is at least 4 years old. Where cars are worth more than £80,000 the benefit is restricted to an appropriate percentage of £80,000 depending on mileage.

5.12 The full charge also applies to any second and subsequent cars used at the same time by the employee or the employee's spouse. In the case of a car made available to a spouse in her own right who also works for the same employer then the spouse is taxed independently. Any contribution towards the purchase cost or running costs made by the employee will be deductible.

5.13 Where fuel is provided for private use then an additional charge is made based on the following scale.

Table 2.2: Car fuel scale charges 1996-97

Cylinder Capacity	Petrol	Diesel
Up to 1400cc	£710	£640
1401-2000cc	£890	£640
2001cc and over	£1,320	£820

5.14 These charges cover any other expenses and costs met by the employer incurred in providing the car and fuel. Any contribution made by the employee will be deducted.

5.15 The employer is liable for NI contributions on car and fuel benefits. However, the employee is not.

Vans

5.16 If an employee has private use of a company van, this is charged as a fixed taxable benefit of £500, or £350 if the vehicle is four or more years old. The benefit is reduced proportionately if the van is not available for the whole year, or by any contribution made by the employee towards private use. This charge applies to vans with a laden weight of 3.5 tonnes or less; there is no charge for the private use of commercial vehicles larger than 3.5 tonnes unless mainly used privately.

Mobile telephones

5.17 These are subject to a fixed benefit charge of £200 per annum provided the phone is not used exclusively for business use. If no private calls are made or the employee fully reimburses the employer for all private calls then the charge will not apply.

Permanent health insurance

5.18 Employers may offer a permanent health insurance (PHI) scheme which provides benefits if the employee is unable to work due to ill health. The benefits are paid in the same way as salary and so are taxable. However, there is no additional taxation on the provision of this as a benefit in kind. Employers can claim the premiums as an allowable business expense.

Medical insurance

5.19　If an employer provides medical insurance such as through BUPA this is treated as a taxable benefit in kind based on the cost to the employer less any contribution paid by the employee. Medical treatment paid for by an employer will be taxable unless it occurs abroad while the employee is working away from the UK. Insurance costs met by the employer for employment abroad are also not taxable.

Life assurance

5.20　Where an employer provides death benefits to employees this is not taxed as a benefit in kind.

Living accommodation

5.21　If an employee is provided with living accommodation by his employer then he is taxed on the value of the accommodation. This value is based on the annual value of the property, or the rent paid by the employee. Annual value is the rateable value.

5.22　If the cost to the employer of the property is more than £75,000 there will be an additional charge to the employee. This is calculated by multiplying the excess of the cost over £75,000 by the official rate of interest (as prescribed by the Treasury) applying at the beginning of the tax year, and then deducting any rent paid by the employee.

5.23　There will be no tax charges if:

(a) It is necessary as part of the employee's duties to live in the accommodation, for example, as a caretaker.

(b) The accommodation allows better performance of the employee's duties and the nature of the employment is one where it is customary to provide accommodation.

(c) There is a special threat to the employee's security and his accommodation is part of special security arrangements.

Loans

5.24　If an employer provides a cheap or interest-free loan to an employee, this is taxable as a benefit in kind for employees earning over the £8,500 limit and directors. The tax charge is based on the difference between the interest paid by the employee (if any) and the interest which would have been paid at the official rate of interest. This official rate is kept in line with typical mortgage rates.

5.25　The tax charge is calculated as the measure of interest saved by the employee, added to the employee's income and charged at his marginal rate of tax. The employee is then able to get tax relief on the loan as if he had paid interest at the official rate. Loans totalling up to £5,000 are exempt.

Workplace nurseries

5.26　If the employer runs a nursery or play scheme on the premises, or jointly with other employers on their premises then the cost of providing a place for an employee's child is not taxable. The employer will normally offer this benefit to employees for a subsidised fee. The employer must be involved in financing and organising the arrangement.

In-house benefits

5.27 Certain benefits may be provided by an employer because of the nature of the business or type of employment. For example, a teacher in a private school may get a reduction in fees for his own children. These benefits will be taxable based on the cost to the employer of providing them.

5.28 An 'in-house' benefit will include goods and services sold or produced by the employer which are offered at a discount to the employees, services and facilities provided at the place of work and assets owned by the business which are used privately by employees.

5.29 The cost to the employer of providing benefits such as these is usually based on the marginal or additional cost he incurs, therefore the following are generally disregarded as taxable in-house benefits.

- Goods sold to employees who pay at least the wholesale price

- Professional services such as legal advice the costs of which are repaid by the employee

- School fees of which a teacher pays at least 15%

5.30 Where an employee uses assets (other than cars, vans or mobile 'phones) owned by the employer, the initial cost of providing the asset is not treated as a taxable benefit if the asset remains the property of the employer. Instead, the annual value of the use of the asset is calculated as 20% of its market value when it was first provided, plus any additional expenses incurred in making it available to the employee.

Lump sum payments

5.31 Lump sum payments are generally made to employees when they begin employment, 'golden hellos', or when they leave, 'golden handshakes'. All lump sums paid to an employee as part of his terms and conditions of employment count as pay for tax purposes. However, certain tax payments made when an employee leaves employment are not taxable.

5.32 Non-taxable lump sums include the first £30,000 of payments made because of injury, disability or death-in-service due to accident but any amount which exceeds £30,000 will be taxed. Other lump sums which are only taxed on the excess over £30,000 include statutory redundancy payments and lump sum payments for loss of employment from an employer's own non-statutory redundancy scheme. Also included are lump sums paid for damages following an industrial tribunal or similar decision of wrongful or unfair dismissal.

Removal expenses

5.33 If an employee changes residence to take up a new job or because of a change of job or location with his existing employer he may be eligible for an exemption from tax provided that the expenses incurred are qualifying. The main rules are as follows:

- The residence must be the sole main residence of the employee

- The new residence must be within reasonable daily travelling distance from the new place of work

- The old residence must not be within reasonable daily travelling distance from the new place of work

5.34 The expenses and benefits which qualify for relief are those provided for the following:

- Disposal of the old residence

- Acquisition of new residence

- Transporting belongings

- Travelling and subsidence

- Domestic goods for new residence

- Bridging loans

Training expenses

5.35 If an employee is attending a training course which is relevant to his employment any costs and expenses paid by his employer or reimbursed to the employee are not taxable. This includes course fees, cost of books and travelling and subsistence costs if temporarily away from work whilst attending the course.

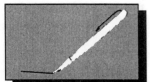

Student Activity 1

You should complete this student activity before reading the next section of the text. Answer the question, then check your answers against the paragraph(s) indicated.

1. Who is liable to pay income tax?   (2.1)

2. Emma has a company car with a list price of £8,000. It is a 2   (5.8-5.13)
    year old 2 litre car and she travels about 10,000 business
    miles a year. Calculate her taxable charge for the current tax
    year.

3. How are the following treated for income tax purposes?

    (a) State pension   (4.4)

    (b) PHI benefits paid by employer's scheme   (5.18)

    (c) Living accommodation provided for a school caretaker   (5.23)

    (d) Golden handshake of more than £30,000   (5.32)

If you are unable to answer any of the questions satisfactorily, you should read the relevant paragraphs again. Your understanding of the text will be further tested in the self-assessment section at the end of this unit.

6 Unearned Income

6.1 This is all income that is earned from investments. Income from certain investments is tax free, for example National Savings Certificates and interest from Tessas. However, most other investment income is liable to tax.

Such income includes:

- Interest on bank and building society accounts

- Dividends from shares, including investment trusts

- Dividends from unit trusts

- Income from government stocks and similar

- Income from trusts (but not pension trusts)

- Some rental income from property, though furnished property rental has been normally treated as earned income if it qualifies as furnished holiday lets

6.2 For the tax year 1996-97 and subsequent years, the tax charge on savings has been reduced to 20%, although higher rate taxpayers continue to be liable for tax at 40%. This brings the tax treatment of savings income in line with that of dividends, which are already charged at the lower rate.

Interest on bank and building society accounts

6.3 Interest on bank and building society accounts is paid after deduction of tax at source. As the tax charge on savings income was reduced from 25% to 20% with effect from 6 April 1996, savers receive interest net of 20% tax. The tax deducted matches the liability of both lower rate taxpayers and basic rate taxpayers, who have no more tax to pay. Higher rate taxpayers are liable for the difference between lower and higher rate tax, i.e. 20%.

6.4 For interest paid or credited before 6 April 1996, tax was deducted at 25%, and lower rate taxpayers could claim a repayment of the difference between basic and lower rates from the Inland Revenue. Higher rate taxpayers had to account for an additional 15%.

6.5 Non taxpayers can avoid paying tax at source by signing a written declaration (Inland Revenue Form IR85), giving them gross interest. If they do not fill this form in, they can still reclaim the tax by completing Form IR95, but will have to wait for a rebate of the tax paid.

Dividends from shares

6.6 All dividends from shares are paid net of a 20% tax charge but come with a 'tax voucher' showing the tax paid. Non taxpayers can reclaim the appropriate amount of tax by sending their tax voucher to the Inland Revenue at the end of the tax year. Both lower rate and basic rate taxpayers are regarded as having covered their full tax liability. Higher rate taxpayers have an extra 20% tax liability on such income.

Income from government stocks

6.7 Income from government stocks (known as gilts) is subject to the lower rate tax charge of 20% on savings income as introduced with effect from 6 April

1996. Until that date, the tax charge was 25%. Higher rate taxpayers are liable for tax at 40%, and must account to the Inland Revenue for the additional tax.

6.8   If the gilts are bought through the Post Office, interest is paid gross, but is still taxable and therefore has to be declared. Tax is deducted from interest at source if gilts are bought through a stockbroker.

7   Tax Schedules and Cases

7.1   Income was originally grouped under different schedules because there were different rules regarding each schedule in relation to offsetting expenses against income and different bases of assessment i.e. current year or preceding year, and different payment dates. With the introduction of self-assessment and current year basis this division is no longer as necessary and it is likely that the schedules will be phased out in the future.

7.2   There are four schedules for tax liability and individuals are assessed via these schedules. These are as follows:

Schedule A
Covers income such as rent from land and buildings in the UK. Allowable expenses such as maintenance costs and rates are deductible.

Schedule D
Tax is charged under six cases:

Case I -   profits from trade

Case II -   profits from profession or vocation

Case III -   interest, annuities or other annual amounts received including income from government stocks

Case IV -   income from foreign securities

Case V -   income from foreign possessions

Case VI -   income not covered by any other schedule or case

Income under Cases IV and V is based on the amount remitted to the UK if the taxpayer is resident but not ordinarily resident and/or not domiciled in the UK.

Schedule E
Case I -   Earnings of employees resident and ordinarily resident in the UK on employment in the UK or abroad. Also covers pension income and social security benefits.

Case II -   Earnings for UK duties by employee not resident or resident but not ordinarily resident in the UK.

Case III -   Earnings of non-UK domiciled employee from non-UK resident employer (known as foreign emoluments) earned by a person resident and ordinarily resident in the UK.

- Earnings abroad of person resident but not ordinarily resident in the UK.

If the money is not brought into the UK there will be no tax charge.

Schedule F
Dividends and distributions of UK resident companies.

Schedules B and C
These two schedules have now been abolished. Schedule B was a charge on woodlands and was abolished in 1988. Schedule C covered income arising from gilts and foreign government stocks. This is now covered under Schedule D Case III or IV.

8 Tax-Free Income

8.1 Some income is tax-free and can be ignored for tax purposes. Examples are:

- Profits from gambling (racing, pools, etc.)

- Premium bond winnings

- Prizes (e.g. lottery, competitions, etc.)

- Interest on certain National Savings accounts

- First £70 interest on National Savings ordinary accounts

- Income from personal equity plans (within agreed limits, as per current legislation)

- Interest on tax exempt special savings accounts (Tessas)

- Certain bonuses in 'save as you earn' contracts

- Certain grants and scholarships

- Certain armed forces allowances and pensions

- Maturity proceeds from a qualifying life assurance policy

- Profit related pay (within legislative limits)

- Shares allocated under an approved profit sharing scheme

- Certain lump sum payments on retirement

- First £30,000 of certain payments for compensation for loss of employment

- Maintenance payments (within legislative limits)

- Capital element received from a purchased life annuity

Tax exempt state benefits
8.2 Some social security benefits are also tax-free, or may be tax-free at a lower level and taxable at higher rates. The main tax-free benefits are listed below:

- Child benefit and allowances

- Wounds or disability pensions

- War widow's pensions

- Disability living allowance

- Severe disablement allowance

- Disability working allowance

- Incapacity benefit (for the first 28 weeks only)

- Maternity allowance

- Widow's payment

- Job release allowance for men aged 64 plus or women aged 59 plus

- Attendance allowance

- Invalidity benefits

- Family credit

- Housing benefit

- Christmas bonus for pensioners

- Industrial injury benefits

8.3   These are particularly significant for people who are marginally non taxpayers and higher rate taxpayers but will have some attractions for everyone.

Student Activity 2

You should complete this student activity before reading the next section of the text. Answer the questions, then check your answers against the paragraph(s) indicated.

1.   What is the current tax rate on investment income?   (6.3-6.7)

2.   Explain which tax schedule the following are taxed under   (7.2)

   (a) Earnings by a UK resident employee

   (b) Trading profits made by a self-employed builder

   (c) Rent from land

   (d) Annuity income

   (e) Statutory sick pay

3.   Give four examples of income you could receive which is   (8.1-8.2)
       classed as tax-free.

If you are unable to answer any of the questions satisfactorily, you should read the relevant paragraphs again. Your understanding of the text will be further tested in the self-assessment section at the end of this unit.

9 Charges and Deductions from Income

9.1 Certain charges and payments made by an individual may be deducted from income before tax. Tax is generally saved at the taxpayer's highest rate of tax, although in some cases, for example mortgage interest payments, relief is restricted.

9.2 Some of the allowable charges are paid net of basic rate tax. If the taxpayer is entitled to higher rate tax relief, this will be given by an adjustment to coding or income tax assessment. Other charges are paid in full and all the tax relief is given in this way.

9.3 The main allowable deductions and charges from income are:

- Interest on qualifying loans

- Pension contributions

- Certain maintenance payments

- Certain expenses (but limited for employees)

- Payments by individuals for qualifying vocational training

- Private medical insurance premiums paid by or for those aged 60 and over and their spouses

- Covenanted payments and qualifying gifts to charity

10 Allowable Interest Payments

10.1 Interest paid on certain loans may be deducted in calculating taxable income. The following loans qualify for tax relief at the top rate:

(a) Loan to purchase a partnership share, introduce capital or lend money to a partnership.

(b) Loan to buy shares in or lend money to a trading company by persons owning share capital who work at least nearly full time for the company.

(c) Loan to buy plant or machinery for use in a partnership or employment. Relief is given on interest paid in the year of purchase and the next three tax years.

(d) Loan to the personal representatives of a deceased person to pay IHT.

(e) Loan to acquire shares in an employee-controlled trading company.

(f) Loan to acquire shares in a co-operative.

Relief is only given as the interest is paid.

Mortgage interest relief at source (Miras)

10.2 Under current legislation, the interest on loans of up to £30,000 for the purchase of a main residence in the UK is eligible for tax relief. Up to 6 April 1994, tax relief was available at full basic rate tax. From 6 April 1994 mortgage interest relief was reduced to 20% and from 6 April 1995 was further reduced to the current level of 15%.

10.3 For individuals age 65 or over, a loan of up to £30,000 secured on their home for the purchase of a life annuity qualifies for tax relief at the basic rate i.e. 24%.

10.4 If the borrower has a mortgage loan over £30,000, interest on the part of the loan over £30,000 does not qualify for tax relief. The tax relief is deducted at source, that is, deducted from the payment that the borrower makes to the lender.

10.5 Lenders do not have to include loans over £30,000 made on or before 5 April 1987 in the Miras scheme. If they do not, the borrower will have to reclaim the relief by sending the certificate of interest which is supplied by the lender each year to his Inland Revenue office. The majority of mortgages fall within the scheme.

10.6 The following example illustrates how the Miras scheme can mean a dramatic cut in the 'real' cost of the interest paid.

Example 2.1: The 'real' cost of interest payments

On a house purchase loan of £30,000 the interest payments in a year carry mortgage interest relief.

If the rate of interest was 8% the interest in the year would be £2,400, but with Miras at 15% this amount would be netted down to £2,040, a cut of £360 p.a. or £30 per month.

In real terms this means that a 8% loan on £30,000 would be charged at the 'real' interest rate of 6.8%.

The part of the loan over £30,000 is charged at full rate with no tax relief.

10.7 Non taxpayers benefit from Miras because they are allowed to retain the tax relief deducted. This is also true, within certain time limits, for persons living or working abroad who are not paying UK tax.

10.8 Before the changes brought about by the Finance Act 1991, higher rate taxpayers could claim higher rate tax relief on the interest on the first £30,000 of their house purchase loan, but this ceased from 6 April 1991.

10.9 Married couples are entitled to tax relief on loans up to £30,000 and are deemed to share the tax relief equally unless an election is made to split this differently. Originally, people buying a house jointly could each claim relief up to £30,000 if unmarried, but this was stopped from 1 August 1988. Loans effected prior to this date were not affected by the change, unless re-mortgaged. The £30,000 limit is now given per property.

10.10 Where unmarried home sharers are receiving tax relief on mortgage interest the limit is divided equally and relief cannot be given to one borrower for interest paid by another. However, the individuals can transfer their limits to another sharer.

Example 2.2: Transferring tax relief

Borrower A and borrower B have a shared loan of £30,000. Each is entitled to interest relief on £15,000. However, borrower A actually pays interest on

£25,000 of the loan and borrower B on £5,000. Borrower B can transfer her remaining £10,000 limit to borrower A to receive full tax relief.

10.11 Mortgage interest relief is only available on loans for house purchase to a limit of £30,000. It is not available on other loans, loans for house improvement or extension, or `top-up' loans. Previously, mortgage relief was available for home improvement loans and is preserved on loans taken out before 6 April 1988, unless the property has been re-mortgaged. For example, if a property was purchased for £20,000 and a re-mortgage was required on that property for £30,000 only the original loan of £20,000 would qualify for mortgage interest relief.

10.12 If a home is partly used for business or letting then different rules will apply to how the relief is given. If more than a third is used for business then the mortgage cannot be in Miras and the individual will have to claim relief from the Inland Revenue.

10.13 If less than a third is used for business then the loan is treated as two separate loans. The private portion will be included in Miras while the business portion can offset interest payments against business profits or letting income.

10.14 There is no mortgage interest relief for the purchase of second homes but bridging loans qualify for tax relief on the interest. A separate limit applies to the bridging loan for a statutory period of one year but is generally extended to two years by the Revenue. Any outstanding loan on the old house will continue to attract tax relief for up to one year from the time the bridging loan is taken.

10.15 The fact that the £30,000 limit has remained unchanged for a number of years and the tax relief has reduced regularly means that it is becoming relatively more expensive to purchase property. The £30,000 limit covered the majority of mortgages a decade ago, but with the sudden rise in property prices in 1986 and 1987 the situation changed. Now the majority of new mortgages will exceed the limit.

11 Allowable Expenses

11.1 There are some allowable expenses that may be offset against income, but these are very restricted for employees. To qualify these must be expenses incurred 'wholly, exclusively and necessarily' for the purposes of the employment.

11.2 The definition of allowable expenses can be difficult, but may include subscriptions to professional bodies, vocational training costs and some special clothing, tools or equipment required by manual workers.

11.3 Employers may need to negotiate dispensations from the Inland Revenue for expenses such as travelling and hotel expenses. Employees need to keep a record of all allowable expenses to be offset against income. This will become more important in the change to self-assessment.

Overseas travel expenses

11.4 Where a UK resident employee incurs expenses when travelling abroad to take up employment he is not taxed on them when they are paid or reimbursed by the employer. If the period of employment outside the UK is more than 60 days (consecutive) than travelling for two return journeys by the employee's spouse and/or children are not taxable either.

Entertainment expenses

11.5   Where an employee pays for entertaining UK customers, these expenses are not taxable as long as they have been incurred wholly, exclusively and necessarily in the performance of his duties.

Incidental expenses

11.6   An employee who has to stay away from home on business is entitled to certain expenses, to cover items such as telephone calls home, which are not taxable. The limits are up to £5 a night in the UK and £10 a night if abroad.

Training courses

11.7   Individuals are able to obtain tax relief at their highest rate on fees paid for vocational training courses, if the course leads to a National Vocational Qualification or Scottish Vocational Qualification. Fees are paid net of basic rate tax to the training organisation, and the individual may keep the tax deducted even if he is a lower rate or non taxpayer. Higher rate tax relief is claimed through the annual assessment. The training providers reclaim the basic rate tax deducted from the Inland Revenue. From 6 May 1996 tax relief will be given on fees paid by individuals aged 30 or over for any full-time vocational course lasting between four weeks and one year.

12   Car and Mileage Allowances

12.1   Employees who use their own car for business travel may claim the business proportion of running expenses, a capital allowance for the cost of the car and relief on the interest on a loan used to buy the car. Some employers pay a mileage allowance, and this is taxable, although an employer can come to an arrangement with the Revenue to have the mileage allowance ignored, in which case the employee does not need to claim the car expenses. If the mileage allowance exceeds the expenses, the profit element is taxed.

12.2   Employers may use an arrangement known as the fixed profit car scheme (FPCS). Under this arrangement, tax-free mileage rates are fixed by the Revenue, based on average allowable costs for a range of car engine sizes. Taxable profits are calculated as the amount the employer pays over the published tax-free rates. This reduces the need for an employee to keep detailed records of motoring expenses, only the business mileage needs to be recorded.

Table 2.3: Fixed profit car scheme (FPCS)

	Tax-free rate per mile 1996-97	
	on the first 4,000 miles in the tax year	on each mile over 4,000 miles in the tax year
Size of car engine		
up to 1000cc	27p	16p

1000cc-1500cc	34p	19p
1501cc-2000cc	43p	23p
over 2000cc	61p	33p

12.3 Employees do have the option to be taxed on the strict statutory basis if they wish.

12.4 From 1996-97, any employee using his own car for business travel will be able to use the FPCS tax-free mileage rates to calculate any tax due on car or mileage allowances paid by their employers, even if the employer has not entered the scheme.

13 Maintenance Payments

13.1 The tax treatment of maintenance payments payable following divorce or separation depends on who they are being paid to, i.e. the spouse or directly to the children. Where maintenance qualifies for tax relief it is paid in full to the recipient and the payer can deduct the tax from income. If applicable the recipient is taxed on the amount received either by an adjustment to the PAYE code if employed, or by including it on a tax return under the self-assessment system.

13.2 Different taxation rules apply to maintenance payments depending on whether the arrangement was set up before or after 15 March 1988.

Maintenance payments to spouse (post March 1988)

13.3 The person paying maintenance can claim a tax deduction of 15% of the first £1,790 (or 15% of the amount payable if less). This limit applies to the aggregate of all payments even if paying maintenance to more than one person. The spouse is not taxed on the money received. The allowance is given in the year of separation as well as the married couples allowance.

13.4 Any payments made to a spouse who remarries do not qualify for relief.

13.5 Relief is available to any EEA national who is resident in the UK, and to any UK national who pays maintenance by order or written agreement of an EEA country.

Maintenance payments to spouse (pre March 1988)

13.6 For arrangements made before 15 March 1988 which are still continuing tax relief is limited on the first £1,790 to 15% (1996-97). The balance qualifies for tax relief at the payer's highest tax rate. The spouse is taxed on the maintenance received, except for the first £1,790 (1996-97).

13.7 If the amount being paid has increased since the 1988-89 tax year, tax relief is only given on the amount which was payable in that year. The spouse is only taxed on the frozen amount less £1,790.

13.8 If the amount of maintenance has increased to more than the current maintenance relief limit it may be better to switch to the new rules. For example, maintenance paid in 1988-89 was £1,000 and has now increased to £2,000. Tax relief under the old rules is limited to 15% of £1,000 whereas under the new rules it would be given on £1,790 in 1996-97.

Maintenance payments to children

13.9 Tax relief is only available on maintenance payments made directly to children under a pre-March 1988 court order. Relief ceases when the children reach 21.

13.10 Tax relief is given in the same way as for spouses with the first £1,790 limited to tax relief of 15%, and the balance relieved at the payer's highest tax rate. The amount which qualifies for relief is frozen at the amount payable in 1988-89.

13.11 The child may be taxed on the maintenance received if it exceeds his personal allowance.

13.12 Maintenance paid under a pre-March 1988 agreement, rather than a court order, ceased to qualify for tax relief from 6 April 1995.

14 Pension Contributions and Medical Insurance

14.1 Anyone who makes contributions to a pension plan or scheme is entitled to tax relief at their highest rate. Employees will pay contributions net of basic rate tax. Higher rate taxpayers obtain the excess i.e. 16% through their tax return. Self-employed individuals pay pension contributions gross and claim tax relief through their tax return.

14.2 Tax relief is also available on premiums paid for private medical insurance where the insured is over 60, or at least one of a married couple jointly insured is over 60. If someone else is paying premiums on their behalf, e.g. a son or daughter, they are eligible for the relief. Relief is only given at the basic rate and deducted from the premium. Tax relief is given even if the premiums are paid by a non taxpayer or lower rate taxpayer.

14.3 Relief is also available on contracts with an insurer within the EEA.

15 Covenants and Gifts to Charities

15.1 A deed of covenant is a written promise to pay a specified sum of money at set intervals for a specified period. It is a legally binding agreement and covenants have to be signed in the presence of a witness.

15.2 If an individual makes a covenanted payment or a gift to charity of at least £250 net of tax (£400 net for gifts before 16 March 1993), this may be deducted from income before tax. Non-charitable covenants established before 14 March 1988 still qualify for relief but at basic rate only.

15.3 A charitable covenant must run for over three years and be to a UK charity to be eligible for tax relief. The payer will pay the gift net of basic rate tax and the charity will reclaim the tax relief from the Inland Revenue. A higher rate taxpayer can claim the additional 16% relief from the Inland Revenue.

Example 2.3: Covenants

Sarah wants to make an annual payment of £1,000 to a charity. She will pay £1,000 and the charity will receive an additional £315.79 making a total donation of £1,315.79.

If Sarah was a higher rate taxpayer she would also be able to reclaim an additional £350.87 in tax relief.

If she pays this to the charity her actual payment would be £1,350.87 and the charity would receive £1,666.67 in total. Sarah would still only be actually making a net payment of £1,000.

15.4 A non taxpayer will not benefit from making a covenant as he will be liable for the basic rate tax relief paid to the charity by the Inland Revenue.

Payroll giving to charities

15.5 Payroll giving is a simple method for employees to make regular donations from their pay to charities of their choice. The payroll giving scheme must be set up by the employer with an agency approved for the purpose by the Inland Revenue. Employees then tell their employer how much they wish to donate each week or month, and the donations are deducted from pay before tax is calculated. The employee therefore receives full tax relief on the donations. The agency distributes the gifts to the charities nominated by the employee.

15.6 There is an annual limit on donations that may be made under the payroll giving scheme, and this is set at £1,200 per year/£100 per month for 1996-97.

Gift aid

15.7 If a single gift is made to a charity, of £250 or more, the payment can be treated in the same way as a covenant and basic rate tax is regarded as having been deducted. Higher rate tax relief is also given if appropriate. The charity can reclaim basic rate tax if the donor completes a certificate (R190(SD)) and gives it to the charity.

Student Activity 3

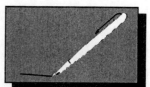

You should complete this student activity before reading the next section of the text. Answer the questions, then check your answers against the paragraph(s) indicated.

1. Jim and Joan are married and buying a house. They are taking out a mortgage of £59,000. Are there any limits on the amount of tax relief available on their interest payments and how will it be given? (10.2, 10.4)

2. Derek is working abroad for three months in the current tax year. His employer has paid for his accommodation and for his wife to fly out to visit him for a long weekend. His employer will reimburse any expenses Derek incurs on his return to the UK. What is the tax position for Derek on these expenses? (11.4)

3. Joanna was divorced from Tony in July 1990 and receives (13.1, 13.3) maintenance payments, currently £3,500, from him for their two daughters. What is the tax position on these payments for:

    (a) Joanna

    (b) Tony

If you are unable to answer any of the questions satisfactorily you should read the relevant paragraphs again. Your understanding of the text will be further tested in the self-assessment section at the end of this unit.

16 Allowances

16.1 Not all of an individual's income is taxable. The first part of any individual's income is normally exempt from tax since everybody has an allowance, decided by the Finance Act every year.

16.2 The main allowances are:

	1996-97 (£)
Personal allowance	3,765
Personal allowance (age 65-74)	4,910
Personal allowance (75 and over)	5,090
Married couple's allowance, Additional personal allowance and Widow's bereavement allowance	1,790*
Married couple's allowance (age 65-74)	3,115*
Married couple's allowance (75 and over)	3,155*
Blind person's allowance	1,250
Income limit for age related allowances	15,200

* Allowances where relief is restricted to 15%.

Personal allowance

16.3 Every person, of any age, has a personal allowance whether single or married.

Age allowance

16.4 The rate applies up to age 65, after which there are two bands of age allowance which increase with age. The bands are age 65-74, and 75 and over. However, the age allowance is subject to certain earnings limits. The allowance is reduced if income is more than £15,200 by £1 for every £2 earned.

16.5 For example, a single person aged 65-74 would lose full age allowance if his income was £17,490 or more. The excess in income over the income limit is £2,290 which divided by 2 equals £1,145 i.e. the amount of age allowance.

16.6 While individuals may be concerned that any income e.g. investment income, may mean that they lose the age allowance the actual cash value at stake is only £274.80 (i.e. 24% of £1,145) and so this problem should be put into perspective.

Married couples

16.7 A married couple will receive an additional married couple's allowance. This is normally given to the husband, but may be allocated to the wife or split equally. The wife has the right to claim half the allowance. Relief on this allowance is now restricted to 15%.

16.8 An age allowance is also given on the married couple's allowance and is subject to the same restrictions. It is given if either spouse reaches the appropriate age in a tax year and can be transferred from husband to wife, or split as required. However, the reduction in age allowance for income over £15,200 (1996-97) is determined by the husband's income only, even if it is the wife's age which determines eligibility for the allowance or she is given the allowance because the husband's income is too low to make use of it. The reduction is applied first to the personal allowance and then to the married couple's allowance.

Additional personal allowance

16.9 Additional personal allowance is available to single, widowed, divorced or separated individuals who have one or more qualifying children living with them for all or part of the year. Relief is restricted to 15% and the allowance remains the same regardless of the number of children.

Widow's bereavement allowance

16.10 This is available to a widow in the tax year in which her husband dies and in the following tax year, unless she remarries before the beginning of the following year. Tax relief is restricted to 15%.

Using allowances

16.11 Allowances only come into use if there is income to be related to them. In other words, a married couple will only qualify for two personal allowances if both have income.

16.12 Under independent taxation legislation this can now be unearned income, so it may be appropriate to have income yielding investments in the name of the non-income producing spouse to use up the allowance.

16.13 From 6 April 1996 entitlement to UK personal allowances and to tax credits from UK company qualifying distributions e.g. dividends paid by a UK company, was extended to citizens of all states within the European Economic Area (EEA).

17 Taxation of Married Couples

17.1 Since 6 April 1990 married couples have been taxed independently. A husband and wife each receive a single person's personal allowance, and as described above the husband also receives a married couple's allowance, although the wife has a right to claim half of this. The couple may both elect to allocate the whole of the married couple's allowance to the wife.

17.2 A husband and wife are each responsible for their own tax affairs, including the completion of tax returns and the payment of tax.

17.3 Any capital gains are taxed separately, and married couples each have their own annual exemption. This will be covered in the unit dealing with capital gains tax.

Joint taxation

17.4 Before 6 April 1990 and the introduction of independent taxation, a husband and wife were treated as one for income tax purposes. This was known as joint taxation.

17.5 Under the old system, a couple could end up paying more tax because their income was aggregated before the tax bill was calculated. Thus, some couples could have had a higher rate tax liability when now they would have none.

17.6 Another drawback of the old system was that all unearned income, no matter whose name it was under, was always treated as the husband's. So again, this could result in a higher rate liability.

Separate taxation

17.7 The pre April 1990 legislation often led to married couples electing to be taxed separately to avoid the potential higher rate tax liability described previously.

17.8 This meant that a married couple would be treated as single individuals for tax purposes, losing the married man's allowance, although unearned income would still be treated as the male's.

17.9 Although this reduced a couple's tax free income it could often lead to a saving in tax.

17.10 Another method was separate assessment where the tax liability of a couple remained the same, but the onus for payment fell on the husband and wife in proportionate shares, rather than just on the husband. This was often requested to allow a wife privacy in her tax affairs.

Marriage and divorce

17.11 The married couple's allowance begins in the year of marriage but is reduced in that year by one-twelfth for each complete tax month before the wedding date. A tax month runs from the 6th to the 5th e.g. 6 August to 5 September.

17.12 The allowance is given in full in the year of divorce, separation or death of either spouse.

18 Taxation of Children

18.1 A child has his own tax allowance from birth and will be liable for tax on any income if it exceeds this allowance. A child can be taken to include an illegitimate, adopted or step child. However, where a parent gives a child income, either directly or indirectly, the parent carries the tax liability. The only exceptions to this are as follows:

(a) If a parent gives a child a capital sum which produces income of no more than £100 gross per annum.

(b) A national savings children's bonus bond bought for child.

(c) Up to £270 per annum can be paid into a qualifying friendly society tax exempt savings plan.

(d) Certain income from an accumulation and maintenance settlement or a bare trust made by a parent for his children.

18.2 The most common example of this is where a parent opens a building society account for his child. If the interest exceeds £100 a year the parent will be liable to tax on it although the child should receive the interest gross.

18.3 These restrictions do not apply to anyone else, e.g. a grandparent, who wishes to give capital to children, or invest it on their behalf.

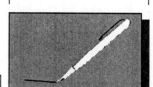

Student Activity 4

You should complete this student activity before attempting the self-assessment. Answer the questions, then check your answers against the paragraph(s) indicated.

1. A married couple are eligible for the additional married couple's allowance. How is this given and what restriction is there on the amount of relief?   (16.7)

2. Andrew and Anita Smith are both employed and pay tax at the basic rate.
    (a) Calculate their total personal allowances   (16.2)

    (b) How would their allowances be affected if they got divorced leaving Anita with custody of their son?   (16.9, 17.12)

3. You are a basic rate taxpayer and have just opened a building society savings account with £500 for your new born baby. Do you have any tax liability on this arrangement? What about the baby?   (18.1)

If you are unable to answer any of the questions satisfactorily you should read the relevant paragraphs again. Your understanding of the text will be further tested in the following self-assessment.

Summary

Now that you have completed this unit, you should be able to:

❑ **Define earned and unearned income**

❑ **Know who is eligible to pay income tax**

❑ **Explain which main benefits in kind are taxable**

❑ **Know the tax schedules and cases**

❑ **Know which income is tax-free**

❑ **Know the main allowable deductions from income and their limits**

❑ **Understand how married couples are taxed**

❑ **Know the tax liability of children and arrangements made for them**

If you can tick all the above boxes with confidence, you are ready to answer the questions which follow.

Self-Assessment Questions

1. Who is taxed under the PAYE system?

2. Give four examples of:

   (a) Earned income

   (b) Unearned income

3. Who is a P11D employee and what is the significance of the term?

4. Sarah has got a new job 100 miles away from where she currently lives. What are the restrictions on tax relief for relocation expenses that her new employer has agreed to pay?

5. A couple have taken out a mortgage to buy a guest house which has five bedrooms to let excluding their own. How will they obtain tax relief on their mortgage interest payments?

6. Joe travels about 3,000 miles for work a year using his own 1,600cc car. How much in mileage expenses can he claim tax-free for a 100 mile trip using the fixed profit car scheme?

7. Debbie wants to make regular payments to a charity using a covenant. She is a basic rate taxpayer and has completed a direct debit mandate for £30 a month. How much is this worth to the charity and how does it reclaim the tax relief?

8. A woman is paying premiums into a medical insurance policy on behalf of her 65 year old mother. The woman is a higher rate taxpayer and her mother is a non taxpayer. Are the premiums eligible for tax relief and if so, how is it given?

9. Eddie and Monica Knight are both 68. Eddie receives a pension income of £18,000. What personal allowances are they entitled to?

10. A couple get married on 30 August. How much of the married couple's allowance for that year will they be eligible for?

Unit 3

Calculating Income Tax Liability

Objectives

Students are required to study the following topics:

- **Tax calculation**

- **Tax assessment systems**

- **Pay as you earn system**

- **Profit sharing, share option and profit-related pay schemes**

- **Taxation of pension schemes**

- **Tax mitigation and anti-avoidance**

1   Introduction

1.1   Now the basics of income tax have been covered, this unit looks at how to calculate an individual's income tax bill and how payment is made by employees.

2   Calculating a Tax Bill

2.1   There are four steps in calculating an individual's tax bill.

- Step one   - bring together all sources of income for the year (earned and unearned)

- Step two   - deduct any allowable charges and expenses

- Step three   - deduct any allowances

- Step four   - the amount remaining will be taxable at the current rates of income tax

All sources of income

2.2   This has to include all income, not just salary and wages but also all bonuses, commission, benefits in kind etc. plus all unearned income.

2.3   This also includes 'tips' if these are expected as part of the job, e.g. as earned by a waiter. If the taxpayer does not include these the Inland Revenue will estimate an amount to be included.

2.4   Often, as explained earlier, unearned income will have been taxed at source. Since this will only be taxed at 20%, it will have to be included to see if there is any higher rate liability.

Allowable expenses

2.5 Allowable expenses such as professional subscriptions can be deducted from the total income.

Allowances

2.6 Allowances are deductible from all sources of income. These include the personal allowance and married couple's allowance.

Taxable amount

2.7 The amount left is taxable at current rates. There are three rates of tax depending on the level of income.

Table 3.1: Income tax rates

	1996-97	Income Band
Lower Rate Tax	20%	On first £3,900
Basic Rate Tax	24%	£3,901 - £25,500
Higher Rate Tax	40%	Over £25,500

2.8 The first 'band' of income will be taxed at the lower rate, the next 'band' of income at the basic rate, whilst any income above that 'band' will be taxed at the higher rate.

2.9 Once these steps have been followed the individual's tax liability can be calculated.

2.10 To recap:

INCOME
less
ALLOWABLE CHARGES AND EXPENSES
less
ALLOWANCES
equals
TAXABLE INCOME

To be calculated at the current rates applicable.

Example 3.1: Income tax calculation 1

Gilbert is 25, single and earns £27,000 p.a. salary. In 1996-97 he also received £2,500 bonus. There are no other sources of income.

His tax bill is as follows:

Total income	£29,500
Less allowable expenses	NIL
Less personal allowance	£3,765
Equals taxable income	£25,735

This is charged as follows (at 1996-97 rates)

Lower Rate Band £3,900 at 20%	£780
Basic Rate Band next £21,600 at 24%	£5,184
Higher Rate Band Balance of £235 at 40%	£94
Total Tax Bill	£6,058

Example 3.2: Income tax calculation 2

Gail is single, aged 27 and earns £17,000 p.a. She also has a 1.4 litre company car, list price £10,500, which has all petrol paid, in which she completed more than 2,500 but less than 18,000 business miles in the fiscal year.

She pays professional subscriptions of £100 p.a.

Her tax bill is as follows:

Income	£17,000
Benefits in kind (car)	£2,450
(petrol)	£710
Total income	£20,160
Less allowable expenses (subscriptions)	£100
Less personal allowance	£3,765
Equals taxable income	£16,295

This is charged as follows (at 1996-97 rates)

Lower Rate Band £3,900 at 20%	£780
Basic Rate Band Balance of £12,395 at 24%	£ 2,974.80
Total Tax Bill	£ 3,754.80

Example 3.3: Married couple's income tax calculation

Angus and Muriel are married and aged 30 and 27 respectively. Angus earns £25,000 p.a. and has a 2 litre company car, list price £16,000, in which he completes 20,000 business miles p.a. He also received £5,500 commission. Muriel earns £13,500 p.a.

Their tax bills in 1996-97 were as follows:

Angus

Income	£30,500
Benefits in kind (car)	£1,867
(petrol)	£890
Total income	£33,257
Less allowable expenses	NIL
Less personal allowance	£3,765
Less married allowance	£1,790
Plus allowance restriction	£1,118
(Relief on Married Couples Allowance limited to 15%)	
Equals taxable income	£28,820

This is charged as follows (at 1996-97 rates)

Lower Rate Band £3,900 at 20%	£780
Basic Rate Band next £21,600 at 24%	£5,184
Higher Rate Band balance of £3,320 at 40%	£1,328
Total Tax Bill	£ 7,292

Muriel

Total income	£13,500
Less allowable expenses	NIL
Less personal allowance	£3,765
Equals taxable income	£9,735

This is charged as follows (at 1996-97 rates)

Lower Rate Band £3,900 at 20%	£780
Basic Rate Band Balance of £5,835 at 24%	£ 1,400.40
Total Tax Bill	£ 2,180.40

Student Activity 1

You should complete this student activity before reading the next section of the text. Answer the questions, then check your answers against the paragraph(s) indicated.

1. What are the four steps in calculating income tax liability? (2.1)

2. Jenny has a taxable income of £32,000 after all deductions (2.10) and personal allowances. Calculate the amount of tax she will have to pay in the current tax year.

3. Fred Baines is single and earns £15,000 a year, he pays his (2.10) mortgage under Miras and is taxed under Schedule E. Calculate his income tax liability for the current tax year.

If you are unable to answer any of the questions satisfactorily, you should read the relevant paragraphs again. Your understanding of the text will be further tested in the self-assessment section at the end of this unit.

3 Notice of Coding

3.1 Every individual has a tax code which is notified to his employer. Where a tax code changes (other than for a change in the personal allowances following the Finance Act each year), a Notice of Coding will be issued. If an individual's circumstances change regularly, they may receive more than one Notice of Coding in a year.

3.2 This confirms the allowances available to an individual and shows his tax free allowance for the tax year. The Notice of Coding gives the taxpayer his tax code. This is an abbreviated form of the amount of allowances available with the last number replaced by a letter. The letter used depends on the allowances.

What the tax code letter means

- L : Basic personal allowance

- H : Basic plus married couple's or additional personal allowance

- P : Age 65-74 age allowance

- V : Age 65-74 age allowance plus married couple's allowance

- T : May be requested by an employee who does not wish his employer to know which allowance is available; also used where no personal allowance is available

- BR : Tax to be deducted at basic rate

- D : Tax to be deducted at higher rate

- K : Benefits in kind (or state pension/benefit for pensioners) exceed allowances

- NT : No tax to be deducted

- OT : No allowances given

3.3 In the left hand column there is a list of available allowances for the individual, e.g. personal allowance £3,765. In the right hand column are benefits in kind and arrears payments, which will be deducted to give a reduced allowance if there are any benefits or back-taxes to collect.

Example 3.4: Tax code number

In example 3.1 previously, Gilbert's tax code number would be as follows:

Personal allowance	£3,765
Single person suffix	L
Gilbert's tax code number will be	376L

In example 3.2 previously, Gail's tax code number would be as follows:

Personal allowance	£3,765
Plus professional subscriptions	£100
Less benefits in kind	£2,450 (car)
	£710 (petrol)
Reduced personal allowance	£705
Single person suffix	L
Gail's tax code number will be	70L

Allowance restrictions

3.4 Certain allowances have relief restricted to 15% for all taxpayers. Basic and higher rate taxpayers will have an allowance restriction added to their tax coding to reduce the value of the allowance.

3.5 A basic rate taxpayer is entitled to $^{15}/_{24}$ths of a restricted allowance, i.e. 62.5% and has a restriction of 37.5% of the allowance. A higher rate taxpayer is entitled to $^{15}/_{40}$ths of a restricted allowance i.e. 37.5% and has a restriction of 62.5% of the allowance.

3.6 For example, if an individual is entitled to a married couple's allowance, the Inland Revenue will use an allowance restriction of £670 (i.e. 37.5% of £1,790) if he is a basic rate taxpayer, and an allowance restriction of £1,118 if he is a higher rate taxpayer.

Example 3.5: Allowance restriction

Cyril is 43 and married to Julia, who is 44 and does not work. Cyril earns £40,000 p.a. and has a 2.9 litre company car, list price £30,000, in which he completes more than 2,500 but less than 18,000 business miles per year. He also has gross investment income of £6,000 p.a.

His tax bill for 1996-97 is as follows:

Income earned	£40,000
Income unearned	£6,000
Benefits in kind (car)	£7,000
(petrol)	£1,320
Total income	£54,320
Less allowable expenses	NIL
Less personal allowance	£3,765
Less married allowance	£1,790
Plus allowance restriction	£1,118
Equals taxable income	£49,883

This is charged as follows (at 1996-97 rates)

Lower rate band £3,900 at 20%	£780
Basic rate band next £21,600 at 24%	£5,184
Higher rate band balance of £24,383 at 40%	£9,753.20
Total Tax Bill	£15,717.20

3.7 A Notice of Coding should be checked to see if it is correct. If it is incorrect, the individual will pay too little or too much tax and their tax office should be contacted. The code number will also usually be shown on a payslip.

Notice of Assessment

3.8 As a Notice of Coding applies to current and future status for the existing or forthcoming tax year, so the Notice of Assessment looks to the previous tax year to see if the correct amount of tax has been paid.

3.9 Often, changes occur during the course of the tax year which can only be corrected retrospectively. These changes can either be in favour of the Revenue or the individual, and the Notice of Assessment is the Revenue's method of adjusting to the changes from the previous year.

3.10 If a Notice of Assessment is received, the recipient only has thirty days to appeal if it is incorrect. If there is no appeal it is deemed to be an accurate view of the previous year.

The tax return - current system

3.11 All taxpayers who receive a Notice of Assessment will also receive a tax return which should be completed and returned within 30 days of issue, although there is an unofficial deadline of 31 October following the end of the relevant tax year. This should be completed accurately by the taxpayer since, if not, the taxpayer could be liable to prosecution.

3.12 Anyone who does not receive a tax return but has taxable profits or gains on which tax is due have a duty to tell the Revenue who will then issue a return. Penalties based on the amount of unpaid tax will be levied if the Revenue is not informed. Notification must be by 5 October following the end of the tax year. The Revenue is informed by employers of any benefits paid to employees and other institutions such as banks and building societies have reporting requirements so that the Revenue is informed of interest payments made and so on.

3.13 There are different tax returns for different circumstances i.e. self-employed, employed and employees with uncomplicated tax affairs who receive a simplified form. The return requires details of income, allowable deductions such as pension contributions and capital gains in the previous tax year and allowances claimed for the current tax year. Married couples will receive separate forms for husband and wife.

3.14 Tax is payable on different dates depending on the type of income.

- Business profits - two equal instalments on 1 January and 1 July

- Rental income - 1 January in the tax year

- Extra tax on investment income including for higher rate taxpayers, capital gains tax etc. - 1 December following tax year

3.15 Where the Revenue has issued an assessment late then payment is due within 30 days and if an appeal is made then payment can be delayed if a postponement is applied for. Interest is charged on any payments not made by their due date.

4 Self-Assessment

4.1 The new tax system was introduced by the Finance Act 1994 to simplify the system of assessing and collecting tax. It means that all individuals, partnerships and companies have a fixed date on which to file their tax returns and fixed dates for payment. The taxpayer can calculate his own liability and can seek advice from new tax enquiry offices which are being set up around the country. For those persons who have fairly simple tax calculations and can complete their returns correctly contact with the Revenue will be minimal.

4.2 The new tax system of self-assessment will affect all taxpayers whether employed or self-employed. However, the impact will only be felt by individuals who have income not taxed through the Pay As You Earn (PAYE) system. This includes higher rate taxpayers with unearned income, anyone with a capital gains tax liability and those receiving income such as rental income. Tax returns for self-assessment will be sent out from 6 April 1997 to cover the tax year 6 April 1996 to 5 April 1997. The effect of the new rules on the self-employed is dealt with in Unit 4 and the notes which follow relate to the employed.

Records

4.3 Although not everyone gets a tax return everyone must, by law, keep records so that they can fill in a tax return if required. For employees these records will include pay slips, notes of expenses and benefits paid by the employer, as well as other sources of income such as building society interest and investment income. Any payments on which the individual wishes to claim tax relief should also be recorded. This includes pension contributions not paid through the employer and payments to charities.

4.4 Some of these documents may need to be submitted with the return as evidence of a claim for tax relief or to support any other information as relevant. These records must be kept for a year after the filing date for employees unless there is any formal enquiry into the return in which case they should be kept until the enquiry is completed if later.

Tax return

4.5 The new style tax return will include a number of supplementary pages (schedules) to complete depending on the type of income involved. The individual will complete his own tax calculation or alternatively the Inland Revenue will do this. However, if the Revenue are doing the calculation the return must be submitted earlier.

4.6 The timescales for submitting the completed tax return for the tax year 1996-97 are as follows:

- Return issued 6 April 1997

- If Inland Revenue calculating tax - submit by 30 September 1997

- If self-calculating - submit by 31 January 1998

- Payment of tax will be made by 31 January 1998

4.7 This system of dates for submission of returns and payment of tax will apply each year. Where income is mostly taxed at source, i.e. through PAYE and investment income paid net, then tax will be payable in one instalment on 31 January following the end of the tax year. A minimum limit has been set by the Inland Revenue to clarify when this will be the case.

4.8 Tax will be payable in one instalment if:

- Income tax and NI contributions or tax credits or dividends liability, net of tax deducted at source, in the preceding year was less than £500 in total or

- More that 80% of income tax and NI contribution liability for the preceding year was met by deduction of tax at source or from tax credits on dividends

Example 3.6: Limits for payments on account

Alan paid £18,000 in tax and National Insurance contributions through PAYE and on share dividends and building society interest in the previous year. He also had an additional £1,000 tax liability on building society interest as he was a higher rate taxpayer.

He does not meet the £500 rule, but his total tax and National Insurance liability deducted at source was more than 80% of the total tax liability so he meets the second requirement and does not have to make payments on account.

4.9   However, in all other instances tax will be payable in two instalments on 31 January in the tax year and on 31 July following the end of the tax year. These are known as payments on account and will be based on the amount of tax paid in the previous year. Where the taxpayer thinks he will be paying too much tax on this basis he can reduce the amount he pays on account. A payment on account will never be more than 50% of the previous year's tax liability even if it becomes obvious that the total tax bill that year will be a lot higher. Where necessary any adjustment involving either an extra payment or a refund will be made the following 31 January. This is referred to as the balancing payment. Capital gains tax is excluded from payments on account and will be collected with the balancing payment. For the tax year 1996-97 the provisional instalments will be based on the tax paid in the tax year 1995-96.

Example 3.7: Timetable for tax payment

Tax year 1998-99

31 January 1999	- first instalment of tax on account for 1998-99 due
April 1999	- tax return issued
31 July 1999	- second instalment of tax on account for 1998-99 due
30 September 1999	- submit tax return if IR to calculate
31 January 2000	- submit tax return for 1998-99, plus first instalment of tax for 1999-2000, or tax payment for 1998-99 if mostly taxed at source, plus any additional balancing payment required

Payment of tax

4.10   Tax will normally be paid by cheque or giro and the Revenue will normally issue reminders before payments on account are due. Statements will be issued each year showing payments made and all outstanding liabilities.

Penalties

4.11   If the tax return is submitted late then there is an automatic penalty of £100. If it is still not returned after another 6 months a further fine of £100 will be imposed. After this time the Inland Revenue can apply to the Tax Appeal Commissioners to impose penalties of up to £60 for each day that the return is outstanding.

4.12   Late payment of tax will carry an interest charge. A balancing payment due on 31 January will be charged at 5% if not paid by 28 February. If it is still outstanding by 31 July then a further 5% surcharge will be made. Tax refunds will be given with interest.

PAYE

4.13   Where possible employees can continue to have any additional tax liabilities collected through PAYE by an adjustment to their coding. In this case the Inland Revenue would prefer to have returns filed by 30 September even where individuals are completing their own calculation. They will then be notified of any adjustment to their code.

Errors

4.14 Where the Revenue wish to amend an error in the tax return they must do so within 9 months of the date on which it was filed. The taxpayer may also wish to make an amendment to the original information and can do so within 12 months of the filing date.

Time limits for self-assessment

4.15 The taxpayer has a total of 5 years 10 months from the end of the relevant tax year in which to make a self-assessment. After this time tax can only be assessed by the Revenue. The penalties above will apply during this time and tax bills will be issued by the Revenue based on estimates. When the self-assessment is filed it will automatically replace the estimate and any overpayment will be refunded.

Death

4.16 On the death of a taxpayer the executors of his estate have 3 years in which to complete a self-assessment.

Example 3.8: Tax payments for tax year 1997-98

Tom is a basic rate taxpayer who pays most of his tax through PAYE. However in 1996-97 he had a self-assessment of additional tax of £900. During the 1997-98 tax year he receives the return from a National Savings Capital Bond of £10,000 plus taxable interest of £4,500 which means a tax liability of £1,080. He also has CGT liability of £700 in that year.

January 1998 - 1st payment on account £450 based on half previous year's assessment
July 1998　　 - 2nd payment on account £450
January 1999 - Balancing payment of £180 (i.e. £1080 - £900)
　　　　　　　 - £700 CGT
　　　　　　　 - £540 1st payment on account for 1999-2000

Employers

4.17 Employers will receive revisions of the PAYE regulations to enable them to deal with the requirements of the self-assessment system. Their main duties towards employees are to provide them with certain information to enable record keeping. This information is as follows:

(a) P60 to be given to employees by 31 May.

(b) Copies of forms P11D and P9D (which provide information on benefits and expenses) to employees by 6 July. This is also the date when these forms must be submitted by employers to the Revenue.

(c) P11D forms must include calculation of the cash equivalent of any benefits in kind.

4.18 Further information will be issued to employers during the 1996-97 tax year.

Student Activity 2

You should complete this student activity before reading the next section of the text. Answer the questions, then check your answers against the paragraph(s) indicated.

1. What is meant by an allowance restriction? (3.4)

2. (a) Under the current system, who receives a tax return? (3.11)

   (b) Jim pays tax through PAYE and does not normally complete a tax return. However, he is a higher rate taxpayer and has received a substantial amount of investment income this year. What should he do regarding tax liability? (3.12)

3. Explain the system for submitting tax returns and making tax payments under the self-assessment system. (4.5-4.15)

If you are unable to answer any of the questions satisfactorily, you should read the relevant paragraphs again. Your understanding of the text will be further tested in the self-assessment section at the end of this unit.

5 Pay As You Earn (PAYE)

5.1 Employees and directors must be taxed through the PAYE system on their Schedule E income. Under the system the employer deducts tax due on a cumulative weekly or monthly basis from pay together with National Insurance (NI) contributions. The Inland Revenue issues tables to employers which tell them how much tax to deduct depending on the amount of taxable pay. Tax is due when earnings are paid and any balance or repayment will be resolved at the end of the tax year.

Who is an employee?

5.2 In most cases it is obvious if someone is classed as an employee and taxed through PAYE. However, there are instances where a person who is carrying out activities for someone else could be either self-employed or employed. The issue is not clear cut and the Inland Revenue provide guidance notes outlining the main criteria to use.

5.3 An individual is likely to be regarded as employed if the following apply:

- He works wholly or mainly for one business
- He needs to carry out the work in person
- He has to take orders as to how and when to carry out the work
- He works at a specified place
- He works set hours at an hourly, weekly or monthly rate
- He is paid overtime, sickness and holiday pay

5.4 An individual is likely to be regarded as self-employed if the following apply:

- He risks his own capital and bears any losses in the business
- He controls when, where and how he does the work
- He provides his own equipment
- He is free to employ others to complete the work

- He bears the cost of correcting anything that goes wrong

5.5 As the decision affects how the individual pays tax and NI contributions it is important that the situation is clarified. An employer who has treated someone as self-employed when it is later decided that they are actually an employee may have to pay tax and NI contributions arrears. Individuals can challenge a ruling made by the Inland Revenue but this can be costly and time consuming.

Employer's role and responsibility

5.6 The employer is responsible for calculating and deducting the correct amount of tax and paying it to the Collector of Taxes each month. He must also send a return to the Inland Revenue at the end of each tax year detailing all payments and deductions.

5.7 The employer must keep a record of all pay, tax, NI contributions and any statutory sick pay or maternity pay made. He must also complete various forms some of which are given to employees and some of which are returned to the Inland Revenue depending on circumstances. The main forms are as follows:

(a) P45 - completed when an employee leaves employment unless due to retirement. It shows total pay and tax to date, and tax code in use, and should be given to a new employer to ensure the correct tax will be deducted.

(b) P11D - this summarises all benefits and expenses payments for directors and employees earning more than £8,500 a year. It is sent to the Revenue at the end of the tax year.

(c) P9D - this form is used to send details to the Revenue of expenses and benefits to non-P11D employees and certain other benefits. This form and the P11D are due by 5 June each year.

(d) P14 - this form is used to summarise an employee's pay, tax, NI contributions and statutory sick pay or maternity pay. Two copies of this form are sent to the Revenue, the third being the P60 which is given to the employee each year.

(e) P35 - this summarises the information given for individuals on the P14 by showing the details for all employees and is what is commonly referred to as the employer's annual return. It is due by 19 May after the tax year.

Procedure

5.8 The employer will use the employee's tax code number to calculate tax due. Most companies will use computers to calculate tax and to print pay slips etc. Payment to the employee is usually by cash, cheque or into a bank or building society account. The employer must pay money owed for tax and NI contributions to the Revenue within 14 days of the end of the tax month. This will also include any employer's NI contributions.

Definition of remuneration

5.9 The general rule is that any amount paid to an employee arising from his employment is taxable through the PAYE system. The following list covers most of the types of payment an employee will receive:

- Salary/wages, bonuses, commission and fees

- Pensions

- Holiday pay

- Maternity pay and statutory sick pay

- Payments under profit sharing schemes

- Certain benefits and expenses such as payments for travelling between home and normal workplace

- Certain lump sum payments

- Payments in the form of marketable assets or vouchers or credit tokens used to acquire these assets. This could include stocks and shares, futures, commodities and fine wine vouchers

5.10 Benefits in kind are usually taxed by adjustment to the tax code.

6 Share Options, Profit Sharing and Profit Related Pay

6.1 The tax treatment given to these types of benefits is intended to ensure that employees and directors are not being indirectly remunerated and thus avoiding tax and NI contribution liabilities. To gain favourable tax treatment schemes must be approved by the Inland Revenue and be set up accordingly.

Profit sharing schemes

6.2 To gain tax advantages a profit sharing scheme must be approved by the Inland Revenue. Approval is given if the scheme provides similar terms to all qualifying employees (usually those who have completed at least five years service).

6.3 The scheme aims to provide employees and directors with shares in their employer's company. The shares are paid for by the employer and bought and held (appropriated) by trustees on behalf of the employees. During this time the employee may receive dividends which are taxable in the normal way. However, there is no tax liability on the shares held for the employees' benefit. The limit on the amount of shares that can be appropriated to an employee each tax year is 10% of salary subject to a minimum of £3,000 and a maximum of £8,000. After three years the shares can be allocated to the employee who is then the owner and can keep them or sell them as he chooses. (Prior to the Finance Act 1996 this period was five years). There will be no liability to income tax on allocation.

6.4 For capital gains tax (CGT) purposes the shares are regarded as belonging to the employee even when held by the trustees. If shares are sold at any time the chargeable gain will be based on the base cost defined as the market value at the time the shares were first appropriated to the employee.

6.5 The trustees are able to allocate shares to employees after two years of purchase but there will be a tax charge if the employee sells the shares within three years of allocation. The tax charge will be based on the market value at allocation or the sale proceeds if less. This is reduced by 50% if disposal occurs within three years because the employee leaves employment due to injury, disability, redundancy or retirement.

6.6   The main benefits of this type of scheme are the tax incentives for employers who can claim the amount provided to buy the shares as a tax deductible expense, and the fact that it is a tax-free alternative to providing a taxable cash bonus. Employees may feel more directly involved in the profitability of the company if they own shares.

SAYE linked share option schemes

6.7   Approved share option schemes can offer employees and directors the opportunity to save over a fixed period at the end of which they have an option to use the money to buy shares in the company at a favourable price.

6.8   Under an SAYE linked scheme the employee saves between £5 to £250 a month in a Save As You Earn (SAYE) contract with a building society, bank or through National Savings. The contributions will usually be deducted from pay but are not eligible for tax relief. The contract will be for three, five or seven years and at the end of this period the employee can exercise the option to buy shares. During the term of the contract the employee will receive tax-free interest and bonuses depending on the terms of the SAYE contract.

6.9   The price the employee pays for the shares must not be less than 80% of the market value of the shares at the time the option was originally granted. No income tax liability will arise on any gain when the option is exercised. If the employee decides not to exercise the option, if for example the share price had fallen below the option price, he is entitled to the SAYE contract proceeds.

6.10   If the employee leaves employment he can only exercise the option if he had been in the scheme for at least three years. In this case he has 6 months to exercise the option. Employees who leave due to injury, disability, redundancy or retirement also have 6 months within which to exercise the option. This is extended to 12 months for the personal representatives of an employee who dies.

6.11   If the company operating the scheme is sold or leaves the group of companies operating the scheme then any employee who joined the scheme less than three years before will be taxed on any gain made if the option is exercised.

6.12   For CGT purposes the base cost is the price paid by the employee for the shares. It is possible to transfer the shares into a single company Pep according to the current limits.

Company share option schemes

6.13   Under these schemes, directors or employees can be given the option to buy shares in the company. Prior to the Finance Act 1996 these approved schemes were known as executive share option schemes and received more favourable tax treatment. However because there has been some controversy over the misuse of this non savings-related option the rules have been changed. Following the Act the options cannot be granted at a discount to the current market value of the shares and the total value of all shares held by the employee or director from this and any other similar schemes must not be more than £30,000.

6.14 If these conditions are met, there is no tax charge when the option is granted. There will also be no tax charge when the option is exercised if this is between three to ten years after being granted and the option is exercised no more frequently than once in three years. When the shares are disposed of then CGT will apply.

6.15 Directors or employees may also have share options under an unapproved scheme. If an unapproved scheme option is exercised, then a tax charge will arise on the difference between the market value and the price paid at the time the option is exercised including any amount paid for the option.

Profit-related pay

6.16 An employee can receive part of his pay tax-free if it is related to the profits of the company that employs him. The scheme must be registered with the Inland Revenue and full details of how the scheme will operate, the profits on which the scheme is based and the formula for calculating the profit-related pay (PRP) must be given.

6.17 The scheme must include at least 80% of employees. However, any employee who, with associates, owns more than 25% of ordinary share capital of the company is excluded. The employer can also exclude employees who have completed less than three years service.

6.18 The 'distributable pool' must be based on the profit and loss account which can be adjusted for certain items as specified in the scheme particulars. This amount can be distributed to employees as a single lump sum or as a series of interim payments with the balance payable after the profits have been calculated at the end of the accounting period.

6.19 PRP cannot exceed 20% of an employee's total pay in a year up to a maximum of £4,000. Therefore the biggest saving available is to a higher rate taxpayer who could save up to £1,600 in tax.

6.20 The pay can be distributed at a flat rate to all employees or linked to levels of pay or length of service. It must be according to a set formula and not at the discretion of the employer.

6.21 Tax relief is given by deducting PRP from pay before calculating tax through PAYE. NI contributions are payable. The employer can treat both the PRP paid and the costs of running the scheme as tax deductible.

7   Pension Schemes

7.1 Employees who contribute to an approved pension scheme will benefit from tax relief on their contributions within certain limits, and receive certain tax-free benefits.

7.2 Employees can either take out a personal pension to which their employer may or may not contribute, or join their employer's occupational pension scheme. If they are members of an employer's pension scheme, they may also contribute to an additional voluntary contribution (AVC) scheme or free-standing additional voluntary contribution scheme (FSAVC) to enhance the benefits they receive at retirement.

8 Personal Pensions

8.1 Personal pensions have several tax advantages:

- Contributions build up in a fund which is not liable to income tax or capital gains tax on its investment returns

- Contributions are given tax relief at the highest rate paid by the policyholder

- Part of the benefits can be taken as a tax-free lump sum

- Any lump sum payable by the policy on death before retirement is normally tax-free

- Additional life assurance taken out in conjunction with a pension enjoys tax relief on premiums

Contributions

8.2 The maximum contributions which may be made in a tax year are as follows:

Table 3.2: Maximum personal pension contributions

Age	Percentage of 'net relevant earnings'
35 or less	17.5
36 - 45	20.0
46 - 50	25.0
51 - 55	30.0
56 - 60	35.0
61 - 75	40.0

8.3 Where contributions are being made by both employee and employer the total contribution is subject to the above limits.

8.4 There is also a maximum limit on 'net relevant earnings' of £82,200 (1996-97) known as the earnings cap.

Tax relief

8.5 Tax relief is available on contributions within the maximum contribution limits, at the highest rate of income tax paid by the individual.

8.6 Self-employed contributions are payable gross with tax relief being claimed through the annual tax return.

8.7 Employees pay contributions to the provider, net of basic rate tax which is 24% in the 1996-97 tax year. Any higher rate relief due to the individual is claimed through his annual tax return.

8.8 If an employee wishes to maintain the level of gross contributions being paid to a pension scheme in 1995-96, net contributions will have to increase by 1% to reflect the change in basic rate tax.

8.9 Employer's contributions are payable gross, but are normally allowable against the taxable profits of the business.

Life assurance

8.10 A maximum of 5% of net relevant earnings can be used to provide a lump sum death benefit in the form of term assurance expiring no later than age 75. Tax relief is given on the premiums comparing favourably with an ordinary term assurance policy where tax relief is not available.

8.11 The 5% limit must be part of the overall limit for pension contributions given above.

8.12 These policies may be written under trust thereby avoiding any liability to inheritance tax.

8.13 Most pension policies also provide a return of premiums paid plus interest or the value of the fund accumulated at time of death if the planholder dies before retirement. This may also be written under trust as above, but more usually will be paid at the discretion of the scheme administrator. This means liability to inheritance tax is avoided.

Lump sum benefits

8.14 Where part of the retirement benefit is taken as a lump sum (commutation) this must not exceed one-quarter of the fund. It is payable tax-free.

Pension

8.15 The pension is taxed as earned income with basic rate tax normally deducted at source.

9 Occupational Pension Schemes

9.1 Occupational pensions i.e. employer related group schemes, executive pension plans, additional voluntary contributions (AVCs), including free-standing additional voluntary contributions (FSAVCs) enjoy similar tax advantages to personal pensions.

- Contributions build up in a fund which is not liable to income tax or capital gains tax on investment returns

- Contributions are given tax relief at the highest rate paid by the member

- Part of the benefits can be taken as a tax-free lump sum

- Any lump sum payable by the scheme on death before retirement is normally tax-free

Contributions

9.2 The maximum amount that an employee may contribute is 15% of earnings each year, including to AVCs and FSAVCs. The earnings cap applies i.e. £82,200 in 1996-97.

9.3 There is no limit to the maximum contribution that an employer may make.

However, contributions are limited to providing maximum approvable benefits.

Tax relief

9.4 Tax relief is available on employees' contributions within the maximum limit, at the highest rate of income tax paid by the individual. Contributions including AVCs are deducted from gross pay by the employer before taxable income is calculated.

9.5 FSAVCs are paid net of basic rate tax to the provider, with the employee responsible for reclaiming any higher rate tax relief at the year end.

9.6 Employer's contributions are deductible from profits as a management expense.

9.7 There is no liability to NI contributions on the amount of contribution paid by the employer and employee. (Note that if that amount was paid as salary instead there would be liability to NI).

Life assurance

9.8 The maximum lump sum on death in service is four times salary. A refund of the employee's contributions, with interest, may also be paid.

9.9 Provided this is paid at the discretion of the scheme trustees it is free of inheritance tax.

9.10 In addition, a pension may be provided for a spouse or dependant not exceeding two-thirds of the maximum pension which could have been provided for the employee. Such pensions are taxed as earned income.

Lump sum benefits

9.11 Part of the benefits can be taken as a tax-free lump sum (commutation). The maximum is equal to $^3/_{80}$ths of final salary (limited to the earnings cap) for each year of service up to 40 years. Alternatively, the lump sum can be calculated as 2.25 times the pension before commutation if this gives a higher figure.

9.12 The earnings cap applies to the definition of final salary. The lump sum is also subject to an overall limit of 1½ times the earnings cap (i.e. £123,300 for 1996-97).

9.13 Benefits secured by AVCs or FSAVCs cannot be commuted and must provide pension benefits.

Pension

9.14 The maximum pension at normal pension age is two-thirds of final salary, provided that the employee has completed twenty years service with the employer. Those with less service are restricted to a maximum pension of 1/30th of final salary for each year of service. The pensions are taxed as earned income.

Refund on leaving service

9.15 If an employee leaves service, having made less than two years contributions, he can take a refund which is taxed at 20%.

Overfunded AVC and FSAVC contributions

9.16 If at retirement, or on earlier death, the combined benefits payable from an employer's scheme and any AVCs or FSAVCs exceed the maximum allowed, this is known as overfunding.

9.17 The refund is taxed at 34% but is only payable to a higher rate taxpayer. Basic rate taxpayers are not entitled to a refund. The higher rate taxpayer will be treated as having received the payment net of basic rate tax and will have a further 16% liability on the gross equivalent.

Example 3.9: Taxation of AVC overfunded refund

Surplus £2,000 gross paid to higher rate taxpayer. He receives this amount less 34%, i.e. £1,320. This is regarded as having been taxed at 24%, i.e. £417. So grossed up, £1,320 is £1,737. Tax at 40% is £694 with £417 already treated as paid. This leaves a further £277 to pay. The taxpayer will actually only receive £1,043.

Student Activity 3

You should complete this student activity before reading the next section of the text. Answer the questions, then check your answers against the paragraph(s) indicated.

1. John is unsure whether he is employed or self-employed. He works at home on a project basis, mainly for one company who pay him on completion of the work. He bases his fee on an hourly rate. How would you define his employment status and why? (5.3, 5.4)

2. Explain how a profit sharing scheme works. How does it compare with a profit-related pay scheme? (6.2-6.6, 6.16-6.21)

3. Outline the main tax advantages of contributing part of earnings to a pension plan or scheme. (8.5-8.9, 9.4-9.7)

If you are unable to answer any of the questions satisfactorily, you should read the relevant paragraphs again. Your understanding of the text will be further tested in the self-assessment section at the end of this unit.

10 Lessening the Income Tax Liability

10.1 It is important to be aware of the difference between evading tax and avoiding tax.

10.2 It is illegal to evade paying tax; it is perfectly legal to mitigate (or avoid) the tax liability by using knowledge and understanding of the tax laws.

10.3 The introduction of independent taxation gave individuals plenty of opportunities to mitigate their income tax liability and make full use of personal allowances. Some of these are summarised below.

Mortgage interest relief

10.4   Under independent taxation legislation, the mortgage interest relief for a couple with a joint mortgage is normally split on a 50-50 basis. It may still be advantageous to make an election to have the mortgage interest relief allocated in a different way, for example:

- If the mortgage is not in Miras and one spouse is a non taxpayer

- If one or both spouse is over 65 or 75 and an election would reduce income below the limit where age allowance would cease to be available

Investment income

10.5   Before April 1990 it was not possible to use income from investments to set against the unused personal allowance of a wife. However, this situation has now changed.

10.6   It may be possible to take advantage of independent taxation to move investments or other assets from husband to wife or vice versa. Such transfers will be effective for tax purposes if they are outright gifts with no conditions attached.

10.7   For example, a non-working wife could take on her husband's investment income (or have her own allocated to her) to realise up to £3,765 p.a. (1996-97) without paying tax.

10.8   The following example shows that there are substantial savings to be made in this way.

Example 3.10: Investment income

Graham is married to Charlotte. He earns £40,000 p.a. and has gross investment income of £3,000 p.a. Charlotte has no income.

His tax bill in 1996-97 is	£40,000 plus £3,000
Less personal allowance	£3,765
Less married couple's allowance	£1,790
Plus allowance restriction	£1,118
Equals taxable income	£38,563

This is taxed	@ 20% £ 3,900	£780
	@ 24% £21,600	£5,184
	@ 40% £13,063	£5,225.20
Total Tax Bill =		£11,189.20

If investment income is given to Charlotte, tax is as follows :

Graham :	£40,000
Less personal allowance	£3,765
Less married couple's allowance	£1,790
Plus allowance restriction	£1,118

Equals taxable income			£35,563
This is taxed	@ 20% £ 3,900		£780
	@ 24% £21,600		£5,184
	@ 40% £10,063		£4,025.20
Total Tax Bill =			£9,989.20
Charlotte: £3,000 less £3,765			= No tax liability
			SAVING £1,200 TAX

Tax saving summary

10.9 If an individual follows the basic steps outlined below, he should be confident that he is not paying too much in income tax. He should ensure:

- All available allowances, exemptions and reliefs are used and claimed

- The Inland Revenue are kept up to date with any changes of circumstances, e.g. marriage

- All current available reliefs are used, e.g. mortgage interest relief and pension reliefs and that the correct relief is given if a higher rate taxpayer, where available

- Pension arrangements are used to their maximum advantage

- All investments are tax efficient, e.g. using Tessas and Peps if appropriate to investment needs

- There is an annual check on the amount of tax paid by an individual

- Consider timing of investments, particularly around the end of the tax year

11 Anti-Avoidance Law

11.1 Although it is valid for individuals to try and lessen their tax liability, the Inland Revenue is concerned with countering what it regards as unacceptable ways of avoiding tax. The tax avoidance law and its interpretation in the courts is very complex and the notes which follow provide a brief overview of the main provisions.

A series of transactions

11.2 Three court cases in the 1980s established the current law relating to the use of a series of transactions to gain a tax advantage. The cases are often quoted so are named here for information; however the subsequent legislation and interpretation is complicated and will only be summarised. The relevant cases are: *Ramsay (WT) Ltd v. IRC* (1981), *Furniss v. Dawson* (1984) and *Craven v. White* (1988)

11.3 The main principle which has evolved is that unless a person can show that a series of transactions which resulted in a tax advantage had a bona fide commercial purpose other than the taxation aspect, or occurred in the course of making or managing investments, then the tax advantages would be lost.

11.4 The transactions are described as 'pre-ordained' thus implying an overall purpose, and investigation into any suspect arrangements will not only look at each step involved and any tax consequences but also look at the scheme as a whole and its final result.

11.5 The interpretation of this principle applies to any tax and not just income tax.

Income on securities

11.6 It is possible to habitually time the sale of certain securities, namely equities and preference shares, so that income is not received but reflected in a capital surplus on sale. In this event, the individual will be treated as having received the income that has accrued on a day to day basis and be taxed at the excess of higher rate tax over basic rate.

Offshore funds

11.7 Where a person resident or ordinarily resident in the UK makes a gain on a disposal of investments in an offshore fund this will be taxed as income under Schedule D, Case V1 instead of attracting a capital gains tax charge. However, if the fund is a distributor fund, normal CGT rules will apply. (See Unit 20 for full details.) Any switches between classes of investment will also attract an income tax charge unless the distributor fund definition applies.

Interest and dividend income becoming attributed to another person

11.8 If the owner of securities sells or transfers the right to receive any interest or dividend income payable without transferring or selling the actual securities, he will be liable to tax on them as the owner. However, if he is not the beneficial owner of the securities, for example under a trust arrangement, then the beneficiaries will be taxed on the income.

Avoidance of PAYE

11.9 As explained earlier in this unit, where an employer makes payments to employees or directors in the form of assets, these will be taxed under the PAYE system. These assets include shares, futures and commodities which can be traded freely in the relevant markets. If the employee can exchange an asset for cash then it falls into these provisions. The reason for the rule is to stop employers from using artificial methods to provide employees with cash and so avoid taxation through PAYE.

Capital receipts treated as income

11.10 In certain circumstances, some so-called artificial transactions in land are taxed as income rather than subject to capital gains tax to ensure that these transactions are not taking place simply to avoid an income tax liability.

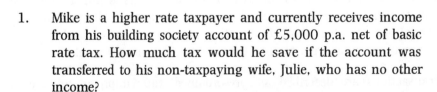
Student Activity 4

You should complete this student activity before attempting the self-assessment. Answer the questions, then check your answers against the paragraph(s) indicated.

1. Mike is a higher rate taxpayer and currently receives income   (10.8)
    from his building society account of £5,000 p.a. net of basic
    rate tax. How much tax would he save if the account was
    transferred to his non-taxpaying wife, Julie, who has no other
    income?

2.   What is the main purpose of the anti-avoidance laws?   (11.1)

If you are unable to answer any of the questions satisfactorily, you should read the relevant paragraphs again. Your understanding of the text will be further tested in the following self-assessment.

Summary

Now that you have completed this unit, you should be able to:

❑ **Calculate an income tax bill**

❑ **Understand the current system for assessing and paying tax**

❑ **Understand the changes under the self-assessment system**

❑ **Explain how employees pay tax through PAYE**

❑ **Explain share option, profit sharing and profit-related pay schemes**

❑ **Understand the main tax benefits of pension schemes**

❑ **Identify how individuals can mitigate their tax liability**

❑ **Understand the underlying principle of anti-avoidance law**

If you can tick all the above boxes with confidence, you are ready to answer the questions which follow.

Self-Assessment Questions

1.   Ben and Fliss Green are both employees and had the following income in the current tax year:

	Ben	Fliss
Earned income	£21,000	£5,000
Unearned income	£ nil	£3,000

They have an endowment mortgage paid under the Miras system. Ben pays pension contributions of £850 a year through his employer's scheme.

Calculate their income tax liability.

2. An elderly married couple, both aged over 75, have one source of income - the state pension.

   (a) Calculate their unused allowances.

   (b) They are considering selling their house and buying a cheaper flat, so that they can use the proceeds to produce income. What, in general terms might you advise them concerning the impact on tax liability?

3. (a) An employee has a tax code of 555H. How much pay each month will not be taxed?

   (b) As well as paying his employees, what related payments must an employer make at the end of each month?

   c) What is a P60?

4. Which of the following lump sum payments are tax-free?

   • Redundancy payment of £30,000

   • Compensation payment of £25,000

   • Long service award of £10,000

   • Pension commutation from an approved pension scheme

5. Tony works for a large company as a training manager. his job involves a lot of travelling and work around the country. He has a company car and a company credit card. Which of the following payments he receives, directly or indirectly, are taxable?

   (a) Petrol for travelling to the office

   (b) Sick pay received for two weeks

   (c) A meal at a service station while en route to a meeting

   (d) The fees for a training course Tony attends to improve his training skills

   (e) Telephone calls to his family while away on business, paid for by his employer

6. In order to comply with the self-assessment rules what types of records should an employee keep?

7. What is the tax treatment of benefits from an occupational pension scheme?

8. An employee has been told he is eligible to join his employer's SAYE linked share option scheme

   (a) What does the employee do under the scheme?

   (b) What timescales are available under the scheme?

(c) What happens when he exercises his option?

9. Calculate your own tax liability for the current tax year. Check your tax coding. Make a note of all the sources of information you referred to, to be able to carry out this calculation.

10. An employer has given a director part of his remuneration in the form of shares. How will this be taxed?

Unit 4

Taxation of Sole Traders and Partnerships

Objectives

Students are required to study the following topics:

- **Preceding year basis of assessment**

- **Current year basis of assessment**

- **Payment of tax by the self-employed**

- **Calculation of taxable profits**

1 Introduction

1.1 The last unit described how most people pay tax on their income as it is earned, under the Pay As You Earn System.

1.2 This unit will look at how the tax system differs for self-employed people and those in partnership. Generally, sole traders and partners can claim more in expenses to reduce the amount of tax they pay. Tax is not deducted from their earnings before they are paid and there is usually a considerable delay before they have to pay the tax which is due on these earnings.

1.3 However, although being taxed as self-employed may seem to have several advantages the Inland Revenue will consider carefully the nature of a person's employment and in some cases insist that tax is deducted under Schedule E as an employee. An employee will have a 'contract of service' whereas a self-employed person will have a 'contract for services' where he will be paid against an invoice for his services.

1.4 As was discussed in the previous unit, it is often difficult to distinguish between the two and the deciding factors will include how much control the individual has over the work done. Similarly, the Inland Revenue will wish to determine that a partnership exists for tax purposes. To do so it will take into account a number of factors, including the written partnership agreement (if any), the firm's stationery, authority to transact bank accounts and so on.

2 The Basis of Schedule D Case I and II Tax Assessment

2.1 The self-employed and those in partnership are assessed under Cases I and II of Schedule D. Tax is not paid on income as it is earned but on an assessment drawn up after the end of an accounting period.

2.2 At the moment, sole traders and partners in businesses established before 5

April 1994 are taxed on what is known as a 'preceding year basis', but this is being replaced with a new simpler 'current year basis' during the year 1996-97. New businesses set up after 5 April 1994 are already using current year basis and all businesses will be taxed on this basis from the 1997-98 tax year.

3 Preceding Year Basis of Assessment

3.1 Businesses that were established on or before 5 April 1994 pay income tax on the trading profits of the accounting year ending in the preceding tax year. The 1995-96 assessment for an established business would therefore have been based on the trading profits of the business for the twelve month accounting period ending at some time during the 1994-95 tax year. However, the 1995-96 assessment is the last one that will be drawn up on the preceding year basis.

3.2 The income tax on trading profits is generally payable in equal instalments on 1 January in the year of assessment and the following 1 July. The individual or partnership chooses the annual accounting date and if an accounting date is early in the tax year, there is a greater interval between earning profits and paying the tax on them.

Example 4.1: Preceding year basis of assessment - payment dates

Up to and including 1995-96, an established business paid tax on the trading profits of the accounting year ending in the preceding tax year.

	Dates for Payment of Tax for 1995-96	**Interval between end of accounting year and payment date**
Accounting year ended 30.4.94	1.1.96 1.7.96	20 months 26 months
Accounting year ended 31.12.94	1.1.96 1.7.96	12 months 18 months
Accounting year ended 31.3.95	1.1.96 1.7.96	9 months 15 months

3.3 In the case of a partnership under the preceding year basis, all of the partners are liable to tax on the profits made by the whole partnership. One, joint assessment is made and addressed to the first named or 'precedent partner', who is also responsible for making the return of the partnership profits and gains. The assessment is then divided between the partners in the proportions that they split the profits of the partnership. However, the joint liability to tax means that each partner can be held liable for any tax that is unpaid. So if partners Bill and Ben have a tax liability and Ben leaves the country, Bill will be liable for the full amount of tax owed by the partnership.

3.4 The tax of a partnership can be paid either out of the partnership account or by the individual partners themselves.

3.5 Non-trading income, for example dividends and interest, and capital gains are not jointly assessed. Each partner is charged on his share and there is no claim against the other partners for unpaid tax.

Opening years of trading

3.6 A special basis of assessment operates in the early years of a new business or partnership established before 5 April 1994. In the first year the assessment is based on the profit from the starting date to the following 5 April. In the second year the assessment is based on the profit for the first twelve month's trading. From the third year onwards, assessment will normally be on the profits of the accounting year ending in the previous tax year.

3.7 A sole trader may alternatively elect to have the assessment for both the second and third years (but not just one of them) based on the actual profits for those years. The election must be made within six years of the end of the third tax year.

Assessment of a business ceasing to trade

3.8 When a business or partnership stops trading permanently, the final assessment is based on the profits from 6 April of the tax year in which the business stopped to the date of cessation rather than profits in the accounting year ending in the previous tax year. Since this will result in some profits not being assessed the Revenue may choose to make an adjustment for the two tax years before the final assessment year, and base assessments on actual profits for those two years. This revision must be made for both tax years or for neither.

Partners leaving or joining

3.9 Under the preceding year basis of assessment, a partnership is treated as ceasing for taxation purposes if a partner leaves through agreement or death or a new partner joins. The final tax assessment is made on a current year basis, with an adjustment for the previous two years in respect of an excess of profit. This could cause chaos to a partnership as the effective tax bill for that year could be far in excess of that expected.

3.10 Provided at least one member of the original partnership remains in the partnership then election can be made for taxation on a continuation basis. This means that the partnership is not treated as ceasing, but continues to be assessed under Schedule D in the normal way. New partners are assessed on their proportion of the profits from the time of joining.

3.11 Since an assessment is divided between the partners in the way in which they share profits in the year of assessment, it follows that where a continuation election is made on a change of partners, the division will be made between different persons from those who actually shared the profits.

3.12 If a continuation election is not made on a change of partners, the closing year rules apply to the old firm.

3.13 If the partners have the right to make a continuation election, but choose not to do so, the assessments for the first four tax years on the new partnership are based on the actual profits made.

Student Activity 1

You should complete this student activity before reading the next section of the text. Answer the questions, then check your answers against the paragraph(s) indicated.

1. Joe Smith has an accounting period of 1 January to 31 December.

    (a) On what accounting period will he have paid tax   (3.1)
    in 1995-96?

    (b) On what dates would the tax be payable?   (3.2)

    (c) If he had set up in business on 1 January 1993,   (3.6)
    what period of profit would his assessment for the
    tax year 1992-93 have been based on?

2. Tom, Dick and Harry are partners being taxed under the   (3.3)
    preceding year basis. If Tom does not pay his tax bill who is
    responsible for payment of this unpaid tax?

If you are unable to answer any of the questions satisfactorily, you should read the relevant paragraphs again. Your understanding of the text will be further tested in the self-assessment section at the end of this unit.

4 Current Year Basis of Assessment

4.1 Businesses and partnerships that were established on or after 6 April 1994 are taxed on the new current year basis of assessment. Existing businesses and partnerships will be charged on the current year basis from 1997-98, with transitional arrangements coming into effect in the 1996-97 tax year. This means they are taxed in the current tax year on profits made in the accounting period ending in that year. So if a sole trader has an accounting period which runs from 1 September to 31 August, he will be taxed in 1997-98 on the profits made in the period ending on 31 August 1997.

Opening and closing years

4.2 On the current year basis of assessment, a new business will be taxed in its first year on the profits from the start date to the end of the tax year. In the second year, tax is charged on the profits of the accounting year ending in the second tax year. By the third year, the business is taxed on the profits of the current year.

4.3 When a business is permanently discontinued, the profits of the relevant accounting period will be treated as if they were the profits of the tax year in which the basis period ends.

Example 4.2: Taxation in opening years - current year basis.

Tom Smith sets up in business on 1 August 1998 and chooses an accounting period of 1 August - 31 July.

Tax Year

1998-99   -   Taxed on profits for 1 August 1998 - 5 April 1999

1999-2000-   Taxed on profits for 1 August 1998 - 31 July 1999

2000-01   -   Taxed on profits for 1 August 1999 - 31 July 2000

The profits taxed in the first year are overlap profits and will be relieved when the business ceases trading or changes its accounting year.

Partnerships

4.4   Under the current year basis there is an important change in taxation of partnerships. Each partner will be assessed individually for tax on his or her share of the partnership profits and income and no longer be jointly liable for tax on the whole of the profits. The profits of the accounting period will be divided between the partners according to the share arrangements in that period. Each partner will be treated as though his profit share accrued to him individually. Any losses will be shared in the same way, as will non-trading income. Each partner will only be responsible for his own tax liability and not for any unpaid tax in respect of another partner.

4.5   Any income of the partnership such as rental income, and any capital gains, will be included in the calculation of each partner's share for tax purposes.

4.6   Although each partner is self-assessed, it is impractical for each one to send full accounts with other details. Therefore the precedent partner will make a tax return with details of each partner and their individual tax districts and reference numbers. The return will also include a statement of each partner's share of profits, losses and charges on income. The accounts must also be sent. Submission must be by 31 January following the tax year.

Partners leaving or joining

4.7   For new partnerships which started after 6 April 1994, and for existing partnerships with effect from 1997-98 a change in partners will no longer mean that the partnership will be regarded as ceasing, unless no existing partners continue in the business. This means that continuation elections will no longer be necessary. However, existing partnerships which change during the period up to 5 April 1997 must choose whether to make a continuation election or not. If they do not then the partnership will cease and the new partnership will be subject to current year basis immediately.

4.8   When a new partner joins, he will be taxed in the first year in the same way as a business is taxed in the opening years, i.e. from the date of arrival until the end of the tax year. Therefore overlap profits may arise, depending on the partnership's accounting dates. This overlap will be relieved when the partner leaves or the accounting date alters (this is explained later on).

Partnership agreements

4.9   Most partnerships have written agreements to establish procedures such as buying out partners who leave, making continuation elections and so on. These need to be reviewed in the light of the taxation changes and may need to be altered.

Transitional arrangements

4.10   For businesses and partnerships in existence at 5 April 1994, the assessment for 1995-96 is the last one drawn up on the preceding year basis. The assessment for 1996-97 will be based on 50% of the combined profits for the two accounting periods ending in the 1995-96 tax year and the 1996-97 tax year. From 1997-98, profits will be assessed on the current year basis. The tax return for the transitional year must be submitted by 31 January 1998.

4.11   Businesses can either prepare a single account for the whole two year period (1995-97) or two separate accounts for each year. If losses are incurred, these will be allowed in full and not averaged.

Overlap relief

4.12   Existing businesses which do not have a year end of 31 March or 5 April will have an overlap of profits which will have been taxed twice due to the way businesses are taxed in the opening years of trading.

4.13   This is represented by the period between the end of the basis period for 1996-97 to 5 April 1997.

4.14   This will be set against profits either in the year the business closes, or if the business changes its year end to 31 March or 5 April and so has a year which is longer than 12 months. It should be noted that the value of this relief is not index-linked and so may lose value due to inflation.

4.15   The following example shows how the overlap arises and how relief is given by a change in accounting date during the transitional period.

Example 4.3: Howe, Wye and Watt partnership

The partnership was set up on 1 November 1992 with an accounting period to 31 October. Profit for accounting year 1 November 1992 to 31 October 1993 was £10,000.

Tax in the opening years was assessed as follows:

Tax year	Basis period	Period in business	Period taxed
1992-93	1 Nov 92 - 05 April 93		5 months
1993-94	1 Nov 92 - 31 Oct 93	12 months	12 months
1994-95	1 Nov 92 - 31 Oct 93		12 months
1995-96	1 Nov 93 - 31 Oct 94	12 months	12 months
1996-97	1 Nov 94 - 31 Oct 96 x 50%	24 months	12 months
Total		48 months	53 months

Overlap = 5 months

The business decides to change its accounting year in the transitional year 1996-97 to end on 5 April. This means that the basis period for this year is 1 November 1994 to 5 April 1997 and tax will be 50% of the average profits for this period. However, this will be reduced by the five months' overlap which is represented by the profits made between 1 November 1996 and 5 April 1997. Tax for the year 1997-98 will be based on profits made between 6 April 1997 and 5 April 1998.

If the change of accounting date had not taken place this overlap relief would have been given when a partner left or the partnership ceased.

Note that if the taxation in 1996-97 took full account of the two years' profits then the overlap relief would be increased to 17 months.

If the partners had not changed their accounting date then their tax liability for the tax year 1997-98 would be based on profits for 1 November 1996 to 31 October 1997.

Anti-avoidance

4.16 The effect of using an average of two years' profits to calculate tax liability in the transitional period is that businesses will want to create large profits for the relevant accounting periods and therefore reduce the amount of tax payable. For example, a business which makes profits of £10,000 in each of the relevant accounting periods will be taxed on £10,000. If it could add in another £5,000 profits which could be taxed under those provisions they would only be liable to tax on £2,500. If, however they were included in the following year's accounts then the full £5,000 would be taxable.

4.17 The Inland Revenue has introduced anti-avoidance provisions to ensure that businesses do not reduce their tax bill by abusing the transitional arrangements. Where it can identify certain transactions such as a change in accounting policy or connected party transactions which do not seem to have any other bona fide commercial reason for having taken place the Revenue can impose an additional 25% tax charge. The business can defend a challenge by the Revenue but must prove its reasons. A change in accounting date to 31 March or 5 April during the transitional period is excluded from the anti-avoidance provisions.

5   Payment of Tax under Self-assessment

5.1 Self-employed persons will pay tax in the same way as was described in Unit 3 for employees except that the PAYE system does not apply. Individuals will complete a tax return based on profits made in the relevant accounting period and any other tax liabilities such as unearned income or capital gains, and make payments on account which will be based on the previous year's liability. Any balancing adjustment will be made the following January. Individuals will be able to make amendments up to 12 months after.

Example 4.4: Payment of tax by a sole trader

Alex Smith's total tax liability in 1997-98 was £6,500. His tax payments for the tax year 1998-99 are as follows.

January 1999 - £3,250 (i.e. half previous year's liability)

July 1999   - £3,250

January 2000 -   balancing amount of £2,000 to pay following completion

of tax return
- plus first payment on account for 1999-2000 tax year
of half x £8,500 = £4,250

Partnerships

5.2 Partnerships have to adjust to both the current year basis and self-assessment during the transitional year. Although each partner will now be responsible for completing his own tax return based on his share of the partnership income it would be impractical for each partner to submit details of accounts and other relevant information relating to the partnership.

5.3 Each business will appoint a 'representative' partner, usually the precedent partner as described earlier, who will be responsible for filing the partnership statement which will give details of the income and allocation of the business together with information to enable the Inland Revenue to link the information with the individual partner's tax returns.

5.4 During the transitional year 1996-97, for businesses which existed before April 1994, each partner will complete a tax return based on his other income and liabilities and will be given a tax credit for his share of the partnership tax for that year. Therefore, his individual responsibility for tax on his partnership share will commence in the tax year 1997-98.

5.5 The payments on account and any balancing payment a partner makes will include his personal tax liabilities on other earned and unearned income as well as on his share of the partnership profits and income. Partnerships may, however, decide to retain part of each partner's profits to meet tax liability on partnership income and release it when tax payments are due.

5.6 The main impact of the change to self-assessment for partnerships is that partners are now only liable for their own share of the tax bill and cannot be made to pay the tax bill of other partners. The partners must agree between them how they will apportion profits for taxation purposes and that share is then treated as though it arose to the individual partner. Losses are also apportioned in the same way. When a partner leaves, he will be taxed on his share arising to him up to the date of leaving. He will also be eligible for his share of any overlap relief. When a new partner joins, he will be liable to tax on his share from the date of joining to the end of the tax year in the first year. This has been explained earlier in this unit.

Example 4.5: Partnership share

The three partners Howe, Wye and Watt have partnership profits in the year 1997-98 of £12,000. The profit share is split in the ratio 2:1:1 so the profits liable to tax for the individual partners are apportioned as follows:

Howe - £6,000
Wye   - £3,000
Watt   - £3,000

Change of accounting date

5.7 The Inland Revenue will only allow a change of accounting date once every five years under the current year basis unless there are sound commercial reasons for a change. A change will mean that an accounting period either longer or shorter than 12 months will occur. If the accounting date in the year of change is less than 12 months then the profits of the 12 months up to the new date are taxed. This may lead to an overlap which can be relieved when the business ceases trading or at a subsequent change of accounting date.

5.8 If more than 12 months profits are taxed in the year of change overlap relief from the opening years of trading can be offset against them. The Inland Revenue will not allow an accounting period of more than 18 months.

5.9 If a self-employed person or a partnership wishes to change the accounting date the Inland Revenue must be notified by 31 January following the end of the tax year in which the new accounting date first falls.

5.10 If a business makes up its accounts to a year end of 31 March the Revenue will treat it as being equivalent to a tax year so a business that sets up on 1 April 1996 will be treated as having no profits for the five days from 1 April to 5 April for the 1995-96 tax year. Tax liability will commence in the tax year 1996-97. There would be no overlap profits and so no relief to apply in later years. The procedure for opening and closing years of business are much simpler if the accounting period coincides with the tax year.

Example 4.6: Changing accounting date

Mary Jones is self-employed and has an accounting period ending on 31 December. She wishes to change to 31 March with effect from 1 April 1988.

The accounting period for the year beginning January 1997 will be extended to 31 March 1998 and her tax liability in 1997-98 will be based on this 15 month period. She may be able to relieve the overlap tax from her opening years against this tax liability.

Her tax liability for the tax year 1998-99 will be based on her profits in the year 1 April 1998 - 31 March 1999.

Student Activity 2

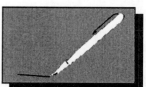

You should complete this student activity before reading the next section of the text. Answer the questions, then check your answers against the paragraph(s) indicated.

Diana White is self-employed. She set up in business on 1 April 1995, and her accounting period is 1 April - 31 March.

(a) On what accounting period will she be assessed for tax for the tax year 1995-96? (4.1)

(b) When will she have to submit her tax return for the 1996-97 tax year? (4.1)

(c) How will she make her payments of tax for the tax year 1997-98? (5.1)

(d) What advantage does Diana have in choosing an accounting period which ends on 31 March? (5.10)

If you are unable to answer any of the questions satisfactorily, you should read the relevant paragraphs again. Your understanding of the text will be further tested in the self-assessment section at the end of this unit.

6 Calculation of Taxable Profits

6.1 As has been shown, self-employed individuals are taxed on their business profits which arise in an accounting period. The notes that follow explain how taxable profits are calculated and the types of allowances and expenses that are available.

6.2 It should be noted that, as well as a liability to business profits, an individual may have other tax liabilities, such as unearned income, which need to be taken into account on a tax return. Whilst an employee will know his salary for the year and therefore know if he is a higher rate taxpayer and liable to marginal rate tax on his investment income, the situation may not be as clear for a self-employed person. He may not know if he is a basic rate or higher rate taxpayer until he has completed his tax return and so tax planning becomes more complicated. Under the preceding year basis of taxation, individuals had more time to adjust their taxable profits, for example, by using carry back and carry forward of pension contributions. Generally speaking, under current year basis, claims for reliefs should be made in the tax return for the year in which they apply.

Deductible business expenses

6.3 Provided an expense is wholly and exclusively incurred for the purposes of business it will be allowed as a deduction for tax. This general rule is, however, subject to some qualifications. Some expenses such as legal expenses relating to the acquisition of capital assets rather than to the running of the business will be disallowed for tax.

6.4 Allowable business expenses are deductible from the gross income of a business before assessment for tax. The following list identifies some of the common deductions:

- The cost of goods purchased for manufacture or resale i.e. stocks
- Wages and salaries paid to employees and National Insurance contributions paid for their benefit
- Pensions paid to past employees and/or dependants, and pension contributions for employees' benefit
- Redundancy payments
- Running costs of the business premises such as rates, light, heat, insurance, cleaning, repairs
- Selling costs such as carriage, packing and delivery
- Printing, postage, stationery
- Repairs to plant and machinery
- Staff welfare expenses
- Business insurances

- Advertising

- Trade subscriptions

- Audit fees and legal charges

- VAT on purchases and expenses if not VAT registered

- Travelling expenses including hotel bills, fares etc., but excluding travel from home to work

- Bad debt arising in the course of trading

- Motor vehicle running expenses excluding private use

- Interest payments including hire purchase

- Cost of obtaining loan finance which carries deductible interest

Expenses not allowed

6.5   The following is a list of the common expenses not allowed when tax assessment is made, but this list is by no means exhaustive:

- Payments or expenses not wholly for business purposes

- If an expense contains a proportional use for business and private, then only the business proportion is deductible

- Capital for improvement of premises

- A loss not connected with the business

- Payment of tax

- Any annuity or other payment made out of profits

- Owner's drawings (these are only an 'advance' against the profit shown in the accounts)

- Certain legal costs, e.g. legal costs on a lease for a new capital purchase

- Charitable donations (as an individual a sole trader could make a tax-free donation of up to £250 but as a business donation it is not an allowable expense)

- Political donations

- Cost of acquiring assets (under preceding year basis only)

Capital allowances

6.6   Under the preceding year basis, expenses incurred in acquiring a capital asset may not be deducted from trading profits. Assuming that the asset has a limited life span, an amount for depreciation can be included in the accounts. However, depreciation in itself is not allowable for tax purposes, but instead there are specific allowances available against certain types of capital expenditure. The most common are for machinery and plant, industrial buildings and agricultural land and buildings.

6.7   Allowances are first given for the expenditure made in a 'basis period' which is usually the relevant accounting period.

6.8   There are two ways of granting allowances; a writing-down allowance each year during the life of the asset and a balancing charge or allowance at the end of the trade or on the disposal of the asset.

6.9　This is to bring the allowances into line with the actual amount spent i.e. the difference between original cost and the proceeds of disposal. If no allowances have been given, and the proceeds are less than the original expenditure then a balancing allowance is given. If proceeds are greater than the original cost then a balancing charge is made.

Writing-down allowance

(a)　Machinery and plant (this can include cars, fixtures and fittings).

- First year : 25% of cost reduced according to length of first year basis period - the net figure of the 'cost less the allowance' is called the written down value

- Next year : Allowance is given of 25% of the written-down value and the same procedure is repeated in subsequent years

(b)　Industrial buildings, hotels

- 4% per annum of construction cost until fully written off

(c)　Agricultural land and buildings

- 4% per annum of cost for 25 years.

(d)　Cars

- 25% allowance if car cost less than £12,000 (£8,000 if bought before 11.3.92)

- £3,000 each year if car costs over £12,000 (£2,000 for cars over £8,000 bought before 11.3.92) until the amount brought forward falls below £12,000, when the 25% rate of allowance becomes applicable

Capital allowances under the current year basis of assessment

6.10　With the introduction of the new current year basis of assessment, there is a change in how expenditure on capital assets is treated. Capital allowances will in future be deducted from profits as a trading expense of the accounting period and will be claimed in the tax returns. Previously, the allowances applied to the tax year rather than the accounting period. The new rules applied immediately to businesses starting up on or after 6 April 1994, and will come into force for existing businesses from 1997-98.

7　Preparation of Accounts

7.1　The accounts produced by a sole trader, or by his accountant/book-keeper do not have to be audited (checked by an independent and qualified source). Similarly, partnerships are not legally obliged to use an accountant to draw up their accounts, although it is advisable.

7.2　The accounts form the basis for self-assessment for income tax payable. As previously described, there are allowable deductions which can be made in arriving at taxable profits. There are, however, deductions made within the accounts which are not allowable against the profit of the business for tax assessment. These will be added back into the figure shown in the accounts before any deductions for capital allowances are made.

Assessable profits

7.3   The accounts will normally require adjustment in the following way:

- Add to the profit figure any non-deductible expenses detailed previously which have been charged in the accounts

- Deduct any items included which make up the profit figure but are not taxed under Schedule D, Cases I and II, e.g. interest received, taxed under Schedule D Case III; capital profits subject to capital gains tax

- Deduct any further allowable expenses not already charged

- Exclude certain grants e.g. those for capital expenditure

- Add any further profit from trading not already credited

- Deduct capital allowances for the year

7.4   This produces the adjusted profit which is the taxable figure.

Trading losses

7.5   Under the preceding year basis of assessment, relief for trading losses could be claimed in a number of ways:

(a) **Set off losses against other income -**
A trading loss could be set off against other income in the same year of assessment, or in the following year of assessment provided that the trade is still carried on in the later year. Losses could also be set against any capital gains where they cannot be set against income. This concession for loss relief against general income is only available for losses incurred in a demonstrably commercial trade.

(b) **Carry forward of losses against subsequent years' profits -**
Losses could be carried forward to a later year to be set against future profits from the same trade. There is no time limit.

(c) **In a new trade, carry back against general income of previous three tax years -**
If a business made a loss in any of the first four tax years, this could be offset against other income, including earnings from a previous employment, in the three years before the year in which the loss was made. The loss is offset against income for the earliest year first. Losses may not be offset against capital gains. Alternatively, losses may be offset against other income, including capital gains, in the tax year of the loss or in the following year.

(d) **When a loss occurs on ceasing to trade, carry back against trading income of previous three tax years -**
If a business which is closing down made a loss in the last twelve months of trading, this could be offset against profits from the same business in the three preceding tax years, starting with the latest year first, or against other income of the same year.

Trading losses under the current year basis of assessment

7.6   The treatment of losses changes for the current year basis of assessment where relief is given for the trading losses of the relevant accounting period. Capital allowances will be included in the loss calculation. Whereas losses under preceding year basis may be set against other income in the year of loss

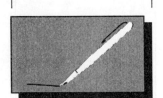

and the following year, this is changed to the year of loss and the previous year. The trade does not need to have been carried on in that previous year. The rules for losses made in the opening and closing years remain the same as for preceding year basis, although it should be remembered that if the loss arising in the relevant tax year relates to the loss made in the basis period for that tax year, claims for either current year or preceding year must be made within 22 months of the end of the tax year in which the loss arose.

Student Activity 3

You should complete this student activity before attempting the self-assessment. Answer the questions, then check your answers against the paragraph(s) indicated.

1. Name four types of business expenses that are tax deductible. (6.4)

2. What is the difference between the way in which capital allowances are given under the current year basis compared with the preceding year basis? (6.10)

3. Partners A and B are taxed under the current year basis and have incurred a loss in the relevant accounting period for the current tax year. How are these losses treated and when must relief for losses be claimed by? (7.6)

If you are unable to answer any of the questions satisfactorily, you should read the relevant paragraphs again. Your understanding of the text will be further tested in the following self-assessment.

Summary

Now that you have completed this unit you should be able to:

☐ **Explain the differences between preceding year basis and current year basis for assessing tax liability of the self-employed**

☐ **Understand the particular changes of relevance to partnerships**

☐ **Define an accounting period and know which tax year an accounting period is taxed in**

☐ **Understand the provisions for opening and closing years of trading**

☐ **Know what is meant by overlap relief**

☐ **Understand the transitional arrangements for the 1996-97 tax year**

☐ **Explain how sole traders and partners arrive at taxable profits and how tax is paid**

☐ **Know how business losses are treated for tax purposes**

If you can tick all the above boxes with confidence, you are ready to answer the questions which follow.

Self-Assessment Questions

1. Under what tax schedule are a self-employed person's business profits taxed?

2. A new partnership is set up on 1 January 1997. What period will form the assessment basis for the 1996-97 tax year?

3. How does a partner know how much of the partnership's profits he will be taxed on when he is completing his tax return?

4. Mike Scott is joining a partnership on 1 September 1997. The partnership has an accounting year of 1 July to 30 June.

    (a) On what period will Mike be assessed to tax in the tax years 1997-98 and 1998-99?

    (b) Will an overlap arise, and if so how is this relieved?

5. Why has the Inland Revenue introduced anti-avoidance provisions for the transitional year 1996-97?

6. Anna Johnson has a total tax liability of £10,000 for the year 1997-98. What are her payments on account for 1998-99 and when will they be due?

7. ABC Partnership decides to change its accounting year from 1 January to 31 December to coincide with the tax year starting on 6 April 1998. How will the tax liability for the tax year 1997-98 be calculated?

8. A self-employed person wants to make a donation to a charity. Is this an allowable expense for tax purposes?

9. What is the purpose of a writing-down allowance?

10. Partners Tom and Jerry have incurred a loss this year. Do they have to claim this loss in the current tax year under the current year basis?

Unit 5

National Insurance

Objectives

Students are required to study the following topics:

* **Introduction to National Insurance contributions**

* **Classes of National Insurance contributions**

* **State benefit entitlement**

1   Introduction to National Insurance

1.1   National Insurance is, effectively, a form of taxation on income. Contributions are paid by individuals on their earnings, and also by their employers where applicable. Contributions are compulsory and are used to help fund the State's social security programmes, run by the Department of Social Security (DSS). These contributions are intended to build up an entitlement to various benefits in the event of certain needs, e.g. disability, unemployment and retirement. Any changes in rates are normally announced at the annual Budget statement in November, and come into effect in the following April.

1.2   The level of National Insurance (NI) contributions due is dependent on a number of different factors, the main one being the level of income received. As we shall see, however, this is not the sole consideration, and the other factors each have their own, important, influence on NI contributions. These include the nature of the individual's employment i.e. whether he is employed or self-employed, the individual's age and residence status.

2   Earnings

2.1   Before considering the types and levels of contributions, it important to ensure a clear understanding of what is meant by the term 'earnings' in this context. This will, obviously, include any salary or wages for the employed, and profits for the self-employed individual. But there are a number of other types of income or moneys received that should also be taken into account when considering NI contributions.

2.2   Earnings that may be subject to National Insurance include:

(a) Bonuses, commissions, overtime and holiday payments.

(b) Benefits in kind, specifically:

* Use-of-own-car allowances, unless the use of the car can be proven to have been on business grounds

* Private petrol provided by the employer

- Payments received for private use of telephone bills and rentals

- Any excess made on subsistence and expenses claims over and above the actual costs incurred

- Various other fringe benefits, including the provision of vouchers, premium bonds, gilts, subscriptions in the individual's name where made by an employer

  It should be noted that a monetary value is attributed to these benefits, which is then added to income, thereby increasing the gross income level subject to NI contributions, working in the same way as the calculation of income tax.

(c) Profit-related pay.

(d) Certain lump sum payments made by an employer:

- As a form of service award for past or future service

- As a 'sweetener' to encourage the acceptance of alterations to employment contracts by employees

(e) Profits from a trade.

Payments not subject to National Insurance

2.3   There are, conversely, a number of payments that can be received without being subject to National Insurance:

(a) Payments received as a result of redundancy.

(b) Ordinary business expenses.

(c) Certain payments in kind.

(d) Pension income.

(e) Tips and gratuities (although these are subject to income tax).

(f) Payments as a result of travel, lodging or board incurred due to industrial action.

(g) Payments received on which contributions may already have been made.

3   Types of Contribution

3.1   There are five types of contribution, known as classes, and it is the class paid that determines the amounts of contribution and relevant rules. The five classes are:

Class 1   -   paid by employees and their employers
Class 1A-   paid by employers only
Class 2   -   paid by the self-employed
Class 3   -   voluntary contributions
Class 4   -   paid by the self-employed in relation to their profits.

4   Class 1 Contributions

4.1   This class of NI contributions is broken into two tiers, primary contributions which are made by employees and secondary contributions made by their employers. The employee's (primary) NI contributions are payable from age 16 to 60 (women) or 65 (men), providing the individual earns above the lower earnings limit (LEL). The employer's (secondary) contributions do not cease at state retirement age if the employee continues to work.

Employee contributions

4.2 An employee will pay NI contributions on gross income received that falls between two levels. Where earnings are above the LEL (£61.00 per week in 1996-97) a percentage will be payable in primary contributions, on all earnings that qualify up to the upper earnings limit (UEL) (£455.00 per week for 1996-97). Above the UEL, no employee contributions are due. The income that falls between the two levels is known as the middle band earnings.

4.3 Where the employee's income exceeds the LEL the percentage payable in NI contributions will be split as follows:

- 2% of earnings up to the LEL

- 10% of earnings between the LEL and UEL

Example 5.1: Calculating Class 1 National Insurance contributions

James Sharp, an employed man, earns £13,000 gross per annum (£250 per week) in the fiscal year 1996-97. His primary Class 1 NI contributions would be due as follows:

First £61.00 per week @ 2%	= £ 1.22 per week
Balance of £189.00 per week @ 10%	= £18.90 per week
Total primary Class 1 NI contributions	= £20.12 per week

Contributions will be affected by whether the individual is contracted-out of the state earnings related pension scheme (SERPS). This is covered below.

Employer contributions

4.4 The employer's (secondary) contributions will also depend on whether the individual has 'contracted-out' but first consider the situation for those employees who are 'contracted-in'. Like the employee, the employer also has the benefit of the LEL for the lower paid employee. However, the major difference is that the employer does not have a cap on the maximum contributions that can be paid, they have no UEL. Secondary Class 1 NI contributions are calculated on a scale, depending on the employee's earnings. The rates for 1996-97 are as follows:

Table 5.1: Secondary Class 1 NI contributions (contracted-in rate)

Employee's Total Weekly Earnings	Contribution (on all earnings)
£ 61.00 - £109.99	3%
£110.00 - £154.99	5%
£155.00 - £209.99	7%
£210.00 and over	10.2%

4.5 Thus for James Sharp earning £13,000 per annum, his employer's secondary contributions would be at 10.2% on his whole £250 per week i.e. £25.50 per week.

Class 1A contributions

4.6 Employers have to pay Class 1A NI contributions where cars are provided for private use for employees earning at least £8,500 per annum, and most directors. Fuel provided for private use is also liable. The rate used is the highest secondary contribution rate in force in the relevant tax year, i.e. 10.2% in 1996-97. The cash equivalent of the car, known as the car benefit, is used to calculate the amount due. The car benefit is based on the manufacturer's list price plus the value of any accessories provided. Adjustments are also made for any business mileage which the car is used for and other elements such as periods of unavailability or payments made by the employee towards private usage.

Tax relief for employers

4.7 Employers can obtain tax relief on their share of NI contributions paid for employees. This is given by allowing the contributions as a tax deductible expense. This also applies to Class 1A contributions.

Contracted-out NI contributions

4.8 Where the employer provides an occupational pension scheme and employees are contracted-out of Serps, National Insurance contribution levels will be reduced. These reduced rates apply to both the employer's and the employee's NI contributions. However, they do not apply if the individual employee decides to 'contract-out' through an appropriate personal pension where the difference between the contracted-in and contracted-out rates is rebated by the DSS into the pension plan. For the employee, the reduction in rates amounts to 1.8% off the contribution on his middle band earnings. The rate for 1996-97 is, therefore, 8.2%.

4.9 The employer benefits from a reduction of 3% from the scale above on earnings between the LEL and UEL so the rates are reduced as follows:

Table 5.2: Secondary Class 1 NI contributions (contracted-out rate)

Employee's Total Weekly Earnings	Contribution (on all earnings)
Under £61.00	none
£ 61.00 - £109.99	none
£110.00 - £154.99	2%
£155.00 - £209.99	4%
£210.00 - £455.00	7.2%
over £455.00	7.2% plus 10.2% on £61 and on earnings over £455.00

Married women and widows

4.10 There are two categories of employees that are treated differently from these standard bases. The first covers married women or some widows who married prior to 1977. Providing their marriage date was before 6 April that year, and they exercised an option to pay reduced NI contributions before 12 May 1977, they were given a certificate of election (CF383). This remains in force until revoked, cancelled or the husband and wife divorced, and therefore some women are still entitled to pay reduced NI contributions as a result. The reduction affects their entitlement to certain benefits that could be received, although they would still be eligible for statutory sick pay, statutory maternity pay or retirement pensions. The election also meant that the woman would not be liable to pay Class 2 NI contributions if she were self-employed.

4.11 The reduced rate payable by the employee for 1996-97 is 3.85% of all earnings up to the UEL provided that earnings exceed the LEL. They are the same irrespective of whether she is contracted-in or contracted-out.

4.12 The employer's liability to NI contributions is not affected by the election, they will pay the rates due dependent on whether the employee is contracted-in or contracted-out.

Special occupations

4.13 The second category that falls outside the normal calculations for Class 1 NI contributions includes specified occupations. These include some company directors, people working on oil rigs, people serving in the armed forces, certain civil servants (typically those working abroad), agency supplied staff (on a temporary basis), and office and telephone equipment cleaners among a range of others. Although these persons will normally be liable for Class 1 NI contributions there may be special rules which apply and employers should seek advice from the DSS.

Payment of contributions

4.14 Employee NI contributions are collected by the employer through the PAYE system. The employer calculates the amount due for each employee and deducts their primary contributions from gross pay. These are then sent, together with the employer's secondary contributions, to the Collector of Taxes in the same way as income tax payments at the end of each month. In certain cases, typically where the amount to be paid is small, this can be submitted quarterly.

Exceptions

4.15 The National Insurance regime covering Class 1 contributions excludes certain employees and their employers from having to pay NI contributions. These include:

(a) Those employed by their spouse or a near relative for a non-business related purpose.

(b) Employees of visiting armed forces, unless they are ordinarily a UK resident.

(c) Employees coming from countries which do not have an agreement with the UK regarding social security arrangements.

Working abroad

4.16 The normal rule is that if an employee goes abroad to work for a UK based employer he will continue to pay Class 1 NI contributions for the first 52 weeks. If the employee takes up permanent or semi-permanent residence abroad then NI contributions will normally cease. If the individual is working temporarily abroad or moving around between countries he may have to pay contributions. It may be advisable to make voluntary contributions to ensure eligibility for state benefits.

4.17 Where an individual is working in a country with a reciprocal arrangement, liability to the UK may continue for a number of years. However, the opposite applies to any European Economic Area (EEA) countries where the employee will be liable to the country of employment. However this does not apply for a short-term visit of up to 12 months (which may be extended, depending on circumstances, up to 24 months or longer) in which case the person will remain liable for making payments to the UK.

4.18 Visitors and new permanent residents in the UK are not normally liable to pay Class 1 NI contributions for the first 12 months. This does not apply to someone coming from an EEA country who will be liable to UK contributions from outset. Anyone from a country with a reciprocal agreement will make payments to their home country.

4.19 Wherever an employee is liable to pay Class 1 NI contributions then his employer will also be liable for secondary contributions. It may be sensible for individuals to renegotiate their employment contracts to gain the best advantage regarding payment of contributions. Any gap in a contribution record may have an effect on eligibility for state benefits.

More than one income

4.20 In some circumstances an individual may have more than one source of earnings that are liable to Class 1. In these cases the employee is liable for primary contributions on each source of income, with each set of earnings being subject to the LEL and UEL as described previously. In a similar way, the employers are also liable for secondary contributions on the income derived from that employment. However, if the sources of income are closely related, perhaps from different companies within the same group, the contributions will be aggregated together, both for primary and secondary NI contributions.

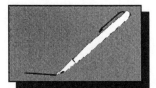

Student Activity 1

You should complete this student activity before reading the next section of the text. Answer the questions, then check your answers against the paragraph(s) indicated.

1. (a) Calculate both the primary and secondary weekly Class 1 NI contributions due on James Sharp's income, assuming he is now contracted-out of Serps, and has just received a £2,000 bonus. (4.8)

   (b) What is the difference between NI contributions payable on 'contracted-in' earnings and 'contracted-out' earnings? (4.4, 4.9)

2. In what situation may certain women pay reduced NI contributions? (4.10)

3. How does an employee pay his NI contributions? (4.14)

If you are unable to answer any of the questions satisfactorily, you should read the relevant paragraphs again. Your understanding of the text will be further tested in the self-assessment section at the end of this unit.

5   Class 2 Contributions

5.1   Class 2 NI contributions are a flat rate payment paid by self-employed individuals aged over 16 and under 60 (women) or 65 (men). Before moving on to consider the detail it is important to clarify the differences between the employed and self-employed individual.

Self-employment

5.2   As has been established in an earlier unit, there may be circumstances in which an individual is, in fact, employed when he believes himself to be self-employed, e.g. services are provided in return for instructions of how, where and when the duties are to be performed. This has a resultant effect on his NI contribution position and may mean an extra liability if the wrong class of contribution is being paid. Additionally, the employer will also be required to make contributions as if the individual had always been employed, together with possible penalties.

Contributions

5.3   Although contributions are made at a flat rate there is still a need to establish earnings levels. The rate for 1996-97 is £6.05 per week, and is often referred to as the 'Stamp'. Contributions are now typically made by either a monthly direct debit arrangement with the DSS, or by a quarterly payment but were previously paid for by purchasing National Insurance stamps each week. This was abolished in April 1993.

Earnings levels

5.4   Class 2 NI contributions are payable by the self-employed if their earnings exceed a set amount which is £3,430 per annum for the year 1996-97. If their earnings are below this figure, no Class 2 contributions are payable. This is known as the small earnings exception.

Special occupations

5.5   In a similar way to Class 1 NI contributions there are specific rules for a number of types of self-employment particularly where there may be elements of both employment and self-employment. An example of this is where persons are employed by the Post Office to run a sub-post office on a salary. They typically also have their own business as well. Class 1 NI contributions are due on the salary they receive, while Class 2 contributions will be due on their own business income.

Payment of contributions

5.6   As noted above, contributions are paid on a regular basis by direct debit or by a quarterly arrangement in arrears, following a bill from the DSS. They will be due in the same way as income tax payments following tax assessments.

Exceptions

5.7 In addition to those outside the age range, below the small earnings exception, and those married women or widows with the certificate of election, there are a number of people who need not pay Class 2 NI contributions:

(a) The DSS allows for those who are not 'ordinarily' self-employed to be exempt. A common example is the person who, while having some form of regular employment, earns less than £800 from spare-time self-employment.

(b) People who anticipate their earnings will be below the small earnings exception (rather than being based on actual earnings).

(c) Those people who work outside the UK in a given week will not have to contribute for that week.

(d) Those people who, for some reason, cannot work. This would include those people in receipt of various state benefits or who are otherwise incapable of working, are in prison or in custody.

Voluntary contributions

5.8 Where a self-employed individual is not required to pay Class 2 NI contributions, e.g. they earn below the small earnings exception, they can choose to make contributions on a voluntary basis. The main benefit of so doing would be to build up entitlement to state benefits that are accrued by Class 2 contributions, but are not available through Class 3 contributions.

5.9 For those who are self-employed outside the UK, but are ordinarily UK resident, there is no requirement to pay Class 2 NI contributions. They may do so, however, if they wish to maintain their contribution record. The same provisions as for Class 1 contributions apply where there are reciprocal agreements or the individual is working in an EEA country.

5.10 For individuals who come to work in the UK there would not, ordinarily, be an immediate requirement to make contributions, but, again, they may wish to start contributing before having been deemed to be resident, to start accruing benefit entitlement as soon as possible.

More than one source of income

5.11 Earnings will be added together to calculate the level of contributions due, provided all the income comes from self-employment. Those situations involving both employed and self-employed earnings are dealt with later in this unit.

6 Class 3 Contributions

6.1 Class 3 contributions are a voluntary class of NI contributions, made by people whose overall contribution record is insufficient to ensure entitlement to certain benefits.

6.2 NI contributions under this class can be paid by those over 16 years of age and under 60 (women) or 65 (men). In certain circumstances people aged 17 or 18 are entitled to credits and may not then contribute. Those married women and widows with the election to pay reduced contributions may not make class 3 contributions.

6.3 Contributions are made at a flat rate which, in 1996-97, is £5.95 per week.

7 Class 4 Contributions

7.1 These contributions are made by the self-employed, based on their profits. The ages for payment are in line with other NI contributions, i.e. over 16 and under 60 (women) or 65 (men). Class 4 contributions do not provide any entitlement to state benefits.

Contributions

7.2 Payments are made based on the profits made by the self-employed, where they fall between two levels, lower profits and upper profits limits.

7.3 For 1996-97 the lower limit for Class 4 contributions is a taxable profit of £6,860 per year, and the upper limit is £23,660 per year. Between these two levels NI contributions are paid at 6% of the profit achieved that falls into the middle band.

Example 5.2: Calculating Class 4 National Insurance Contributions

A self-employed man makes a taxable profit of £12,500 in the year 1996-97. His Class 4 contribution will be:

£12,500 - £6,860 = £5,640

6% of £5,640   = £338.40

Married women and widows

7.4 Where the election has been made to pay reduced NI contributions, resulting in exemption from Class 2 NI contributions, care must be taken to note that Class 4 contributions are still required from self-employed women whose profits fall into the band described above.

Payment of contributions

7.5 Class 4 NI contributions are collected in the same way as income tax payments on profits, with the due amounts shown as two payments on the individual's income tax assessment. The contributions are payable at the same time, therefore, as the tax instalments i.e. January and July. For the 1996-97 year the payments due are based on the previous year's Class 4 contributions due to the change to self-assessment.

7.6 As with income tax, 1996-97 is a transitional period during the change to self-assessment and Class 4 contributions will be the same as those paid in the 1995-96 tax year. Any balancing adjustment will be made in the following January.

Exceptions

7.7 The following people are not liable to pay Class 4 contributions:

- Anyone over state pension age at the beginning of the tax year

- Persons not resident in the UK for tax purposes

- Trustees and executors who are chargeable to tax on income received on behalf of other people

In addition income from holiday letting of property is not liable to Class 4 NI contributions.

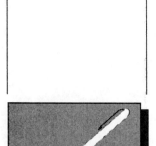

Student Activity 2

You should complete this student activity before reading the next section of the text. Answer the questions, then check your answers against the paragraph(s) indicated.

1. Brian Bounds is self-employed and has net trading profits of £28,000.

    (a) Calculate the Class 4 contributions he will have to make for   (7.3)

    the year covered by the profits.

                                                                                            (7.3, 7.7)

    (b) What will the contributions be if half of his income is derived from holiday letting?

2. If a self-employed person goes to work abroad for two years   (5.9)
    how will this affect their NI contribution record?

3. Who pays Class 3 NI contributions?   (6.1, 6.2)

If you are unable to answer any of the questions satisfactorily, you should read the relevant paragraphs again. Your understanding of the text will be further tested in the self-assessment section at the end of this unit.

8   More Than One Income

8.1   There are some people who receive income from both an employed and a self-employed source. This requires them to pay Class 1, Class 2 and Class 4 NI contributions if their incomes from each source exceed the LEL and lower profits limits. This could result in a complicated set of rules and requirements in some cases.

8.2   In practice where the person is liable for Class 1 and Class 2 NI contributions the total payable for his primary Class 1 contributions, together with his Class 2 NI contributions will not exceed an amount equivalent to 53 weeks of Class 1 contributions. Therefore, if the earnings he derives from his employment are in excess of the UEL (£455.00 per week in 1996-97), he will be deemed to have paid the maximum in NI contributions, and no Class 2 contributions will be due.

8.3   Note that annual liability is always based on 53 weeks to allow for the extra

1 or 2 days at the end of a year. These are treated as a whole week.

8.4 As far as Class 4 NI contributions are concerned, the situation is less straightforward. If the maximum in Class 1 NI contributions have been made, there will be no liability to Class 4 contributions. Likewise, if the Class 1 NI contributions together with the Class 2 NI contributions are at the maximum payable, there is no Class 4 liability. The complication arises where the maximum has not been reached. In this case the Class 4 contributions payable are based on a limit. This is expressed as the excess of the sum of maximum Class 2 and Class 4 contributions over the sum of Class 1 and Class 2 contributions.

8.5 Note that although there is a maximum limit for the amount of NI contributions an employee can pay in a year this does not apply to the employer.

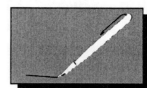

Student Activity 3

You should complete this student activity before reading the next section of the text. Answer the questions, then check your answers against the paragraph(s) indicated.

Calculate the annual NI contributions payable by Simon Fisher on his employed earnings of £10,000 and self-employed profits of £15,000. Show each class of contributions separately.   (8.2, 8.4)

If you are unable to answer any of the questions satisfactorily, you should read the relevant paragraphs again. Your understanding of the text will be further tested in the self-assessment section at the end of this unit.

9   State Benefits

9.1 Payment of NI contributions entitles the individual to certain state benefits. In order to build entitlement to benefits a record of contributions will have to be established. The DSS will compile a record of the class and contributions received based on earnings or in some cases credited as having been paid. Different classes of NI contributions are credited towards different benefits, with some not counting at all. Everyone has a National Insurance number to enable a record to be kept.

No entitlement to benefits

9.2 The following contributions carry no entitlement to benefits:

(a) Secondary class 1 contributions, from the employer.

(b) Reduced contributions payable by some married women and widows with the election. They can only claim entitlement to retirement and widows pension on their husband's contribution record.

(c) Self-employed class 4 contributions.

Limited entitlement to benefits

9.3 Class 2 and Class 3 contributions have a limited range of benefit credits as shown in the table below.

Benefits provided

9.4 A brief overview of the main contributory state benefits provided by NI contributions is detailed below.

Table 5.3: Contributory state benefits

| State Benefit | Class of contribution | | |
	1	2	3
Basic State Pension	✓	✓	✓
Incapacity Benefit	✓	✓	
Maternity Allowance	✓	✓	
Serps	✓		
Statutory Maternity Pay	✓		
Unemployment Benefit	✓		
Widowed Mother's Allowance	✓	✓	✓
Widow's Payment	✓	✓	✓
Widow's Pension	✓	✓	✓

9.5 As no study of National Insurance can be complete without including the benefits that the contributions, and credits, entitle the individual to, an overview of the main benefits now follows.

Basic state pension

9.6 The amount of pension payable to an individual is currently £61.15 per week (1996-97) with an additional allowance for married couples of £36.30 per week based on the spouse's contributions for a non-contributing wife.

9.7 To qualify for the maximum level of pension, an individual must contribute 90% of Class 1 NI contributions due during his working life. Any less will result in a lower pension being paid.

9.8 Each spouse is entitled to the maximum if both have contributed throughout their lives, thus the maximum a married couple could receive in basic pension is £61.15 each, i.e. £122.30 per week.

9.9 A widow who has paid reduced rate NI contributions can claim a widows pension based on her husband's contribution record. This will be 60% of the husband's basic pension if he is over 65 and she is over 60.

State earnings related pension scheme (Serps)

9.10 The level of benefit is dependent on the amount of contributions and length of service of the individual. The DSS can provide a forecast of the entitlement built up to persons who submit form BR19.

9.11 For those retiring during, and after, the year 2010 the pension payable will be based on 20% of an average of their middle band earnings over their working lives. The situation regarding future Serps entitlements is a large topic, beyond the scope of this unit, but in summary, the retirement age that is applied to the individual employee will also affect the amount of pension he can expect to receive.

9.12 Individuals who are contracted-out of Serps are not entitled to this benefit but should have made equivalent provision either through their employer's scheme or by an appropriate personal pension. It is common, however, for individuals to have some Serps entitlement to cover periods when they were not contracted-out.

9.13 Note that only Class 1 contributions count towards Serps so the self-employed are not eligible.

Incapacity benefit

9.14 Claimants must be ineligible for statutory sick pay (SSP) paid by their employer and unable to work due to illness for more than 3 days. The current lower rate is £46.15 a week (1996-97) for the first 28 weeks if assessed as incapable of working

9.15 If a claimant has already been in receipt of SSP, incapacity benefit or statutory maternity pay for 28 weeks then he will receive the middle rate benefit of £54.55 a week (1996-97) for weeks 29 -52. Neither the lower nor the middle rate benefit will be paid to anyone over state pension age unless the period of incapacity began before that age.

9.16 The higher rate (long term incapacity) benefit will commence after 52 weeks and is only payable to claimants who are under 45 at the start of the period of incapacity. It must cease at state pension age. The current benefit is £61.15 a week (1996-97).

9.17 An additional payment will be made to claimants whose spouses are caring for children or are aged over 60.

9.18 Although the benefit is contributory it is non-contributory if the incapacity was caused by an accident at work or an industrial disease.

Unemployment benefit (jobseekers allowance)

9.19 Claimants for unemployment benefit (to be replaced by the jobseekers allowance from October 1996) must be unemployed but actively seeking employment and fit and able to work. The current benefits are £48.25 a week if under state retirement age and £61.15 a week if over retirement age.

9.20 The amount payable is for one year, provided the claimant is available to look for work, following which it is replaced by income support. If the claimant receives an income from some form of pension, the amount of benefit is reduced proportionately.

9.21 The jobseekers allowance will replace both unemployment benefit and income support and will be directly linked to the extent to which an individual actively seeks and accepts work. It will be available on either a contributory or means tested basis.

Statutory maternity pay

9.22 The claimant must have worked for her employer for at least six months. The employer pays the benefit and reclaims it from the DSS. The rate depends on the length of employment. If less than two years the current weekly rate is £54.55 for 18 weeks (1996-97). If over two years the rate is 90% of earnings for 6 weeks then £54.55 a week for the next twelve weeks (1996-97).

Maternity allowance

9.23 If a claimant is ineligible for SMP she can claim maternity allowance. The current rates are £47.35 a week (1996-97) for a maximum of 18 weeks for the self-employed or non-employed or a higher rate of £54.55 a week (1996-97) for employed women.

Widow's pension

9.24 The claimant must be aged 45 or over on her husband's death unless receiving the widowed mother's allowance or the allowance ends. The benefit is based on her husband's NI contributions and is payable until she is 65 or claims a state pension after age 60. It will cease if she remarries or cohabits.

9.25 The amount payable at the standard rate is £61.15 a week (1996-97) but a lower rate of £18.35 is payable if the husband's contributions were insufficient for the full rate. An additional earnings related pension may be payable unless the husband was contracted-out of Serps.

Widowed mother's allowance

9.26 If the widow under age 45 has children she can claim a widowed mother's allowance which will continue as long as she is entitled to child benefit. It is dependent on her late husband's contribution record.

9.27 The amount payable is £61.15 a week (1996-97) with additional payments for each child of £9.90 a week for the eldest child and £11.15 for each subsequent child.

Widow's payment

9.28 A lump sum is payable on the death of a husband to widows under 60, or over 60 if the husband was not receiving retirement pension when he died. The amount is £1,000 and is dependent on the husband's NI contributions. However, the eligibility level is very low so most widows qualify for this payment.

Taxable benefits

9.29 Certain benefits are taxable and some are liable for NI contributions. These are:

- Unemployment benefit - taxable

- Incapacity benefit - taxable on middle and higher rates

- Statutory maternity pay - taxable and NI contributions payable

- State pension - taxable

- Serps - taxable

- Widows pension - taxable

- Widowed mother's allowance - taxable

9.30 Statutory sick pay is now the responsibility of employers and is not contributory. It is taxable and employees have to pay NI contributions on the benefit.

Student Activity 4

You should complete this student activity before attempting the self-assessment. Answer the questions, then check your answers against the paragraph(s) indicated.

1. Which state benefits are available to individuals who pay Class 2 NI contributions?   (9.4)

2. What benefits are provided by the reduced rate contributions paid by women with a certificate of election?   (4.10, 9.9)

3. What state benefits are available for widows?   (9.9, 9.24-9.28)

If you are unable to answer any of the questions satisfactorily, you should read the relevant paragraphs again. Your understanding of the text will be further tested in the following self-assessment.

Summary

Now that you have completed this unit you should be able to:

☐ **Ascertain the different types of earnings and their effect on the National Insurance contributions that will be payable**

☐ **Identify the difference between the classes of contributions payable, and the people they affect**

☐ **Recognise the levels at which NI contributions are payable, and their purpose**

☐ **Identify the main benefits provided by NI contributions, and their part in the social security system in the UK**

If you can tick all the above boxes with confidence, you are ready to answer the questions which follow.

Self-Assessment Questions

1. Give examples of three types of earnings, other than basic salary, which may be subject to Class 1 NI contributions.

2. What National Insurance contribution responsibilities does an employer have?

3. What is the effect on an employee's NI contributions if he becomes contracted-out of Serps and how is his employer affected? What difference would it make if the employee was contracting-out using an appropriate personal pension?

4. Jenny Smith is an employee earning a salary of £22,500. She also earns approximately £2,500 in bonus each year and has a company car which she only uses for work. She is a member of her employer's contracted-out occupational pension scheme. Calculate her own and her employer's National Insurance contributions.

5. Tony is employed by a UK based company but is going to work in their European offices in Brussels for an indefinite period. What is the likely position regarding his NI contributions?

6. Maria is a self-employed physiotherapist. She makes taxable profits of about £15,000 a year.

   (a) Calculate her Class 2 and Class 4 NI contributions for the year 1996-97.

   (b) Her sister is intending to come back to England after 10 years in the USA and work with Maria. What will her NI position be?

   (c) How will Maria pay her contributions now that she is paying tax under the new self-assessment regime?

7. Explain the NI contribution position for individuals who have earnings from more than one source in the following cases:

   (a) Gordon MacLean is a teacher employed by the local education authority on a salary of £18,000. He also writes text books on a self-employed basis, earning about £3,000 a year.

   (b) Simon Case is a partner in a firm of solicitors. He also does some freelance private work for local charities for which he charges a fee.

   (c) Theresa Howlett has three part-time jobs. She works at a local supermarket five mornings a week, is a cleaner three evenings a week and works full-time as a garage cashier at weekends. Her earnings are £100, £33 and £72 respectively.

8. Explain which state benefits a self-employed person is eligible for.

9. You are discussing state benefits with a friend who tells you that because some benefits are contributory they won't be taxable when in payment. What would you say to this statement?

10. Explain the following terms and their relevance to NI contributions:

   (a) Lower earnings limit

   (b) Upper earnings limit

   (c) Middle band earnings.

Unit 6

Capital Gains Tax (CGT)

Objectives

Students are required to study the following topics:

- **Definition of CGT**

- **Liability to tax**

- **Exemptions, reliefs and allowances**

- **Indexation**

- **Calculating tax liability**

- **Mitigating tax liability**

1   What is CGT?

1.1   Capital gains tax (CGT) is a tax levied on the profits made on the disposal of an asset. In simple terms, if an individual sells an asset and makes a profit he will be liable to tax on that profit if it falls within certain limits.

1.2   CGT was introduced on 6 April 1965 and all gains realised on disposals after that date are chargeable regardless of when the asset was acquired. The legislation affecting CGT can be changed in each Finance Act.

2   Chargeable Assets

2.1   With the exception of certain exempt assets which will be covered later, all forms of property are treated as chargeable assets for CGT including:

- Land and buildings

- Investments, options etc.

- Jewellery, antiques, works of art etc.

- Any currency other than sterling

- Any property created by the person disposing of it

3   Disposal

3.1   Although the normal 'disposal' will be a sale of an asset (e.g. shares, property, etc.) there are other circumstances which are treated as a disposal or part disposal of an asset. The principal types of disposal are:

- Sale of an asset, be it a whole sale or part sale

- Gift of an asset, be it whole or part

- Destruction of an asset, be it whole or part

- Sale of any right in an asset, or money received to forfeit any right

3.2 Disposals also occur when:

- A capital sum is received as compensation for damage or injury to assets

- A capital sum is received under an insurance policy for damage, injury or loss of assets

- A beneficiary under a trust becomes absolutely entitled to settled property against the trustees

Sale

3.3 This is the normal way of disposing of an asset. There are certain exemptions for CGT purposes and certain allowances and reliefs that are available to reduce the tax liability.

3.4 In some circumstances the Inland Revenue will value the asset at current market prices at the time of disposal rather than sale proceeds. This means individuals cannot sell low to avoid CGT.

Gift

3.5 CGT cannot be avoided by gifting assets. If an asset is gifted it is treated as a disposal, with the Inland Revenue valuing the asset at the market price at the time of disposal. Certain gifts, however, are exempt and are discussed later in this unit.

Destruction

3.6 If an asset is destroyed or lost, it is deemed to be a disposal since valuable assets should be well insured. This avoids the loophole of destroying assets to avoid CGT.

Negligible value

3.7 If a company has become insolvent and a liquidation will leave the shares worth virtually nothing, a shareholder can treat this as a disposal. A loss can be claimed without actually disposing of the asset. The Inland Revenue publish a list of shares which they accept have become of negligible value.

Settlements

3.8 CGT may also be charged on the creation of a settlement or a payment out of a settlement. Settlements and trusts are discussed in more detail in a later unit.

4 Liability to CGT

4.1 Those who are resident or ordinarily resident in the UK are liable on all gains, including gains made overseas, and all gains arising in or remitted to the UK if domiciled elsewhere. If the disposal proceeds are received in a foreign currency they are converted to sterling at the exchange rate current at the date of disposal.

4.2 Many countries charge a version of CGT on local property held by non-residents which may lead to a UK resident being charged a foreign tax as well as UK CGT. However, if there is a double taxation treaty with the country concerned, this may give relief, generally by making the foreign tax a credit against the UK tax. This could eliminate any UK tax if the foreign rate is higher. CGT will only be charged on foreign assets of a UK resident who is not domiciled in the UK if the gain is remitted to the UK.

4.3 Individuals who are not resident or ordinarily resident in the tax year of the disposal are not liable to UK CGT. However, a disposal is taxable when someone who is non-resident is carrying on a trade or profession through a branch or agency in the UK and disposes of assets used in that branch.

4.4 Companies are liable for tax on capital gains but pay via the corporate tax system. There is no entitlement to annual capital gains exemption. Trustees are also chargeable persons for CGT. Trusts generally have an annual exemption of half the individual exemption, i.e. £3,150 for 1996-97. Most trusts are charged CGT at 24%, but accumulation and discretionary trusts are charged CGT at 34%.

When the tax is paid

4.5 The normal due date of payment for CGT is the 1 December after the end of the tax year in which the disposal occurred.

4.6 It is therefore a good tax-saving hint to use the personal exemption before 6 April and put off any further disposals until 7 April wherever possible as this will defer any tax payment by 12 months.

Example 6.1: Deferring tax payment

Disposal 5 April 1995

Tax to be paid 1 December 1995

Disposal 7 April 1995

Tax to be paid 1 December 1996

Note that the payment date will change with the introduction of self-assessment.

Student Activity 1

You should complete this student activity before reading the next section of the text. Answer the questions then check your answers against the paragraph(s) indicated.

1. Give three examples of when a disposal may occur. (3.1, 3.2)

2. Tony makes a gift to a friend of an asset worth £8,000. How is this treated for CGT purposes? (3.5)

3. A UK resident makes capital gains on assets held abroad. What is his CGT liability on these gains? (4.1, 4.2)

If you are unable to answer any of the questions satisfactorily, you should read the relevant paragraphs again. Your understanding of the text will be further tested in the self-assessment section at the end of this unit.

5 Exemptions from the Tax

5.1 All forms of property are chargeable assets for CGT purposes, with the exception of certain exempt assets.

Major exempt assets

5.2 Gains on the following are not liable to CGT:

- An individual's only or main private residence will receive principle private residence relief, provided various conditions are satisfied

- Private motor cars

- Winnings from betting, pools, competitions, etc.

- National savings certificates and premium bonds

- Personal equity plans

- Venture capital trusts

- Government stocks (gilts)

- Enterprise investment schemes or business expansion schemes

- Most life assurance policies

- Gifts between husband and wife

- Gifts to charities, heritage and in the national interest

- Decorations for gallantry (unless purchased)

- Compensation or damages for personal or professional wrong or injury

- Sterling currency and foreign currency for an individual's own spending and maintenance of assets abroad

- Woodlands

Principle private residence relief

5.3 An individual's home is usually exempt from any capital gains tax, although part of the gain may be taxable if it has not been the seller's main residence throughout the period of ownership.

5.4 The following periods of absence can be ignored:

- A delay of up to a year between purchase and residence

- Any period up to 31 March 1982

- Up to three years if lived in before and after that period

- The last thirty six months of ownership if it has been used as the owner's main residence at some time previously

- Up to four years if employment elsewhere in the UK prevented residence if lived in before and after that period

- Any period of absence working abroad if both preceded and followed by residence

- Any period of living in job-related accommodation when the individual intends to return to the main residence

5.5   If the conditions are satisfied for only part of the time of ownership, only a proportion of the gain is exempt. For example, if the period of qualifying use was three years out of nine years of ownership, a third of the gain would be exempt.

5.6   If an individual has two houses, only the chosen place of residence will be exempt. The individual can choose which should be deemed to be the chosen place of residence, even if he does not live there, based on the house that will make the largest potential gain. The choice must be made within two years of the purchase of the second property. The choice can be changed if necessary but cannot extend back beyond two years before the change. If the Inland Revenue are not informed of the choice within this period they will decide which property should be treated as the main residence for CGT purpose.

5.7   When a married couple live together, they can only claim the exemption for one property at a time. Where both spouses own a residence when they marry a new two year period starts for notifying which is the main residence.

5.8   If a part of a home is used exclusively for a business (e.g. a room used as an office) and expenses claimed against tax, this part of the house will be liable to CGT on disposal. However, this rule does not apply where parts of the house are used partly for personal and partly for business reasons. For example a person who uses a spare bedroom to do sewing for income on a part time basis will not lose the exemption.

5.9   If you live in a property while letting part of it, your CGT exemption is not affected if the boarders live effectively as part of the family. However, if the letting extends beyond this but is still for residential use, the gain on the part which is let is exempt up to the lesser of £40,000 and the exemption on that part occupied by the owner.

Example 6.2: Partial letting of property

(a)   The gain on the sale of a property is £95,000.

(b)   The proportion applicable to the let part is £50,000.

(c)   The exempt gain is £45,000.

(d)   The £50,000 on the let part is reduced by the lower of

    (i)   £40,000 or

    (ii)   £45,000 (the exempt gain).

Therefore a further £40,000 is exempt leaving £10,000 chargeable.

This can be further reduced by the £6,300 annual exemption if not already used.

The exemption cannot be used where a property was purchased for the purpose of making a gain, for example where a person buys a house to renovate then sell without a genuine intention to live in the property.

Gifts between spouses

5.10 Before the introduction of independent taxation, there was only one relief for married couples. The positive aspect of this was that gains of one spouse could be offset against the losses of the other spouse. Now that both spouses have their own tax-free allowance this is no longer possible. This is discussed later in this unit.

5.11 As well as the above, there are certain allowances and reliefs available to mitigate the tax liability.

6 Allowances and Reliefs

Personal exemption

6.1 Every individual in the UK has his/her own personal exemption. Married couples are entitled to an exemption for each spouse. For the tax year 1996-97 the exemption is £6,300 for individuals, while trusts have an exemption equal to half this, i.e. £3,150. So, the first £6,300 of any individual's gains are completely exempt for CGT. However, if the exemption is not fully used in a tax year, it cannot be carried forward to the next year.

Example 6.3: Calculating liability

Johns sells an asset in May 1996 and makes a gain of £7,800. His CGT liability will be as follows:

Gain	£7,800
Less exemption	£6,300
CGT liability	£1,500

Personal chattels

6.2 There is a personal chattel exemption of £6,000 which, as the name suggests, refers to personal belongings which are tangible, moveable assets as opposed to stocks, shares, property, etc. This includes coins, furniture, jewellery, works of art and cars.

6.3 If the proceeds from the disposal of a chattel exceed £6,000 the capital gain is restricted to five-thirds of the excess.

Example 6.4: Personal chattels exemption

Anthony sells an antique chair for £7,000 which originally cost £700.

His gain is £7,000 less £700 which is £6,300.

The excess of its value over the £6,000 exemption is £1,000 (i.e. £7,000 less £6,000) so the gain is as follows:

£1,000 x 5/3 = £1,666.67

6.4 If a chattel is bought for more than £6,000 but sold for less than £6,000, the allowable loss is restricted to the excess of the cost over £6,000.

Allowable expenses

6.5   There are certain allowable expenses that can be deducted from any gain to reduce the size of the gain.

6.6   Typically, these are the costs of acquisition and disposal, including legal costs, advertising, transport, etc., and any enhancement expenditure, that is the costs of any capital improvements to the asset such as the cost of building an extension to a house.

7   Indexation Allowance

7.1   Indexation allowance is an allowance that is designed to offset the effects of inflation to give a true reflection of the real gains made on an asset, going back to 31 March 1982.

Using indexation allowance

7.2   All assets owned prior to 31 March 1982 are revalued at the market value at that date and only gains made after this date are taken into consideration to calculate the CGT liability. All gains are then 'inflation-proofed' by applying the indexation allowance. Acquisition costs and any enhancement expenditure may also be indexed.

Calculation of indexation allowance

7.3   This allowance is calculated as follows:

Indexation allowance

equals

Original cost multiplied by indexation

7.4   Where a March 1982 rebasing election is made, or where March 1982 market value is used to calculate indexation, then:

Indexation Allowance

equals

31 March 1982 market value multiplied by indexation

7.5   This indexation allowance can then be taken from the gross gains to leave the net, or indexed gain.

7.6   The 'indexation' factor can be obtained from periodicals or newspapers, which print monthly tables. However, it can also be calculated by using the retail prices index which is also published regularly.

7.7   The formula to calculate the 'indexation' factor is as follows:

$$\frac{RD - RI}{RI}$$

7.8   This is where RD is the retail price index in the month of disposal and RI is the retail prices index for March 1982, or the month of acquisition if later.

Where enhancement expenditure is being indexed, the date of the improvements is taken as RI.

Example 6.5: Calculating indexation factor

Original cost January 1985 was £100,000

Disposal August 1995 was £250,000

Unindexed gain £150,000

Using the formula $\frac{RD - RI}{RI}$ to calculate indexation factor

Where RD is retail prices index in month of disposal i.e. August 1995

RI is retail prices index in month of acquisition i.e. January 1985

Indexation factor $= \frac{149.9 - 91.20}{91.20} = 0.644$

Indexation allowance   = Original cost x indexation factor
                        = £100,000 x 0.644

Indexation allowance   = £64,400

This amount can then be deducted from the gain to give the indexed gain.

Indexed gain is therefore

£150,000 - £64,400 = £85,600

Example 6.6: Calculating taxable gain on asset acquired prior to March 1982

An asset was acquired in November 1970 for	£ 10,000
Its value at 31 March 1982 was	£ 50,000
It was sold in March 1995 for	£100,000

Giving a capital gain before indexation of £50,000

Using the formula $\frac{RD - RI}{RI}$ to calculate indexation factor

Where RD is retail prices index in month of disposal i.e. March 1995

RI is retail prices index in March 1982

Indexation factor $= \frac{147.50 - 79.44}{79.44} = 0.857$

Indexation allowance   = March 1982 value x indexation factor
                        = £50,000 x 0.857

Indexation allowance   = £42,850

This amount can then be deducted from the gain to give the indexed gain.

Indexed gain is therefore

$$£50,000 - £42,850 = £7,150$$

7.9 There are some instances where the general rule re-basing to 31 March 1982 will not apply. For example, if a smaller gain would result from using the original cost rather than March 1982 value, the lower figure may be taken unless an irrevocable election has been made by the taxpayer to use March 1982 value for all assets.

Losses

7.10 There will be disposals which result in a loss. Generally speaking losses can be offset against chargeable gains to reduce tax liability. However, indexation can only be used to reduce a gain to zero but not to create or increase a loss.

Example 6.7: How loss can be created by indexation

Using the example given in 6.5, but assuming a sale price of £150,000, indexation will produce a loss as follows:

Unindexed gain	£50,000
Indexation factor	0.644
Indexation allowance	£100,000 (original cost) x 0.644 = £64,400

This would produce a loss of £14,400. However, the gain can only be reduced to zero and the loss cannot be offset against any gains made that year or in the future.

7.11 Previously, indexation could be used to reduce a gain, create a loss or increase an existing loss. The Finance Act 1994 changed the rules and reduced the limit for indexation losses on disposals made between 30 November 1993 and 6 April 1995 to £10,000. After 6 April 1995 no indexation losses were allowed.

Student Activity 2

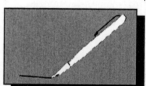

You should complete this student activity before reading the next section of the text. Answer the questions then check your answers against the paragraph(s) indicated.

1. Which of the following events may incur a CGT liability? (5.2, 5.6, 6.2)

   (a) Sale of main home

   (b) Winning a large sum on the National Lottery

   (c) Sale of holiday cottage used for about two months a year

   (d) Sale of an antique clock for a profit of £3,000

2. George owns an antique dining table and six chairs. He bought the set in January 1980 for £15,000 and it was worth £18,000 in March 1982. He sold the set in July 1995 for £38,500. The RPI in March 1982 was 79.44 and 149.1 in July 1995. Calculate the taxable gain. (7.7)

3   Alison inherited a cottage in July 1990, which had a market   (7.7)
     value at the time of £80,000. She sold it in January 1996 for
     £92,000. The RPI was 126.8 in July 1990 and 150.2 in
     January 1996. Calculate the taxable gain.

If you are unable to answer any of the questions satisfactorily you should read the
relevant paragraphs again. Your understanding of the text will be further tested in
the self-assessment section at the end of this unit.

8   Calculating the Tax Bill

Calculation process
The tax is calculated as follows:

> Final value
> *less*
> Initial value (or 31 March 1982 market value)
> *less*
> Allowable Expenses
> *equals*
> Gross Gain
> *minus*
> Indexation
> *equals*
> Chargeable Gain
> *minus*
> Annual exemption
> *equals*
> Capital Gain (or allowable loss)

Example 6.8: Calculation of capital gain

Original price of asset	£100,000
Current market price	£250,000
Capital gain (unindexed)	£150,000
Less expenses	£ 1,000
Less indexation allowance	£ 64,000
Less personal exemption (1996-97)	£ 6,300
Equal capital gain	£ 78,700

Payment of tax
8.1   Any capital gains (or losses) are communicated to the Inland Revenue via the
      annual tax return and, under the current system, are paid on the 1 December
      in the tax year following the gain.

8.2   The tax is charged at income tax rates as if it were the top slice of the
      taxpayer's income, with the actual gain after exemptions being added to that

year's income to see the amount payable and at which rate or rates. It should be noted that personal allowances and charges on income cannot be offset against capital gains.

8.3   Therefore, a basic rate taxpayer will probably pay basic rate tax on the first part of the gain but, dependent on the amount of the gain, may well find that he has to pay higher rate tax on the 'top-slice' of the gain.

8.4   Where income already incurs a liability to tax at higher rate, net chargeable gains will be taxed at the higher rate too.

8.5   For 1996-97 there are three rates of CGT for individuals:

- Lower rate   20%

- Basic rate   24%

- Higher rate 40%

The lower rate does not apply to trusts.

Example 6.9: When a basic taxpayer may be liable for higher rate tax

In 1996-97 a married man makes a gain of £15,000 (after indexation and expenses). His tax liability for CGT is as follows:

Income	£25,000
Less allowances	£ 5,555
Plus allowance restriction	£ 670
Equals	£20,115
Chargeable gains	£15,000
Less annual exemption	£ 6,300
Equals gain	£ 8,700

This charged as follows:

£25,500 - £20,115 = £5,385	@ 24% = £ 1,292.40
£8,700 - £5,385 = £3,315	@ 40% = £ 1,326.00
	Total = £2,618.40

Effects of self-assessment

8.6   Following the introduction of self-assessment from 1996-97, any capital gains tax payable will be included in the balancing payment due on the 31 January following the end of the tax year. Relief for losses will usually be claimed in tax returns, with an overall time limit to make the claim of 5 years 10 months from the end of the tax year in which the loss occurred. There will be no restriction on the time over which losses may be carried forward.

8.7   Interest on underpaid tax will be charged from the due date. A repayment supplement of overpaid tax will apply from the date of overpayment to the date the repayment order is issued.

9 Mitigating the CGT Liability

9.1 There are many ways to mitigate the tax liability for CGT, most of which involve good forward planning. This includes offsetting losses against gains, spreading ownership of assets and making best use of the annual exemption.

Using capital losses

9.2 In the same way that an individual can make a capital gain in any year, so a loss on the sale of an asset (as long as it is a genuine loss at current market values) can be made. If this is so, losses can be offset against gains and the tax can be 'aggregated' in any tax year. The loss only needs to be used to reduce a gain where it exceeds the annual exemption.

9.3 Remember, however, that indexation losses can only be used to reduce a gain to zero, not to create or increase a loss.

9.4 Capital losses made can be carried over indefinitely into future tax years to mitigate the tax liability of future gains.

9.5 It is vital that any losses are used to minimise the tax liability on gains.

Example 6.10: Using capital losses to reduce tax liability

George makes a loss of £3,000 on a disposal in 1995-96 but makes no capital gains to offset it against.

In the following year, 1996-97, he sells a property and makes a chargeable gain of £11,000. This can be reduced by the annual exemption of £6,300 and the previous year's loss of £3,000, leaving £1,700 which is liable to tax.

Spreading ownership

9.6 Since all individuals have an annual exemption it may be possible to spread ownership of assets around a family to utilise all personal allowances.

9.7 Gains of a husband and wife are calculated and charged separately so the losses of one spouse cannot be set against the gains of the other. However, disposals between a husband and wife in a tax year when they are living together are exempt from CGT, which provides opportunities for tax savings. If one spouse pays tax at a higher rate than the other, an asset which will make a profit can be transferred to the lower taxpaying spouse before it is sold, so that the gain will accrue to the lower taxpayer. Note that if assets are transferred following divorce, then CGT will be chargeable in the normal way.

9.8 An asset can be transferred to a spouse before it is sold in order to utilise an unused annual exemption. Equally if one spouse is selling an asset which is expected to make a loss, it could be transferred to the other spouse, if he or she has already realised gains against which the loss can be set.

9.9 Through advance planning and transfer of assets between them it is possible to ensure that one spouse is not left with unrelieved losses while the other has gains in excess of the exemption.

9.10 Holding assets jointly can also save tax by using both a husband's and wife's exemptions on any subsequent gain.

9.11 All transfers of assets to other family members e.g. children, parents, brothers, sisters will be regarded as at open market value. However, if a loss arises on disposal to a family member (other than a spouse), the loss cannot be set against general gains but only against a later gain on a transaction with the same person. This also applies to any other 'connected' persons which includes business partners and their spouses and relatives, and the settlor, if the individual is a trustee.

'Bed and breakfasting'

9.12 This is the process of selling assets, usually quoted shares, one day and re-buying the next to utilise an annual exemption. The sale and repurchase must be genuine and evidence must be kept of this. The stockbrokers' costs will have to be considered as well as the possibility of prices increasing between selling and buying transactions. However, bed and breakfasting can lead to substantial savings over a period of years especially for someone who has no other gains and so has a full annual exemption which will be lost if not used.

Example 6.11: Bed and breakfasting

Oliver has a portfolio of quoted shares which originally cost £6,000 in January 1993. He wishes to realise capital gains each year without paying capital gains tax by 'bed and breakfasting'.

Sells and repurchases in March 1994 for £9,000
Gain = £9,000 - £6,000 = £3,000 which is below the annual exemption so no tax to pay.

Sells and repurchases in March 1995 for £13,000
Gain = £13,000 - £9,000 = £4,000 which is below the annual exemption so no tax to pay.

Sells in March 1996 for £18,000
Gain = £18,000 - £13,000 = £5,000 which is below the annual exemption so no tax to pay.

If Oliver had not used bed and breakfasting and had sold for £18,000 in March 1996, his indexed gain would have been £11,412 which, after deducting his annual exemption of £6,000, would have left £5,412 liable to tax.

Using all allowances

9.13 As illustrated by bed and breakfasting it is important to use a client's annual exemption every year, if gains are a normal occurrence. It is also important that all other allowances (e.g. indexation, costs of acquisition, etc.) should be fully used to mitigate any tax liability.

Timing the disposal

9.14 The tax liability can be delayed by the timing of the disposal and this should always be considered when making a gain.

Investments

9.15 As certain investments are free of CGT, it makes sense for an investor to consider these if he is trying to reduce his CGT bill, or is likely to make returns above his annual exemption. The CGT treatment of different investments is covered in detail in later units.

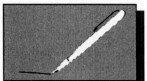

Student Activity 3

You should complete this student activity before reading the next section of the text. Answer the questions then check your answers against the paragraph(s) indicated.

Eleanor Price invested £25,000 in a portfolio of shares in June 1990. Since May 1993 she has annually bed and breakfasted her shares to mitigate her CGT liability, particularly important as she is a higher rate taxpayer. The portfolio has been very profitable and was worth the following: May 1993 - £29,000, May 1994 - £33,000, May 1995 - £38,000 and May 1996 - £39,000.   (9.12)

(a) Calculate the gain each year and whether there was any CGT liability.

(b) Compare the situation if she had not bed and breakfasted but had sold the portfolio in May 1996. What tax would she have to pay?

If you are unable to answer any of the questions satisfactorily you should read the relevant paragraphs again. Your understanding of the text will be further tested in the self-assessment section at the end of this unit.

10 Reliefs

Business retirement relief

10.1 There is relief for people owning businesses or parts of businesses who sell the business subject to certain conditions being met, including a minimum qualifying shareholding. The relief is available to taxpayers who have reached age 50, or who retire earlier due to ill-health. There is an exempt gain and half of the amount over that is also exempt, to certain limits. The exemption is reduced if the individual has been running the business for less than 10 years and is affected by whether he has been working part-time for the business some time before.

Table 6.1: Business retirement relief limits

First £250,000 gain	- exempt
Next £750,000	- 50% exempt
Excess over £1,000,000	- taxed at full rate

Example 6.12: Business retirement relief

Jim Smith owns a manufacturing company and wishes to sell it to his son John. The gain he will make on the sale is £1,200,000. His relief will be calculated as follows.

First £250,000	- exempt
£250 - £1,000,000	- 50% exempt
Next £200,000	- taxed at full rate

Rollover relief and holdover relief

10.2   When a business sells an asset and purchases another within a specified period it can postpone payment of CGT on the original disposal. The specified period is the rollover period and is defined as extending from one year before sale to three years after. The relief applies to sole traders, partnerships and companies.

10.3   The assets must be qualifying, i.e. agreed to be eligible by the Inland Revenue for relief but do not have to be the same type. Therefore, a company may sell some land and use some of the proceeds to buy some machinery. This would qualify for relief. There can be one disposal and several acquisitions or the opposite could apply. It is also possible to rollover or holdover part of the disposal proceeds rather than the full amount.

10.4   The type of relief given depends on the type of replacement asset.

10.5   **Rollover relief** is given if the replacement asset has a life of more than 60 years e.g. land. It is used to reduce the cost of the replacement asset and indexation is calculated on the cost of the replacement asset less the rolled over gain.

Example 6.13: Rollover relief

Qualifying asset original cost	£90,000
Sale price	£150,000
Gain (after indexation)	£40,000

Qualifying asset bought for £60,000.

The full gain has been reinvested so the cost of the replacement asset for CGT purposes will be £20,000.

10.6   **Holdover relief** is given if the replacement asset has a life of less than 60 years and is referred to as a depreciating asset. The gain does not reduce the cost of the replacement and so does not affect the calculation of indexation, but is held over for up to ten years and becomes chargeable when the replacement asset is disposed of or at the end of the ten years. It can be used as rollover relief for a non-depreciating asset during this period if the timescales are appropriate.

10.7   A company must claim rollover or holdover relief within six years of the end of the relevant accounting period. Individuals (i.e. the self-employed) have five years from the 31 January following the relevant tax year to make a claim on their tax return under the self-assessment rules.

Reinvestment relief

10.8 Individuals may defer paying tax on any gains arising from the sale of shares in their own unquoted trading companies if they reinvest the proceeds in other such companies. This includes companies on the Alternative Investment Market (AIM). Any gains will remain deferred where a holding of qualifying shares is sold and another is acquired. The deferred gain will be taxed if the claimant emigrates, sells the shares without replacing them with other qualifying shares or if the company involved ceases to carry on a qualifying trade within three years of the reinvestment being made.

10.9 From 30 November 1993 the reinvestment relief was extended to make it available for all chargeable gains realised by individuals. Trustees are also eligible for the relief unless the beneficiaries of the trusts are not individuals. To qualify for reinvestment relief, the chargeable gain arising on any disposal must be reinvested in unquoted trading companies or in the holding company of a trading group. The investor does not have to take a stake in the unquoted company. The deferred gain will be taxed under the same circumstances as the original relief for entrepreneurs.

10.10 The Finance Act 1995 extended the relief to reinvestment in enterprise investment scheme (EIS) shares and venture capital trusts (VCT), this applies to any disposals since 29 November 1994. Both EIS and VCT have the added advantage of 20% income tax relief on up to £100,000 invested. The gain on the original asset is deferred until the disposal of the EIS or VCT shares, any subsequent gain on the shares will be exempt.

Gift relief

10.11 When a gain arises following the gift of an asset by an individual or trustee, gift relief may apply and the gain is deferred. The gifts which qualify for relief are as follows:

- Business assets - including assets used in the donor's company, farm land and buildings which would qualify for inheritance tax agricultural property relief (see Unit 7); shares and securities in unquoted trading companies (not dealt with in the AIM) and shares or securities in the donor's personal trading company

- Gifts of heritage property (works of art, historic buildings, etc.)

- Gifts to funds for the maintenance of heritage property

- Gifts to political parties

- Gifts that are immediately chargeable to inheritance tax or would be if not covered by the annual exemption

10.12 If relief is being claimed, the donor is not charged to tax on the gain, and the value at which the donee is treated as having acquired the asset is reduced by the gain.

11 Assets Passing on Death

11.1 No CGT is payable on death. If losses have arisen in the year of death, these may be carried back and set against gains in the three previous tax years and tax will be refunded accordingly. Those to whom the asset is bequeathed will acquire it at the market value at the date of death, leaving any previous gain untaxed. If the persons entitled to the estate vary the way it is distributed within two years and notify the Revenue within six months of variation, the variation will not be regarded as a disposal and so no CGT charge will arise on any increase in value since death.

Student Activity 4

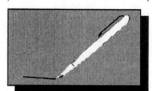

You should complete this student activity before attempting the self-assessment. Answer the questions, then check your answers against the paragraph(s) indicated.

1. Suggest three ways in which a married couple can keep their   (9.7-9.10)
    CGT liability to a minimum.

2. Bill is a partner in a firm of brokers. He is due to retire and is   (10.1)
    selling his partnership share to the new incoming partner for
    £200,000. Will Bill be liable for CGT on this sale?

3. A company director sells his shares in his own unquoted   (10.8)
    company. How could he qualify for reinvestment relief?

If you are unable to answer any of the questions satisfactorily, you should read the relevant paragraphs again. Your understanding of the text will be further tested in the following self-assessment.

Summary

Now that you have completed this unit you should be able to:

❑ **Define a disposal**

❑ **Know when a liability to CGT arises**

❑ **Know which gains are exempt**

❑ **Know what allowances and reliefs are available**

❑ **Explain the purpose of indexation and how it is calculated**

❑ **Calculate a CGT tax bill**

❑ **Suggest ways in which individuals can mitigate their tax liability**

If you can tick all the above boxes with confidence, you are ready to answer the questions which follow.

Self-Assessment Questions

1. Why may a disposal occur if an asset is destroyed?

2. What liability to CGT do trustees have?

3. Norman has incurred a chargeable gain in the current tax year. Under self-assessment rules when must he pay his tax?

4. What are the time limits for claiming relief for losses against taxable gains?

5. The following taxpayers all have a taxable capital gain of £7,000. How much tax will each have to pay?

   (a) Alan has a taxable income of £3,000

   (b) Andrea has a taxable income of £15,000

   (c) Albert has a taxable income of £32,000

6. An investor wants to utilise the bed and breakfasting method to reduce CGT liability on his share portfolio. What should he consider other than the potential for tax saving?

7. What is the difference between rollover relief and holdover relief?

8. What CGT liability do the personal representatives of a deceased person have:

   (a) If the deceased made capital gains in the year of death?

   (b) If the deceased made capital losses in the year of death?

9. James and Barbara Mundy ask you to explain how much they can make in capital gains in a tax year before incurring any tax. What would happen if they sold an asset for less than it cost to buy?

10. What is the personal chattels exemption?

Unit 7

Inheritance Tax (IHT)

Objectives

Students are required to study the following topics:

- **What inheritance tax is and what it is levied on**

- **Types of transfers**

- **Reliefs and allowances available**

- **How to mitigate the tax**

- **Making a will**

1   Introduction

1.1   Inheritance tax (IHT) is often referred to as a voluntary tax since, with the correct planning, it is one that can be avoided quite legally. IHT can be a complicated tax in its calculation and, by nature, is a tricky tax to plan for since it is based on non-guaranteed future events, but it is not a difficult tax to understand.

1.2   This unit will look at IHT, when it is payable, and at the available exemptions, reliefs and allowances. It will also look at how to calculate an IHT liability, and at certain basic steps an individual should be aware of in order to mitigate the tax liability. Individuals and advisers need to be aware of the potential tax problems so that steps can be taken to solve them, though it is not their role to calculate the tax.

1.3   Many years ago, IHT was seen to be a tax on the rich and the super-rich, since it is a tax on an individual's estate. However, since that estate contains the house, and levels of UK house ownership are high, it is becoming a tax that everybody needs to be aware of.

1.4   The 1995-96 nil rate band was £154,000 and with average house prices in certain areas being around or above that level, many people have been concerned with a potential IHT liability. Coupled with this is the increased wealth of offspring inheriting houses and estates from parents. In 1996-97 the inheritance tax threshold has risen by 30% to £200,000 removing the liability of IHT from some people, but still leaving a genuine concern.

Table 7.1: Tax man's share of an estate on death 1996-97

Estate	Tax man's slice	%
£250,000	£ 20,000	8%

£300,000	£ 40,000	13.3%
£400,000	£ 80,000	20%
£500,000	£120,000	24%

2   What is IHT Levied on?

2.1   IHT is a tax on an individual's estate. It will be charged on certain transfers or gifts from the estate during the individual's lifetime and on the value of the estate on death. Certain transfers in and out of trusts are also chargeable to IHT.

2.2   Individuals domiciled in the UK are chargeable to IHT on property anywhere in the world, and those not domiciled in the UK are chargeable on property in the UK. Husband and wife are treated separately so any available exemptions apply separately to each of them and each can make transfers free of tax up to the nil rate threshold.

What is an estate?

2.3   The estate is the complete wealth of the individual, comprising all assets. This means the following:

- The house and other property

- Savings in banks and building societies

- Investments, premium bonds, etc.

- Possessions

- Unpaid salary

- Debts

- Any life assurance not written in trust

- Debt from others

- Transfers of value in the past seven years, etc.

Excluded property

2.4   The main examples of property excluded from the value of the estate are:

- Property outside the UK for non UK domiciled individuals

- Certain reversionary interests

- Cash options under approved pension schemes

- Interest on certain UK government securities paid gross to non UK residents or non UK domiciled individuals

- National savings certificates and premium bonds for individuals domiciled in Channel Islands or Isle of Man

Valuation of the estate

2.5   For IHT purposes the value of the property is taken as the amount it might reasonably raise if sold on the open market. No reduction of this value is allowable on the grounds that if the whole property, e.g. a large shareholding, were put on the market at one time, this would reduce the price.

2.6 The only exception to this general valuation rule applies in certain cases involving the valuation of development sites or where building work on a property has not been completed. The property will normally be valued at the relevant date as if the work had been completed, the cost of completion will then be deducted as a charge against the deceased's estate.

2.7 Changes in the value of the estate by reason of the death (e.g. life assurance monies receivable or loss of goodwill) are included as if occurring before death except:

(a) The termination on the death of any interest.

(b) The passing of any interest by survivorship.

(c) A decrease in value resulting from an alteration of a close company's unquoted share or loan capital or any rights attached thereto.

Claims for reduction in value may be made where:

(a) Quoted shares are sold at a loss within one year of death.

(b) Land is sold at a loss within three years of death.

The IHT charge

2.8 IHT will be charged on an estate when the estate exceeds the current nil rate band. The estate includes any transfers made in the seven years prior to death so the first step in calculating an IHT liability is to check the tax liability on any transfers in the past seven years.

2.9 It is a cumulative tax with transfers more than seven years old falling out of the tax calculation. This is explained in detail later in this unit.

Rates of IHT

2.10 IHT is charged at the following rates:

- Nil rate (£200,000 threshold 1996-97)

- Lifetime rate 20% (for chargeable lifetime transfers)

- Death rate 40%

3 Transfers

3.1 There are three types of transfer which it is important to be aware of, and how they will be taxed. They are :

- Exempt transfers

- Potentially exempt transfers

- Chargeable transfers

3.2 A transfer that is neither exempt nor potentially exempt will be chargeable and if this takes the seven-year cumulation total over the nil rate band the excess is taxable at the lifetime rate of 20%.

Exempt transfers

3.3   There are many exemptions from IHT which should be fully used to minimise the effects of tax on an estate. The full list is given below and an individual with a potential IHT liability should make use of the major exempt transfers if he wishes to avoid taxation.

3.4   Many of the transfers can be made in the individual's will, e.g. gifting to charity, but individuals with a potential IHT liability should make full use of their annual exemption and the exempt nature of transfers between spouses.

3.5   These exemptions only apply to lifetime transfers:

(a)   Annual exemptions of £3,000 in any tax year. Any unused portion from the previous year can be added but will be lost if not used in that year.

(b)   Small gifts. Any gift to one person not exceeding £250 is exempt and any number of these gifts to different individuals can be made but must be outright.

(c)   Gifts in consideration of marriage. These gifts are limited to £5,000 by a parent, £2,500 by a grandparent, £2,500 by the bridegroom to the prospective spouse and £1,000 by another person.

(d)   Normal expenditure out of income. Expenditure has to be habitual and regular to rank as normal and needs to be proven to be so, as well as not reducing the individual's standard of living. A good example of this is regular premiums to a life assurance policy.

(e)   Waivers of dividend are exempt from IHT, e.g. if a director does not take dividends this is not seen as a transfer for IHT purposes.

(f)   Capital transfers for family maintenance are exempt, e.g. to provide for a family following divorce where the normal spouse exemption does not apply.

These exemptions apply both to lifetime transfers and transfers on death:

(g)   Transfers between husband and wife. The only exception to this is where the receiving spouse is domiciled abroad where the amount exempted is restricted to £55,000.

(h)   All transfers to charities are exempt. These need to be registered charities.

(i)   Gifts to political parties are exempt. A political party is one that has two members of parliament, or one MP and at least 150,000 votes in the last general election.

(j)   Gifts to housing associations, for national purposes and for heritage are also fully exempt.

(k)   Inheritance tax is also avoided if there is death on active service.

Potentially exempt transfers

3.6   The Inheritance Tax Act of 1984 introduced the concept of potentially exempt transfers (Pets) and most transfers made after 18 March 1986 will be Pets. It should be noted that before this date all transfers that were not exempt were deemed to be chargeable.

3.7 A potentially exempt transfer is a lifetime transfer made from one individual to:

- Another individual

- Any interest in possession trust (as long as a trust has a beneficiary who is entitled to the income, the trust has an interest in possession regardless of whether the trust actually generates any income)

- An accumulation and maintenance trust for disabled persons

3.8 Such transfers are potentially exempt in that should the donor survive seven years there will be no tax liability whatsoever on the transfer. If the donor dies within seven years from the date of the Pet the gift becomes chargeable retrospectively and there is a potential IHT liability. Tax will be chargeable on the value of the Pet on the day it was actually made, based on the donor's seven-year cumulation at that date. The rule on Pets ensures that estates cannot be given away to avoid tax.

3.9 Transfers are brought into account in chronological order. Some or all of the transfers may escape IHT to the extent that they are within the nil rate band. However, their presence in the overall total for IHT assessment will have the effect of increasing the amount of IHT payable on the estate on death.

3.10 The nil rate band has to be used first in calculating the tax liability of transfers. If the transfer(s) is below the nil rate band there will be no tax liability for the donee, but the amount of the transfer will be added to the value of the estate.

3.11 If there is a tax liability on the transfer(s) i.e. the transfer(s) exceeds the nil rate band then the excess transfer is taxed and so is not included in calculating tax on the estate. This avoids any double taxation. The annual exemption for lifetime gifts may be applied to reduce the IHT liability. Up to two annual exemptions may be applied where a deceased person made a gift in the previous seven years and has not used the full allowance from the previous year. In addition, tapering relief may decrease the tax liability further.

3.12 Example 7.1 illustrates the calculation of a fairly simple tax liability as there is only one transfer. In this example, there is no tapering relief on the transfer as this relief only applies to the tax on the transfer, on which there is no liability. Note the use of two annual exemptions.

Example 7.1: Calculating the tax liability on a transfer

Mr. Moore died in January 1996 leaving an estate of £130,000. He gave £50,000 to his son in 1995 (this was a Pet).

The gift in 1995 is below the 1995-96 nil rate band of £154,000 so there is no tax liability and the transfer of £50,000 is added into the estate.

Tax is due as follows:

Estate	£130,000

Gift	£ 50,000
Total	£180,000
Less two annual exemptions	£ 6,000
Total estate	£174,000
Less nil rate band	£154,000
Taxable amount	£ 20,000 @ 40%
	= £ 8,000

3.13 In the following example where there are multiple transfers, the calculation can be more complex and the effects on the estate and the final donee more marked.

Example 7.2: Calculating the tax liability on multiple potentially exempt transfers

Mr Clark died in January 1996 leaving an estate of £200,000. He made three gifts (Pets) to his daughter and two sons during the seven years prior to his death.

1st gift	- 6 years before death	£ 54,000
2nd gift	- 4 years before death	£100,000
3rd gift	- 2 years before death	£ 50,000

1. The donees of the first two gifts escape IHT on death by using up the whole of the 1995-96 nil rate band (£154,000).

2. The third gift, made two years before death is taxable as follows:
   £50,000 less unused annual exemptions for lifetime transfers available from the current year and previous year (2 x £3,000) = £44,000

3. The tax payable by the donee of this gift = £44,000 x 40% (IHT death rate) = £17,600. There is no tapering relief as the gift was made less than three years before death.

4. The beneficiaries of the estate will be liable for IHT on the whole of the estate, the nil rate band being fully used above.
   £200,000 x 40% (IHT death rate) = £80,000

Chargeable transfers

3.14 These are transfers with an immediate liability to IHT. Now that most lifetime transfers are potentially exempt, the main examples of chargeable lifetime transfers are:

- A lifetime transfer into or out of a discretionary trust where no one has a right to income (trusts will be covered in more detail in Unit 9)

- Gifts involving companies

3.15 Such transfers will attract IHT at the lifetime rate if above the nil rate band. If the donor pays the tax, the amount can be grossed up to deduct from the value of his estate, shown in Example 7.4 below.

Example 7.3: Chargeable transfers

Percy makes a chargeable lifetime transfer of £210,000 in November 1996. His IHT liability is as follows:

	£210,000
Less nil rate band	£200,000
Equals	£ 10,000
IHT at lifetime rate 20% =	£ 2,000

Example 7.4: Grossing up

Percy makes a further chargeable lifetime transfer of £8,000 and the nil rate band has been previously used. He pays the tax.

His estate is therefore reduced by:

- The £8,000 gift

- £2,000 tax payable

i.e. £10,000 in total.

3.16 If death occurs within seven years of a chargeable transfer, tax will be recalculated at the death rate with a tapering relief deduction if appropriate, and any tax already paid can be deducted from the final liability. However, if the tax already paid is greater than the liability, no refund will be due. The death rates of tax in force at the date of death are applied to the transfer.

3.17 Most transfers are now deemed to be potentially exempt so this category of transfer is now rarely encountered, although all transfers made before 18 March 1986 were chargeable.

Example 7.5: Cumulative tax

Joan Wilson, a widower, died on 1 July 1996 leaving an estate worth £450,000.

She had also made the following gifts during her lifetime. (These amounts assume that all available reliefs and exemptions such as the annual exemption have already been taken into account).

June 1988	£100,000 to discretionary trust
July 1990	£ 20,000 to son
January 1992	£ 20,000 to charity
May 1994	£180,000 to discretionary trust
September 1995	£ 50,000 to daughter

(a) The gift in June 1988 was a chargeable lifetime transfer but was under the nil rate threshold at the time (£110,000) so was not taxed.

(b) The gift to her son in July 1990 is a Pet, and will only come into consideration if Joan dies within seven years.

(c) Gift to charity in January 1992 is an exempt transfer.

(d) Gift in May 1994 is a chargeable lifetime transfer. The previous chargeable transfer of £100,000 is added to the May 1994 gift of £180,000 as it occurred less than seven years previously. The first £150,000 is not taxed as that was the nil rate threshold at the time. This leaves £130,000 to be taxed at 20% i.e. £26,000 payable at the time the gift is made.

(e) The gift to her daughter in September 1995 is a Pet.

(f) On Joan's death the situation is as follows:

- Transfer in June 1988 falls out of the calculation as it occurred more than seven years ago

- Gift to son is below the nil rate threshold so is not taxable; leaves £180,000 threshold

- Gift to trust in May 1994 also falls under the nil rate threshold so no further tax to pay

- Gift to daughter becomes taxable at 40% i.e. £20,000; no tapering relief applies as death occurred within a year of making the gift

- Plus tax on the estate is £450,000 at 40% = £180,000

4 Gifts with Reservation

4.1 The Finance Act 1986 introduced provisions for gifts with a reservation of benefit. In effect this invalidates the potential inheritance tax saving of a gift of property, if the possession and enjoyment of the property is not taken by the donee for at least seven years prior to the death of the donor or the property is not enjoyed to the entire or virtual exclusion of the donor.

4.2 If the benefit enjoyed by the donor is small the gift will not be subject to reservation. For example a gift of a valuable picture would not be a gift of reservation if the donor 'enjoyed' the picture on short visits to the donee. Similarly a house which becomes the donee's residence but where the donor then stays, in the absence of the donee for not more than two weeks each year, or stays with the donee for less than one month each year will not be subject to reservation.

4.3 However, if the donor stayed in the donee's house most weekends or for a month or more each year the reservation rules would apply, as they would if the gift was a holiday home which the donor and the donee both used on an occasional basis. In both of these cases there is no outright gift. As the donor retains a benefit in the transfer it is a gift with reservation. It would be regarded as a lifetime transfer and could be exempt, potentially exempt or chargeable depending on the circumstances. In the event of the donor's death, the gifted property will be treated as part of the donor's estate and will be taxed accordingly. If the donor had already paid any tax on the original transfer this will be credited against the tax on death.

4.4 There are some transfers which cannot constitute a gift of reservation:

- Gifts between spouses

- Gifts in consideration of marriage

- Gifts to charity

- Small gifts

- Gifts to political parties

- Gifts to housing associations

- Gifts for public or national benefit

- Employee trusts

4.5 Before the introduction of the gifts of reservation rule many life policies were sold when the donor could be a potential beneficiary. An amendment has been made so that any policies effected before 18 March 1986 which have not been varied since, cannot be treated as gifts of reservation.

4.6 These provisions only catch benefits reserved to the donor and to his spouse, however, great care should be taken to ensure that any benefit reserved to a spouse cannot be treated as a benefit to the donor. For example, a wife who receives capital from a discretionary trust of which her husband was settlor should not pay the money into a joint account. She should not maintain him with the money or pay any bills which would normally be his responsibility.

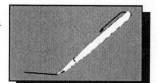

Student Activity 1

You should complete this student activity before reading the next section of the text. Answer the questions, then check your answers against the paragraph(s) indicated.

1. How are premiums to a life policy written for the benefit of another person, treated for IHT purposes? (3.5)

2. John Smith wishes to give his two children an equal cash sum, he has not made any previous gifts. How much can he give them exempt from IHT in the current tax year? (3.5)

3. Paul Western died in July 1996 leaving an estate of £300,000. He gave his two sons £50,000 each in 1995 and £30,000 to his favourite charity. Calculate the IHT tax bill on his estate. (3.13)

4. Ruth Millar gave her son Sam a house worth £60,000. For one week at Christmas and two weeks in summer she visits her son and stays in the house with him and his family. How would this be regarded for IHT purposes? (4.2)

If you are unable to answer any of the questions satisfactorily, you should read the relevant paragraphs again. Your understanding of the text will be further tested in the self-assessment section at the end of this unit.

5 Reliefs and Allowances

5.1 There are several reliefs and allowances available if there is a tax liability on the estate. These are:

- Tapering relief

- Quick succession relief

- Business property relief

- Agricultural property relief

Tapering relief

5.2   This is a relief that will decrease the tax liability of a transfer if a donor dies within seven years. It should be noted that it is only the tax liability that is reduced and not the size of the transfer. The relief is designed to decrease the tax on a transfer in line with the time elapsed from the date of the transfer.

5.3   The percentage of the full scale rate payable if death occurs within seven years of the transfer being made, is as follows:

Table 7.2: Tapering relief

Within death to 3 years of transfer	100% of full scale
More than 3, but less than 4 years	80% of full scale
More than 4, but less than 5 years	60% of full scale
More than 5, but less than 6 years	40% of full scale
More than 6, but less than 7 years	20% of full scale

Example 7.6: Using tapering relief

A transfer of £400,000 is made by a father to his son, there are no previous transfers and no exemptions. After allowing for the nil rate band of £200,000 IHT payable on death of the father would be as follows:

Years survived until death	IHT after tapering relief
0 - 3	£80,000
3 - 4	£64,000
4 - 5	£48,000
5 - 6	£32,000
6 - 7	£16,000
7 and over	0

5.4   It should be stressed that the relief does not reduce the size of the transfer, only the tax liability on the gift. The full value of the transfer is included in the donor's cumulation for the purpose of calculating the death tax on the estate. This will be given as a credit against IHT payable as a result of death.

Quick succession relief

5.5   This is a relief to avoid unnecessary double charging of tax if a donee dies shortly after receiving a transfer that has attracted IHT. Where death occurs within five years of the original transfer relief is available. There is no requirement to retain the actual asset obtained by that transfer.

5.6 The total tax on the chargeable estate is calculated in the normal way and reduced by the quick succession relief. The amount of relief is found by making the following calculation:

$$\frac{\text{Previous transfer net of tax}}{\text{Previous gross transfer}} \quad x \quad \text{Tax paid on previous transfer}$$

5.7 A percentage is then taken of the calculated amount as in the following table:

Table 7.3: Quick succession relief

Period between transfer and death	Percentage relief
Less than 1 year	100%
1 - 2 years	80%
2 - 3 years	60%
3 - 4 years	40%
4 - 5 years	20%

Example 7.7: Calculating quick succession relief

Ronald died on 26 May 1996 leaving an estate of £350,000. He had received a gift of £70,000 from an uncle in December 1993, on which he had paid tax of £28,000 following his uncle's death on 30 June 1995. Ronald died four years after the gift; the tax on his estate will therefore be reduced as follows:

$$\frac{£42,000}{£70,000} \times £28,000 \times 40\% = £6,720$$

Where there are successive charges within five years on trust property in which there is an interest in possession, quick succession relief is also available at the same rates as those quoted above.

Business property relief

5.8 This relief is available on the valuation of lifetime and death transfers of business property providing that the property has been owned for certain specified periods and is 'relevant business property' .The relief aims to enable businesses to be preserved intact through successive generations.

5.9 To be 'relevant business property' it must have been owned for two years prior to the transfer, but it does not apply to businesses dealing in securities, stocks or shares, dealing in land or buildings or holding investments.

5.10 The reliefs available are listed below:

Table 7.4: Business property relief

Business or interest in a business	100%
Shareholding in an unquoted company	100%
Controlling shareholding interest in a quoted company	50%
Land, buildings, machinery or plant used by a controlled company or partnership	50%

Agricultural property relief

5.11   This relief only applies to the agricultural value of the property and is available on lifetime and death transfers. Agricultural property includes agricultural land, growing crops and farm buildings but not the animals or equipment. The relief applies to the agricultural value of the land, but not any development value. In calculating that value, any loan secured on the agricultural property must be deducted.

5.12   Owner-occupied farms and tenancies will receive 100% relief and landlord's interests in let farmland 50% relief. The 50% relief is increased to 100% for land let under new leases on or after 1 September 1995, where transfers are made on or after that date.

5.13   In order to qualify for the relief the agricultural property must have been either:

- Occupied by the transferor for the purposes of agriculture for two years prior to the transfer, or

- Owned by the transferor for seven years prior to transfer and occupied by him or another person for the purposes of agriculture

Growing timber

5.14   Where an estate on death includes growing timber, the timber but not the land on which it stands can be left out of the value of the estate. The relief only applies to transfers on death not lifetime gifts and it operates by deferring the tax until the timber is disposed of. However, where woodlands are managed on a commercial basis they qualify for 100% business property relief so long as they have been owned for two years.

6   Payment of the Tax

6.1   IHT is not dealt with by the local tax office but by the Capital Taxes Offices, based in London, Edinburgh and Belfast. Once the size of the estate has been established, the first task is to calculate and pay the IHT liability. Probate cannot be granted until this is done.

6.2   Payments of the tax have to be made six months after the end of the month in which the death occurs. However, the legal personal representatives cannot get their grant of representation to administer the estate until they have delivered an account of the deceased's assets and paid the tax, so in practice tax is often paid before the due date.

6.3 Tax on chargeable lifetime transfers between 6 April and 30 September has to be paid by 30 April in the following year; tax on transfers between 1 October and 5 April has to be paid six months after the end of the month in which the transfer was made. There are provisions for paying tax in instalments on certain property, such as land.

Responsibility for paying the tax

6.4 The responsibility for paying the tax on a lifetime chargeable transfer rests with the donor, although the donor and donee may agree between them who should pay the tax. Where the transfer is of property within a discretionary trust however, the trustees are responsible for paying the tax.

6.5 Where IHT is payable on death, the personal representatives or executors of the estate are liable for the tax. The estate is therefore reduced by the amount of the tax and the beneficiary or beneficiaries receiving the estate, after all other specific bequests have been made, effectively suffer the tax. Trustees are again responsible for tax on trust property arising on death.

6.6 If a potentially exempt transfer becomes liable for tax or chargeable lifetime transfers are to be reassessed at the full rate on the death of the donor within seven years, the donee is responsible for the tax or additional tax payable. If the donee does not pay the tax it will be deducted from the estate.

Student Activity 2

You should complete this student activity before reading the next section of the text. Answer the questions, then check your answers against the paragraph(s) indicated.

1. James Wilks transfers £300,000 to his son, there are no previous transfers or exemptions. Four and a half years later James dies. What will the IHT liability be? (5.3)

2. Charles Hey is left £100,000 by an aunt, 18 months later Charles dies leaving his total estate of £300,000 to his daughter. Calculate by how much quick succession relief will reduce the IHT tax bill. (5.7)

3. What is the aim of business property relief? (5.8)

4. If a lifetime chargeable transfer was made on 20 May 1995, when would IHT need to be paid? (6.3)

If you are unable to answer any of the questions satisfactorily, you should read the relevant paragraphs again. Your understanding of the text will be further tested in the self-assessment section at the end of this unit.

7 Mitigating the Tax

7.1 As with any other tax the first step in mitigating liability to IHT is to make sure that all available allowances and exemptions are used. The position with IHT differs from other taxes, however, in that the liability to tax on death cannot be known for certain. Even if an individual has an estate which is simple to value, the nil rate threshold may increase before death and property values can rise and fall unpredictably.

7.2 A variety of arrangements exist to attempt to reduce or avoid an IHT liability, most of which involve either funding for the eventual tax bill, or removing assets from an estate to reduce its value.

7.3 This section aims to look at some of these arrangements in more detail. However, the following points should always be taken into account first:

- Use all available allowances

- Use all exemptions, especially gifts to spouses and charities

- If gifting assets, choose assets that are increasing in value and protect the potential gift liability with a simple life assurance policy

- Redistribute assets to utilise business and/or agricultural reliefs

- Use trusts to ensure that the proceeds of life assurance policies are not included in the estate

- Ensure a will is written and kept up to date

- For large estates, bequests to children on the death of the first parent, up to the current nil rate band, will reduce the IHT liability on the estate on the death of the second parent

7.4 The important aspect of IHT for an individual is planning to avoid it as shown in this simple example:

Example 7.8: Who benefits on death?

If there are four equal beneficiaries to an estate of £420,000 the tax man will get the biggest share if no provision for IHT has been made.

£420,000 less £200,000 nil rate band (1996-97)

= £220,000 @ 40% = £88,000

Each beneficiary receives a quarter of the remainder, i.e. £83,000 each, which is £5,000 less than the Capital Taxes Office.

8 Use of Exemptions and Reliefs

8.1 Where an individual wishes to reduce the value of his estate he should take full advantage of the gift exemptions each year. Any number of small gifts of up to £250 per person can be made each year, as well as the annual exemption of £3,000.

Example 7.9: Using gifts

Tony White needs to reduce the value of his estate as he is concerned about the potential tax burden for his family. He has three sons who are each married, and two teenage grandchildren.

In the current year Tony could gift £6,000 using this year's and the previous year's annual exemptions, plus he could gift £250 to each member of his family. This would total £8,000 which he could give away without tax liability for the donor or donee.

Nil rate threshold

8.2   If a husband and wife leave everything to each other on death, they will lose the benefit of the nil rate band on the first death. When the surviving spouse dies only one nil rate band will apply to the total estate. It may be more tax-efficient to leave the nil rate band direct to the couple's children on the first death and the balance to the surviving spouse. No tax would be paid on the first death but the surviving spouse's estate would be reduced by £200,000.

Example 7.10: Husband and wife

Mr and Mrs Harrison each have an estate worth £250,000. If they have written their wills giving each other the full estate on death and Mr Harrison dies first the tax situation on Mrs Harrison's death would be as follows:

Total estate	£500,000
Less nil rate band	£200,000
	£300,000
Tax at 40%	£120,000

If the couple set up a trust for their children and transfer £200,000 then the tax liability will be reduced as follows:

Mr Harrison's death

Estate	£250,000
Nil rate band	£200,000
covered by transfer to	
trust for children	
Remainder passes to wife	£ 50,000
	No tax to pay

Mrs Harrison's death

Estate	£300,000
Nil rate band	£200,000
	£100,000
Tax to pay at 40%	£ 40,000

The couple could also take out a £40,000 joint life last survivor whole life policy written under trust to cover the tax liability.

Business property relief

8.3   Where a business property qualifies for 100% relief, it would be sensible to leave this to someone who might otherwise be taxable i.e. a son or daughter rather than to an exempt spouse.

Student Activity 3

You should complete this student activity before reading the next section of the text.

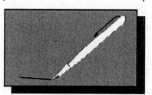

Answer the questions, then check your answers against the paragraph(s) indicated.

1. What should an individual consider first when trying to   (7.1)
    mitigate IHT?

2. How can trusts be used in connection with life assurance   (7.3)
    policies to reduce or avoid IHT?

3. How can the small gift exemption help to reduce the value of   (8.1)
    an estate?

4. Joe Brown has a business property which will qualify for 100%   (8.3)
    relief. In order to get the most benefit from tax relief who could
    he leave it to?

If you are unable to answer any of the questions satisfactorily, you should read the relevant paragraphs again. Your understanding of the text will be further tested in the self-assessment section at the end of this unit.

9   Using Life Assurance and Annuities

Funding for tax

9.1   When death occurs the deceased's legal personal representatives will need access to some cash to pay the tax prior to obtaining the grant of representation, which is needed before title can be proved. A whole life policy is the most common life assurance contract used for this purpose as the sum assured is payable whenever death occurs. If the policy is written under trust for the beneficiaries of the estate there will be no liability to tax on the policy proceeds and payment can be made by the insurance company to the trustees immediately on notification of death.

9.2   The sum assured should initially be equal to the predicted tax liability. With-profits and unit-linked policies are both available and the value of the sum assured should increase over time although this cannot be guaranteed under a unit-linked policy. Most policies are flexible and allow sums assured to be increased, with a corresponding increase in premiums, if it is likely that the sum assured will be insufficient for its purpose.

Joint life policies

9.3   Where a married couple wish to pass on their estate to their children, and have made use of the nil rate exemption as discussed earlier, they should effect a joint life last survivor policy as the proceeds will not be required until both partners have died.

9.4   Other joint life policies may be used in trust arrangements (see below) where the lives assured are not married but have another relationship such as settlor and beneficiary.

Potentially exempt transfers

9.5   Where a potentially exempt transfer has been made it is important to fund for the potential tax bill if the donor should die within seven years. This is most commonly met by a decreasing term assurance where the sum assured decreases in line with the increase in tapering relief. The donee will be responsible for payment of the tax if the donor dies and can take the policy out on the life of the donor. The donor could make gifts to the donee to pay the premiums or alternatively take out an own life policy written under trust for the benefit of the donee. The premiums are likely to come under the normal expenditure exemption or the annual exemption. It is important that the policy proceeds are not paid into the estate on death or they will increase the value of the estate.

Example 7.11: Funding for a Pet

Martin makes a gift to Sally of £250,000 which is a Pet. Based on the current threshold of £200,000 (1996-97) £50,000 will be taxable if Martin dies within seven years.

Sally takes out a decreasing term to cover the tax liability and the sums assured will be as follows:

Years 0 - 3	£20,000
Years 3 - 4	£16,000
Years 4 - 5	£12,000
Years 5 - 6	£ 8,000
Years 6 - 7	£ 4,000

After seven years the policy will cease as cover will no longer be needed.

If Martin dies after four years, with an estate worth £500,000, the policy will pay out £16,000 to Sally to meet the tax liability.

However, it should be remembered that when the value of Martin's estate is being assessed for IHT the full value of the Pet should be taken into consideration. So on death his estate is worth £500,000 plus £250,000 i.e. £750,000.

Using pension life cover

9.6   As well as the use of whole life assurance it may be suitable for individuals to consider their death-in-service benefits paid under an occupational pension scheme. This sum is usually payable free of IHT as the benefit is available under a discretionary trust and the scheme trustees will have discretion as to whom it is payable. The money could be used to meet an IHT liability and can be a considerable sum as the maximum benefit is four times salary. The tax relief available on contributions to this type of scheme make it an advantageous method of funding.

9.7   Where an individual has a personal pension he can take advantage of the tax treatment of contributions to a pension term assurance where there is no limit on the sum assured although contributions are limited. The policy can be written under trust with the main disadvantage being that cover must cease at age 75 if not earlier.

9.8   In both instances if the individual has a change in employment circumstances this may change their death benefit provision and an alternative method of funding IHT tax liability may have to be found.

Reducing the size of the estate

9.9   As mentioned above a whole life policy is generally the best type for funding for IHT as the policy pays out on death whenever it occurs. Term assurance is cheaper but will need renewing at the end of the term if the life assured is still alive.

9.10   These policies will provide funds for meeting any IHT liability on death. However, life assurance arrangements can also be used to reduce the size of an estate and therefore minimise the tax liability or even reduce it to nil. These arrangements will normally involve the use of trusts. The value of a particular arrangement to a customer will depend on how much control he requires over the proportion of the estate that he is putting into a trust. Some arrangements allow the settlor to take income from the trust whilst others restrict the settlor from having any access to the money once it has been removed from the estate. While an individual may wish to mitigate the potential tax liability for his family on his death he may not want to hand over large sums of money to them before his death without retaining some control.

Settlements

9.11   The term settlement means a type of trust where the trust property is held for a succession of interests e.g. 'for my wife for her life, and then for our children in equal shares' .The person who creates the settlement is the settlor, although this term is also used to describe someone who creates any kind of trust.

9.12   The beneficiaries may or may not have an interest in possession to the trust property. An interest in possession generally means a present right to present enjoyment. In the example above the wife has an interest in possession but the children do not. The beneficiary will be regarded as owning the property.

9.13   Placing a life policy under trust where there is an interest in possession constitutes a transfer which will be a Pet and may be chargeable if death occurs within seven years. If a beneficiary dies then there will be an IHT liability because there will be a transfer of value.

9.14   The transfer chargeable on a transfer of an existing life policy is normally based on the market value of the policy. This is usually the greater of the surrender value or the total premiums paid less any previous sums paid out e.g. part surrenders. For unit-linked policies any fall in value of the units since they were first allocated can be deducted from the total premiums paid.

9.15   This valuation rule does not apply to term assurances of three years or less, or for terms over three years, where premiums are payable for two thirds of the term, and premiums payable in any one year do not exceed twice those payable in any other year.

9.16   Where a premium is paid net of tax relief it is the net premium which is classed as the value transferred because this is the actual loss to the estate.

9.17 Where there is no interest in possession the settlement will normally be a discretionary trust, where the trustees have discretion on how to allocate income to a group of beneficiaries. For example, a discretionary trust may be set up for the benefit of the settlor's children and grandchildren, but the trustees can decide when and to whom to make payments. In this case if a beneficiary dies there will be no transfer of value and so no inheritance tax is payable. The trustees of a discretionary trust may be subject to a periodic IHT charge every 10 years on the value of the trust fund. It is currently 30% of the lifetime rate (i.e. 6%). There will also be a tax charge every time a distribution or appointment of capital is made to a beneficiary (see Unit 9 for further details on trusts).

Tax planning arrangements

9.18 Obviously individuals with large estates are likely to have quite complex tax planning needs and expert advice should always be sought in individual cases. The notes that follow explain the principles behind the main types of arrangements currently in use. It should also be remembered that changes in the law can make an excellent arrangement useless in the future and individual customers should be made aware that recommendations can only be based on current law.

9.19 These arrangements may have different names when offered by different companies and new arrangements are regularly being developed as the associated law changes, or different needs of customers become apparent.

Loan trusts

9.20 Under this arrangement an individual creates a trust and makes an interest-free loan to trustees. The loan is still part of the estate's assets.

9.21 The trustees then use the loan to buy a single premium bond and the funds grow in the bond outside the estate thus freezing the tax liability to the amount of the outstanding loan. The trustees make loan repayments to the customer using the bond withdrawal facility and if the withdrawal does not exceed the 5% limit (see Unit 21) there will be no income tax liability at that time.

9.22 When the customer dies:

(a) The bond pays out the value of units to the trustees.

(b) The trustees repay the loan from the bond proceeds and pay the remainder to the beneficiaries of the trust. This portion will be free of IHT.

(c) The loan repayment will form part of the deceased's estate and be liable to IHT.

(d) If the encashment of the bond creates a chargeable gain to income tax the liability must be met by the settlor's estate if it occurs in the same tax year as death (dead settlor rule).

(e) If the trust is set up so that the bond does not pay out on the death of the settlor then, provided the bond is not encashed until the tax year following death there will be no income tax liability. This could be arranged by writing the bond on a joint life last survivor basis with the youngest beneficiary as the other life. Assuming the settlor dies first the beneficiary can continue to take withdrawals or encash the bond in full without incurring an income tax liability.

9.23 If the settlor lives long enough for the loan repayments to substantially reduce the size of the loan then the value of the estate will also be reduced substantially. This arrangement also allows the settlor to receive income. Any growth in the value of the bond will not be liable to IHT and so allows the settlor to increase the value of the sum he passes on to his beneficiaries.

9.24 The main use of this type of arrangement is to freeze liability. For example, if someone has a sum of money equal to the nil rate threshold that they wish to invest to achieve capital growth then by using a loan trust they can ensure that any growth will not form part of the estate for IHT purposes. If the income received is spent on receipt it will not add to the value of the estate either.

Gift trust

9.25 Under this type of arrangement the settlor gifts capital to the trustees. By doing this he creates a Pet. The settlor cannot be a beneficiary under the trust and the trustees will use the gift to buy an insurance bond. On death of the settlor the bond will be paid out to the beneficiaries free of IHT and having reduced the settlor's estate by the amount of the gift.

9.26 Of course, where large sums are involved the IHT problem of the settlor may then be passed on to the next generation who may then have to look at their own IHT planning arrangements. It is possible to write trusts to cater for this problem.

Example 7.12 Tax planning over successive generations

Jack Jones wishes to pass on his estate to his son Gregory. Gregory is also quite wealthy and would be faced with an IHT problem of his own following his inheritance. He has a son Tom. Jack could set up a gift trust and be a trustee thus retaining control over the trust property. Gregory could also be a trustee and a beneficiary. Tom would have an interest in possession as a beneficiary.

Control over the trust would pass to Gregory on Jack's death. Gregory could then appoint some or all of the money back to himself if he wished. The investment bond would be written on the three lives on a last survivor basis therefore keeping growth outside the estate over a long period of time.

Gift and loan trusts

9.27 Some life companies offer a trust which combines a gift and a loan. In this case, the settlor creates a trust by making a gift, which can be a very small sum and is often less than or equal to the annual exemption to avoid tax, and then make a much bigger loan to the trustees. This means that the tax treatment of the gift portion may differ from that of the loan portion.

Split trust bond

9.28 Another arrangement which uses a single premium bond is a split trust. The customer pays a single premium to a bond which is written under a split trust, this splits the beneficial ownership into a retained portion for the settlor absolutely and a gifted portion for the intended beneficiaries. The initial transfer is a transfer of value for IHT and may be partly exempt (e.g. by using £3,000 annual exemption) and partly a Pet.

9.29   The customer can take withdrawals from the bond, subject to the 5% rules and taxation will be based on the full initial investment. However, the withdrawals reduce the value of the retained portion only. In this way the retained portion is progressively reduced or eventually eliminated altogether.

9.30   On death the gifted portion is paid to the beneficiaries free of IHT. The retained portion is paid to the settlor's estate and is subject to IHT. Any higher rate income tax liability is payable by the customer's estate and so reduces the value of the estate for IHT purposes.

Use of annuities

9.31   Certain arrangements known as 'back to back' plans combine a whole life policy and an annuity. The individual pays a lump sum into an annuity which pays an income for life. He also pays the first premium to a whole life policy written under trust for the beneficiaries. The premium is a gift for IHT purposes but should fall under the normal expenditure exemption. The annuity income is used to pay the whole life premiums each month (or annually). Part of the annuity may be available as income for the individual.

9.32   When the annuitant dies the annuity ceases and the whole life policy proceeds are paid to the beneficiaries free of IHT. This has effectively removed the amount of initial investment from the individual's estate. The policy can be written on a joint life last survivor basis if the customers wish to pass the estate on to their children.

9.33   Provided the individuals are in good health, to avoid underwriting problems, this arrangement is suitable for anyone requiring IHT mitigation as well as an income for life. The only disadvantage is that under current tax law the two contracts must not be associated otherwise the chargeable transfer of value at the time the arrangement is set up will be based on the lesser of the total initial lump sum and the whole life sum assured. This would mean the plan would not be effective in reducing IHT liability. The contracts will not be regarded as associated if they are issued on the same terms as if they were individual arrangements e.g. the whole life policy is subject to full medical underwriting. Plans can be taken out using the same company, who must take care to ensure the two elements are treated separately or with two different companies. The latter method may mean that the best rates can be obtained for both the annuity and the whole life assurance.

Using offshore policies

9.34   Some inheritance tax planning arrangements use offshore bonds to take advantage of the tax-free roll-up of investments available thereby allowing the value of the bond to grow at a faster rate outside the estate if written under trust. This is covered in more detail in Unit 20.

Taxation implications of trusts

9.35   When an individual transfers assets from his estate into a trust there is a chargeable transfer. The value transferred when the trust is set up will usually be the first premium or single premium paid. Regular premiums will be transfers of value each time they are paid. However, as mentioned earlier, these are likely to be covered under the annual or normal expenditure exemptions. If the policy is joint then two exemptions will apply.

9.36 If the trust has an interest in possession then there will be a potentially exempt transfer. If the trust is discretionary then there will be a chargeable lifetime transfer.

9.37 Where an existing policy is assigned to a trust during its lifetime then this will also be a transfer of value based on the higher of the surrender value or the total premiums paid less any sums previously paid out.

9.38 Where an offshore bond is used, this has the advantage that it is not regarded as an income bearing investment and so can benefit from the roll-up of investment growth (see Unit 20).

9.39 Where a chargeable event for income tax occurs under a life policy written in trust the gain will be taxed as if it were the income of the settlor. If the gain arises when the settlor is dead it will only be taxable if the gain occurs during the same tax year as death (see para 9.22). This 'dead settlor' rule is likely to be changed in the near future, and changes may be applied retrospectively.

9.40 Capital gains tax does not usually apply where life policies are written under trust as there is not usually a capital gain.

Advantages of writing a policy under trust

9.41 As described the purpose of writing a life policy under trust is to remove the sum assured from the life assured's estate. It also provides other advantages which can be summarised as follows:

(a) Allows the settlor choice and flexibility in who can receive the policy proceeds.

(b) Allows proceeds to be paid almost immediately on death.

(c) Where a person becomes bankrupt the policy is outside the bankrupt's property so cannot be claimed by creditors. This is of particular use in businesses i.e. by self-employed and partners.

(d) Trust arrangements can be arranged to suit particular needs.

Disadvantages of writing a policy under trust

9.42 Where a person writes a policy under trust he may feel he no longer owns the policy proceeds and may see this as a disadvantage. However, this can be overcome by the settlor becoming a trustee.

9.43 If a policy is written under the Married Women's Property Act (see Unit 9) then the policy may only be single life and the beneficiaries are restricted. The arrangement also lacks flexibility.

9.44 A trust must be worded correctly to ensure it achieves its aim. Individuals may be deterred from writing a policy under trust if it appears to be complicated.

9.45 There must be other trustees to ensure that there is someone to make a claim in the event of the settlor's death. If a husband and wife, for example, are the only trustees this will create problems in claiming and administering the policy proceeds when the last survivor dies.

10   Equalisation of Estates

10.1   Where a husband and wife own an estate of considerable size they should ensure that they equalise ownership of their assets to reduce the potential tax liability. If one partner owns a larger proportion he or she can gift part of it to the other spouse taking advantage of the inter-spouse exemption.

Example 7.13: Equalisation of estate

Charlie and Diana Smithson own the following assets:

	Charlie	Diana
House	£ 80,000	£80,000
Personal effects	£ 5,000	£ 5,000
Building society account	£ 3,000	£ 1,500
Bank	£ 800	-
Partnership interest	£ 85,000	-
Premises used for workshop	£ 35,000	-
Anticipated inheritance	£700,000	-
Total	£908,800	£ 86,500

It would be sensible, when Charlie receives his inheritance, to spread the assets between them. This would ensure that if Diana died first she could make full use of the nil rate tax band by leaving £200,000 of her estate to their children under trust. At present she cannot take advantage of this. Charlie should also do the same. The couple would then have to look at further ways of mitigating their potential tax liability on the death of the last survivor.

11   Disposal of Increasing Value Assets

11.1   A further factor to be considered by the donor of a potentially exempt transfer is that it is the value of the gift at the time of transfer that is taken into account rather than its value at the time of death. Therefore, it may be advantageous to gift an appreciating asset which will increase in value in the hands of the donor. This removes the value of the increase from the estate. Any insurance cover taken will need a sum assured equal to the value of the gift at the time of transfer.

11.2   Conversely it would not be sensible to gift a depreciating asset as the value which may be chargeable on death would be more than the asset was actually worth.

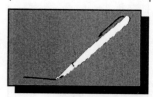

Student Activity 4

You should complete this student activity before reading the next section of the text. Answer the questions, then check your answers against the paragraph(s) indicated.

1. Why is cash needed in order to prove title and how can a life   (9.1)
    assurance policy help to provide this?

2. If a married couple wish to pass their estate after death to their   (9.3)
    children what type of policy should they effect?

3. Why would some individuals not wish to use a trust to   (9.10)
    mitigate the potential IHT liability?

4. Charles Watson is considering effecting a life policy under   (9.41-9.45)
    trust, explain the advantages and disadvantages of doing this.

If you are unable to answer any of the questions satisfactorily, you should read the relevant paragraphs again. Your understanding of the text will be further tested in the self-assessment section at the end of this unit.

12   Making a Will

12.1   In the United Kingdom, seven out of ten people who die do so 'intestate', that is without having made a will. Dying intestate is not always a problem for an individual's dependants but where it could be a few simple steps can often alleviate the quite serious difficulties that can arise. Making a will is a first important step in gaining control over an estate and is therefore a vital part of financial planning.

12.2   If an individual does not make a will, the laws of intestacy will apply, giving control of how the deceased's estate will be distributed on death to the law of the land, rather than to the dependants.

12.3   If an individual would like to control what happens to his estate on death he needs to make a will and keep it up to date. A properly drafted will can also be an important weapon in mitigating inheritance tax, although deeds of variation can be used after death to restructure an estate despite a will having been made.

If no will is made

12.4   Without a will, when a person dies he will be termed to die 'intestate' and certain rules apply for the distribution of the estate. These rules will not necessarily provide what the deceased would have wanted and are unlikely to be very tax-efficient.

12.5   When a will has been made the deceased's estate can be distributed exactly as he intended and it can be done with a view to minimising inheritance tax. This is particularly relevant where minor children are involved, because instructions can be left in the will for their care and custody which the laws of intestacy do not provide for.

12.6   In effect, if someone dies intestate he hands over control of the distribution of his estate to the particular laws of the country in which he lives. The law is slightly different in Scotland, but both sets of intestacy laws are shown below.

Table 7.5: Intestacy in United Kingdom, excluding Scotland

Surviving spouse only	Spouse takes everything (but only if he/she survives the deceased by at least 28 days if tenants in common).
Surviving spouse and children	Spouse takes personal chattels together with £125,000 plus life interest in half of residue. Children share half of residue immediately plus the half in which the spouse had life interest on his or her death.
Surviving spouse and parents	Spouse takes personal chattels together with £200,000 and half of residue absolutely. Parents share half of the residue absolutely plus balance on spouse's death.
Surviving spouse and brothers, sisters and their issue	Spouse takes personal chattels together with £200,000 and half of residue absolutely. Brothers, sisters or their issue share half of residue absolutely, plus the balance on spouse's death.
No surviving spouse	Children or issue take whole estate absolutely.
No surviving spouse, children or their issue	Whole estate goes to following in order of precedence: • Parents • Brothers/sisters • Half brothers/half sisters • Grandparents • Uncle and aunts • Uncle and aunts of half blood • The crown

Intestacy in Scotland

12.7 If a will is made:

- Spouse gets one-third of moveable estate

- Children get one-third divided amongst them

- Other third distributed according to will

- Or if no issue, widow gets half moveable estate

12.8 If no will is made:

- Everything goes to descendants, children first if no spouse

- But if spouse survives 'prior rights' and 'legal rights' come into use

- 'Prior rights' are the house (or £65,000 if it is worth more than that) plus £12,000 for furniture plus £35,000 if no children or £21,000 if there are children

- 'Legal rights' are *jus relictae* - the right of a widow to half her husband's estate, *jus relict* - the right of a widower to half his wife's estate and *legitim* - the right of the children to one-third of the estate if there is a surviving spouse, or a half if there is no surviving spouse.

12.9 It could be that dying intestate may not be a large concern for an individual. In most cases, however, the unforeseen death of a potential inheritor could lead to a different inheritor benefiting from the death of the testator, which may not be desired.

Making a will

12.10 The legal definitions and complicated terms often used in drawing up a will should not be regarded as a barrier to making a will. Banks and some other specialist companies offer will writing services at reasonable prices and, of course, the family solicitor can also be used to draft a will. An individual can also draft his own but this is not always recommended except in fairly straightforward estates as errors can be made by the inexperienced.

How to make a valid will

12.11 The Wills Act of 1837, amended by the Wills Act of 1963, lays down UK (excluding Scotland) law for wills. To make a valid will two formalities must be followed:

- It has to be in writing

- It has to be properly executed

12.12 The only exception to this is in the case of privileged wills which can be made verbally by soldiers on active service.

12.13 The terms of the will must be 'reasonable', i.e. no strange conditions laid down for the inheritor, and the will must be signed by the person making the will (testator or testatrix), although a cross or a thumb print will do if that person cannot write, in the presence of two witnesses. This signature has to be 'at the foot or end of the will' for obvious reasons.

12.14 A beneficiary under a will or a spouse of a beneficiary should not act as a witness, as this would result in the beneficiary losing his entitlement under the will. Amendments to wills can be made by codicil which must be signed and witnessed in the same way as the original will.

The content of the will

12.15 The content of the will should be a clear and unambiguous explanation of the deceased's directions for his estate. It should distribute the estate according to his wishes, as long as there is an estate to distribute, of course.

12.16 It is a sensible precaution to include 'survivorship clauses' in a will. For example, it is usual for one spouse to leave his estate to the surviving spouse. This will not create a problem unless the two die together or within a short time span. If two spouses die together one of them will inherit the entire estate which will be free of inheritance tax until it is passed on to their beneficiaries. The size of the estate could then entail an IHT charge.

12.17 It is sensible, therefore, to include such a 'survivorship clause', which simply states that the spouse will inherit if he survives the deceased by, for example, thirty days, otherwise a named individual or individuals will inherit the estate.

12.18 It should also be noted that if the two spouses do die together the elder is deemed to have died first if actual time of each death cannot be determined.

12.19 If a survivorship clause is not included and part of the estate is left to someone who has died recently this will create 'partial intestacy' and this residue will be distributed under the rules of intestacy.

Deeds of variation

12.20 Sometimes when property passes on death by will or intestacy it can be advantageous for the recipients to vary the disposition for tax reasons or family reasons. This can be done by executing a deed of variation. All those who would have benefited from the original provisions must be over 18 and must agree to the variation. The deed must be executed within two years of the death and the Inland Revenue must be informed within six months. The variation must not be made for any consideration in money or money's worth.

12.21 If these conditions are met the variation is treated for IHT purposes as if made by the deceased and the variation is not treated as a transfer of value.

Disclaimers

12.22 A person cannot be made to accept a gift if he does not want it. He has the right to disclaim the gift at any time before he accepts, but he will be treated as having accepted the gift if he takes any benefit from it. The gift must be disclaimed within two years of the death and again there must be no consideration in money or money's worth. The disclaimer can be withdrawn but only if it has not been acted on by any party relying upon it.

12.23 If a legacy is disclaimed it will return to the deceased's estate and if this is not effectively disposed of by will, it will pass on intestacy. If an individual disclaims a gift he will have no influence on its ultimate destination. The ultimate beneficiary of the disclaimed gift is treated as having received the gift from the deceased and not from the person disclaiming.

Updating a will

12.24 Since individual circumstances do change regularly it is a wise precaution to ensure that a will is up to date and still reflects the testator's wishes. Any updates or codicils have to be signed and witnessed as before.

Revoking a will

12.25 There are four ways to revoke a will:

- Subsequent will or codicil

- A writing executed like a will

- Subsequent marriage

- Destruction of the will, if intended

12.26 A new will should be written on marriage or remarriage, unless it appears from the will that at the time it was made the testator was expecting to be married to a particular person and that he intended that the will should not be revoked by the contemplated marriage.

12.27 Although divorce will not revoke a will, a former spouse cannot take any gift under the will unless a contrary intention is shown in the will. In addition, any appointment of the former spouse as executor or trustee is revoked on divorce. If a will is destroyed it has to be proven that there was intention to destroy the will for it to be revoked. Accidental destruction is not a revocation.

Family provision claims

12.28 Individuals can make claims against wills to revoke them, often on the basis of 'unsound mind' and there are normally cases going through the courts which would illustrate this. It is up to the courts, in these cases, to uphold or dismiss any claims made.

12.29 Dependants who have not been mentioned in the will, or for whom inadequate provision has been made, may be able to claim reasonable provision from the estate under the Inheritance (Provision for family and dependants) Act 1975.

12.30 It should be noted that a 'common law' spouse has no legal claim on a will or an estate unless judged to be a dependant under the above Act. Before 4 April 1987, illegitimate children had no legal claim on a will since the law did not recognise them. After that date, illegitimate children were put on the same footing as legitimate children.

Will trusts

12.31 A trust can be set up under the provision of a will to ensure that the estate is administered as the deceased wished. A discretionary trust may be set up which has several advantages:

(a) It allows a settlor to leave his estate to a group of beneficiaries but without the need to specify who should benefit and by how much. The trustees can decide this at the time depending on family circumstances and tax considerations.

(b) Under the IHT Act 1984 S144 any distributions made within two years of death will be free of IHT. However, if a distribution is made to the surviving spouse within three months of death an IHT charge will be incurred so it is advisable to delay beyond this period.

(c) The trust can be used to take advantage of the nil rate band by settling £200,000 and including the spouse as one of the potential beneficiaries. This would mean that instead of passing the full estate to the remaining spouse and thus increasing the estate on his or her eventual death the discretionary trust can be used to pass this amount indirectly. The trustees can use their discretion to decide whether income should be paid to the remaining spouse from the trust.

(d) The trustees can be given powers to make loans to beneficiaries which is a method of passing capital to beneficiaries without declaring it as an outright intention and thereby incurring a tax charge.

(e) Discretionary trusts can be written to ensure that an investment such as a bond or unit trust by the settlor will become subject to the trust on the settlor's death. The trustees then have power to deal with the investment as they see fit.

12.32 As with all other trust arrangements the actual tax treatment will depend on the circumstances of the individual arrangement. The ten-year charges and exit charges will apply as for other discretionary trusts and these should be taken into consideration.

Scots law

12.33 As explained previously the law in Scotland is somewhat different to the law in the rest of the United Kingdom in relation to wills.

12.34 The major differences are as follows:

- A Scottish will is not revoked by subsequent marriage

- A cross or mark is not allowed for a Scottish will and only a Justice of the Peace, solicitor or parish minister can sign on behalf of the testator

- A will may be 'holograph', that is a will in the testator's own handwriting and signed with no witness required

13 Wills - A Summary

13.1 A will is an important part of any individual's financial plan to ensure control over the distribution of his estate after death. It can also be a very useful method for mitigating inheritance tax. The following points should be remembered:

- Always store a will where it can be found, preferably in a safe place, e.g. bank, solicitor, etc.

- Include survivorship clauses to mitigate the potential inheritance tax liability

- Remember that wills are annulled on marriage, subsequent will revocation or intended destruction

- Review wills regularly

Student Activity 5

You should complete this student activity before attempting the self-assessment. Answer the questions, then check your answers against the paragraph(s) indicated.

1. What problems may a deceased's family face if he has not made a will?   (12.4-12.6)

2. Sam Jones dies intestate leaving a wife and two children. He leaves an estate of £300,000, how will this be shared?   (Table 7.5)

3. Why should survivorship clauses be included in a will?   (12.16)

163

4.   John Smales dies, leaving some of his property to his nephew   (12.20)
     and niece. Chris Smales is left a large old property in need of
     major repairs. Chris can't afford to fund the repairs, however
     his sister Jane has the funds and has been left a small holiday
     cottage at the coast which she doesn't want. She would enjoy
     the challenge of the renovation and Chris would like a holiday
     cottage. What could they do?

If you are unable to answer any of the questions satisfactorily, you should read the
relevant paragraphs again. Your understanding of the text will be further tested in
the following self-assessment.

Summary

Now that you have completed this unit, you should be able to:

☐ **Define inheritance tax and know what it is levied on**

☐ **Know the major exempt transfers and any conditions or limits associated with them**

☐ **Know how potentially exempt transfers arise, in what circumstances they may be taxed and how tapering relief operates during the liable period**

☐ **Define a gift with reservation and understand the purpose of the rules governing such gifts**

☐ **Know which lifetime transfers may be chargeable**

☐ **Understand the special considerations of spouses for IHT purposes**

☐ **Know the rates of IHT, and the nil rate band**

☐ **Know when inheritance tax is payable, and by whom**

☐ **Know the principal reliefs from IHT**

☐ **Understand the methods available to mitigate IHT liability, including lifetime gifts, life assurance and annuities, estate equalisation, settlements and trusts**

☐ **Understand the importance of making a will and the main elements of a will**

☐ **Know the laws of intestacy, and the consequences of intestacy**

If you can tick all the above boxes with confidence, you are ready to answer the questions which follow.

Self-Assessment Questions

1. Mr Williams recently died. Included in his estate is a property on which the building work has not yet been completed. How would this property be valued for IHT purposes?

2. Jeremy and Sarah have recently divorced and Jeremy is making maintenance payments for their two children who live with Sarah. How are these payments treated for IHT purposes?

3. Maria made a transfer of £300,000 to her daughter in January 1992 and subsequently died in May 1996. Calculate the IHT liability after the current nil rate band and tapering relief are taken into account.

4. David Jones wishes to transfer some of the agricultural land which he owns to his son. What two conditions must apply for the transfer to qualify for agricultural property relief?

5. Sophie asks you whether she could use the death-in-service payment under her occupational pension scheme to fund for IHT. What could you tell her?

6. Briefly describe the main purpose of a loan trust and how it operates.

7. Adam Blake owns assets totalling £800,000 and his wife Teresa owns assets worth £60,000. They have two children. What action could they take to mitigate potential inheritance tax liability?

8. Alan Jones dies intestate leaving a wife and four children who are all aged over 18. His estate is worth £600,000. How will this be distributed?

9. Describe the two formalities which must be followed for a will to be valid and name the exception to this rule.

10. Richard does not want to accept the legacy which his father has left him in his will. What can Richard do and what timescales apply?

Unit 8

Taxation of Investment Income

Objectives

Students are required to study the following topics:

- **Overview of corporation tax**

- **Advance corporation tax**

- **Franked and unfranked income**

- **Stamp duty**

1   Introduction

1.1   So far in this module the emphasis has been on taxation of the individual. Corporate taxation is outside the scope of personal investment planning but is briefly touched on in this unit because of its impact on the way dividends received by individuals are taxed. The notes that follow give a brief outline of corporation tax and advance corporation tax and how companies are taxed on investment income received and paid out. It also explains how individuals are taxed on dividends paid by these companies.

1.2   The ways in which companies pay dividends and the types of shares available to individuals is covered in more detail in later units.

1.3   This unit also gives an overview of stamp duty and its relevance to the personal investor.

2   Corporation Tax

2.1   Corporation tax is the tax on the world-wide profits of companies which are resident in the UK. Overseas companies trading through a branch or agency in the UK will pay corporation tax on the profits arising in this country.

2.2   Corporation tax is charged both on a company's profits and its capital gains.

2.3   Profits are worked out in much the same way as for the self-employed, but income and gains from all sources are included. The gross amount of investment income the company receives is included and if tax has already been deducted it can be offset against corporation tax. However, the company does not have to include dividends from UK resident companies because the underlying profits of the paying company have already suffered corporation tax before the dividend was paid. Such dividends and their related tax credits are called 'franked investment income'.

2.4   Expenses which are wholly and exclusively for business purposes, and capital

169

allowances are deducted. Any payments that the company has made where income tax is deducted before handing over the money, such as royalty payments and some interest payments, are also deducted before arriving at the profit assessable for corporation tax.

2.5   Companies are not entitled to any annual capital gains tax exemption.

When the tax is payable

2.6   Corporation tax is worked out on a current year basis. A company's income is charged to corporation tax on the basis of the actual income assessable for each accounting period. The accounting period will normally be the period for which the company prepares annual accounts but cannot exceed twelve months.

2.7   A system called 'Pay and File' has been in force from October 1993. Under this system companies are required to pay tax on their own estimate of the amount due within nine months of the end of the accounting period, and to file their returns and accounts for assessment within twelve months.

Rates of corporation tax

2.8   The rate of corporation tax is fixed for each financial year which runs from 1 April to 31 March. For example, the financial year 1996 runs from 1 April 1996 to 31 March 1997.

Small companies rate

2.9   If a company's profits are below a certain level in a given accounting period, a lower rate of corporation tax is charged. The special definition of profits for the small companies rate includes the profits chargeable to corporation tax (basic profits) plus dividends received from other UK companies with their related tax credits (franked investment income). The level of profits for the small companies rate to apply is set at £300,000. The small companies rate was reduced with effect from 1 April 1996 from 25% to 24% in line with the revised basic rate of income tax.

Marginal rate

2.10   If the profits of a company fall between the stipulated amount for a small company and an upper maximum of £1,500,000, marginal relief is available.

2.11   Although the calculation of marginal relief is beyond the scope of this unit, it has the effect of taxing profits up to £300,000 at 24% and profits between £300,000 and £1,500,000 at a marginal rate of 35.25%.

Table 8.1: Corporation tax rates

| Year beginning 1 April | Full rate % | Small Companies | | |
		Rate %	Upper Profit Limit (£)	Upper Profit Limit (£)	Effective Marginal Rate (%)
1992	33	25	250,000	1,250,000	35
1993	33	25	250,000	1,250,000	35
1994	33	25	300,000	1,500,000	35
1995	33	25	300,000	1,500,000	35
1996	33	24	300,000	1,500,000	35.25

3 Dividends and Advance Corporation Tax

3.1 When a company pays a dividend, it has to pay some corporation tax at the same time. This is called advance corporation tax (ACT), since the company is paying part of its corporation tax before it is normally due.

3.2 As a result of paying this ACT, the shareholder receives the dividend with a tax credit. This is known as the 'imputation system' since shareholders are imputed, or attributed, with tax at the appropriate amount of their dividends. The dividend plus the ACT is known as a franked payment made by the company.

3.3 The rate of ACT on dividends is 20% for the tax year 1996-97 and the tax charge is also 20%. Previously it was 25% up to 5 April 1993 and then a transitional rate of 22.5% for 1993-94.

3.4 Both lower rate and basic rate taxpayers will therefore receive a tax credit that matches the income tax charge exactly, and there will be no repayments or tax to pay. Higher rate taxpayers will be liable to a further 20% tax on the amount of dividend received and the tax credit (equal to 25% of the dividend).

3.5 Non taxpayers can reclaim the tax deducted.

Example 8.1: Tax liability for individuals

Dividend of £300 plus tax credit of £75 is received.

Matthew is a non taxpayer so he can reclaim the £75 tax credit and will receive a total of £375.

Mark and Luke are lower rate and basic rate taxpayers respectively and have no further tax liability to pay. They receive £300.

John is a higher rate taxpayer. He must pay a further 20% on £375, i.e. £75 and so will have a net payment of £225.

The effect of ACT on the company's total tax bill

3.6 The payment of ACT is, as its name implies, a payment on account of the eventual total corporation tax liability. The amount of ACT will be offset against the corporation tax on the profits of the accounting period in which the dividend was paid, subject to a maximum set-off limit. There are provisions to carry back and carry forward any surplus ACT so that it can be offset against previous or future corporation tax.

Accounting periods for ACT

3.7 Unlike mainstream corporation tax, ACT must be paid within 14 days of every quarter, i.e. 31 March, 30 June, 30 September and 31 December.

3.8 If a company's accounting period does not end on one of these dates, the period of three months during which it ends is divided into two separate periods for which returns must be submitted.

ACT returns to the Inland Revenue

3.9 Form CT61 is used to make returns to the Revenue and must show:

- The franked payments

- The franked investment income received (see below)

- The amount of ACT payable plus certain other details

3.10 A cheque in settlement of ACT is normally sent with the return. In calculating the ACT, companies may deduct tax credits on receipt of franked investment income during the relevant period. Any foreign income dividends paid or received will be detailed in a separate section of the form.

Surplus ACT

3.11 This is any ACT which is not relieved against corporation tax payable for the accounting period in which the relevant distribution is made.

3.12 This can be carried back and offset against corporation tax payable for any accounting periods beginning in the six years preceding that in which the relevant distribution is made.

3.13 A claim must be made within two years of the end of the period for which the surplus ACT arises.

3.14 Any surplus ACT which is not carried back, as above, may be carried forward without time limit, to be offset against future corporation tax payable.

Other distributions

3.15 ACT is payable on dividends and 'other qualifying distributions'. This normally means other distributions in respect of shares in the company. Non-qualifying distributions broadly cover those that confer a future rather than a current claim on a company's assets. For example, a bonus issue of redeemable shares is only liable to ACT when the shares are redeemed. When the distribution is made, the shareholder has a marginal rate tax liability if a higher rate taxpayer. This can be offset against any tax due at redemption.

4 Franked and Unfranked Income

4.1 Franked investment income, as mentioned earlier, is the income received by a UK resident company as dividends from shares invested in another UK resident company. The ACT deducted by the distributing company is given in the form of a tax credit. This means that franked investment income does not have to be included in a company's profits for corporation tax purposes because the tax credit is equal to the amount of ACT paid on it by the distributing company.

4.2 Certain income received by a company is not treated as franked because tax has not already been paid on it. This is known as unfranked income and includes the following:

(a) Group income i.e. dividends from a company within a group of companies where both the distributing company and the receiving company have elected not to pay ACT on dividends being distributed.

(b) Dividends or interest received from building societies.

(c) Foreign income dividends. If a company both pays and receives foreign income dividends it can offset one against the other and will only be liable to pay ACT on the excess.

4.3 If a company has more franked investment income (FII) than it has franked payments to make, the excess FII can be carried forward to the next accounting period

Example 8.2: Franked investment income exceeds franked payments

A company receives a dividend of £200,000 and a tax credit of £50,000 making total franked investment income of £250,000.

It also pays dividends to its own shareholders of £150,000 with an accompanying tax credit of £37,500. Total franked payments are £187,500.

A surplus FII of £62,500 can be carried forward to the next accounting period and be offset against further franked payments.

Example 8.3: Franked payments exceed franked investment income

The same company receives franked investment income of £250,000 but makes franked payments of £375,000 (i.e. dividends of £300,000 plus tax credits of £75,000).

The FII can be offset against franked payments leaving £125,000 liable to ACT at 20% = £25,000.

Losses

4.4 If a company has made a trading loss and all other reliefs available have been exhausted surplus franked investment income can be used to obtain a refund of dividend tax credits in the current year and the previous three years.

Foreign income dividends (FIDs)

4.5 Foreign income dividends paid and received by a company are not franked payments or franked investment income. ACT is payable on them but shareholders do not receive a tax credit although they are treated as being paid net of tax at 20%. This means that non taxpayers cannot reclaim repayment of tax and that higher rate taxpayers have a further 20% liability.

4.6 The company will be liable for ACT on the excess of FIDs paid over FIDs received in the same way as franked payments. Any surplus can be carried forward to the next year as it cannot be offset against mainstream corporation tax.

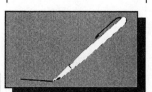

Student Activity 1

You should complete this student activity before reading the next section of the text. Answer the questions, then check your answers against the paragraph(s) indicated.

1. What is the difference between the financial year and the tax year? (2.8)

2. Andrea is a basic rate taxpayer and receives a cheque for £500 (3.4)

in respect of dividends on her shareholding. What tax credit will have been given?

3. Why must a company pay advance corporation tax? (3.1)

If you are unable to answer any of the questions satisfactorily, you should read the relevant paragraphs again. Your understanding of the text will be further tested in the self-assessment section at the end of this unit.

5 Stamp Duty

5.1 Stamp duty is the oldest tax administered by the Inland Revenue having been in existence since 1694. The present stamp duty law was introduced by the Stamp Act 1891 and is payable on certain legal documents completed in the UK or relating to UK property or transactions. The document should normally be stamped before it takes effect although no penalty will be levied if stamping takes place within 30 days. It should be noted that the duty is being levied on the document and not the actual transaction.

5.2 Documents which are subject to stamp duty cannot, except for criminal proceedings, be given in evidence or be available for any other purpose, including registration of title (such as following house purchase) unless they are stamped.

5.3 The stamp duty is either fixed or based on the value of the transaction (known as ad valorem duties). The main heads of charge and rates are as follows:

Table 8.2: Stamp duty

Heads of charge	Rate of duty
Bearer instruments	
Inland and overseas(but excluding deposit certificates for overseas stock)	1.5%
- those excluded above	10p per £50 or part
Conveyances or transfers of sale	
Stock and marketable securities	0.5%
Other transfers (including house purchase)	1%
Duty on certified transactions not exceeding £60,000	Nil
Various share transactions	
Includes take-overs, mergers, demergers, reconstruction and amalgamation schemes	0.5%
Leases	
For definite term less than one year of furnished dwelling house rent over £500 per annum	£1
Any other rental leases	0 to 24% on sliding scale depending on average rent

5.4 Documents for most other types of chargeable transactions attract a fixed duty of 50p.

Sales of property

5.5 Sales of property come under the heading of conveyances and transfers on sale. The main sale of relevance to most individuals is a house sale and these transactions are exempt up to £60,000. Where a person buying a newly built house trades in his old house as part payment stamp duty used to only be payable on the cash difference. However, because this is becoming more common practice in a depressed housing market stamp duty is now payable at 1% of the full sale price of the new house if it is worth more than £60,000. The house given in part payment will only have a 50p stamp duty.

Trusts

5.6 There is no stamp duty where a trust is created by a will. Any written declaration of a trust made in an individual's lifetime will attract stamp duty of 50p. This includes writing a life assurance policy under trust. Once the trust has been created the trustees will be liable to pay stamp duty on any chargeable transactions in the same way as individuals.

Family arrangements

5.7 Any qualifying deeds of family arrangement and deeds which convey property on separation or following a divorce are exempt from stamp duty.

Payment and penalties

5.8 Stamp duty is administered by the Commissioners of the Inland Revenue through the Office of the Controller of Stamps. Any documents which are submitted late for stamping will incur a penalty of up to £10 plus interest plus the duty payable. Documents can be sent or taken to any of the ten stamp offices in the UK.

5.9 Payment is made at the local stamp office where the document is impressed with a stamp to show that duty has been paid. If there is doubt as to whether stamp duty is applicable then the stamp office will adjudicate the document and either stamp it as adjudged not chargeable or as duly stamped.

Exemptions

5.10 There are several types of documents which are exempt from stamp duty including transfers of gilts, conveyances, transfers or leases to approved charities, transfers brought about by wills, contracts of employment, deeds of covenant, and insurance policies and related documents (excluding life policies written under trust).

Stamp duty reserve tax

5.11 Stamp duty reserve tax (SDRT) was introduced by the Finance Act 1986 and is applied at a rate of 0.5% to share transactions which escape stamp duty e.g. transactions within the same stock exchange account. The introduction of CREST on 15 July 1996 on the London Stock Exchange means that shares which would have attracted stamp duty of 0.5% will attract SDRT at 0.5% instead. Unit 10 explains the system for buying and selling shares through the London Stock Exchange and the CREST system.

5.12 Liability arises at the date of the agreement and the tax is payable at the end of the following month. If duty is paid after reserve tax has been paid then the tax will be refunded. The tax is collected by market makers, brokers and dealers.

5.13 Overdue reserve tax will be charged interest and further penalties may be levied by the Commissioners where notice of a liability is not given and no tax has been paid.

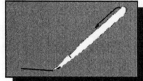

Student Activity 2

You should complete this student activity before attempting the self-assessment. Answer the questions, then check your answers against the paragraph(s) indicated.

1. On what is stamp duty levied? (5.1)

2. Mr and Mrs Hurst take out a mortgage of £80,000 for a property worth £92,000. How much stamp duty must they pay on the sale? (5.5)

3. What penalty may be levied if a document is submitted late for stamping? (5.8)

If you are unable to answer any of the questions satisfactorily, you should read the relevant paragraphs again. Your understanding of the text will be further tested in the following self-assessment.

Summary

Now that you have completed this unit you should be able to:

❑ **Explain why companies pay ACT on dividends**

❑ **Know the current rates of corporation tax and ACT**

❑ **Explain the differences between franked and unfranked investment income**

❑ **Understand the effect of corporation tax and ACT on the personal investor**

❑ **Calculate the tax credit on a dividend payment**

❑ **Explain on what stamp duty is levied**

❑ **Know the types of stamp duty rates**

❑ **Know the main documents which are exempt**

If you can tick the above boxes with confidence, you are ready to answer the questions which follow.

Self-Assessment Questions

1. What is the pay and file system for corporation tax.

2. What are the current rates for:

   (a) corporation tax (full rate)?

   (b) ACT?

3. Explain the difference between how a higher rate taxpayer pays tax on dividends and the position for a basic rate taxpayer.

4. What is a 'franked payment'?

5. What can a company do if it receives more in franked investment income than it makes franked payments?

6. If a company pays out dividends from foreign income what is the tax position of the individual?

7. What are the two types of stamp duty rate?

8. Why do documents need to be stamped?

9. Give three examples of when stamp duty would be imposed.

10. What is stamp duty reserve tax?

Unit 9

Trusts

Objectives

Students are required to study the following topics:

- **Principles of trust law**

- **Parties to a trust**

- **Role of the trustee**

- **Types of trust**

- **Taxation and trusts**

- **Uses of trusts**

- **Legislation and case law**

1 Introduction

1.1 There are many different definitions of a trust, but essentially they all point to the fact that a trust is a method of asset distribution for the benefit of people, usually other than the owner of the asset, without allowing them to exert control over that asset. The asset then becomes the legal property of the trustees, although it cannot be used for their personal benefit, but is held for the benefit of the beneficiaries.

1.2 The beneficiaries' interests can be laid down formally, in a trust deed, when the trust is created or they can be implied by trust law. Thus trusts can be created by deed, by will or by statute, and can be in writing, oral or implied by the conduct of all parties involved. While the majority of law regarding trusts is now contained in the Trustee Act 1925 there are also other notable areas of legislation that apply as discussed later in this unit. It is this range of different governing requirements that often causes confusion regarding the nature, and principles, of trusts.

1.3 It is important to remember that the ownership of the asset rests with the trustees as this will be reflected in any relevant property register, e.g. company share lists, and reflected in the taxation of the trust.

2 Reasons for Creating Trusts

2.1 Before moving on to look at the intricacies of trusts themselves it would be prudent to consider the reasons for their creation. The most commonly held belief surrounding the creation, and use, of trusts is the effect of minimising taxation, especially favoured by financial planners in the avoidance of inheritance tax. This is not, however, always the only reason for the serious consideration of setting up a trust.

2.2 Often an asset can be settled into a trust with the trustees being given the choice of how best to use the income or capital value accruing to the trust for the beneficiaries, or a class of beneficiaries. These 'discretionary' powers give the trustee the flexibility to respond to future changes in circumstances without having to risk breaking the trust's terms.

2.3 Trusts can be extremely useful in ensuring property succeeds to others, the main purpose for trusts. An example may be where an asset is placed in trust for the benefit of children, but the intention is to ensure that on their death the asset can be enjoyed by their children (i.e. the settlor's grandchildren).

2.4 Where an asset is to be used for the benefit of a child, or perhaps someone who is mentally handicapped and unable to manage their own affairs, a trust becomes a method through which their interests can be protected and maintained. Under UK law a minor is not entitled to hold land, but the trust gives them beneficial ownership, and thus the right to enjoy the income that land may produce.

2.5 Trusts can also be used to meet certain types of charitable aspirations. Laid down in 1891, the rules for gifts to charitable trusts allow for exemptions from capital gains tax and inheritance tax, while the funds are free from tax as well and may, unlike other trusts, run in perpetuity. In order for the trust to qualify for charitable status it must meet certain conditions, the main ones being that it must be set up for the advancement of education, the relief of poverty, the advancement of religion, or any other purpose deemed to be of general benefit to the community.

2.6 An occasional reason for the creation of a trust could be to protect the asset from the financially indisciplined. Usually lasting for the lifetime of a specified individual this would be intended to protect the 'family inheritance' from a spendthrift.

2.7 Finally, trusts are used where the intended beneficiary's identity is to be kept secret. In this case an individual is obliged, by the trust, to make a gift to the beneficiary subsequent to their having received it. Thus, a solicitor may be the person named in the deed, but the beneficiary to whom they pass on the property will remain unnamed. This avoids the possibility of the beneficiary being identified when the will has been granted probate and is open to public inspection.

3 Certainties

3.1 In order for a trust to be valid it must possess three certainties, *Knight v. Knight* (1840):

(a) Certainty of intention - The wording used must make clear the intention to create a trust, although there is no prescribed form that must be used.

(b) Certainty of subject matter - The property that is the subject of the trust must be clearly identified and set out.

(c) Certainty of objects - The beneficiaries must be readily identified by the trust, or identifiable, except where the trust is for charitable purposes.

This often leads to 'classes' of beneficiaries being specified such as 'my children'.

3.2   In *Knight v. Knight* (1840) Lord Langdale specified that if any one of the three certainties were not present, or fulfilled, the trust would be invalid. In the case of a lack of the wording to create the trust, the asset would pass automatically to the beneficiary. If either of the other two certainties were not present the gift would lapse and be assumed to have never taken place. This could have serious consequences, especially if, say, the settlor's aim had been to minimise a large tax position.

4   Trust Deed Wordings

4.1   While there are no predetermined, specified, wordings that must be used in the creation of a trust, there are certain phrases and words that would be more likely to achieve the desired result:

(a)   To state that the settlor's 'partner' is to be the beneficiary does not provide enough detail, as it could be construed a domestic partner is intended. This would need to be specified, by stating, perhaps, 'the partners in the Acme Agency'.

(b)   The use of the word 'children' may be intended to include all children that the settlor has, but it does not, in legal parlance, include stepchildren. Thus, if the intention was to make sons and daughters, both legitimate, illegitimate and adoptive, the beneficiaries then the intention will be satisfied.

(c)   'Children and remoter issue' is often used in trust wordings to cover those mentioned above, together with grandchildren and so on down the descending family line.

(d)   The term 'husband' or 'wife' in connection with trusts applies to those to whom the settlor is legally married at the time the trust comes into force. So, for example, if a husband names his 'wife' as beneficiary and subsequently divorces and remarries, his 'new' wife will become the beneficiary under the terms of the trust. Had he named his first wife, saying 'my wife Gladys', then his second wife would not be the beneficiary, unless she could prove it had been his intention that his legally married wife at the date of his death was to be the beneficiary.

4.2   This reflects the fact that beneficiaries can be placed into 'classes', which should be specific enough to clearly identify who the intended beneficiaries are, but not so vaguely worded as to be open to misunderstanding.

5   Parties to a Trust

The settlor

5.1   The person who initiates the trust, the original owner of the property being placed in trust, is the settlor. By creating a 'deed of trust' the legal ownership is transferred to the trustees, as previously discussed. This is also sometimes known as a 'settlement'. It is not uncommon for the settlor also to be a trustee in order to retain some control over the trust. In Scotland the settlor is known as the granter, or truster.

The trustee

5.2　The trustee, as mentioned, is the person (or people) to whom legal ownership of the asset is transferred, in order that it may be used for the benefit of the trust's beneficiaries. The role of the trustee is, therefore, crucial to the execution of the trust's requirements. This is covered in detail later in this unit. It is possible for the trustee to be a beneficiary under the trust.

The beneficiary

5.3　The trust's beneficiary becomes the ultimate, or beneficial, owner of the property subject to the trust, and is entitled to benefit from anything that takes place within the trust. The trust may contain any number of beneficiaries, with any sole beneficiary obviously being entitled to all the trust property. Joint beneficiaries will, unless the trust deed's wording says otherwise, be entitled to equal shares.

5.4　The trust may grant the beneficiary an absolute interest, which provides a 'full equitable interest' that cannot be subsequently removed.

5.5　A life interest provides an income from the trust for the beneficiary, but the capital cannot be used by them. Under English law this type of beneficiary is known as a life tenant, while in Scotland is called the life renter with the life interest known as life rent.

5.6　On the death of the life tenant the property may pass to another type of beneficiary. This is someone who, while the life tenant was alive and entitled to the benefit, held a reversionary interest in the trust. These beneficiaries are known as 'remaindermen'.

5.7　A further type of beneficiary is one called a 'contingent beneficiary'. This refers to someone whose interest in the trust is dependent on the occurrence of a specified event. This could, for example, apply to a situation where a man intends his children to be the beneficiaries with his wife to be the beneficiary should the children predecease him. In this case his wife would be the contingent beneficiary.

6　Rights of Beneficiaries

6.1　Where the beneficiary is under the age of majority he cannot demand his share of the trust's property. The trustees can, however, use the trust income for the maintenance or education of that beneficiary under the terms of the Trustee Act 1925. The Act also allows for capital to be used for the beneficiary's advancement.

6.2　Provided all the beneficiaries are over the age of 18, and unanimously agree, the trust provisions can be varied, the trust can be brought to an end, or the trustees can be required to deal with the assets in line with the beneficiaries' wishes. Under *Saunders v. Vautier* (1841), provided all the beneficiaries are of sound mind and they have all been identified, the trust property can be handed to them. This would effectively end the trust.

6.3　While the beneficiaries cannot usually directly control the trustees, they can demand any information relating to the trust, having the right to inspect the trust documents and accounts. This allows them to require the proper

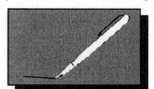

processes of administration to be employed by trustees, and for them to be in full accordance with the trust's terms. If unsatisfied the beneficiaries have the right to go to court to seek redress for a breach of trust, or even seek the removal of a trustee.

Student Activity 1

You should complete the student activity before reading the next section of the text. Answer the questions, then check your answers against the paragraph(s) indicated.

Mike has a whole life policy written under trust. He appoints his bank manager and a close friend to look after the trust; they are also the executors of his will. He wishes the policy proceeds to go to his two children on his death.

For each of the following, explain their formal title, including any different Scottish terms, and their main duties and/or rights.

(a) Mike   (5.1)

(b) The bank manager and the close friend   (5.2)

(c) The two children   (5.3)

If you are unable to answer any of the questions satisfactorily, you should read the relevant paragraphs again. Your understanding of the text will be further tested in the self-assessment section at the end of this unit.

7   Role, Duties and Responsibilities of the Trustee

7.1   Anybody who is over 18 and who is of sound mental capacity can become a trustee. It is possible to use a corporate body to act as a trustee, often a service offered by banks to their customers. The government also have a trust department, the Public Trustee, which often administers settlements made on behalf of minors through the courts, especially those made as a result of criminal actions or negligence.

7.2   The trust's deed and provisions lay down the beneficiary's entitlements, and the trustee's first responsibility is to administer the trust and its property in accordance with those terms. The only exception is where the courts have varied the trust terms. This means that the trustee must act 'bona fide' and as if he were a prudent business person managing his own affairs, *Speight v. Gaunt* (1883).

7.3   In order to administer the trust properly and to reflect his ownership, the trustee must ensure that the trust property has been vested in him, that is, the legal ownership of the property has been transferred to him. This should not be taken to imply that the trustee can either purchase, or use, the property for his own benefit. Rather, it is held for the beneficial interest of others, namely the beneficiaries.

7.4 As mentioned, trustees are not normally permitted to benefit financially from their position, but they may be allowed to recover expenses incurred in administering the trust. The trust deed may, in some cases, specify that the trustee can be remunerated, through a 'charging clause', or the courts may make such a provision. This will usually relate to a corporate trustee rather than to a private individual assuming the role.

7.5 The trustee is required to ensure that any actions taken are not in breach of his using utmost diligence to protect the interests of the beneficiaries. Any loss so caused may result in the trustee being held personally liable to make good the shortfall. The beneficiary can monitor this behaviour by using his right to inspect the trust's documentation as referred to in 6.3.

7.6 Where the property subject to a trust generates cash, whether it be due to dividends, asset sale, or to a gift into the trust, the trustee is bound to invest those monies as soon as is practicable. The only exception is where the beneficiary is due to receive the money straightaway, in which case it will be paid out of the trust. The subject of trust investment will be covered when considering the Trustee Investments Act 1961.

7.7 The trustee is required, unless excepted by the trust deed or the Trustee Act 1925, to act personally on all matters concerning the trust, and not to pass the responsibility on to a third party.

7.8 When acting on behalf of the trust the trustee must act together with the other co-trustees, particularly when signing cheques and selling trust property. Thus all decisions must be made unanimously, unless the trust deed has made a specifically clear intention that this is not required.

7.9 The trustee also has a duty to ensure that each class of beneficiary is treated equally, even though their interests may be different. For example, the life tenant of the trust may be entitled to an income payable throughout his lifetime, with the capital reverting to the remaindermen on the life tenant's death. With changing investment conditions and the effects of inflation on the capital value, causing possible capital erosion, the remaindermen may suffer as a result of a trustee attempting to maintain a constant income level for the life tenant. The trustee must bear this in mind when making investment decisions.

7.10 As part of the trustee's duty to ensure that each class of beneficiary is treated equally, he has a 'duty to convert'. This means that if an asset has a finite timespan, the trustee should realise its value into cash so that it can be invested. This will avoid a remainderman receiving property which has significantly depreciated in value or has no value at all.

7.11 The duty to convert only applies to personalty, i.e. property which does not include land or intangible rights in land. It does not apply if there is a contrary intention, for example an instruction in the will, or if the property has been settled by deed or on intestacy.

7.12 Until the asset can be converted to cash and invested, any income derived can be apportioned by the trustee in order to achieve, or maintain, a balance between providing income and protecting capital. This is subject to the trust's wording not precluding such a course of action. This has, then, the effect of helping the trustee to protect the interests of the beneficiaries, as far as possible.

7.13 As can be seen, the trustee's responsibilities are many, and complex. These can often be clarified when looking at the terms and provisions of the Trustee Act 1925.

Delegation of Trustee Responsibility

7.14 In certain circumstances the trustee may be allowed to pass powers and responsibilities on to a third party. Should he so wish S23 of the Trustee Act 1925 does allow him to appoint an agent in relation to certain transactions. An example could be that of appointing a stockbroker to deal with an equity portfolio. In this instance the agent, the stockbroker, takes on the responsibility for any defaults caused as a result of his actions, provided he was used as an agent by the trustee in good faith.

7.15 Again under the Trustee Act 1925, S25, and as later amended by S9 of the Powers of Attorney Act 1971, the trustee can delegate his duties to another person. This allows the trustee's own duties to be assumed for up to one year should his circumstances so require.

Trustees' investment powers

7.16 Trustees are given their powers of investment in one of two ways. Either the trust deed itself will express their powers, or trust law will provide the investment parameters by which they must abide.

7.17 The deed setting up the trust contains details of investment powers which will overrule those provided in law, mainly those laid down in the Trustee Investments Act 1961 which is described later in this unit. The notable exceptions are where the trust is silent on trustees' investment powers, where the statutory powers exceed those in the trust deed, or in cases of intestacy.

7.18 Most modern trusts contain wide powers of investment for trustees although not all allow the trustee to invest in life policies. This is commonly available through a specific, clearly worded, power. These wide powers are often known as 'beneficial owner clauses' as the trustee is given the power to invest 'in all respects as though he was the beneficial owner of the trust'.

7.19 Older trusts contain a variety of investment powers and instructions, known as 'special powers of investment', which overrule the statutory powers. These may include the requirement that the property is sold, but at a time of the trustee's choosing, or they may specify the types of investment the trust can make, for example into family companies only.

7.20 Irrespective of the trustee's powers of investment, there are certain issues to which they must constantly, and consistently, attend:

- The investments made by the trust must be of a 'suitable' nature

- The trustees must attend to the need to diversify the trust's investments, where appropriate

- The trust's investment portfolio should be regularly reviewed to reflect changing investment conditions and beneficiary needs

8   Appointment of Trustees

Initial trustees

8.1   When a new trust is created by deed or will, the appointment of the initial trustees will usually be by the settlor or testator, who names the trustees in the deed or will. The settlor may appoint himself, either as a sole trustee or as one of the nominated trustees. The trust property vests in the initial trustees, and they hold it jointly until they die, retire or are removed. The trust property continues to vest in the survivor or surviving trustees.

8.2   If a situation arises where a trust is declared but no trustee is appointed, the trustee will be considered to be the person in whom the trust property has been vested. If a settlor declares a trust but does not make an effective transfer of the trust property to the trustees, then he holds the property as trustee.

Under an express power in the deed

8.3   The trust deed may give an express power to the settlor or another named person to appoint trustees, in which case the scope and conditions of the power of appointment will be set out in the deed. New trustees will be appointed by this nominated person, although if he fails to do so then the existing trustees, or the personal representatives of the last surviving trustee, may make appointments under the Trustee Act 1925 S36 (1).

Statutory provisions to replace trustees

8.4   The Trustee Act 1925 also provides for the appointment of new trustees, should the need arise. The situations where this may occur include the death of the trustee, but also allows for:

- The replacement of a trustee who leaves the UK and remains abroad for more than one year

- The replacement of a trustee who resigns, or retires, or who no longer wishes to act

- The discharge of a trustee who refuses to act, perhaps never having wanted to in the first place

- The replacement of those trustees who may not have attained the age of majority at the time the trust becomes effective

- The replacement of those who are, or who become, unfit or incapable of acting as a trustee

8.5   The appointment may be made by whoever is nominated in the trust instrument to appoint new trustees. If there is no nominated person, or no-one able or willing to act, then the surviving or continuing trustee, or the personal representative of the last surviving trustee has the power of appointment.

8.6   Under S36(1) of the Trustee Act 1925 the appointment of new trustees must be made in writing. Although there is no required format, a deed of appointment is usually the most convenient as, subject to some exclusions, it will operate to vest the trust property in the new trustees jointly with any continuing trustees.

By the court

8.7   If there is no trustee or the nominated trustee refuses to take up the position, then the trust will not necessarily fail. The Trustee Act 1925 S41(1) gives the court the power to appoint new trustees, either to replace a trustee or to act with the existing trustees. The court can only exercise this power in cases where it is 'inexpedient, difficult or impracticable' to appoint trustees in any other way. A trustee may be removed by the court even if he disagrees, although in cases where the court does act to remove a trustee, it must also appoint a replacement. Where a trustee is appointed by the court, he has the same power and authority to act as if he had been appointed trustee from the outset.

By beneficiaries

8.8   Beneficiaries do not have automatic power to appoint or replace trustees, although they may be granted the power expressly.

9   Duration of Trusts

9.1   The length of time over which trusts may run has been an area over which both the courts and common law have exercised some forms of control, particularly in relation to perpetuities and accumulations. 'Perpetuities' refers to the period before which the trust capital is vested in the beneficiaries, while 'accumulations' relates to the duration over which income can be accumulated in the trust. In order to bring about an equitable situation the Law of Property Act 1925 and the Perpetuities and Accumulations Act 1964 were introduced.

Perpetuities

9.2   Before the Perpetuities and Accumulations Act 1964 came into being common law stated that unless a contingent interest vests in a life already in being at the time of the trust deed being created, or at the date of the testator's death, plus 21 years, then the gift would be void. Thus, if a grandchild were to be the beneficiary on attaining age 25, but was not yet born at the date of the settlor's death, his interest would fail as it was outside the 21 years.

9.3   Under this requirement a life in being is someone who is living at the date the gift takes effect, and the trust's duration is based on his lifespan. In order for this to be the case an individual must be clearly identifiable for the period to be tested, he must either have been implied or expressly nominated as a beneficiary.

9.4   The main implications of the Perpetuities and Accumulations Act 1964 are:

(a)   An express period of up to 80 years may be selected as the perpetuity period, instead of a period related to lives in being.

(b)   Where it can be shown that it is unlikely that children may be born in the future and fall outside the perpetuity period, the gift will be valid under the Act.

(c)   A gift can now be treated as valid until it actually falls outside the perpetuity period. Previously the gift was invalid from the outset if it may have fallen outside the period in the future. This 'wait and see' principle means that the event must be a reality, rather than a possibility.

(d) Where a contingent interest would have caused the gift to fail, the vesting age can be reduced to bring it within the perpetuity period. This is subject to a minimum age of 21. By doing this, an otherwise void gift can be made valid.

(e) The Act presumes that only males above the age of 14 can father children, and that only females between the ages of 12 and 55 can bear children.

(f) Where the 'wait and see' principle applies and no perpetuity period was nominated, the Act defines the lives in being, and their classes. These include the donor, the donee, the donee's parents and grandparents, and the owner of a prior interest.

Accumulations

9.5 Originally subject to the same rules as perpetuities, the rules which apply were later altered by the Accumulations Act 1800 and the Law of Property Act 1925. The Perpetuities and Accumulations Act 1964 further amended and updated the provisions for accumulations.

9.6 Under the Law of Property Act 1925 income can be accumulated for one of four periods, which will either be specified in the settlement or will, or be construed from the wording to ascertain which should apply. These are:

- The settlor's life

- A period of 21 years following his death

- The minority of any persons who were living at the date of the settlor's death

- The minority of beneficiaries to the settlement (minority being the period of being a minor i.e. until the age of maturity has been reached)

9.7 The Perpetuities and Accumulations Act 1964 extended the time periods available for those gifts which came into effect after 15 July 1964, including a further two periods:

- A period of 21 years from the gift's taking effect

- The minority of any person in being at the same date

9.8 Furthermore, if the stated accumulation period exceeds the maximum allowable accumulation period, then only that portion which is in excess will be invalid. Where the period exceeds the perpetuity period then the whole accumulation will be void and the income must pass to those entitled to receive it as if no accumulation had been directed.

10 Variation

10.1 As previously discussed beneficiaries can, in certain circumstances and under certain conditions, vary the terms of the trust. The settlor only has the option of altering the trust if it is a revert to settlor trust.

Variation by the court

10.2 Trusts can be varied in other ways, perhaps the major one being under the

Variation of Trusts Act 1958. This allows the court to alter trusts for the benefit of:

- Those beneficiaries who, by reason of incapacity or infancy, are incapable of consenting to the unanimous decision by beneficiaries requirement under *Saunders v. Vautier* (1841)

- Beneficiaries with contingent interests

- Unborn beneficiaries

- Beneficiaries under a protective trust who hold a discretionary interest, i.e. those who would be entitled to an interest if the protective trust ended and became a discretionary trust (these types of trust are defined later in this unit)

10.3 A further method permitting variation would take place under a court's direction. This could come into effect as a result of situations that were highlighted by *Chapman v. Chapman* (1954):

(a) Where an infant beneficiary's interest in the trust was potentially threatened due to an alteration in the nature of the trust property.

(b) Where the beneficiary cannot agree to certain transactions that take place within the trust where they fall outside the trust deed. This would only be possible in circumstances that require emergency action that could not have been foreseen by the settlor.

(c) Where income that was to have been accumulated can be redirected for the maintenance of an infant beneficiary.

(d) Where the court establishes a compromise in favour of infants in the event of a beneficiary dispute.

Statutory variation

10.4 There are a number of statutory provisions for the variation of trusts. Examples of these statutes include:

(a) The Mental Health Act 1983 which allows the Court of Protection to become involved.

(b) The Matrimonial Causes Act 1973 which allows divorce courts to alter marriage settlements.

(c) The Settled Land Act 1925 which allows variations to be made for the benefit of the beneficiaries or the land in the trust, provided these variations could have been validly effected by an absolute owner.

10.5 Sections 53 and 57 of the Trustee Act 1925 also allow statutory variation. Under S53, if the beneficiary is an infant, variation can be made to release capital or income for the maintenance, education or benefit of the infant. This could involve selling an infant's reversionary interest and using the proceeds for his benefit.

10.6 Under S57, the court can authorise trustees to effect a transaction, which the trust instrument does not cover, providing the whole trust will benefit. The transactions involved are those which the trustees might need to effect when managing and administering trust property e.g. buying and selling.

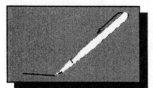

Student Activity 2

You should complete the student activity before reading the next section of the text. Answer the questions, then check your answers against the paragraph(s) indicated.

1. Where are the powers of a trustee set out?   (7.2, 7.13)

2. What would happen if a trustee, chosen by the settlor,   (8.1)
    subsequently died?

3. If a trustee is unable to fulfil his duties for a short period, e.g.   (7.15)
    six months, can he delegate his powers?

4. What is meant by a trustee's duty to convert?   (7.10, 7.11)

5. Why would a trustee use his power to apportion?   (7.12)

If you are unable to answer any of the questions satisfactorily, you should read the relevant paragraphs again. Your understanding of the text will be further tested in the self-assessment section at the end of this unit.

11 Types of Trust

11.1 There is a wide range of different trust terminology, some of which has already been covered. This is reflected in the names of the different trust types. Some trusts are actually known by more than one name. The principles behind the different types of trust are relatively straightforward.

Bare trusts

11.2 This is the simplest type of trust in many ways. Often there is one, sole, beneficiary for whose benefit the assets are held in trust. As he is then absolutely entitled to the trust's proceeds and ultimately to its property these trusts are also known as 'absolute trusts'. The trustee has no obligations, apart from passing the trust property to the beneficiary when the beneficiary has attained majority, is free from disability and the trustee has fulfilled his duties.

11.3 The bare trust's beneficiary must be a clearly identified, named individual. For example, a bare trust may state that the settlor's son is to receive the property on reaching the age of 25.

11.4 Typical uses of a bare trust, where the trust fund is often seen as being held in nomineeship, are for those who have not yet reached the age of majority and cannot legally deal with investments, those who want secrecy and those who require simple convenience.

Interest in possession trusts

11.5 Sometimes referred to as 'life interest' trusts, these confer a right on the beneficiary to claim an income from the trust or to use the property in the trust. This may, for example, cover a situation where a house has been settled in the trust and the beneficiary is entitled to occupy it rent-free during his lifetime. Ultimately, however, the property will revert to someone else.

11.6 Income received may be available to a specified age only, after which the capital from which it was generated may pass to others. A typical use would be for a husband to provide an income for his wife during her lifetime, or until she remarried, and then for their children to receive the capital in equal shares.

11.7 Many interest in possession trusts are set up as a result of a will and are called 'will trusts'. A will trust could apply to the example above, or it may apply if the husband had been married previously and there were children from that marriage. The fact that he stated 'our children' may allow all his children to benefit from an equal share when their interest reverts.

11.8 The protective trust is a type of interest in possession trust and this creates a life tenant of the spendthrift. Any attempt on the life tenant's part to dispose of the trust property will end the trust, which then becomes a discretionary trust.

Discretionary trusts

11.9 Under a discretionary trust the trustees are given the power or discretion to appoint beneficiaries from a specified group. For example, the beneficiaries could include the settlor's 'wife, children and any of their offspring'. From this list the trustees can choose the beneficiaries who they feel it is most appropriate to include, and any who may not have been born at the time of the settlement.

11.10 None of the beneficiaries, under these trusts, normally has a predetermined right to claim the benefits. The trust deed would determine their right to income or capital, or both. Once appointed by the trustees, the beneficiary would then receive whichever is his interest in the trust.

11.11 The trust allows the trustee to reflect possible changes in beneficiary circumstances between the date of settlement into the trust, and the time at which the benefits are due to be paid. Thus, if some of the beneficiaries are financially stable, while others are less well able to cope, the trustee can appoint accordingly.

Accumulation and maintenance trusts

11.12 These are a type of discretionary trust which allow the settlor to transfer property to minors, without the minor having access to that property at too young an age. The beneficiaries can include children, or grandchildren, whether born or unborn.

11.13 In order for the trust to be deemed an accumulation and maintenance trust it must satisfy certain conditions:

- The beneficiary can have no interest in possession at the outset of the trust, although he must gain one at some stage

- Where the income from the trust is not applied for the beneficiary's maintenance, education or benefit, it must be accumulated

- One or more people must become beneficially entitled to the settled property, or to an interest in possession, on or before an age not exceeding 25

- No more than 25 years must elapse since the settlement date, or since it became an accumulation and maintenance trust if converted from another settlement

- Where all the beneficiaries are, or were, grandchildren of a common grandparent, or where a beneficiary dies before attaining a vested interest, then his children or spouse may take his beneficial interest

Flexible trusts

11.14 Also known as power of appointment trusts, flexible trusts are increasingly used to provide for changes in future circumstances. Often available from life assurance providers, the flexible trust allows for beneficial interests to be varied if required in a similar way to discretionary trusts.

11.15 Typically the beneficiaries are not named specifically by the trust, rather, they are included as a 'class'. Thus, the settlor's 'children' could allow for any that may be born after the trust has been set up, or the settlor's 'wife at the date of death' would allow for the possibility that the settlor may divorce and remarry.

11.16 A further method by which the settlor can use a flexible trust is to include himself on the list of potential beneficiaries, known as a 'revert to settlor trust'. This allows the settlor, provided the trustees agree, to recover the trust property. Due to the tax implications of this type of trust these are not common; the original settlement will be a gift with reservation for inheritance tax purposes.

Other trusts

11.17 A constructive trust is one where a person, who was not necessarily a trustee originally, holds property in trust for beneficiaries as a result of a legal imposition upon him. For example, he may have received trust property to which he was not entitled as a result of a breach of trust. Under the court's decision he would then be deemed to be holding that property under a constructive trust.

11.18 An express trust is one where there is an express intention to create a trust. Except in the case of personal property which can be expressed orally, a trust deed or will would be drafted to reflect the settlor's intention to create the trust.

11.19 Another type of trust is an implied trust. As previously discussed, a trust can be deemed to have been created by the actions of the parties involved. This could occur where one person holds property on behalf of a group, for instance, where no deed has been created.

11.20 An overseas or offshore trust is one created outside the UK. Mainly used as a tax planning vehicle it is governed by the law that relates to the trustees; thus, most overseas trusts will have trustees who are situated offshore.

11.21 A presumptive trust involves property being purchased in the name of one person by somebody else. This is, however, not the case where the person in whose name the acquisition is made is the purchaser's spouse, child or is his ward, i.e. the purchaser is his guardian.

11.22 A successive trust involves property passing through a succession of beneficial interests. A trust that provides for property to pass to the settlor's children and then to their children, would be a form of successive trust. The final beneficiaries, the grandchildren in this example, would be entitled to what is known as the 'ultimate interest'.

11.23 A will trust, or testamentary trust, is one which is established under the terms of a will. A will does not necessarily give rise to a trust; the personal representative will deal with the estate of the deceased person in accordance with his will (or intestacy) and although he has a similar role to a trustee there are differences in their powers. However, the personal representative may be directed under the will to hold certain property on trust, and he then acts as a trustee on the terms specified by the will trust. A will trust may also be created if the personal representative is unable to distribute some of the property, for example because the beneficiary is an infant, but the administration of the estate is otherwise at an end.

Student Activity 3

You should complete the student activity before reading the next section of the text. Answer the questions, then check your answers against the paragraph(s) indicated.

> Brian has inherited his family home. He does not wish to live there but wants to ensure the property stays in the family and can be passed on to his children, and possibly grandchildren. If he should die when his children are still under 18, he would like his wife, Mary, to have control of the property until they have all reached age 18. He has two children, Frances and Emma who are aged six and three, but Brian and Mary have not decided whether to have any more children.
>
> (a) Explain the advantages of a flexible trust to Brian.   (11.14)
>
> (b) If Brian wanted to be included as a potential beneficiary, what problem might this raise?   (11.16)
>
> (c) How does a flexible trust differ from a bare trust?   (11.2, 11.15)

If you are unable to answer any of the questions satisfactorily, you should read the relevant paragraphs again. Your understanding of the text will be further tested in the self-assessment section at the end of this unit.

12 Taxation of Trusts - Income Tax

12.1 The income received by a trust on the assets of the trust is assessed for tax on the trustees. This means the trustees are responsible for accounting for the income tax. Under the self-assessment rules the trustees must assess the amount of tax payable on the trust income and gains and make payments on account in the same way as individuals. Where discretionary trusts have an additional rate of tax to pay, as discussed below, this will also be paid in the same way.

12.2   Where a beneficiary has absolute right to the trust income, i.e. under a bare trust, then the tax position will depend on the beneficiary's circumstances rather than that of the trust. The beneficiary will be responsible for payment of the tax and can make use of his personal allowances.

Interest in possession trusts

12.3   The trustees pay the tax on the trust income at 24%. Savings income is taxed at 20% as for individuals. Trustees are not liable for higher rate tax and there are no personal allowances available for trusts. Expenses incurred by the trustees in managing the trust are treated as being paid for out of income after tax has been deducted and cannot be reclaimed by the beneficiary. Expenses will be offset against savings and dividend income before any other income such as rental income.

12.4   When a beneficiary receives the income he is entitled to a tax credit for tax paid by the trustees. If he is a non taxpayer he can reclaim the tax paid; if he is a higher rate taxpayer he will have a further liability.

Example 9.1: Beneficiary's income

The trust receives income of £5,000 which is to be paid to the beneficiary. The trustees will deduct tax at 24% i.e. £1,200. They have also incurred expenses of £250. The beneficiary will receive £3,550. This is equivalent to a grossed up income of £4,671. If he is a higher rate taxpayer he will have an additional liability of 16% of £4,671 i.e. £747.36. If he is a non taxpayer he can reclaim tax of £1,121.

12.5   It may be possible for trustees to avoid meeting expenses out of trust income by arranging for certain income such as dividends to be paid directly to the beneficiary and so avoid incurring administration costs.

Discretionary trusts

12.6   Where the trustees have discretion over the distribution of income and no-one has a right to it, the trustees are taxed on income in the same way. However, there is an additional rate of tax to pay, currently 10% (1996-97), making a total liability of 34%. Expenses can be deducted first before determining the amount chargeable at 34%.

12.7   If the income is treated as the settlor's income than the additional rate is not payable. Any income paid to beneficiaries is net of 34% tax and they can reclaim tax if their personal rates are lower. A higher rate taxpayer will have an additional rate of 6% to pay. As investment income is received net of 20% the additional rate of tax is effectively 14%.

Settlor's income

12.8   Where a settlor or his spouse retains an interest in the settlement then any income will be treated as his for tax purposes. This also applies if the settlement transfers income but not capital. Spouse includes a future, former or separated spouse but not a widow or widower.

12.9   In addition, if the settlor is a parent and applies capital or income from the trust to his unmarried children aged under 18, the income is treated as the parent's income for tax purposes. The £100 exemption applies, so if income is less than £100 in a tax year there will be no tax liability.

12.10 Any tax paid by the settlor can be reclaimed from the trustees or the person who received the income.

Accumulation and maintenance trusts

12.11 These trusts are a type of discretionary trust so the trustees have to pay the additional rate of tax. Parents who settle funds on their children who then receive income either directly or indirectly, e.g. payment of school fees by trustees will be taxed as described above. This does not apply to income accumulated and held within the trust.

13 Taxation of Trusts - Capital Gains Tax

13.1 As described in Unit 6 on capital gains tax (CGT) trustees are eligible for an annual exemption of half the individual rate i.e. £3,150 (1996-97) and have a tax rate of 24%. If the settlor has created several trusts this exemption will be divided between them subject to a minimum exemption of £630 per trust. So if, for example, a settlor had set up three trusts then an exemption of £1,050 would apply to each. Trusts for the disabled are eligible for the full exemption of £6,300 (1996-97).

Interest in possession trusts

13.2 If the settlor has transferred assets to the trustees but he or his wife have retained a present or future right to trust income or property, then any gains made by the trust are taxed on the settlor as his personal gains. He may therefore have a higher rate liability which the trust would not otherwise incur.

13.3 When the beneficiary becomes absolutely entitled to the trust property on the death of the settlor the trustees are regarded as disposing of the property to the beneficiary at its current market value; however, no CGT liability will arise.

13.4 If the beneficiary becomes entitled to the property for any other reason then this will be treated as a disposal at market value. CGT will be payable on any gain made due to the increase in value since the date the property was transferred to the trust. Indexation will apply.

13.5 If the beneficiary transfers his interest to someone else this is not normally treated as a chargeable disposal.

Discretionary trusts

13.6 Where trustees dispose of chargeable assets there will be a CGT charge of 34% i.e. the same rate as an income tax liability. If a beneficiary becomes absolutely entitled to any chargeable assets of the trust, the trustees are treated as having disposed of the asset at its current market value. The trustees and beneficiaries can, however, make a joint election to treat the gains as reducing the beneficiary's acquisition cost for CGT, thus deferring the tax liability until the beneficiary disposes of the asset.

Accumulation and maintenance trusts

13.7 The CGT position is the same as for other discretionary trusts except for the availability of gift relief. As the transfer is potentially exempt for inheritance tax purposes gift relief is not available when the assets are transferred to the trust unless they are qualifying business assets. There is also a problem with gift relief when the assets are transferred out of the trust.

13.8 If a beneficiary becomes entitled to the capital and has not previously received any income from the trust, it is possible to use hold-over relief for non-business assets transferred to him out of the trust. This would reduce the beneficiary's acquisition cost. However, in practice hold-over relief cannot often be claimed as beneficiaries usually become entitled to income before they are entitled to the capital.

14 Taxation of Trusts - Inheritance Tax

Interest in possession trusts

14.1 Where someone is entitled to the income from a trust he is regarded as being entitled to the underlying capital so on death he will be treated as making a chargeable transfer of the underlying capital. If the trust assets pass to someone else during his lifetime this is a Pet and will only be chargeable if he dies within seven years of the transfer. Any tax due is payable by the trustees even though it is based on the individual's situation. The reason for this tax treatment is to prevent trusts being used to avoid IHT on wealth. However, once the seven years has passed then the trust property will not be included in the settlor's estate and so IHT liability will not apply.

14.2 It is possible for life tenants to take steps to minimise their IHT liability. For example, a life tenant could surrender his interest in possession in tranches over a number of years making use of the annual exemption, currently £3,000, each year. If he assigns or surrenders his interest this will be a Pet but if the beneficiary is likely to survive a further seven years IHT will not be a problem.

Discretionary trusts

14.3 As no-one can be treated as being entitled to the underlying capital of the trust this means an IHT charge cannot be levied on a particular individual. Because of this a charge is made on the trust funds every 10 years. There is also a charge when funds leave the trust, i.e. an exit charge and when an individual becomes entitled to the fund or to income from the trust. The charge is 15% of the IHT rate at the appropriate scale so the maximum payable is 40% x 15% = 6%.

14.4 The trustees may want to consider making distributions from the fund before the ten-year anniversary comes up to reduce the size of the trust property for the ten-year charge.

Accumulation and maintenance trusts

14.5 There is favourable IHT treatment of accumulation and maintenance trusts where one or more of the beneficiaries will become entitled to the trust property or income not later than age 25. The settlement must either terminate no later than 25 years after its creation or all the beneficiaries must have a common grandparent. If the beneficiaries do not live long enough then their children or widows can take their place.

14.6 The advantages of this type of settlement for IHT are:

- Transfer of assets into the trust are potentially exempt

- There is no ten-year charge

- There are no exit charges when the beneficiary becomes absolutely entitled to the trust property or income from it

15 Conversion and Apportionment of Trust Assets

15.1 As well as the tax implications when the trust assets are distributed there are considerations to be made when the trustees exercise their duties to deal with the trust assets to the best advantage of the beneficiaries.

15.2 Trustees usually have a duty to convert wasting trust assets to cash. This is to protect the interests of any remaindermen who are entitled to capital in the future. However, the trustees can also convert assets to save tax. For example, it may be possible to convert assets which would carry an IHT liability on transfer to ones which are eligible for relief e.g. agricultural land. In this way they will reduce IHT liability. The only problem which may arise, however, is that if property is sold to acquire other property there may be a CGT charge.

15.3 The trustees' power of apportionment is their power to change the way the trust assets are used to produce income for the life tenant, so that there will be adequate capital for the remaindermen. If the life tenant surrenders part of his interest to the remaindermen this will be treated as a transfer of value for IHT purposes equal to the value of capital he is deemed to have given up. This will be a Pet. The income tax treatment will alter depending on the level of income now received by the life tenant. The trustees will still continue to pay tax on the income even though they are reinvesting more of it to increase capital value.

16 Life Policies in Trust

16.1 As discussed in Unit 7 on inheritance tax there are various ways of writing life policies under trust, usually for tax reasons. The two main types of trust used in connection with life policies are statutory trusts e.g. the Married Women's Property Act (MWPA) 1882, and non-statutory trusts.

Married Women's Property Act 1882

16.2 This allows a life policy to create a trust if, without the Act, no trust would have otherwise been created. Section 11 lays down the provisions under which life policies may be established under the MWPA:

(a) The policy must be taken out by a man or woman on his or her own life, for another's benefit; they do not have to be a married person, but can be a widow, widower, spinster or bachelor. It should be noted that only single life policies are eligible for inclusion under MWPA.

(b) The policy must be expressed to be for the benefit of the proposer's spouse or children, or for the spouse and children, or any of them.

(c) Only the policy contract need be governed by English law; a customer who lives abroad and takes out a policy from a UK based company can set up a policy under the Act.

(d) The policy must provide life assurance benefit, which generally excludes annuities and PHI.

(e) The Act does not necessarily have to be mentioned, although it is advisable to do so.

(f) The interests of the beneficiaries are protected against the life assured's creditors in the case of bankruptcy, provided that the trust has not been established deliberately to defraud creditors.

16.3 Beneficiaries can be any of the following:

- Spouse

- Children, which includes grandchildren, illegitimate and adopted children, but excludes stepchildren

- Named or unnamed beneficiaries i.e. classes of beneficiaries provided these are only spouse and children

16.4 The beneficiaries' interest is not necessarily absolute, it can be limited e.g. a policy for the husband who only receives the benefit if the wife dies, otherwise she receives the benefits. Children's interest can be contingent on their reaching majority. Power of appointment trusts can be used if there is uncertainty over how to split the benefits now. This gives trustees the flexibility to choose later.

16.5 The trustees of a policy placed under trust through the MWPA can be appointed by the policy. The life assured may also retain the power of appointment of additional trustees or name an appointor. This allows flexibility to be retained in the trust. Where no trustee is appointed the assured will remain as the sole trustee, and upon his death his personal representatives will assume the trustee's duties.

16.6 The Act does not have to be specifically mentioned or specified for a policy to be written under the MWPA, nor do the words have to declare a trust is being created. In *Gladitz, Guaranty Executor and Trustee Co Ltd v. Gladitz* (1937) it was held that a policy written on a man's own life which provided life and incapacity benefits fell under the terms of the Act, even though this was not expressly mentioned in the policy.

16.7 However, the trust is usually created by the completion of a trust form at the time of proposing the policy. The form is issued by the provider of the life assurance policy.

Non-statutory trusts

16.8 Where a life policy is written under a non-statutory trust, generally some form of interest in possession trust will be used. The two types of interest in possession trusts most commonly used by insurance companies are absolute trusts and flexible trusts.

16.9 Under an absolute trust, the trustees hold the life policy for one or more beneficiaries absolutely and irrevocably. In other words, once the trust has been declared, the beneficiaries or their interests under the trust cannot normally be altered.

16.10 If the settlor wishes to include the power to change the beneficiaries or their shares at a later date, a flexible trust should be used. A flexible trust enables the settlor to place a life policy in trust for the default beneficiaries i.e. the people he currently wishes to benefit from the trust proceeds. However, it also permits the trustees or settlor to change the beneficiaries by appointing benefits away from the default beneficiaries to any one of a range of people known as discretionary beneficiaries. As such, the beneficiaries' interests are not fixed and can be altered to suit changing circumstances. Under this type of trust the default beneficiaries hold an interest in possession.

16.11 While it is clear a flexible trust allows the trust to cope with changing circumstances, there are some important points that must always be borne in mind. Because the default beneficiaries hold an interest in possession they are treated as owning the trust property for inheritance tax purposes. If trust property is appointed away from a default beneficiary to one or more discretionary beneficiaries this is treated as a transfer from the default beneficiary to the discretionary beneficiary. This will be treated as a Pet. The value transferred is equal to the surrender value of the policy for temporary assurance and the greater of the surrender value or premiums paid for other policies.

Example 9.2: Transfers by default beneficiaries

A temporary assurance policy is held in trust with John and Matthew being default beneficiaries each holding a 50% interest. An appointment is made by the trustees as a result of which Matthew and Laura, a former discretionary beneficiary, hold 50% each. John is treated as making a gift to Laura of 50%.

16.12 If the appointment takes place before the life assured's death the transfer is equal to the surrender value and therefore probably nil or a minimal amount. However, if the appointment takes place after the life assured's death the transfer is equal to half the sum assured. This can be a considerable sum. As with all Pets, inheritance tax is not payable immediately and provided the transferor survives seven years after the transfer, the transfer will become fully exempt and no IHT will be payable.

16.13 If the benefits are appointed to the settlor's spouse or the settlor's widow within two years of the settlor's death no transfer will take place.

16.14 If the settlor is named as a default or discretionary beneficiary a gift with reservation is created. This means the value of the trust assets, normally the life policy, remains within the settlor's estate for inheritance tax purposes. The trust is thus not effective for inheritance tax planning.

16.15 If both husband and wife take out the policy and create the trust this means neither can be a beneficiary. If there is a single applicant then that person's spouse can be included as a beneficiary. Caution must be exercised if benefits are to be passed to a spouse beneficiary during the settlor's lifetime to ensure a gift with reservation is not immediately created.

Premiums

16.16 Premiums are regarded as gifts by the payer to the trust. Where regular premiums are paid these will normally be exempt from IHT under the normal expenditure from income or £3,000 annual allowance. If the premium is not covered by either of these allowances it will be a Pet to the extent that the policy increases in value.

16.17 The excess, if any, will be a chargeable transfer. If this will cause inheritance tax problems for the payer, premiums can be paid direct to the trustees who can pay the insurance company. In this case the whole of the premium will be a Pet.

17 When to Write Policies Under Trust

17.1 It is normally advisable to consider using trusts whenever writing a policy for a customer. A life policy will normally be placed under trust using standard trust documentation available from the life company.

(a) An absolute trust should be used when a beneficiary is a known individual and the contract is for that individual's benefit absolutely.

(b) A MWPA trust cannot be used in the case of joint life policies, but can be used for the benefit of the individual herself, for the benefit of the spouse or for the benefit of the spouse and children.

(c) A flexible trust should be used when flexibility is required concerning the beneficiary of the policy proceeds; this is the most common use of a trust.

(d) Pension contracts cannot be placed under trust for another's benefit as the proceeds must be solely for the policyholder. The trustees of an occupational pension scheme will have discretion as to who receives the death benefits, so that they do not form part of the deceased's estate. The employee will normally be given the opportunity to express his non-binding wishes as to who should receive the death benefits.

(e) Personal pension term assurance and the return of fund under a personal pension may be written under trust.

Existing policies

17.2 If existing policies are not written under trust the adviser must be aware of the potential tax traps of now rewriting them under trust.

17.3 If an existing contract is assigned to a trust, it is treated as a transfer for inheritance tax purposes. The amount of the transfer is the current value of the contract. Therefore, it is always advisable to write a policy under trust from outset.

Student Activity 4

You should complete the student activity before reading the next section of the text. Answer the questions, then check your answers against the paragraph(s) indicated.

1. Which one of the following arrangements can be taken out   (16.2, 16.3) under the MWPA?

(a) A widow taking out an own life policy for the benefit of her children.

(b) An unmarried couple taking out a joint life first death

policy.

(c) An unmarried couple each taking out an own life policy for the benefit of the other.

(d) A married women taking out an own life policy for the benefit of her two business partners.

(e) A married man taking out an own life policy for the benefit of his wife and two adopted children.

2. Briefly describe the main methods by which the trustees of a policy, which has been placed under trust through the MWPA, can be appointed. Explain what happens in situations where no trustee is appointed. (16.5)

3. What inheritance tax considerations should be borne in mind when writing a life policy under a flexible trust? (16.11)

If you are unable to answer any of the questions satisfactorily, you should read the relevant paragraphs again. Your understanding of the text will be further tested in the self-assessment section at the end of this unit.

18 Trustee Act 1925

18.1 This Act consolidates and combines much of English trust law. It is the key piece of legislation which describes how trustees are appointed and how they operate thereafter. Having been discussed earlier, the most relevant sections are now described in detail.

18.2 Section 18 governs the death of trustees. If one, or more, trustees die their powers can be transferred to surviving trustees, except that 'a sole trustee cannot give good receipt for the proceeds of a sale of land unless that sole trustee is a trust corporation'. This section also allows that where a sole or the last surviving trustee dies, their personal representatives can act as trustees until the appointor makes another appointment. If the appointor is also dead, the personal representatives can either continue as trustees or appoint replacements themselves under S36 which covers powers of appointments.

18.3 Section 23 enables trustees to employ or pay an agent to transact business on the trust's behalf, e.g. a stockbroker acting in relation to a share portfolio, or a solicitor.

18.4 Section 25 provides trustees with the power of delegation for a period of up to one year where they may be unable to act for the trust, perhaps due to their going abroad. Amended by S9 of the Powers of Attorney Act 1971, this states that the attorney 'cannot be a sole co-trustee unless that trustee is a trust corporation'.

18.5 Section 30 enables the trustee to be reimbursed for reasonable expenses incurred in running the trust, e.g. postage.

18.6 Section 31 provides the trustees with the power to apply trust income for the maintenance or education of any infant.

18.7 Section 32 allows the trustee to apply trust capital for the advancement of a beneficiary, even if his interest is a contingent interest. The trustee would do this if the beneficiary's interest is likely to be diminished by an increase in the class of beneficiaries to which he belongs, or if it is likely to be defeated by the exercise of a power of appointment or revocation. The trust capital which is applied would have to be brought into the beneficiary's share if he later become absolutely entitled to the property jointly with other beneficiaries.

18.8 Section 36 covers the replacement of trustees who:

- Have not attained the age of majority

- Are incapable of acting

- Refuse to act

- Wish to be discharged

- Leave the UK, and remain abroad for more than one year

This section also states that, where there are less than four trustees in a trust, a new appointment cannot increase the number above four.

18.9 Section 39 provides for a deed of retirement to allow a trustee to retire from the trust and not to be replaced. At least two other trustees, or a trust corporation, the appointor and the co-trustees must agree to the retirement.

18.10 Section 53 governs property held for the benefit of infants.

18.11 Section 57 provides that the court can allow a transaction to proceed if it will benefit provided that the trust as a whole, but was not included in the trust wording as it was unforeseen by the settlor. This cannot be used to change the beneficial interests under the trust, nor can it apply to the settlement of land. It relates to transactions involved in the management and administration of the trust.

19 Trustee Investments Act 1961

19.1 Prior to the introduction of the Trustee Investments Act 1961, trustees had restricted powers of statutory investment and could generally only invest in gilt-edged securities, National Savings products and a small range of other investments and fixed-interest securities.

19.2 The introduction of this Act has increased the range of investments in which trustees can invest where their investment powers are not specified. It has given trustees the power to invest in equities, certain industrial debenture and unsecured loan stocks.

Principles of the Trustee Investments Act 1961

19.3 The main aim of the Act is to protect the interests of all beneficiaries. It states that the trustee must obtain written investment advice from a person who he believes to be qualified in financial matters before making investment decisions. The need to seek advice applies to most trustees, including those whose investment powers are not governed by the Trustee Investments Act 1961. If the trustee himself or one of the other trustees in a group is an investment expert, the need for advice can be overridden. Advice should be sought in the following areas:

- Suitability - the investments in the trust must be suitable with regard to the beneficiaries' interests

- Diversification - the trustees must ensure adequate diversification across a range of investments whilst also adopting a relatively conservative policy

- Regular review - the trustees must have the portfolio reviewed at regular intervals by an expert to ensure that the objectives of the trust are being met by the assets held

Permitted investments

19.4   The Act specifies the investments in which the trustees may invest. These are divided into two categories known as 'narrower range investments' and 'wider range investments'. Narrower range investments are then further split down into investments for which financial advice is required and those for which financial advice is not required.

19.5   The types of investment permitted in each of these categories are:

(a)   Narrower range without advice - this includes Defence Bonds and National Savings except premium bonds.

(b)   Narrower range with advice - this includes EU government stock, EU public authority fixed-interest securities, EU company debentures, local authority loan stock, building society deposits, mortgages over EU freehold property and gilt unit trusts.

(c)   Wider range - this includes EU company shares where there is a paid-up share capital of at least the equivalent of £1 million, and dividends have been paid for at least the last five years and they are quoted on a recognised stock exchange, building society shares (Pibs) or the EU equivalent, authorised unit trusts or the EU equivalent (Ucits and Oeics).

19.6   In addition to these categories of investments specified in the Act, the trust deed may give the trustees authority to hold certain other investments, such as shares in a family business, in 'special range funds'.

19.7   It should be noted that life policies are not permitted investments under the Act; however, trustees can invest in life policies if this is permitted by the trust deed. It is now common for trust deeds to contain a specific power for the trustees to effect and maintain life policies.

Practical application of the Act

19.8   Any part of the trust fund may be invested in narrower range investments but, if the trustee wishes to invest in wider range investments, the trust fund must be divided equally between narrower range and wider range investments. Special range funds are excluded from this calculation. Once the fund is divided into narrower range and wider range investments, only investments authorised within each range may be held.

19.9   Any investments in the narrower range which are not authorised must be sold for reinvestment in authorised narrower range investments. Narrower range investments may be held in the wider range but not vice versa. Any investment in the wider range which is neither an authorised wider range investment nor a narrower range investment, must be sold for reinvestment in authorised wider range investments.

19.10 Subsequent additions to the trust must be similarly divided and any proceeds from realisation of assets in special range funds which are not reinvested in special range funds must be allocated equally to the narrower range and wider range funds.

Disadvantages of the Act

19.11 The division of the trust fund into two equal parts can be complex and difficult to administer. Furthermore, once the division has been made, the narrower range and wider range often cease to have the same value due to factors such as the market forces having a different effect on the value of equities and fixed-interest securities.

19.12 Balancing the interests of a life tenant and any other beneficiaries is often difficult because the former will usually require income during life and the latter will normally require maximum capital on the death of the life tenant. The trustee needs to invest the trust fund to produce moderate income for the life tenant whilst also achieving capital growth for the remaindermen; this could be achieved by investing part of the fund in fixed-interest stocks and part of the fund in equities, or unit trusts in the case of smaller trust funds.

19.13 The narrower range and wider range investments which are specified in the Act do not cover all major investments, for example freehold and leasehold land or buildings are excluded. In addition, the investments which are authorised in each range are sometimes viewed as restrictive, for example overseas investment is prohibited. Another restriction which applies is that investment in partly paid shares is only permitted if they are fully paid up within nine months; this often precludes investment in privatisation issues.

19.14 The Act does not always fully protect the interests of the beneficiaries, for example, though a company in which a trustee decides to invest must have paid a dividend for the last five years, it may still be in decline and may have been paying a reducing dividend each year.

20   Administration of Estates Act 1925

20.1   This Act contains the statutory rules of intestate succession for both total and partial intestacy. It gives details of how the personal representatives must deal with an intestate's estate. It lists who is entitled to the intestate's property and the amounts which the surviving spouse, for example, is entitled to receive. Other information which the Act covers includes what happens if it is unclear which spouse survived the other.

20.2   Section 33 of the Act describes the statutory trust for sale which is created on the intestate's death. The personal representatives hold the estate in trust and they have the power to sell assets for conversion to cash, before paying the necessary expenses and distributing the estate in accordance with the rules of intestate succession.

20.3   The Act also provides for statutory trusts to be created for the issue of the intestate, once the surviving spouse has received her entitlement. The remaining property is divided equally between the issue and then is held on the statutory trusts until they reach age 18 or marry before reaching this age.

21 Scottish Trust Law

21.1 This relies mainly on case law, the Trust (Scotland) Act 1921, Trusts (Scotland) Act 1961 and the Married Women's Policies of Assurance (Scotland) Act 1880.

21.2 There are three ways of creating a trust:

- The subject property or related documents can be 'delivered' to the trustees or beneficiaries, which signals irrevocability

- It can be 'intimated' to the beneficiaries

- The trust deed, which only needs one signature, can be registered in the Books of Council and Session

21.3 A trust can be in perpetuity, but income accumulation is the longest of:

- The granter's life

- 21 years from the date of the granter's death

- 21 years from creation of the trust

- Minority of any person living at the death of the granter

- Minority of any person living at creation of the trust

22 Summary of Case Law

(a) *Beningfield v. Baxter* (1886)   A trustee who buys property from a trust, or sells property to the trust, could be acting for personal gain and the beneficiary can ask the court to declare the transaction void.

(b) *Knight v. Knight* (1840)   Three certainties must be present for the creation of a trust.

(c) *Macadam* (1946)   Where a trust owns shares in a company a trustee could become a director of the company, but any redemption received from the company must be passed to the trust.

(d) *Saunders v. Vautier* (1840)   Beneficiaries can require trustees to hand the trust property over to them, provided all beneficiaries agree.

(e) *Speight v. Gaunt* (1883)   The trustee must act diligently and as a prudent man of business would act if managing his own affairs, where fulfilling his duties as a trustee.

Summary

Now that you have completed this unit, you should be able to:

☐ **Explain the reasons for creating trusts**

☐ **Know what constitutes a valid trust**

☐ **Know the rights of beneficiaries**

☐ **Understand the role, duties and responsibilities of trustees**

☐ **Understand how trusts can be varied**

☐ **Know the main types of trust**

☐ **Understand the tax implications for trusts**

☐ **Know how and why life policies are written under trust**

☐ **Know the main relevant legislation and case law**

If you can tick all the above boxes with confidence, you are ready to answer the questions which follow.

Self-Assessment Questions

1. What are the three certainties which must exist for a trust to be created?

2. Briefly define the following terms:

   (a) Life interest

   (b) Life tenant

   (c) Remaindermen

   (d) Contingent beneficiary

3. What are the three factors relating to investments which a trustee must consider, irrespective of his investment powers?

4. For the benefit of whom does the Variation of Trusts Act 1958 allow the court to alter a trust?

5. Define an accumulation and maintenance trust.

6. Julia has a life interest in a trust which receives income of £7,000 and

incurs expenses of £300. Julia is a higher rate taxpayer. Calculate the amount of income which Julia will receive from the trust and any further tax liability.

7. Tom, aged 20, is entitled to receive accumulated income, when he is 24, from an accumulation and maintenance trust set up by his father. What is the income tax position while the income is accumulating?

8. Trust A makes gains of £25,000 in a tax year. The settlor has also created Trust B. Calculate the CGT payable on Trust A.

9. Martin creates a trust giving his wife a life interest, with the property then passing to his children. How is this treated for IHT purposes both when the trust is set up and if Martin dies soon after?

10. When writing a life policy under trust, in what circumstances would the following types of trust be suitable?

    (a) An absolute trust

    (b) A flexible trust

Unit 10

Background to Investment

Objectives

Students are required to study the following topics:

- **Building an investment portfolio**

- **Risk**

- **Reward**

- **Inflation, interest rates and exchange rates**

- **The London Stock Exchange**

- **The Alternative Investment Market**

- **Buying and selling**

- **Crest**

- **The gilts market**

- **Stock market indicators**

1   Introduction

1.1   Personal investment planning involves a great deal of analysis of individual customer needs, wants and circumstances. The considerations to be made cover both the individual's particular situation such as his tax status, and external influences such as inflation and exchange rates.

1.2   The first part of this unit looks at both the internal and external influences on a customer and his investment choice, how a balanced portfolio should be compiled and the relationship between each of the factors to be considered. The second part of the unit gives an introduction to the different markets through which investments are bought and sold, including the London Stock Exchange and the Alternative Investments Market. An explanation of investment terminology, theory and analysis follows in Unit 11.

1.3   The remainder of the Personal Investment Planning and Advice module looks at each of the main investment types and their own particular risk profiles so these will only be discussed in general terms here. Previous units have looked at the different taxes and briefly discussed their effect on investments. This will be further developed in discussion of the different investment types.

2   Building an Investment Portfolio

2.1   Only a small percentage of people in the UK will have any type of investment portfolio although the majority will have investments such as a house, long-term building society accounts, shares in companies, pension plans, etc.

2.2 A vast majority of people will, therefore, have a disorganised investment portfolio that pays little attention to the time factors, the balance of risk and reward, the impact of inflation and changes in interest rates, or their tax position. The role of the adviser is to organise this portfolio to meet the needs and objectives of his customer.

2.3 For example, what are the long-term objectives of the customer? Does he wish to build capital from his investments, perhaps to part-fund early retirement, or has he a need for extra income? Is he saving for a specific date, a special occasion, or just for a 'rainy day' ?Has he got an emergency fund to finance any short-term problems or are all his investments long-term ones?

2.4 The adviser should also establish whether the customer has any strong ethical views. Some investors would not wish to invest in particular sectors of the market, for example, breweries, tobacco companies, distilleries or gaming organisations. Other investors may object to investment in a company which operates in a country whose government they see as politically unacceptable. These views can, of course, be sometimes difficult to satisfy since the underlying investment structure of, say a unit trust or investment trust is not usually known.

2.5 Details of ethical funds can be obtained from the Ethical Investment Research Information Service (EIRIS) and the performance of these funds, to date, has been comparable to that of conventional funds.

2.6 Every customer is different and every customer has constantly changing circumstances, so any investment portfolio needs constant updating and reviews. With this in mind, the adviser will need to establish whether the investor is intending to adopt an active or a passive approach to the management of his portfolio. If an active approach is envisaged, then the investor will be responsible for availing himself of all the necessary information enabling him to review his portfolio. If the portfolio is to be passively managed, then the most suitable products would be those where the risks are spread, for example, unit trusts and investment trusts.

The investment portfolio

2.7 There is no such thing as perfect investment advice since most investments have in-built risk based on the unpredictability of future events. Therefore, any investment strategy can only be judged as correct on completion and that strategy may be unrepeatable given the changing circumstances of the economy.

2.8 However, if the following strategy is adopted in building a portfolio it should avoid the potential pitfalls that can arise whilst providing a sound base to achieve a customer's aims and objectives.

2.9 Any portfolio should fall into three separate areas depending, of course on the customer's attitude to risk:

• Low risk, immediate access, low return

• Medium risk, longer access, higher return

- High risk, long access, best return

2.10 By spreading a portfolio over these three areas the problem of 'eggs in one basket' is avoided, the risk is minimised whilst good returns are anticipated. However, it would be quite incorrect to suggest to a customer with a very low attitude to risk to put anything into the riskier areas. Risk will be discussed in more detail later in this unit.

Part one of the portfolio

2.11 The first part of any investment portfolio really falls into the savings area, being made up of low-risk, short-term savings. This is, in effect, an emergency fund that will provide for unforeseen problems in income or expenditure, e.g. a sudden halt to salary through redundancy, an urgent repair to the house, replacing a large domestic item, etc. Short term is generally taken to mean up to five years.

2.12 The emergency fund is normally estimated to be around two or three months' income, as this will give enough time to access the second part of the portfolio without undue penalties or loss. Not everybody can afford, or would want, an emergency fund of this size, but this is the ideal position to be aimed for. In reality, most people will have different amounts which will alter through their lives.

2.13 This part of the portfolio should be easily accessible, i.e. in hours or days rather than months, and as such will normally comprise of bank or building society accounts. These accounts should be those that give the best returns and use should be made of tax-free accounts for non taxpayers. Taxpayers should consider using the available concessions in National Savings accounts, where some accounts are completely tax-free.

2.14 The returns from this part of the portfolio will not be exceptional and returns can vary throughout the period of the investment. This part of the portfolio should at least keep pace with inflation and provide a feeder fund for part two of the portfolio with total security.

Part two of the portfolio

2.15 The second part of the portfolio should comprise medium-risk investments with longer access times that give higher returns. It should be used to fund for specific events in a set time-frame, using returns that are safe if not always fully guaranteed and are higher than the rate of return from the first part of the portfolio. These events will usually be within five to fifteen years i.e. medium-term needs.

2.16 This part of the portfolio will be more likely to make capital gains than the first part and taxation should be taken into consideration when planning the investments. With careful investment choice, it should be possible to avoid a capital gains tax liability.

2.17 The second part of the portfolio would normally consist of such investments as gilts (which have guaranteed returns but some risk if sold on the stock market), Tessas (which offer valuable tax advantages with the only risk being the variation in the rate of interest) and the like. Some endowment policies may be included here, dependent on their time span, but excluding any unit-linked policies which will fall into part three of the portfolio. However, unitised with-profits policies can be included in this part of the portfolio.

Part three of the portfolio

2.18 The third part of the portfolio is a high-risk area giving high returns over a longer time scale, i.e. at least 15 years, and attention must be paid to tax implications here, especially for capital gains.

2.19 Typically, this part of the portfolio will include any direct stock market investments but will also include other investments that have no guarantee of return. This can include such articles as antiques, gold, silver, paintings, etc., but most commonly will include property.

2.20 Indirect equity investments such as personal equity plans, unit trusts and unit-linked insurance policies should be included in this part, although some of the risk is dissipated when put into collective investments.

2.21 This is the most creative part of the portfolio but its aggressive nature necessitates the more defensive back-up of the other parts of the portfolio.

Summary

2.22 Part one of the portfolio:

- Emergency fund

- Complete security

- Immediate access

2.23 Part two of the portfolio:

- Low-risk with guaranteed returns

- Realisable at short notice

- Look for the higher net income

2.24 Part three of the portfolio:

- Higher-risk, therefore higher reward

- Medium to long-term investments

- Aim for good spread of investments

Balancing the three parts

2.25 Is impossible to decide on the split of the three parts of the portfolio without knowing the customer's attitude to risk. Only this filtering device can accurately tailor the portfolio to meet the needs and objectives of the customer, reflecting his attitudes to the investments and their degree of risk.

2.26 However, it can be said that there has to be a fair balance between the three areas and all have to be represented in any portfolio that is going to be successful in all circumstances. There should be flexibility, though, to allow a shift in investment split depending on the current economic climate.

2.27 For example, in a booming economy there could be a greater emphasis on the riskier end of the spectrum to take advantage of greater gains, whilst in a recessionary economy perhaps the emphasis should be in the more guaranteed end of the investment spectrum to minimise potential losses.

2.28 It is important to remember that an investment portfolio needs constant monitoring to ensure it continues to achieve the objectives of the customer over time.

3 Factors to Take into Consideration

3.1 Having discussed how a balanced portfolio can be created it is important to look at each of the influences on investment choice in more detail.

Customer specific details

3.2 Information on the customer will normally be obtained during a fact find interview where regulated products are under consideration, or otherwise in discussion with the customer, for example, where a purchase of shares is being made. An adviser should ensure that any investments made by a customer fit in with his overall needs and are affordable otherwise problems may develop in the future and a loss may be made by early encashment.

3.3 The customer has to be able to afford the commitment, either to regular savings or to invest a lump sum. Are there any changes envisaged which may affect future levels of income such as marriage, house move, children, change of job, retirement, inheritances etc.? If a lump sum is invested what effect would this have on easy access capital? Will the investment leave an adequate emergency fund?

3.4 The choice of investment type will depend on the customer's requirement i.e. for income or capital growth or a combination of both, as well as his attitude to risk and his tax status. An individual may require a high income which could be provided by direct equity investment but is not prepared to take the risk that his investment could also fall in value. The degree of security offered by an investment, usually expressed in terms of guaranteed returns is very important and a well balanced portfolio will have elements of both high risk (i.e. no guarantee) and low risk (but high guarantee) as discussed earlier.

3.5 The individual's tax status is another important factor with higher rate taxpayers being particularly affected by the tax treatment of different products both for income tax and capital gains tax purposes. Portfolios should ensure that full use of tax-free investments is made if suitable and appropriate and that any change in tax status can be catered for. For example, a basic rate taxpayer may find that a salary increase takes him into the higher rate tax band and consequently he has a further tax liability on his investments. If this change can be predicted then adjustments to the portfolio can be made in advance.

3.6 Conversely advantages can be made of tax changes such as the case of a higher rate taxpayer who retires and takes a drop in income. This will prove advantageous where investments that defer tax liability until encashment, such as non-qualifying investment bonds, are involved.

3.7 So the tax status of the individual should be considered at the time of initial investment, while the investment is attracting interest, while income is being withdrawn or reinvested and when the accumulated capital is finally paid out.

PERSONAL INVESTMENT PLANNING AND ADVICE

3.8 If the customer has existing investments these must be taken into consideration as they will have an impact on any financial planning recommendations made both in the overall balance of the portfolio and because of the various restrictions on certain types of products. An obvious example of this is where a customer has already invested the maximum amount in a Pep in the current year. An adviser cannot recommend further Pep investments until the following year. Another example where an existing investment will be important is where a customer has inherited some shares perhaps but has no emergency fund.

3.9 Finally some customers will have more knowledge of investments and have clearer ideas on what they require and how to achieve it whereas other customers may prefer to 'leave it to the experts' and have little input on how the portfolio is constructed. Some individuals may wish for more control than others over their investments and take a more active part in their management. This may have an effect on the type of investments selected.

4 Risk

4.1 The term risk has been referred to regularly in this unit and is now described in more detail. There are a number of types of risk to be considered as follows:

- Customer's attitude to risk

- Market risk

- Product risk

- Provider risk

- Tax risk

- Offshore risk

Customer's attitude to risk

4.2 An adviser will establish a customer's attitude to risk at a fact-finding interview. This may be difficult for an individual to define but can usually be established by discussing the factors involved. These include:

(a) Customer's degree of wealth - it is probably an obvious statement that the more money a person has the more likely they are to be willing to take the risk that they may lose some of their capital. An individual with little capital to spare will require a higher degree of security.

(b) Timescale - where returns are required over the long term this may be achieved by the more risky investments and customers may be willing to take that risk as fluctuations should even out over the long-term. Where short-term investment is required only those who can afford to make a loss will usually consider investments with little or no guarantee.

(c) Past experience - customers who have made a loss in the past may tend to be more cautious over any future investments they make.

(d) Degree of security required - individuals may have a different attitude to risk on different parts of their portfolio. For example, where a customer is depending on an investment for a particular purpose such as retirement income or to meet school fees then he is likely to be more cautious. He may, however, be prepared to take more of a risk with other investments.

(e) Couples - it is important to remember that financial planning for couples should take both their positions into consideration. It may be that each partner has a different attitude to risk and any resulting portfolio may have to combine the needs of each partner if they cannot agree on a joint approach.

4.3 Customers can normally be grouped into having a cautious, balanced or speculative attitude to risk. Cautious means requiring no or little risk. The customer will not want to see his investment fall in value and will want to ensure that he will at least receive a return of his capital at the end of the investment term. The most suitable types of investment here are fixed-interest securities such as cash deposits in bank and building society accounts including Tessas and National Savings products as well as with-profits life assurance products. The cautious investor should be aware that he will not make high returns on his capital and that any income produced from these types of investments may fluctuate and cannot usually be guaranteed.

4.4 The balanced investor is someone who is prepared to take more risk with part of his portfolio while requiring a greater degree of security in other parts as discussed in (d) above. Investments which may be suitable include Peps and unit trusts as well as unit-linked life assurance and pension products. In this case a higher proportion of the portfolio is being invested in asset-backed investments which allows the opportunity for both capital growth and income.

4.5 The speculative investor will require a high degree of asset-backed investments and have little need for managed funds or with-profits contracts. He may choose specialist areas of investment such as overseas investments in a particular sector or in emerging markets where the potential for a high return is greatest. Investment in futures and options will also fall into the speculative category as will unquoted shares.

Table 10.1 Ranking of risk

Investment Type		Products
Derivatives and highly speculative shares	**Speculative** **High Risk** 6	Futures, options and highly speculative shares
Funds invested in speculative units, or in minor market funds	5	Quoted non blue chip shares Unquoted shares Emerging markets

Funds invested in specialist areas	**4**	Quoted blue chip shares Unit trusts, investment trusts, Peps, bonds and regular premium contracts invested in international smaller companies and recovery funds
Funds invested in broadly spread assets which may rise and fall	**Balanced risk** **3**	Unit trusts, Peps, bonds and regular premium life assurance and pension in UK growth, UK income, UK general or managed funds
Minimal risk to capital if kept for recommended term, rate of growth may fluctuate (inflation may erode capital value)	**2**	Gilts and fixed-interest securities, bonds and regular premium contracts invested in traditional with-profit or unitised with-profit contracts or guaranteed growth bonds, pensions deposit funds
No risk to capital. Interest rates may vary for certain contracts (inflation may erode capital value)	**1** **Low Risk** **Cautious**	National Savings Tessas Deposit accounts Guaranteed income bonds

Market risk

4.6 This is an external risk, i.e. the customer has no influence over it, and has two elements. One is the broad risk that the market can fall or rise, and the other that a particular share or investment will fall or rise in value in relation to the market as a whole. There are great rewards to be had by careful investment in the stock market, but it is important to be aware of the risks involved, and therefore make plans to minimise them.

Spreading the risk

4.7 Most people who lose money on the stock market do so because they do not have a spread of investments and therefore have "all their eggs in one basket". An investment in one company only, for example, heightens risk because all reward is dependent upon the performance of one company. There is no insurance against a neutral or poor performance and there can be every chance of losing the entire investment should that one company fold. A portfolio should be spread across investment in a number of companies in a variety of sectors to spread the risk.

4.8 For example, a spread of investments in companies that is limited to the electrical sector will suffer if that sector suffers. If one company suffers there is insurance against loss but, in most cases, one company will reflect problems throughout the industry.

4.9 The best spread of shares in companies is around 12-15 for this should give a good return whilst spreading ownership sufficiently to minimise risk. It can never be a guarantee, of course, but it is a strategy used by fund mangers to maximise returns whilst minimising risk.

Timing of investments

4.10 To offset the risk of general peaks and troughs in the stock market it is again wise to spread investments, but in this case the spread is over time. No expert can accurately predict when the peaks and troughs will occur, although predictions are now becoming more accurate, so it is wise to spread realisation of assets over time.

4.11 The time element is vital in spreading the need for realisation and also in the timing of the cashing in of assets. By analysing trends, decisions can be made as to whether the market is a bear or a bull one, so maximising gains by holding on to assets or minimising losses by selling assets.

4.12 Time should also be noted for other reasons, especially in terms of patience. Real gains can be made on the stock market by regarding it as a genuine long-term investment for capital growth. This means an investment of probably eight years upwards with any dividends reinvested to boost the capital content of the investment. In the 1970s it took six years for an average UK share to out-perform the top-rate building society accounts. Since then shares have consistently out-performed such forms of investment.

Stock market movements

4.13 Most shares will move up or down in direct relation to movements in the stock market; some more so, others less so. This is known as their "volatility". The more volatile a share, the more the investor stands to lose or gain dependent upon movements; the less volatile, the less he will lose or gain.

The bulls and the bears

4.14 There are few guarantees on the stock market and gains and losses can be made because of sweeping optimism, or sweeping pessimism from buyers and sellers of securities. Emotion can be a real driving force in the London Stock Exchange as feelings drive prices up or down, depending on economic reports, the threat of war, a potential change of government, movements in other stock exchanges, etc.

4.15 There are three market states:

- Neutral
- Bull
- Bear

4.16 The neutral state is self-explanatory, with little movement on a daily basis for various reasons.

4.17 The terms "bulls and bears" originated in history but are used now as a short-hand to indicate an optimistic or pessimistic market. A bull market is one where investors are optimistic about an increase in prices and values. This will show a great increase in activity from a neutral market with prices rising as investors buy in anticipation of gains.

4.18 In a bear market the pessimists take over and prices begin to tumble in anticipation of losses and investors sell to minimise these potential losses. These two terms are now used in wider context but traditionally a bull is a buyer and a bear a seller.

Example 10.1: Remember Polly Peck?

The risk and subsequent fall of Polly Peck illustrates the risks (and rewards) faced by investing in one company.

For those who invested in 1979, a £500 holding would have risen to £160,000 by 1983 and even after the problems of 1987 the Polly Peck shares hit a peak in September 1990 at 462p.

By 20 September trading was suspended on the shares at a price of 108p.

As you can see, great gains for some can mean great losses for others.

Black Monday

4.19 The swings in moods and the dominance of the bears or the bulls have led to large gains for many investors, but what has normally made headline news are the huge crashes in the stock market leading to disastrous losses for many investors.

4.20 The best known downturn was the one in October 1987 when huge losses were felt around the world. The FT-SE 100 index reached a low of 1200 from a high of 2100 in that year, reflecting the size of the "crash", with an overall loss in the year of 36.6%. It took 21 months to recover from this and reach "pre-crash" levels.

4.21 There were many reasons for this, including concern about American and German talks about European currency and the effect of computer trading, which led to certain securities being automatically sold when share prices reached a certain level. The gales in the United Kingdom which cut off communication lines further disrupted trading and diminished opportunities to respond to the situation.

4.22 Since that date there have been two further potential "Black Mondays", the effects of which were diminished by frantic efforts to boost confidence over the non-trading weekend.

4.23 There have been previous market declines, the original one being in September 1869, which led to a depression in the UK economy, although this was a "Black Friday". The other "Black Monday" occurred in 1929.

Product risk

4.24 When an investor has chosen a particular product he then has to bear the risk that the value of that product may fall and returns may not be as high as predicted. The products which carry this risk are either directly or indirectly linked to shares and prices can fall and rise unpredictably. External influences across the world can have an effect on the world's various stock markets and it is impossible for anyone to predict what may happen in the future.

4.25 Investment in a pooled or collective investment such as a unit-linked insurance plan or in unit trusts and investment trusts may cushion the impact of changes in share prices but investors must be prepared to risk the possibility that they may lose some or all of their investment.

4.26 The risk profile of the different types of products is covered in the following units which also discuss the comparable risks involved in choosing between products of the same type. This will include choice of different types of share offered by a company, choice of fund for a unit trust or unit-linked policy or choice of savings account.

Provider risk

4.27 The investor will also be concerned with his choice of provider and the degree of security offered. Following the recent collapses of the Bank of Credit and Commerce International (BCCI) and Barings Bank no investment provider can be regarded as totally safe. The government and the National Savings Bank may be regarded as being the most unlikely to fail as they are both national institutions, although the National Savings Bank has become a privatised offshoot of the Treasury. Therefore, as far as provider risk is concerned gilts and National Savings products may be regarded as the safest form of investment.

4.28 Investor protection for bank account holders is covered by the Deposit Protection Scheme while building society savers are covered by the Investor Protection Scheme. These provide compensation for investors in case of insolvency or collapse of the bank or society. Further details can be found in Unit 12.

4.29 For firms authorised by the Securities and Investments Board (SIB) there is an Investor Compensation Scheme which provides investors with compensation in the event of financial loss on the insolvency of an authorised firm. This does not include insurance based investments however. Each self regulating organisation (SRO) organises its own levy on its members to fund the scheme. Each SRO will handle claims relating to its members. An investor can claim up to 100% of the first £30,000 and 90% of the next £20,000 for any one loss, giving a maximum claim of £48,000.

4.30 Insurance based products are covered by the Policyholder's Protection Act 1975 which was brought about following public concern over the failure of certain life companies. The purpose of the Act was to protect policyholders against the collapse of insurance companies and set up a compensation scheme for policyholders whose insurers cannot meet their liabilities.

4.31 The scheme applies to authorised insurance companies and is financed by a levy on all UK insurers. It is administered by the Policyholder's Protection Board. In the event of failure of an insurance company the following levels of compensation may be paid to policyholders:

(a) 100% of the insolvent insurer's liability in respect of compulsory insurance, e.g. Road Traffic Act section of motor policies.

(b) 90% of the insolvent insurer's liability under non-compulsory general business.

(c) 90% of the value of life policies, although excessive benefits may be reduced or ignored. The Board will first attempt to find another insurer to take over life business from an insolvent insurer.

4.32 Where investments are bought through the London Stock Exchange certain rules in how business is conducted on the exchange and the requirements for companies applying for a listing are aimed at ensuring investor protection. However, there are no compensation schemes available for investors who hold shares in a company which goes into liquidation. Their financial position will be decided by the types of share they hold and how that affects their claim as a creditor on the company. See Unit 14 for further details.

Tax risk

4.33 The tax risk means the risk associated with exposure to tax liability and, as discussed earlier, relates to both the investor's tax position and the tax treatment of the particular investment. Both these can change over time. As far as the tax treatment of investments is concerned the Finance Act each year may change certain aspects of taxation, as evidenced by the Finance Act 1996 which reduced the tax charge deducted at source on savings income to 20%.

4.34 The risk to the investor when his own tax status changes has already been discussed. However, the risk that the tax treatment of a particular investment may change is less predictable and may have a considerable effect on an individual's portfolio.

4.35 For example, an investor may have built a portfolio heavily based on producing income to meet specific needs. An increase in the tax deducted at source on this income will reduce the net income received by the investor and changes may need to be made to the portfolio.

4.36 Some tax changes brought about by legislation may be applied retrospectively and can have a devastating effect on complex arrangements such as investments used in trusts. In this case the risk may be great but is unpredictable and the individual needs to weigh up the possibility that this might occur against the present benefits being enjoyed.

4.37 The tax risk can also vary depending on how the investment is packaged. For example, a unit trust holding will be free of tax if it is held in a Pep but otherwise the investor will be liable to income tax and capital gains tax. Where an investor does not use his annual CGT exemption he may be better off investing in an investment where he is directly liable for the tax rather than one where the underlying funds are subject to CGT anyway e.g. life assurance funds.

Offshore risk

4.38 Where an investor chooses offshore investments he is taking more of a risk as far as any of the above types of risk are concerned. Depending on where the investment is based there is likely to be less investor protection and regulation so the investor may have no entitlement to compensation in the event of collapse of the provider. The taxation of offshore investments may lead to a higher tax bill depending on the treatment applying at the time the income or capital gain is received by the investor and the investor's residence status. As with other types of investment the investor needs to consider the risk associated with different products of the same type to decide which is most suitable for his needs and attitude to risk.

Diversification

4.39 It has already been mentioned that a balanced portfolio includes a good spread of investments both in terms of types of investment e.g. deposit accounts for low-risk savings and unit trusts for a higher potential for growth, and also in terms of sector e.g. across a range of UK and worldwide funds. It is possible to reduce or eliminate some of the risks described in the preceding paragraphs by diversification.

4.40 For example, if two shares are chosen which both offer the same level of return but are influenced by opposite factors then the risk of each will be negated by the other, i.e. when one rises in value the other falls. This is a simplistic view but illustrates the principle behind the reason for diversification. Where the returns on any two securities are not directly related their combined risk is less than a weighted average of their individual risks.

4.41 The more a selected investment is 'managed' for the investor the more likely it is to have in-built diversity. An insurance policy such as a with-profit endowment will have an investment spread across equities, gilts, property and cash. A unit-linked policy will have less diversification depending on the fund or funds selected. Where direct investment is involved the investor will have to take responsibility for ensuring an adequate spread himself.

Student Activity 1

You should complete this student activity before reading the next section of the text. Answer the questions, then check your answers against the paragraph(s) indicated.

1. A customer wishes to review his investment portfolio. He currently owns a Pep, bought two years ago and some life assurance policies and, following the sale of some property, now has £12,000 to invest.

    (a) What questions would you ask regarding his objectives?   (2.3, 2.4

    (b) What are the three areas a balanced portfolio should have?   (2.9)

    (c) Briefly explain the types of details you would require about   (3.2-3.9, the customer to be able to suggest what investment types   4.2-4.5) would be most suitable.

2. How would you define what is meant by product risk?   (4.24)

If you are unable to answer any of the questions satisfactorily, you should read the relevant paragraphs again. Your understanding of the text will be further tested in the self-assessment section at the end of this unit.

5 Reward

5.1 In considering the risk involved in a particular investment it is important to remember the other side of the picture where the degree of risk affects the potential for reward. A high risk may also mean potentially high rewards while low risk will mean lower reward. Investors with different attitudes to risk will have to accept that the potential reward they are aiming for may not be possible if they are not prepared to take some risk in their investment choice.

Income

5.2 Investors can choose the type of reward they require from their investment i.e. income, capital growth or a combination of both. Where income is required it can be provided annually, monthly or at other intervals as required. It will be provided by interest from vehicles such as deposit accounts or gilts or as dividends from equity based investments. Where a particular product only produces income on an annual or half-yearly basis, for example, it may be possible for the investor to buy several products of the same type but with different distribution dates if a more frequent income is required.

5.3 Income can be paid directly to investors by cheque or into a bank or building society account. For example, a building society account holder may set up an arrangement where the interest on his savings account is paid into a separate account from which he can withdraw money as and when required.

Capital

5.4 Capital growth can be achieved in two ways. First, any investment income arising from the capital can be automatically reinvested in the investment. For example, unit trusts offer distribution units which provide income or accumulation units which reinvest the income. In some cases income which is reinvested is used to purchase further units such as with an investment trust savings scheme.

5.5 Secondly the value of the underlying investment can also increase (or fall). For example, the price of a share can rise or fall but this may not have a direct impact on the dividends paid out as they relate to the company's profits rather than its performance on the stock exchange. An investor may gain considerable capital growth on his shareholding but dividends paid out remain relatively low. Obviously this is a simplification of a more complex subject which is discussed further in the relevant units.

Combination

5.6 Often investors require a combination of income and growth from their investment portfolio and this can be achieved by a spread of different types of investments. It is important to remember that where the same product is being used to produce both capital growth and income they will have an effect on each other. For example, if a building society saver withdraws all his interest every month the value of his initial capital investment will fall due to inflation as no reinvestment is being made. For other types of investment too much income may erode the underlying capital and result in a capital loss. This in turn will reduce the amount of income that can be produced in the future.

5.7 If income is taken too soon from a product which is designed to achieve growth over the long term this will have a similar effect. This could occur in the case of a Pep where investors may want to produce an income but also take a capital sum in the future. By taking too much in income, or too early on in the life of the Pep, they will reduce the potential for capital growth.

5.8 Certain investments offer a regular fixed income over a specified period, often five years, and guarantee return of the original investment at the end of the term. It is important to remember that while this means the investor will not lose his original investment, its value in real terms will have been reduced by inflation.

Secure investments

5.9 Certain customers require security of their capital above any other types of reward. This means that the value of their capital is guaranteed not to fall. However, as described earlier, this may mean that the returns on the investment may not be as great as if the capital itself was at risk of losing value.

5.10 Where a return of capital is guaranteed the income it produces may not be and can rise and fall in value. The types of investment which provide capital security include indirect investments such as single premium bonds. A growing number of guaranteed bonds offer a return of capital at the end of the term, usually five years, plus an additional return based on the rise in the performance of a stock market indicator such as the FT-SE 100. These are commonly known as tracker bonds and allow investors to gain indirectly from stock market growth. Of course there is the possibility that the index may actually fall over the five years and this is a risk to be taken into consideration. The guaranteed return in these types of investments is usually provided by zero dividend preference shares which provide a fixed payment at a specified date in the future.

Protection

5.11 When a customer is considering his investment portfolio and the amount he has available to invest he will need to fit this into the context of his overall financial plan. The first part of this will be to protect his income and his assets, usually by insurance, and then to establish the amount available to invest for the future. The degree of protection required by an individual will depend on his personal circumstances and will change over time.

5.12 For example, a young married couple with children are likely to have a number of protection needs including protecting their mortgage and protecting income. Protection will be their priority and investing for the future may not be within their financial capabilities at the present time other than setting up an emergency fund such as a building society account. An older couple without dependent children may have repaid their mortgage and consider investing to provide income in the future to be their priority. They may also need to consider protecting their assets to pass them on to a future generation.

5.13 Where investment is through a life assurance product the customer can provide both protection and savings. For example, an endowment policy pays out either on death during the term (protection) or at maturity (investment return). Of course the downside to this is that part of each premium is paying for the protection and if the policyholder wants to cash the policy in early he is unlikely to receive a full return of the premiums paid.

5.14 Capital protection can be best achieved by investments such as index-linked National Savings certificates and index-linked gilts where the capital value is protected against inflation. However, protection of capital is often at the expense of income and so their suitability has to be weighed against the need to produce income. Protection of income can be obtained through life assurance products such as term or whole life assurance, health insurances such as permanent health insurance (PHI) and other products such as loan payment protection and redundancy protection policies.

6 External Influences on Financial Planning

Inflation

6.1 The main influence on the value of investments over time is, of course, inflation. Inflation can be defined as the sustained increase in the general level of prices and costs and the fall in the purchasing value of money. A temporary increase in prices, for example one which is seasonal, is not inflation.

6.2 Inflation is measured by the movement of the retail prices index (RPI) which was 100 in January 1979 and tracks the cost of selected consumer goods and services. The RPI is calculated monthly and the inflation rate is the annualised increase in RPI. Basically, the RPI is calculated on the difference between the cost of a specific 'basket' of goods at two different times. So if the prices over the specified period rise by 5% a person will be able to buy 5% fewer goods at the end of that period for the same amount of money.

6.3 There are two measures of inflation, 'headline' inflation which includes the cost of housing and associated borrowing, and 'core' inflation or the 'underlying' rate of inflation which is the calculation of inflation excluding these housing costs. The 'average earnings index' means the increases in earnings which tend to be higher than the RPI.

Table 10.2: RPI and inflation rates

	1995	1996				
	Dec	Jan	Feb	Mar	Apr	May
Retail Prices Index	150.7	150.2	150.9	151.5	152.6	152.9
Inflation	3.2%	2.9%	2.7%	2.7%	2.4%	2.2%
Underlying inflation	3.0%	2.8%	2.9%	2.9%	2.9%	2.8%
Average Earnings Index	129.2	129.8	130.8	135.5	131.2	-

6.4 There are three main influences on inflation:

(a) **Increase in money supply.** This is known as the monetarist theory whereby inflation increases because of excessive increases in the money supply. The government try to reduce this by imposing measures such as increasing interest rates, imposing lending restrictions on banks and stopping the printing of money. By reducing the money supply, money will increase in value and so prices of goods and services will reduce. This in turn restores investors' and businesses' confidence in the pound.

(b) **Cost-push.** Inflation will occur when a rise in production costs pushes up prices to consumers. Production costs may rise due to a number of factors such as increases in the price of raw material due to shortages, increase in labour costs due to scarcity of skilled workers or demand for pay increases, rises in interest rates, inflation in other sectors of the economy at home and abroad and other changes such as fashions, world prices, or the weather (effect on crops etc.).

(c) **Demand-pull.** In this case inflation occurs when demand exceeds supply. This may be caused by falling interest rates or a reduction in tax rates which gives people more money to spend.

Deflation

6.5 Where the general price level of goods is falling this will cause deflation. This may arise due to rising unemployment, falling prices or rising bankruptcies and liquidations and indicates that supply is greater than demand. Once deflation occurs it is self-perpetuating because as sales fall so businesses may have to reduce their workforce thus creating more unemployment and so reducing the general level of spending power. This will lead to further reductions in sales and so on. To counteract deflation the government has to stimulate demand, create more jobs and so increase income and sales.

Effect of inflation on investments

6.6 The effect of inflation on investment return will depend on the interest rates available. The individual has to consider the real rate of return on an investment by taking inflation into account. So, for example, if an investor could invest in a Tessa with an interest rate of 7.45% and inflation was 2.2% this would represent a real rate of return of 5.25%.

6.7 One problem for investors in considering the 'real' return on an investment is that this is only an indication of the current position and inflation rates and interest rates can rise and fall in the future.

6.8 Low inflation generally means good news for investors but bad news for people living off their savings as inflation tends to have an effect on interest rates. If inflation is low then interest rates will tend to fall because investors will not be looking for such a high return to keep up with inflation. High inflation will benefit borrowers such as individuals with a mortgage as the value of their property will rise and increase their equity. However this may lead to the problems of negative equity seen in the UK in the last decade as inflation begins to fall again.

6.9 Inflation has an effect on both capital and income. If inflation rises over the term of an investment then its capital value will be eroded. Investments with a long-term aim are less likely to be affected by fluctuations in inflation as it is the overall increase, or decrease, when the investment is realised that will be most important.

6.10 Savings accounts that offer a variable interest rate mean that the income available will tend to rise and fall in line with increases and decreases in the inflation rate. Where it is important to keep pace with inflation it may be appropriate to use index-linked investments such as National Savings index-linked certificates.

Interest rates

6.11 An interest rate can be defined as the price a borrower pays in order to gain a resource now rather than in the future. This price can be calculated by totalling the repayments made over the term of a loan and subtracting the amount of original loan. The interest rate is usually expressed as a percentage of the loan. In the case of investors saving their money and gaining interest it is the product provider who is the borrower and the interest rate will depend on how much the provider needs to attract new sources of funds.

6.12 Interest rates are affected by the supply and demand of future claims on resources, so where, for example, demand for loans is low a building society may drop its interest rates for borrowers to attract business. Conversely, where there is a fall in the number of people opening savings accounts the building society may raise interest rates for savers to attract business. This will also be affected by the interest the building society is gaining on investment of the account holders' money.

6.13 As with inflation there is a 'real' interest rate and a 'nominal' interest rate. The nominal rate is that actually paid or received by the individual while the real rate takes inflation into account. For example, an investor receives 8% nominal interest on his savings account over the year. However, inflation is 3% so his real return is only 5%.

6.14 Some of the influences on changes in interest rates on investments are as follows:

(a) Size of investment: usually higher deposits which are invested over longer periods with notice required for withdrawal will attract higher interest rates. This is due to the economies of scale as the institutions can themselves attract better interest rates on their investments for larger sums. Returns will also be better on long-term investments.

(b) Other economies: interest rates will reflect the state of the UK and overseas economies. Exchange rates also have effect as shown below. One example in recent years of the influence of overseas economies was the Third World debt crisis which led to a rise in interest rates charged by financial institutions on international lending.

(c) Inflation: where inflation is expected to rise or fall this will have an effect on the demand for investments and so on the interest rates offered. Where inflation is expected to remain low then interest rates are likely to remain low.

(d) Political influences: Financial regulation influences the interest rates available, for example, interest rate ceilings may be introduced on certain types of investment. The government may operate a monetary policy which has a direct influence on interest rates.

Bank base rates

6.15 Bank base rates have a high profile in the media and are often referred to as a good indicator of the state of the economy. Their high profile is probably due to their influence on mortgage lending rates. The base rate is used as the starting point from which a bank determines its lending rates. The base rate has fallen from 6.75% in July 1995 to 5.75% in June 1996.

6.16   Lending rates have to take into account the cost to the bank of acquiring funds as well as the cost of the overheads involved. The cost of acquiring funds includes the interest rate that the bank has to offer depositors. Bank base rates tend to be similar for all the major banks otherwise loans and deposits would be constantly switching from one bank to another. Changes in base rates also tend to be announced by the major banks at the same time as each other.

Interest rates and investments

6.17   As far as investments are concerned the risk of changes in interest rates are most marked on fixed-interest investments. A rise in interest rates will mean a fall in the value of the investment. A fall in interest rates means an increase in value of the investment. This particularly relates to gilts and is discussed further in Unit 13. Where an investment has a variable interest rate any fall in interest will mean lower returns.

6.18   As has been discussed previously the effect of the interest rate quoted on a particular product will depend on an individual's particular circumstances and take other factors into account. For example, the need for an emergency fund means money has to be easily accessible. Therefore it cannot be tied up in a long-term investment which may obtain a better interest rate.

6.19   The investor's tax position also influences the 'real' rate of return gained and this will be illustrated in later units.

Market economy

6.20   Supply and demand are the controlling factors on the market economy as a whole and the price or return on investments will depend on the level of demand. If there are more borrowers than lenders interest rates will rise, but if there are more lenders (or investors) than borrowers the rate of return will fall.

6.21   An example of this occurred in Germany after unification. The demand for money to rebuild East Germany meant that interest rates almost trebled to attract investors to lend their money.

6.22   Market economy means that if one market is more attractive than another investors will move their money between them. So, for example, if gilts look more attractive than shares for whatever reason, money will move into gilts and out of shares. This will lead to a fall in share prices and a rise in the price of gilts.

Exchange rates

6.23   An exchange rate is the price at which two currencies are traded in the foreign exchange market. The demand for the British pound is affected by the desire of foreigners to buy British goods, services and assets. The supply of the pound to the foreign exchange market depends on the desire of the British to buy foreign goods, services and assets. In a simple world the exchange rate would rise and fall depending on supply and demand.

6.24   However, governments will have an effect on the exchange rate because they may wish to adjust the balance of their country's imports and exports due to internal inflation rates and economic policies. They can do this by fixing interest rates and so influencing the levels of supply and demand for their country's products.

6.25   Other influences on the exchange rate of a country include economic policies of areas such as the EU. The exchange rate mechanism (ERM) was introduced by the EU as part of the European Monetary System (EMS) and means that each country fixes a nominal exchange rate against each other ERM participant, while the group floats collectively against the rest of the world. Limits are set on the amount by which each participant's currency can fluctuate against the others. The ERM was introduced to reduce the volatility of exchange rates and it has been successful in creating some stability in Europe. However, one of the main criticisms has been that it has tended to undermine the economic growth of the participating countries.

6.26   For the ERM to work effectively the participating members need to have similar economic performances and so certain domestic policies may have to be suspended and replaced by EU policies. This implied loss of sovereignty has led to some of the problems which resulted in the UK withdrawing from the ERM in 1992.

6.27   Further negotiation on exchange rates will need to take place before the single European currency can be introduced. The future of the European economic unit (the Ecu) and the proposal to set up a European Central Bank have yet to be decided and the British government will need to judge the effect on the British economy of any participation in the EMS.

6.28   The effect of exchange rates not only in Europe and the EMS, but worldwide have an impact on investment return. Where interest rates on foreign investments are higher than on domestic products this will make overseas investments more attractive. However, if exchange rates are not favourable then any profit may be lost when the money is exchanged into sterling.

6.29   The main buyers and sellers of currencies are companies who conduct international business and the banks. Private investors usually exchange currency through their bank. Currency is also bought and sold as an investment with investors speculating on the profits to be made from changes in exchange rates.

6.30   Changes in exchange rates arise from a number of influences. The main one is the basic economic forces of supply and demand. Inflation is also an important economic factor as can be illustrated by the following example.

Example 10.2 Effect of inflation on exchange rates

A French car and a German car both cost the same in their own countries. However France has an inflation rate of 10% while Germany only has an inflation rate of 3%.

After a year the French car costs 7% more in French francs to buy than the German car does in Deutschmarks. So it will cost more to buy the French car in Germany than the German one. This means French car manufacturers will find it harder to sell their cars in Germany while the German car manufacturers will find it easier to sell their cars in France.

If France allowed the value of the franc to fall against the Deutschmark then this imbalance would be removed.

6.31 Exchange rates are also influenced by interest rates. Where a country has high interest rates this may attract investors because they see it as a sign that the economy is growing. High interest rates tend to push currency prices upwards. However, there may be times when high interest rates indicate high inflation and so the currency is weakened.

6.32 Private investors will be affected by changes in exchange rates if they invest in any investment which includes foreign investments. However, the fluctuations in return due to exchange rates may be levelled out in the case of pooled investments. Where an individual has the choice of investment areas he may be influenced by personal preferences in his choice as well as his financial needs and the degree of risk he is willing to take. As with all other risks an investor must take the risk that he may lose money by changes in exchange rates but the speculative investments in more volatile economies carry the potential for higher rewards.

Student Activity 2

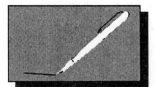

You should complete this student activity before reading the next section of the text. Answer the questions, then check your answers against the paragraph(s) indicated.

1. Elaine Wright has £5,000 in a building society high interest   (5.9, 5.10) deposit account and £5,000 in a Pep. What is the difference in the security of her capital between these two types of investment and why?

2. An investor has been quoted an interest rate of 6.75% on a   (6.6) savings account. If inflation is 3% what will be the real rate of return?

3. A customer wants to know what affects the changes in interest   (6.14) rate on his variable rate deposit account. Briefly explain the main influences on interest rates.

If you are unable to answer any of the questions satisfactorily, you should read the relevant paragraphs again. Your understanding of the text will be further tested in the self-assessment section at the end of this unit.

7 The London Stock Exchange

7.1 The stock market is a free market where securities (equities, gilts, etc.) are bought and sold by or on behalf of investors. Great publicity has been given to the tremendous gains that can be made on the stock market and also to the large losses that can occur.

7.2 The stock market is a risky place to do business because few of the securities that are bought and sold have any guaranteed return at all. However, for years now, institutionalised investors have used the stock market on behalf of customers and have realised significant gains on their behalf. Although risk is high it does mean that reward is also potentially high and a well structured portfolio can minimise losses and maximise gains. There is also a large number of people who invest indirectly in the stock market through collective investments.

7.3 There are stock markets throughout the world but perhaps the three most important ones are in Japan, America and Great Britain. Traditionally, the buying and selling of securities, or shares, was carried out in an open trading area or floor but new technology has meant a phasing out of the dramatic crowd scenes often televised in times of crisis or upswing in economy. Trading in Great Britain is now mostly carried out by computer.

7.4 The London Stock Exchange Limited (LSE) is the formal name for the International Stock Exchange of the UK. Its main activities are:

- Organising and regulating the UK securities market

- Listing the shares which can be traded and administering the rules for listing

- Organising and regulating the international equity market

- Providing settlement facilities for transactions in UK equities

Regulation

7.5 The FSA designated the LSE as a recognised investment exchange (RIE) which allows it to provide markets for the issue of new securities and the trading of existing securities. It is responsible for issuing and administering rules covering listing and investor protection. The Exchange is in charge of regulating the securities markets.

Listing

7.6 A company may decide to list its securities on the LSE for a number of reasons. The main reason is to raise capital. There are other sources of capital a company can use, such as bank loans, but by having its shares listed on the stock exchange it can stimulate increased trading in its shares and raise capital without the need to pay interest or similar penalties.

7.7 The other main reasons are as follows:

- Investors will be more attracted to a well known market-place where there is likely to be a demand to buy and sell the shares

- Increases the standing of the company both nationally and internationally by promoting its name, products or services and reputation

- Provides access to overseas investors

- Allows the company to provide information to the public via the LSE's information services, and gain useful publicity

7.8 Of course, the converse to this is that some companies may perceive some of these reasons as disadvantageous, particularly in the areas of publicity and public access to information. Small, family-owned businesses may not want outside ownership of their company and so will not apply for listing on the LSE.

Obtaining a listing

7.9 The application procedure is quite lengthy and detailed. A brief summary of the basic requirements of a company which wishes to be listed are as follows. Note that not just UK companies can apply, listing is open to international companies as well, and a company can be listed on more than one stock exchange.

(a) Sponsorship. An applicant must be represented by an approved sponsor, e.g. a merchant bank.

(b) It must have a three-year trading record. There are, however, a few exceptions to this.

(c) The percentage of shares to be offered to the public must be at least 25% and equity capitalisation should be in excess of £700,000.

(d) There should be no controlling shareholders as this may represent a conflict of interest. Discussion with the LSE will be required if a controlling shareholder owns 30% or more of the company.

(e) A prospectus for potential investors must be prepared.

7.10 When a company is applying for listing, the particulars must be advertised in at least two newspapers, including a national paper. Usually they will be in all the main newspapers, e.g. Daily Telegraph, The Times, Financial Times, etc. The details must include the following information:

- A statement that the particulars have been submitted to the Registrar of Companies

- A statement that application has been made to be listed on the stock exchange

- Details of the history, principal activities and planned development of the company

- Management details of the company, including names and roles of directors, details of their service contracts and shareholdings

- Capital structure and capital history of the company, including the company's and the director's borrowing powers

- The price at which shares are being issued

- An analysis of the company's assets and liabilities, and financial position, including information on the results of the previous three years and a statement as to the adequacy of working capital

- Details of any major contracts the company has entered into

- Purpose of the share issue and how the capital raised is to be used

- Names and addresses of the company's auditors, bankers, legal advisers and issue sponsors

Setting a price for a new issue

7.11 Company directors will follow the direction of the listing sponsor in setting the price. The sponsor will use analysts to look at market trends to determine the potential demand. If the share price is set too low, the company will have lost out on the extra capital which could have been raised by setting a higher price. If the share price is set too high, future prices will remain depressed for a while. The company will receive the capital they require because issue will be underwritten.

Ground rules

7.12 Once the relationship between the company and the London Stock Exchange has been established, a set of important regulations ("the ground rules") must be complied with. These rules are concerned with the obligations of the company to protect investors.

7.13 The first main obligation is that any price sensitive information (e.g. profits, dividends and new issues) must be notified to the LSE as soon as possible after the information has been decided. This information is then made available to investors (usually via brokers) through the Regulated News Service (RNS) information system of the Companies Announcement Office.

7.14 The second obligation to protect investors is concerned with insider dealing.

Insider dealing

7.15 The definition of insider dealing is trading shares on the basis of unpublished price-sensitive information obtained as part of a person's job.

7.16 A company employee may overhear information about a takeover and so sell his shares in the company. He will be guilty of insider dealing because the information had not been made public when he sold his shares. He would also be guilty of insider dealing if he told someone else this information and that third party acted upon it.

7.17 It is a criminal offence to be involved in insider dealing and the Criminal Justice Act 1993 contains the legislation to deal with this. One of the most risky areas for this crime involves key personnel within a company, particularly directors, who know a great deal of information in advance which could have a major impact on a company's share price. Therefore, they are restricted as to when they can buy and sell shares in their company, and this time is limited to 'dealing windows', usually the periods immediately after the price-sensitive information has been published. They are prohibited from dealing in their company shares for the two months up to this publication date.

Detection and prosecution

7.18 All share transactions are monitored by the LSE enabling it to identify unusual transactions which may be due to insider dealing. Prosecution will be instigated by the Department of Trade and Industry or the London Stock Exchange. Penalties range from fines to up to seven years imprisonment.

8 The Alternative Investment Market

8.1 The Unlisted Securities Market (USM) was set up in 1980 to allow newer companies (only a two-year trading record) to raise capital via a share issue, but without having to meet all the listing requirements. However, changes in regulations meant that the USM requirements were almost as complex as those for a full listing, and no new entrants were accepted after 1994. The USM is due to be closed at the end of 1996.

8.2 The Alternative Investment Market (AIM) was launched in June 1995 to replace the USM. The purpose of AIM is to allow smaller, younger and developing companies to raise capital and trade their shares without having to fulfil all the LSE listing regulations. The cost of belonging to AIM is lower than being admitted to the Official List, and the rules and application process are as simple as possible. Companies have certain ongoing obligations such as publishing interim and annual accounts, and providing price-sensitive information.

The conditions for entry to the AIM are:

(a) The company is a legally constituted public company. This includes non-UK companies.

(b) The company must have published accounts which meet UK accounting standards.

(c) The securities traded on AIM are freely transferable.

(d) The company must adopt a code of share dealings for its directors and key employees.

(e) Where the company's main activity has been earning revenue for less than two years, the directors must agree not to dispose of their interest in the company for a further 12 months.

(f) The company must retain the services of a nominated adviser and a nominated broker at all times. The adviser can assist the company in complying with AIM rules. The broker must be a member of the stock exchange, and must try to match buyers and sellers of the company shares. Investors should be reassured that at least one broker will always trade in that company's shares.

8.3 A prospectus must be issued giving full details of:

• The company

• Financial information about the company

• Management details, including information on the company directors

• Substantial shareholders (more than 10% of the company's votes)

• A statement that the company is satisfied that it has sufficient working capital to meet its present requirements

9 Dealing

9.1 The term dealing is used to describe events which take place when a customer wishes to buy or sell shares. Once the deal has been made, it is 'settled' by transfer of ownership to the buyer and payment to the seller by the buyer.

9.2 Deals and settlements are made on behalf of investors by brokers and market makers who must be members of the LSE. There is a set of rules which they must abide by. They must also follow the rules of the Securities and Futures Authority (SFA).

Stockbrokers

9.3 Stockbrokers act both as brokers and dealers. In their capacity as brokers, they act as agent for their customers, buying and selling shares on their behalf. They are able to offer a variety of services, the most straightforward of which is a dealing or execution-only service, carrying out the customer's instructions to buy or sell shares but not offering any advice. Alternatively, they may provide investment advice on the merits of buying, selling or holding particular shares.

9.4 Brokers also provide portfolio management services. A discretionary service enables the stockbroker to buy and sell investments without consulting the investor on each transaction. The investor will receive a regular report on how the portfolio is progressing. Non-discretionary management of a portfolio requires the agreement and instructions from the investor before any investments are bought or sold.

9.5 Stockbrokers acting as dealers buy and sell shares for their own business. This is known as 'running their own book' .The aim of this is to make a profit for the business by careful timing of transactions and choice of stock.

Market makers

9.6 Market makers are firms which quote prices for certain shares. They buy and sell the shares and 'make a market' in the shares they have chosen. They make their profit from the difference between the bid and offer prices in the shares in which they deal. They must maintain their quotes, and stockbrokers wishing to deal in a particular share will know who the relevant market makers are. The more popular shares will have a larger number of market makers. When a firm wishes to become a market maker in a particular stock, it must give notice to the stock exchange and this will become effective the following day. Gilt-edged market makers need Bank of England approval before registering on the stock exchange.

Regulations

9.7 The regulatory duties of those involved in the dealing process include the provision of 'Chinese Walls' and money laundering procedures.

Chinese Walls

9.8 The Compliance Officer of a large securities house has a regulatory duty to ensure that there are adequate 'Chinese Walls' in place within the organisation. These are meant to separate the different functions to ensure that price-sensitive information is not passed on to the market makers or brokers. An example of this would be where a firm's analysts passed on details of a particular company's prospectus to the market-making department before telling their customers. Criminal proceedings may arise from breaches of these regulations.

Money laundering

9.9 Money laundering is the process of making "dirty" money "clean". Dirty money can be generated by the following crimes: drug trafficking, terrorism, theft, tax evasion, burglary, criminal deception, forgery, handling stolen goods, blackmail and extortion.

9.10 The three stages of money laundering are:

(a) Placement - exchange cash for other form, e.g. insurance bond, unit trust, Pep, gilts.

(b) Layering - to separate the funds from their original source a number of transactions are used, e.g. buying a Pep and then cancelling it within cooling-off period for a refund. The refund is then used to purchase something else, e.g. equities.

(c) Integration - the funds are then cashed in to remove the money from the system, having "cleaned" it. No-one should suspect its origin.

9.11 As well as carrying out the transactions, it is also a criminal offence to assist, tip-off or fail to report a knowledge or suspicion of money laundering.

9.12 All financial institutions have a responsibility, under the UK Money Laundering Regulations 1993 and Criminal Justice Act 1993, to identify suspicious transactions and report them. The institutions must appoint a Money Laundering Reporting Officer and set up procedures to verify customer identity and to report suspicious transactions. Failure to comply with the Money Laundering Regulations is a criminal offence.

9.13 This means that when an intermediary or broker is dealing with a customer's instructions to buy or sell shares, he must comply with his company's regulations.

10 Buying and Selling

10.1 An investor can buy or sell shares through a broker or through a bank or building society which has its own stockbroker or stockbroking firm.

10.2 The investor should explain exactly what he requires and the broker will then complete the following procedure. This procedure will also apply where an intermediary, e.g. member of bank staff, is taking instructions to then pass on to a stockbroker.

Broker's procedures

(a) He will check the customer's instruction to ensure it is clear, e.g. the customer instructs the broker to buy 2,000 shares in XYZ company. Does he mean 2,000 shares or £2,000 worth of shares?

(b) What type of shares does he require if XYZ company has more than one type?

(c) Clarify the company name. Is there more than one company with XYZ in its name? If so, establish which one the customer is referring to.

(d) What price does the customer want to buy at? He may specify 'at best', i.e. the lowest price at the time, or have a price limit above which the purchase should not take place.

(e) How long do the instructions last? The instruction may refer to one day, or over a longer period of time as a standing instruction to continue buying the shares at a price below the limit set. This must be specified.

10.3 The broker, or intermediary, should also ensure that the customer has the funds to complete the purchase. Banks will have some knowledge of this for their own customers, but where a customer is not known, he may be asked to put the funds on deposit until settlement.

10.4 The procedures for an instruction to sell will be similar to those above. However, the broker or intermediary needs to be satisfied that the customer does own the shares and has the authority to sell them.

10.5 Once the broker is satisfied with the instructions, he must execute the deal as soon as possible to ensure that the customer gets the best price (either to buy at or sell at) as prices are changing constantly. If there is a delay, the customer may lose money.

Best execution

10.6 When acting as a broker, stockbrokers have a duty to obtain the highest available price when selling and the lowest price when buying. This is known as the best execution rule.

10.7 Stockbrokers make use of SEAQ to do this. SEAQ is the Stock Exchange Automated Quotations system and provides on-screen information to brokers on the current market prices for all listed shares. The best prices at any time are highlighted on SEAQ by a 'yellow strip'.

10.8 The following information is provided:

- Prices quoted by market makers

- Number of trades above £1,000

- Best bid and offer prices, and up to three market makers quoting this price

10.9 Both the LSE and SFA rulebooks contain regulations to ensure customers are given the best deal. A broking firm may only place an order with its own market-making department if it can prove that the price is better than any price offered elsewhere.

Placing the order

10.10 The broker will place the order with the market maker, quoting the best price, usually by telephone. The market maker must report the trade within three minutes to the stock exchange.

10.11 If the customer is only executing a small order, i.e. where the number of shares is lower than the normal market size, the broker will use SAEF (SEAQ Automatic Execution Facility). The broker enters the order into the system and it will automatically match the order against a market maker making the best price at the time. Market makers must indicate on SEAQ whether they are willing to match the best price currently on offer to accept a SAEF order or whether they will only accept an order if they are currently quoting the best bid or offer price.

10.12 The SAEF system immediately notifies both parties that they have traded and a report is generated automatically. This will take place within seconds.

10.13 There are also similar facilities such as the Best system established by Kleinwort Benson in 1987, and the Trade system, operated by BZW since 1988 which are in competition with SAEF. They take around 10% of orders.

Settlement

10.14 Settlement takes place when the investor pays for his shares or the broker pays out the proceeds from selling shares. The settlement date is five working days after the date of the transaction. Where a customer is buying shares, they will be registered in his name in return for payment of the purchase price (the consideration monies), plus the broker's commission and fees. Where the customer is selling shares, they must be passed to the market maker to forward to the buyer in return for the consideration monies. The broker will pass this on to the seller after deducting his commission and fees. All this is carried out by Talisman at present, but the system is being changed to Crest - see below.

Contract note

10.15 All sellers and buyers must receive a contract note detailing the transaction from the broker. There are LSE and SFA regulations regarding the information which must be shown on a contract note.

10.16 The contract note is evidence of the contract for sale or purchase between the customer and the broker. It is usually required for establishing capital gains tax liability. The information to be shown on a contract note is as follows:

- Name and address of the broking/dealing firm

- Names of the partners in the firm

- Whether the transaction was a purchase or a sale

- The number of shares or amount of stock

- The name of the company or authority, and the type of share or stock dealt in

- The price at which the bargain was done

- The consideration paid

- The commission charged by the broker/dealer

- The transfer stamp duty or stamp duty reserve tax (only on purchase)

- Contract levy

- The total cost of purchase or net proceeds of sale (whichever applies)

- The settlement date

- The contract date

- The customer's name

- The time of the deal

Stamp duty

10.17 The current rate is 0.5% of the consideration paid by the purchaser.

Contract levy (PTM levy)

10.18 This is used to finance the Panel for Takeovers and Mergers and is currently £2 for purchases or sales of equities where the consideration exceeds £10,000.

Ex dividend shares

10.19 When companies are due to pay out share dividends, they 'close their books' for a period prior to the payment date. During this period (normally 37 days) the shares are traded 'ex-div' .Anyone buying the shares does not have the right to the dividend which is due to be paid, this will go to the previous owner.

11   Talisman

11.1   Most securities listed on the London Stock Exchange are currently settled using the Talisman (Transfer Accounting Lodgement of Investors, Stock Management for principals) computer system. It is not used for settlement of new issues and gilts. However, the Talisman system is being replaced by the Crest system over a transitional period from July 1996 to April 1997. Details of Crest are given below.

11.2   Under Talisman when stock is sold, it is registered with SEPON Ltd (Stock Exchange Pool Nominees) which has an undesignated shareholding account for every company participating in the scheme. All sold stock is transferred from the seller into the 'pool' account. Buyers receive their stock when it is transferred out of the 'pool'.

11.3   Talisman has a separate account for each market maker dealing in the stock, and these record the movement of stock during the settlement process.

How settlement is made

11.4   Using the example of a stockbroker dealing with a sale on behalf of a customer, the process will be as follows:

- Broker gives customer a Talisman 'sold transfer' form to sign, recording details of the shares being sold

- Customer gives form and share certificate to broker

- Broker stamps 'sold transfer' form as valid and genuine

- Sends to Talisman centre where it is checked for 'good delivery' (i.e. that it is in good order, not a fraud, etc.)

- Talisman centre forwards form and share certificate to the company registrar to change registration from customer's name to SEPON

- Stock held in nominee account in SEPON until settlement (account) day

- On settlement day, the stock is transferred to the market maker's trading account by Talisman

- Selling broker receives payment from the Talisman centre (paid on behalf of market maker)

- Broker passes payment on to customer (less his fees, etc.)

11.5   When a broker is acting for a customer who is buying shares, he must register details of the buyer with the Talisman centre before settlement day.

11.6   A 'bought transfer' form is used to authorise the transfer of stock from the SEPON account into the buyer's name. The registrar will issue a new share certificate.

11.7   On settlement day, the movement of shares between the market maker's trading accounts and the broker's/dealer's accounts takes place. This is known as 'apportionment'.

11.8 During the whole process, the stock exchange acts as trustee of the stock, on behalf of the seller until settlement day, and then on behalf of the buyer. However, the legal title to the shares is passed to SEPON on registration.

12   Crest

12.1 Crest became operational on 15 July 1996. It is owned and operated by CrestCo Limited and provides a fully electronic means of transferring ownership of shares. It will replace the Talisman system over a nine month transitional period ending in April 1997.

12.2 CrestCo has been recognised as a recognised clearing house by the Securities and Investments Board (SIB) and anyone who sends instructions to Crest on behalf of someone else is carrying out investment business under the terms of the Financial Services Act 1986 and so must be authorised. CrestCo is made up of participants including small stockbrokers, settlement banks and market makers. It is owned by its shareholders.

12.3 Crest aims to reduce the settlement period to three days by autumn 1997 thus streamlining its operation and moving the London Stock Exchange in line with New York and Tokyo. Its main benefits will be seen by the institutions and the City. The effect on smaller private investors is not so favourable.

12.4 This is because the system is designed to do away with the need for share certificates and encourage investors to use nominee accounts. Under a nominee account, the shares are held on behalf of the investor by a stockbroker who deals with all the paperwork involved in running the account and will send dividend payments and tax credits to the investor. They can be used to hold equities, unit trusts, investment trusts and international stocks.

12.5 The main disadvantage is that the shares are registered in the name of the nominee company rather than the individual. This means that some companies who give perks to shareholders, such as Eurotunnel and P&O, do not offer them to investors who hold their shares in nominee accounts. These investors may also lose out on other offers and the right to receive information about annual meetings and rights issues. When an investor opens a nominee account he should find out whether he will lose out on these types of perks and whether he will have to pay for shareholder information to be sent to him.

12.6 Investors who want to have shares registered in their own name can become sponsored members. They must be sponsored by a full member of Crest such as a bank or stockbroker who will be charged £20 for every member they sponsor. Individuals are responsible for organising their own tax and dividend payment records. Because of this and the fact that the £20 will often be passed on to the investor by the sponsor, it is only the experienced active investors who are likely to choose this option.

12.7 Where individuals want to keep their share certificates they are entitled to do so but they will incur brokers' costs and be responsible for keeping their own records. It is likely that brokers will charge more for dealing with certificates and settlement could take a longer time. Also when these investors wish to sell their shares they may find they are less competitive.

12.8 Where individuals already have their shares in a nominee account they will notice little difference in the change to Crest. To be able to hold and transfer shares electronically other investors will have to open a nominee account with a stockbroker and transfer their shares into it by completing a transfer form, or alternatively, become a sponsored member. It should be noted that investors are not forced to use Crest and the move to nominee accounts is purely voluntary. However, it may be advantageous to do so.

12.9 If an investor buys shares through Crest he will still receive a contract note from the broker to confirm the purchase. If an investor retains his share certificates and wants to trade he will sign a Crest transfer form rather than a Talisman form. Brokers will keep supplies of these. When the investor buys shares he must tell the broker if he wants certificates. Investors are covered by the Investors Compensation Scheme in the event of any loss arising due to failure of the Crest system.

12.10 The effects of the Crest system on private investors will not be fully known until the system has been running for a year or so. However, it is likely that investors will be forced into moving into nominee accounts as the costs and delays involved in dealing through the alternative methods will be prohibitive. It is likely that representations by the stockbroking industry to the government may influence the future treatment of shareholders' rights and perks and companies may be forced to give all shareholders the same treatment.

Student Activity 3

You should complete this student activity before reading the next section of the text. Answer the questions, then check your answers against the paragraph(s) indicated.

1. A customer holds his shares in a nominee account. How will he   (12.8)
    be affected by the change to Crest?

2. Why are company directors particularly at risk of becoming   (7.17)
    involved in insider dealing and what restrictions are in place to
    try and reduce this risk?

3. Why might a company want to be listed on the Alternative   (8.2)
    Investment Market?

4. A customer has asked you, as a member of staff of a   (10.2)
    stockbroking firm, to arrange the purchase of some shares.
    What information will you require before you can go ahead
    with the instruction?

If you are unable to answer any of the questions satisfactorily, you should read the relevant paragraphs again. Your understanding of the text will be further tested in the self-assessment section at the end of this unit.

13 Buying and Selling Gilts

13.1 Gilts are not listed on the London Stock Exchange as they are issued by the Bank of England through gilt-edged market makers (GEMMs). The GEMMs only deal in gilts and are often subsidiaries of larger securities houses.

13.2 Brokers can only obtain an indication of likely prices for a gilt from SEAQ and have to telephone the GEMMs for a quote. This can be a lengthy process because the broker must ensure the best price for his customer (best execution rule). The broker will charge the customer commission based on the consideration. As gilts can be dealt with to the nearest penny, this can be an advantage for customers who wish to invest a specific amount.

13.3 Institutional investors can deal direct with the GEMMs rather than going through a stockbroker.

13.4 Inter-dealer brokers (IDBs) are also involved in the gilt market by allowing market makers to deal indirectly with each other. One market maker may hold an unwanted block of a particular gilt which another market maker might want. An IDB can arrange a deal between both parties, keeping their identities unknown. IDBs also operate in the same way in the equities market.

13.5 Stock exchange money brokers (SEMBs) provide liquidity in the gilt market by lending and borrowing stock to and from the GEMMs.

How is settlement made?

13.6 Unlike the equity settlement procedure, there is no nominee account involved. A transfer form is completed, and includes space for the buying broker to indicate the name and address of his customer. The form and certificate are lodged with the Bank of England which records the transfer and issues a new certificate to the buyer. Settlement is in cash on the day following the transfer.

13.7 Some of the larger institutions, including banks and discount houses, together with the GEMMs, IDBs and SEMBs have computerised accounting facilities with the Bank of England's Central Gilts Office. This means transfers can be made without the need for transfer forms or other documentation.

National Savings Stock Register

13.8 Small investors will usually buy gilts through the National Savings Stock Register. This is covered in detail in Unit 13.

Buying and selling fixed-interest securities

13.9 Trading in other fixed-interest securities is similar to trading in gilts. Most GEMMs and some equity market makers will deal in fixed-interest securities. There is a five working day settlement period and again, like gilts, there is no nominee company involved.

Table 10.3: London Stock Exchange member firms

Statistics of member firms in 1994

Total	SEAQ Internat. makers	UK equity market makers	Gilt-edged market makers	Broker/ dealer agents
334	51	30	22	214

Source: London Stock Exchange Fact Book (1995)

14 The Stock Market Indicators

14.1 The stock market exists to deal in individual securities of the United Kingdom and as such involves itself with all major financial, commercial and industrial concerns in the UK, as well as British government stocks.

14.2 At any one time there are around 7,000 securities listed on the London Stock Exchange. All will have their own fluctuations but it was thought sensible to have an 'indicator' as to how the market was going at a particular point in time. This would show investors if the trend was up or down, giving an indication of the mood of the market.

14.3 There are several major indicators used in the United Kingdom which all stem from the Financial Times. Some are used to give a general indication of the market, e.g. the FT Ordinary Share Index, while others are used for analysing individual share or sector performance, e.g. FT-Actuaries All Share Index.

The main FT indices are as follows:

- **FT Ordinary Share:** 30 companies (calculated by hour)

- **FT-SE 100 Index:** 100 largest companies by market share (calculated each minute)

- **FT-SE Mid 250:** Next 250 companies after top 100 (calculated each minute)

- **FT-SE-A 350:** Combines FT-SE 100 and mid 250 (calculated each minute)

- **FT-SE Small Cap:** Reflects movements in share prices of between 500 and 600 small companies (calculated at end of day)

- **FT-SE All Share:** Over 900 securities - sub-divided into sectors (calculated at end of day)

- **FT/S&P Actuaries World Indices:** Nearly 2,400 world-wide companies, sub-divided into national and regional markets

The FT Ordinary (30 Share) Index

14.4 This was the first index to be calculated and started in 1935. It is an index of the shares of 30 leading British industrial, commercial and financial companies. These companies are chosen as being leaders in their field and represent a large proportion of the equity market. The index has been varied recently to include oil companies (e.g. BP), financial companies (Nat West

Bank and Royal Insurance) and privatisation issues (British Gas and BT).

14.5　The index is calculated by dividing the current share price of each member of the index by its base price (100). The geometric mean of the 30 figures is then calculated. Each price is given equal weight.

14.6　The index reflects movements in the stock market and has been criticised for underestimating the impact of changes in share prices. This is because of the effect of using a geometric mean rather than an arithmetical mean. However, its main use is to show the general trend in the stock market.

14.7　The index is calculated hourly and was 2694.5 at 4 p.m. on 30 July 1996. Since it began in 1935, its highest value was 2885.2 on 19 April 1996, and its lowest 49.4 on 26 June 1940.

Constituents of the FT Ordinary Share Index

- Allied-Lyons
- ASDA Group
- BICC
- Blue Circle Industries
- BOC Group
- Boots
- BP
- British Airways
- British Gas
- BT
- BTR
- Cadbury Schweppes
- Courtalds
- Forte
- General Electric
- Glaxo Holdings
- Grand Metropolitan
- GKN
- Guinness
- Hanson
- ICI
- Lucas Industries
- Marks & Spencer
- National Westminster Bank
- P & O

- Reuters

- Royal Insurance

- Smith Kline Beecham

- Tate and Lyle

- Thorn-EMI

Source - Financial Times

FT-SE 100 Index (Footsie)

14.8   This index was established in 1984 by the Financial Times (FT) and the stock exchange (SE), together with the Institute of Actuaries and the Faculty of Actuaries. (Hence the reference in the Financial Times to the FT/SE Actuaries Share Indices.)

14.9   The index consists of the 100 largest UK companies in terms of market share (70% of value of UK equities). The 100 companies are reviewed quarterly to ensure they are still representative, and will be removed if they drop below 111th position. A new one will be added if it reaches at least 90th position. The reason for this is to avoid constant changes in the member companies.

14.10 The FT-SE 100 Index was introduced because the FT30 is limited in the information it gives and the fact that it is calculated hourly. The FT-SE 100 is re-calculated continuously, each minute, between 8.00 a.m. and 4.30 p.m. Its base rate was set at 1000 and it was calculated at 3668.5 at close of business on 30 July 1996.

14.11 It is used for several different purposes, the main ones being:

- A basis for options and futures contracts

- A basis for index tracking funds marketed by a variety of institutions

- A benchmark to measure performance of individual portfolios

FT-SE Actuaries All Share Index

14.12 This is used as the yardstick to measure performance of an equity fund. It includes less than half the quoted companies but represents around 98% of the total market value of UK equities listed on the stock exchange. It is a weighted index as the larger companies have a relatively greater influence on the index if their share price alters.

14.13 The make up of sectors included is detailed in the Financial Times and includes over 900 companies.

FT-Actuaries World Indices

14.14 This is a weighted index based on the prices of around 2,200 equities of major companies from 24 countries, making up around 70% of the world's equity markets.

14.15 The Financial Times publishes indices for each country, for regional areas, e.g. the Pacific Basin, and an overall world index. The indices are quoted in dollars, sterling, yen and deutschmarks as well as the local currency.

14.16 The world indices are used to measure performance of international funds, such as specialist unit trusts.

World markets

14.17 The different indicators throughout the world do impact on each other as optimism or pessimism filters through to affect the day's trading on the other side of the world.

14.18 As well as quoting its own world indices described above, the Financial Times also quotes foreign stock market indices. The major foreign stock market indicators are the Dow Jones in the United States, the Nikkei Dow in Japan and the Hang Seng in Hong Kong.

Student Activity 4

You should complete this student activity before attempting the self-assessment. Answer the questions, then check your answers against the paragraph(s) indicated.

1. A customer instructs his broker that he wants to invest in a particular gilt. What procedure does the broker follow to ensure the best price? (13.2)

2. What does an inter-dealer broker do? (13.4)

3. A customer has invested in an index tracker Pep which is linked to changes in the FT-SE 100 Index.

    (a) What types of company make up the FT-SE 100 index? (14.9)

    (b) What is the purpose of the index? (14.11)

    (c) What makes the index rise and fall? (14.9)

    (d) Does the customer have any guarantee that the index will have risen in the future when he wants to cash in his Pep?

If you are unable to answer any of the questions satisfactorily, you should read the relevant paragraphs again. Your understanding of the text will be further tested in the following self-assessment.

Summary

Now that you have completed this unit you should be able to:

❑ **Explain how an investment portfolio should be structured**

❑ **Understand the customer specific influences on investment choice**

❑ **Understand the types of risk and their effects on investment choice**

❑ **Rank investments in order of risk and suitability for different customer attitudes to risk**

❑ **Understand the types of reward investments offer**

❑ **Explain the effects of inflation and interest rates on investment return**

❑ **Know how shares become listed and are bought and sold on the LSE**

❑ **Understand how small investors are affected by Crest**

❑ **Know what is traded on AIM**

❑ **Know how gilts are bought and sold**

❑ **Know the main types of stock market indicators**

If you can tick all the above boxes with confidence, you are ready to answer the questions which follow.

Self-Assessment Questions

1. What types of investment would you recommend to a cautious investor?

2. You have ensured that a customer has an adequate emergency fund and are now looking at medium-term needs. What considerations should you take into account when selecting appropriate investment types?

3. George Smith has a great deal of capital and wants to speculate on the stock market by investing in shares of companies in developing countries. What types of risk is he exposing his investment to?

4. Sarah Randall is a basic rate taxpayer currently receiving a net income from dividends of around £3,000 a year. If she becomes a higher rate taxpayer how much will this reduce her dividend income by?

5. What factors can erode the capital value of an investment?

6. Why may a company want to be listed on the London Stock Exchange?

7. How does a stockbroker use a market maker?

8. Alan Morris is making his first share purchase. He is using a nominee account run by a stockbroker.

   (a) Within how many days will the settlement be made?

   (b) Will Alan receive any share certificates?

   (c) Who will be named as the share owner?

   (d) Who will Alan receive his dividends from?

9. An investor has a large shareholding in food retailing companies. How could he use the FT-SE All Share Index to track the market risk of his investment?

10. Why were the stock market indicators introduced?

Unit 11

Analysing Equities

Objectives

Students are required to study the following topics:

- **Fundamental analysis**
- **Net asset value**
- **Gearing**
- **Investment ratios**
- **Technical analysis**
- **Chartism**
- **Sources of information**

1   Introduction

1.1   The main objectives of investment analysis are to establish the characteristics of an investment and its suitability for a particular investor; and to establish whether a security is cheap or dear in relation to other investments and whether it should be bought, sold or held at any given time. This unit will concentrate on the latter objective with regard to equity investments. Methods which would enable an investor to analyse securities with a fixed-interest yield and redemption date, such as gilts and company fixed-interest securities are covered in later units.

1.2   The analysis of equities is a difficult task since their performance depends on the fortunes of the underlying company. The information available to support such analysis can come from a variety of sources and can be interpreted through fundamental analysis or technical analysis.

1.3   Briefly, fundamental analysts look forward; they are concerned with the future earnings and dividends of a share and the risk attached to them, while technical analysts look backwards, basing their analysis on past patterns in price movements.

2   Fundamental Analysis

2.1   The information derived from fundamental analysis can help an investor to compare the return from an ordinary share with the return from a fixed-interest stock. A fundamental analyst will aim to assemble all the necessary published information needed to estimate the true or intrinsic value of a share for the purpose of comparing it with the market value of the share.

The share is deemed 'dear' if the market value is above the true value or 'cheap' if the market value is below the true value. Fundamentalists believe that the true value of the share is represented by the value of all the dividends the investor can expect to receive. This approach, of course, has one main disadvantage in that it is difficult to forecast individual dividends. In addition, a discount factor has to be applied to future dividends to reflect their buying power as a result of inflation. To make this method credible, an assumption must be made of the future growth and discount rates.

2.2 Rather than relying solely on this approach, many analysts will endeavour to get to know a company thoroughly. The annual report and accounts are the major source of information on a public limited company, although the analyst will want to assess the management of the company and the market sector within which the company conducts its business. Further to this, the analyst will want to forecast the company's profits in future years and compare them with other companies in the same industry.

2.3 In order to practise these methods of valuation, the analyst will need to extract figures from both the company's balance sheet and the profit and loss account.

3 Net Asset Value

3.1 The net asset value of a share compared with the market value can be a good indicator of whether the company will earn an acceptable return on capital, or that it will be liquidated, or become the object of a takeover bid.

3.2 There are two ways of calculating the net asset value; the book value or the break up value.

Book value

3.3 The 'book value' or 'balance sheet value' of the net asset value per share is the value of the ordinary shareholders' assets after deduction of prior claims on liquidation, for example, secured and unsecured creditors and preference shareholders. Analysts will generally pay little attention to the 'book value' considering it to be unreflective of the exact value of the underlying assets. In the following example balance sheet, the book value of Beaumont Plc is £710 million.

Example 11.1: Balance sheet for Beaumont Plc as at 31.12.95

	£m	£m
Fixed assets		
Intangible assets		
Goodwill		100
Tangible assets		
Land and buildings		250
Plant and machinery		250
Investments		50
		650

Current assets

Stock and work-in-progress	400	
Debtors	250	
Cash	75	
	725	

Less Creditors due for payment within one year

Bank overdraft	75	
Trade creditors	300	
Current taxation	40	
Proposed final dividend	25	
	440	

Net current assets		285
Total assets less current liabilities		935

Less creditors due after one year

-7% loan capital		225
	Net assets	710

Capital and reserves

200m ordinary £1 shares fully paid	200	
Share premium account	50	
Other reserves	460	
Ordinary shareholders' interest		710

Break up value

3.4 A company in liquidation may find that many of its assets will not realise their balance sheet value. For example, the value of a factory might be very much higher as a going concern than as an empty building. Similarly, trade investments in the balance sheet may be more or less than that shown, a situation which can arise with many balance sheet items. Conversely, property may be entered with its historic cost and may realise more than its book value. Therefore, the break up value, or liquidation value of a company will always be seriously considered by analysts. The example below illustrates that if the current and fixed assets of Beaumont Plc realised only £535 million against their balance sheet value of £1.375 million, then the break up value of the share would be £2.68, compared with a book value of £3.55.

Example 11.2: Beaumont Plc - net asset values

	Book Value £m	Break-up Value £m
Fixed assets	650	
Current assets	725	
	1,375	1,200
Less creditors		
within 1 year	440	440
after 1 year	225	225
Net assets	710	535
Net asset value per share	710,000,000	535,000,000
(200m ordinary shares)	200,000,000	200,000,000
	= £3.55 per share	£2.68 per share

3.5 These figures are, of course, only appropriate when a company faces liquidation. When considering the value of a share in a takeover situation, the analyst may assess the company's assets on a replacement basis, a calculation which would require specialist information and is beyond the scope of this unit.

4 Gearing

4.1 Gearing measures the ratio of borrowed funds to overall capital and shows the relationship between the company's creditors and its shareholders. The creditors and preference shareholders must receive their interest payments and dividends before any payment can be made to the ordinary shareholders. Indeed, some creditors may hold a charge over certain of the company's assets which they can call on if interest payments are not met; this could be catastrophic for a company. Gearing is, of course, a voluntary risk in the sense that a company could have a clean balance sheet, i.e. no borrowed funds, but most companies would argue that the risk attached to gearing justifies the enhanced return to shareholders. Provided that the company can earn a higher return on its total assets than the servicing costs of its borrowing, then gearing remains positive. The following example illustrates both the pros and cons of gearing.

Example 11.3: The effect of gearing

Sparkes Electronics has 400,000 £1 ordinary shares in issue and £200,000 worth of 7½% loan capital. The following table illustrates the effect of gearing over a five-year period.

	Profits Before Interest Payments Deducted £	Fixed- Interest Payments £	Profit/(Loss) £	Pre-Tax Profit/(Loss) Per Share Pence
Year 1	11,000	15,000	(4,000)	(1p)
Year 2	27,000	15,000	12,000	3p
Year 3	51,000	15,000	36,000	9p
Year 4	91,000	15,000	76,000	19p
Year 5	111,000	15,000	96,000	24p

In year 1 the ordinary shareholders suffer a loss of 1p per share. Between years 2 and 5 the company's profits increase over four fold; however the returns to shareholders increase by eight fold, after the payment of the fixed-interest charge.

4.2 The gearing ratio of a company is commonly estimated using the following formula:

Loan Capital - Cash
Net Asset Value of Ordinary Shareholders

4.3 So, for example, JVZ Plc has loan stock of £220m, cash of £65m and total net assets of £500m, and a gearing ratio of:

$$\frac{£220m - £65m}{£500m} = \frac{£155m}{£500m} \times 100 = 31:1 \ (31\%)$$

4.4 Gearing calculations must also include any bank loans and/or preference share issues, if applicable, together with the loan capital.

4.5 JVZ Plc does not have a particularly high level of gearing, some companies will pitch gearing at over 100%.

5 Liquidity

5.1 A prime concern of analysts is the liquidity of the company. Most companies will make use of short-term revolving credit from banks and trade creditors to accommodate fluctuation in their cash flow and will continue to enjoy this facility provided that the lenders are confident that the company is trading profitably and able to meet its debts. There are two methods of evaluating a company's liquidity, the current ratio and the liquid ratio and the analyst will compare one company's ratios with other companies in the same industry.

Current ratio

5.2 The current ratio is calculated by dividing current assets by current liabilities and indicates the extent to which the claims of the bank and trade creditors are covered by assets that are expected to be realised during the next year. For Beaumont Plc, the current ratio is:

$$\frac{£725m}{£440m} = 1.65 : 1$$

5.3 A current ratio of 1.5:1 is considered acceptable, although the nature of a company's business will be influential in deciding an acceptable level. For example, large chain stores where the turnover of stock is brisk will manage on a lower ratio while companies who traditionally experience delays between the receipt of an order and payment will require greater liquidity.

5.4 The disadvantage of this method is that it treats all current assets as being equally liquid.

Liquid ratio

5.5 The liquid asset ratio excludes stocks and other non-liquid assets from the calculation. Stock is likely to be the least liquid of a company's assets and a company will need to maintain a certain level of stock to trade effectively. For Beaumont Plc, the liquid ratio is:

$$\frac{\text{Current Assets - Stock}}{\text{Current Liabilities}} = \frac{£725m - £400m}{£440m} = 0.74:1$$

5.6 The traditionally acceptable value for the liquid ratio of a company is 1:1.

6 Cash Flow

6.1 A cash flow statement will enable the analyst to assess whether a company is in a position to meet its liabilities or whether it will have to sell assets or borrow from a bank to meet these commitments or sustain its growth intentions.

6.2 Cash flow is calculated by adding the retained profits to the depreciation charge. Such figures can be extracted from a company's profit and loss account.

Example 11.4: Minster Plc - Profit and loss account for the year ended 31 December 1995:

	£(000s)	£(000s)
Turnover		4,000
Less cost of sales		2,000
Gross profit		2,000
Less distribution costs	328	
Administrative expenses	600	
Depreciation	200	1,128
		872
Less interest paid		72
Profit before tax		800
Taxation		
- on UK profits	106	
- on overseas profits	158	264
Net Profit after taxation		536
Less ordinary dividend		
(10p per share 2m in issue)		200
Retained profit for the year		336
Retained profit brought forward		250
Retained profit carried forward		586

The cash flow for Minster Plc is:
Net profit retained + depreciation
£336,000 + £200,000 = £536,000

Thus the cash flow is representative of the company's savings during the year and the funds available for expansion projects and reinvestment.

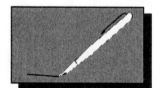

Student Activity 1

You should complete this student activity before reading the next section of the text. Answer the questions, then check your answers against the paragraph(s) indicated.

1. Why is the break up value of a company usually different from the book value? (3.3, 3.4)

2. Calculate the gearing ratio of RHA Construction plc. It has loan stock of £300m, cash of £100m and a net asset value of £650m. (4.2, 4.3)

3. Why should a company with a quick turnover of goods be able to manage on a lower current ratio than a company with a slower turnover? (5.3)

If you are unable to answer any of the questions satisfactorily, you should read the relevant paragraphs again. Your understanding of the text will be further tested in the self-assessment section at the end of this unit.

7 Earnings

7.1 Earnings is the term used to describe the profits earned by the ordinary shareholders. Companies will often produce figures to reflect the increase in profits and the net asset value per share for the purpose of impressing shareholders. Earnings are generally expressed as net profits after payment of tax, less preference share dividends and minority interests. Extraordinary costs, for example losses due to currency fluctuations in a country where a subsidiary operates, are excluded from the calculations as they distort the picture.

7.2 Analysts will generally place more importance on the expected future earnings of a company than on the past year's earnings, even though an increase in such earnings will have the effect of increasing the net asset value per share. A company which maintains a healthy dividend against a falling level of earnings may find that the situation for its shareholders becomes unsatisfactory in future years. On the other hand, a company which pays a small dividend and retains the majority of its earnings for future projects can expect healthy share prices and earnings for its shareholders in the future.

7.3 Whether a share performs well, or not, will only become apparent over a period of time. To perform well, the ordinary share will be expected to yield a return that is comparable with the average return of a long-dated gilt plus, of course, an additional return to reflect the greater risk attached to direct investment in ordinary shares.

7.4 The definition of earnings can be further broken down, when the impact of taxation is taken into account, into nil, net and full or maximum earnings.

Nil earnings

7.5 Nil earnings represent the net profit of the company, available for the ordinary shareholders, after the payment of corporation tax. From the example, Minster Plc, the nil earnings are £536,000. Whatever size of dividend the company decides to pay, the nil earnings figure remains unaffected. This basis, however, is little used.

Net earnings

7.6 When a company pays a net dividend to a shareholder, it has deducted advance corporation tax (ACT) at a rate of 20% of the gross dividend. This represents part payment of the company's full corporation tax liability at the current rate of 33% (1996-97). However, a maximum limit is imposed on the amount of ACT that can be offset in this way. For this reason, net earnings are expressed as nil earnings less unrelieved ACT.

7.7 The maximum amount of ACT that can be offset, for Minster Plc, is as follows:

$$\frac{\text{ACT Rate}}{\text{Corporation tax rate}} \quad \text{x} \quad \text{Actual corporation tax}$$

$$\frac{20\%}{33\%} \quad x\ £106,000 = £64,242$$

The actual ACT due is:

$^{20}/_{80}$ths x £200,000 = £50,000

7.8 From these examples, it can be seen that Minster Plc will have no unrelieved ACT, therefore nil and net earnings are the same figure.

Full or maximum earnings

7.9 Full or maximum earnings are defined as the sum of the nil earnings plus the maximum amount of recoverable ACT. Full earnings are used when calculating investment ratios, as detailed in the following paragraphs. For Minster Plc, the full earnings are:

	£
Nil earnings, plus	536,000
Maximum amount* of recoverable ACT	50,000
Full earnings	586,000

* from ACT calculation above

8 Investment Ratios

8.1 The calculation of four main investment ratios can enable analysts to look at share prices and dividends in a number of ways.

Gross dividend yield

8.2 Gross dividend yield calculations are normally based on the latest annual dividend paid, interim and final. The formula is:

Gross Dividend Yield = $\frac{\text{Grossed-Up Dividend per Share}}{\text{Market Price per Share}}$ x 100%

8.3 When a dividend is declared, it is declared 'net' of the tax credit which the shareholder receives. Therefore, in order to apply the above formula, the 'net' dividend has to be grossed up at the current rate of advance corporation tax, i.e. 20%. For example, if Minster Plc declares a dividend per share of 10p and the current market price of the share is £3.20, then the gross dividend yield would be:

$$\frac{10p \times 100/(100-20)}{£3.20} \times 100\% = 3.91\%$$

8.4 The gross dividend can also be extracted from this calculation as:

10p x 100/(100-20) = 12½p

8.5 Fluctuations in the average gross dividend yield of a cross-section of major equities are measured by the FT-Actuaries All-Share Index. The index is said to be 'cheap' when the yield is over 5% and 'dear' when the yield is under 4%.

8.6 A high gross dividend yield for an individual company's shares does not automatically mean that the shares are 'cheap' - remember that a high yield is often associated with high risk. Thus the reasons for a high yield could be that dividends are likely to be reduced or not paid; or that the prospect of a dividend rise is small; or that profits are likely to fall or the company is about to make a loss.

8.7 Conversely, a low yield may suggest that the current share price is relatively high when compared with current profits, with the expectation of increased profits and dividends over the next few years.

8.8 The gross dividend yield enables an investor to compare the current return on his investment with other securities, for example, the gross interest yield on gilts.

8.9 Historically, and with adjustments for inflation, the returns on ordinary shares have by far exceeded interest payments from building society accounts. As a historic measure, the calculation of gross dividend yield is accurate; however, it fails to make allowances for the total profits available to the ordinary shareholders.

Earnings yield

8.10 The earnings yield is regarded as a more accurate measure of the shareholders' returns since it calculates the potential dividend yield, i.e. the dividend yield assuming that all the profits are distributed to shareholders. Therefore, using the example for Minster Plc, the calculation of the earnings yield is similar to that of the gross dividend yield but substituting full earnings for dividends:

$$\frac{£586,000}{£6,400,000 \text{ (2 million shares @ £3.20 each)}} \times 100 = 9.16\%$$

8.11 Alternatively, this calculation can be calculated per share, as follows:

$$\frac{\text{Full Earnings per Share}}{\text{Share Price}} = \frac{£586,000/2m}{£3.20} \times 100 = 9.16\%$$

Dividend cover

8.12 The dividend cover represents the number of times a dividend is covered by the company's full earnings. A low cover level may suggest that the current level of dividend cannot be maintained while a cover level of less than 1 suggests that the dividend is being paid out of past retained profits. This may certainly be the case where a company is paying a dividend that exceeds that year's full earnings. For Minster Plc the dividend cover is calculated as follows:

$$\frac{\text{Full Earnings}}{\text{Grossed-Up Net Dividend*}} = \frac{£586,000}{£250,000} = 2.34 \text{ times}$$

*(£200,000 /0.80)

8.13 The higher the dividend cover, the greater the security of the dividend. Of course, if a company makes a loss, the calculation cannot be carried out for that particular year.

Price/earnings (P/E) ratio

8.14 The P/E ratio is used to show how well a share is doing in relation to the rest of the market. It is calculated as the market share price divided by the company's nil or net earnings. The Financial Times uses net earnings per share to calculate P/E ratios. For Minster Plc, the P/E ratio using both nil and net earnings is the same:

Nil/Net Earnings

$$\frac{\text{Share price}}{\text{Earnings}} = \frac{320p}{(£536,000 / 2m)} = \frac{320p}{26.8p}$$

$$= 11.94 \text{ times}$$

8.15 A high ratio, e.g. 20, 25 or more, indicates that a share is doing well and can be expected to increase in value in the future. These shares will be relatively more expensive, but have greater growth potential.

8.16 A low ratio, e.g. around 3.5 or 4, indicates poor prospects or that the market has doubts about a share. A period of high inflation will produce lower P/E ratios as future dividends will be worth less in real terms.

8.17 P/E ratios should be used to compare shares within a sector, rather than across the market.

8.18 Fluctuations in P/E ratios and dividend yields over a lengthy period are charted in the Financial Times FT-Actuaries 500 Share Index.

Reverse yield gap

8.19 The concept of the reverse yield gap compares the guaranteed return on gilts with equities. At any one time, it is the measure of the minimum required growth in the current market price of a share, and its dividend, to compensate for the shortfall in immediate returns. Generally, the wider the reverse yield gap, the greater the attraction of gilts.

8.20 It is usually measured by taking the gross redemption yield on a 20 year high coupon gilt and deducting the FT-Actuaries All-Share Index dividend yield. Both figures are published daily in the financial papers. Unit 13 covers gilts in more detail.

9 Income Gearing

9.1 Income ratios measure directly the ability of a company to pay the interest on its borrowed funds, for example, debentures and loan stocks. The two most common types of income ratio are:

- Interest cover

- Income priority percentages

Interest cover

9.2   The extent to which a company's profits can decline before it is unable to meet its borrowing costs can be calculated as follows:

$$\frac{\text{Interest}}{\text{Cover}} = \frac{\text{Profit Before Interest and Tax}}{\text{Gross interest payments}}$$

For Minster Plc interest cover is:

$$\frac{£872,000}{£72,000} = 12.11 \text{ times}$$

9.3   This calculation therefore shows that the profits of Minster Plc could fall to just less than one-twelfth of the current level before interest payments would have to be met out of capital.

Income priority percentages

9.4   Income priority percentages (IPPs) show the particular slice of a company's total profits that is used to remunerate a specific stock in order of priority.

Example 11.5: Income priority percentages

ABC Plc has the following three ranked claims on its income:

Loan interest £134,925 (net cost £90,400*)

Preference share dividend £37,500

Ordinary share dividend £127,500

Retained profits of £900,000 make up the balance.

* The net cost of the loan interest assumes corporation tax relief at 33% so that interest payments, which are paid out of pre tax profits, and dividend payments, which are paid out of post tax profits, can be compared on a like basis.

Income Priority Percentages

	£	%	Cumulative %	Overall Income Cover
Loan interest	90,400	7.82	7.82	12.78
Preference dividend	37,500	3.25	11.07	9.03
Ordinary dividend	127,500	11.04	22.11	4.52
Retained profit	900,000	77.89	100.00	1.00
Total profits	1,155,400	100.00		

Income priority percentages are illustrated on a cumulative basis because each 'claim' cannot be settled until the claim or claims that rank ahead of it have been fully covered

9.5   Such calculations will give an indication to the investor of the security of the income payments for different classes of capital and will enable him to compare, for example, similar ordinary shares issued by different companies. The shares may be currently paying a similar level of dividend but one may appear far more secure than the other if its income cover is higher.

10 Capital Gearing

10.1 Earlier in this unit, the effect of gearing and the impact it could have on the dividend paid to an ordinary shareholder was considered. This paragraph briefly looks at a different approach of measuring a company's capital gearing, known as capital priority percentages. Using this approach, it is possible to calculate the capital priority percentages for each type of capital on a cumulative basis. The example below illustrates what percentage of assets belong to different classes of capital, in descending order of priority.

Example 11.6: Capital priority percentages

The capital structure of company XYZ Plc is:

8% Debentures £500,000

4% Preference shares £250,000

Ordinary shares and reserves £2,500,000

Capital priority percentages

	£	%	Cumulative %	Overall Capital Cover
8% Debentures	500,000	15.38	15.38	6.50
4% Preference shares	250,000	7.69	23.07	4.33
Ordinary shares and reserves	2,500,000	76.93	100.00	1.00
	3,250,000			

Capital priority percentages are illustrated on a cumulative basis since each class of capital is ranked and cannot be redeemed, for example on liquidation, until capital with a prior ranking has been covered.

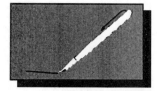

Student Activity 2

You should complete this student activity before reading the next section of the text. Answer the questions, then check your answers against the paragraph(s) indicated.

The AZ International plc has just declared a gross dividend on its ordinary shares of 25p. It has 1.5 million shares. The current market share price is £4.50 and the company has net profit available for distribution of £800,000. Calculate the following ratios and explain what each one could tell you about AZ shares.

(a) Gross dividend yield

(8.2)

(b) Earnings yield

(8.10)

(c) Dividend cover

(8.12)

(d) Price/earnings ratio

(8.14)

If you are unable to answer any of the questions satisfactorily, you should read the relevant paragraphs again. Your understanding of the text will be further tested in the self-assessment section at the end of this unit

11   Technical Analysis

11.1   Technical analysis involves the study of stock exchange information mainly in the form of price and volume data. It concentrates solely on market information, and uses historic information about shares and indices to assess whether a share is cheap or dear at its current market price. It is used by a minority of investors.

11.2   Chartism is the main form of technical analysis and is based on the belief that share prices trace out patterns over time. The patterns reflect investor behaviour and chartists believe that, if a certain pattern of activity produced a certain result, a similar pattern now should produce similar results in the future. After identifying patterns, analysts make investment decisions based on estimated probability.

12   Types of Chart

12.1   The three main forms of chart which plot the movement of the prices of individual shares and market indices are:

* Line charts

* Bar charts

* Point and figure charts

12.2   Share prices can be plotted on either an arithmetic scale, which is calibrated in equal sections for equal absolute changes, or a logarithmic scale which is calibrated in equal sections for equal percentage changes. The different scales used will produce different charts for the same information.

Line charts

12.3   A line connects the actual closing prices of a share, or the average prices over a week or month, for a period. A moving average (ma) is often used to smooth out fluctuations; this is calculated as follows for a four-day moving average:

Share price

Day One	60p
Day Two	52p
Day Three	53p
Day Four	55p
Day Five	48p

Ma days 1-4, ma = $\frac{220}{4}$ = 55p

Ma days 2-5, ma = $\frac{208}{4}$ = 52p

12.4   An example of a line chart is given below. The index for the appropriate market sector is often plotted on the same chart.

Example 11.7: Line chart (using arithmetic scale)

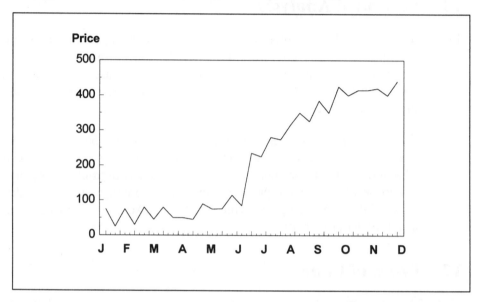

Bar charts

12.5   A bar chart shows the lowest and highest prices a share reaches each week, joined by a vertical line or bar. These charts usually try to show the volume of business each week in the share, along the bottom of the chart. Bar charts can often be found in a company's annual report to demonstrate movement in dividends and continuing earnings per share.

12.6   The example below illustrates the bar chart resulting from the following share price ranges:

	1995
Jan	60-72
Feb	70-79
Mar	65-70
Apr	70-78
May	77-80
June	65-80
July	77-80
Aug	66-78
Sep	70-79
Oct	62-67
Nov	70-71
Dec	62-74

Example 11.8: Bar chart

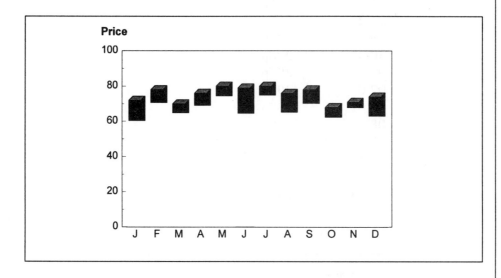

Example 11.9: Bar chart from a company's annual report

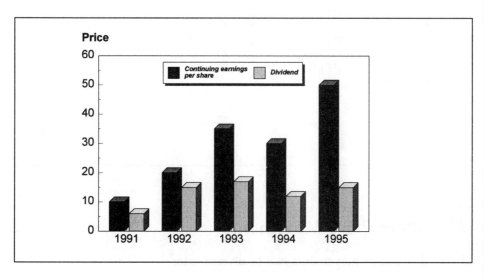

Point and figure charts

12.7 This type of chart does not use a time scale and only price movements are plotted. When the share price rises, a cross is plotted in a vertical column until the share price falls, when a circle is plotted in the next column. A new vertical column is started each time the share price movement changes direction, usually by three or more units (one unit may be a price change of one penny). Usually, the beginning of each month is indicated by the month number.

12.8 The example below illustrates how a point and figure chart works for the following figures:

Company Share Prices:

March   15-18   300p
        19   301p

	20	302p
	21-25	301p
	26-28	300p
	29	299p
	30-31	298p
April	01	297p
	02-03	296p
	04-07	297p
	08	298p
	09	299p
	10-15	300p
	16	299p
	17-18	298p

Example 11.10: Point and figure chart

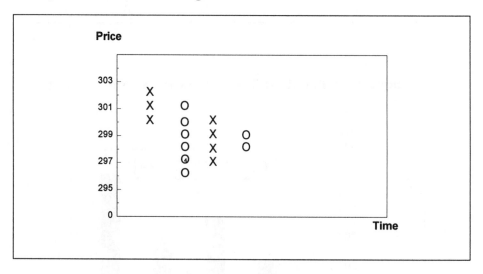

13 Share Price Movement

13.1 Share price movements can be divided into:

- Primary movements

- Secondary movements

- Tertiary movements

Primary movements

13.2 The chartists aim is to identify when a primary movement has occurred. A primary movement is a long-term trend over a period of several months, and is often made up of several secondary movements. An upward primary movement indicates to the chartist that the shares should be bought. A downward primary movement indicates the opposite.

Secondary movements

13.3 A secondary movement is a price movement lasting for a period of several weeks. If an upward secondary movement does not develop into an upward primary movement, it is known as a 'false dawn'.

Tertiary movements

13.4   These are day to day price movements and may become significant if they develop into secondary movements.

14   Chart Patterns

14.1   There are two main common trends which chartists have identified in line charts. These are called:

- Head and shoulders

- Support and resistance

Head and shoulders

14.2   This is probably the best known chart pattern and is illustrated below. The share price rises due to buying pressure from investors with specialist knowledge of the company and other investors following this lead. Some investors then decide to take the profit and the 'left shoulder' forms. There is then another upsurge when investors take advantage of the cheap share price and the 'head' forms. Buying support then becomes exhausted and the price falls again. A small increase in volume of deals then follows and results in the 'right shoulder'; however, this is usually short lived and the price falls again.

14.3   If the 'neckline' is broken, it signifies an important change in sentiment for the share and the start of a major decline in share price. Chartists usually expect the price to fall by an amount equivalent to the vertical distance from the top of the head to the neckline.

14.4   The head and shoulders pattern can also occur in reverse, in which case it is called a 'triple bottom formation' and the final break through the neckline indicates that shares should be bought.

Example 11.11: Head and shoulders

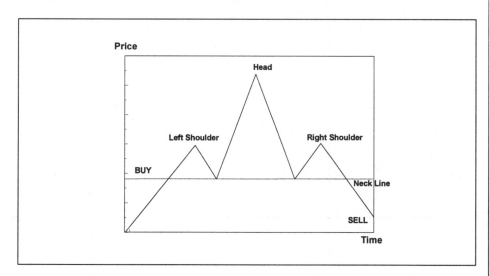

Support and resistance

14.5   A share price moves between two limits. The area between these two limits is called the 'consolidation area'. The consolidation area moves up or down over a period of time, depending on whether the share price rises or falls.

14.6   When the share price rises above the upper limit of the consolidation area, the consolidation area is called the 'support area'. Buyers keep buying the shares at a price near this upper limit so prevent the price dropping any lower.

14.7   If the share price falls below the lower limit, the consolidation area becomes known as the resistance area. The share price persistently fails to rise above this level and the price remains low. One of the reasons for this could be that investors saw the price fall and took the opportunity to sell shares at the price they previously paid.

Example 11.12: Support

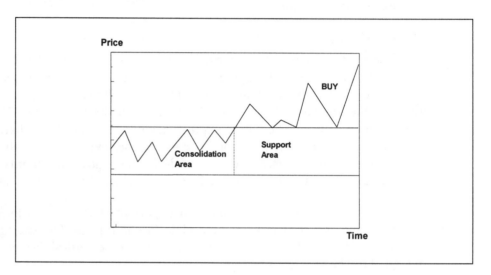

Example 11.13: Resistance

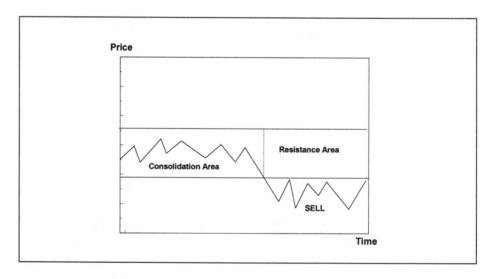

15   Efficient Market Hypothesis (EMH)

15.1   This hypothesis states that investors receive the best returns on a 'passively managed' portfolio. Passively managing a portfolio involves selecting a well balanced, diversified portfolio at outset and avoiding transaction costs by leaving the portfolio unaltered. It is the opposite method to 'actively managing' a portfolio.

15.2 The three forms of EMH are:

- Weak

- Semi-strong

- Strong

Weak form of EMH

15.3 This form of EMH emphasises the importance of fundamental analysis, which was described earlier, and the lack of importance of technical analysis. It believes that the market has already taken into account historical share price movements in the current share price, and that future share price movements will be random.

Semi-strong form of EMH

15.4 This form of the hypothesis states that both technical analysis and fundamental analysis results are already reflected in the share price.

Strong form of EMH

15.5 This form of EMH states that a passively managed portfolio produces the best returns, even if the investor has inside information.

16   Factors Affecting Share Prices

16.1 The influences on investment choice and performance were discussed in Unit 10. This section looks at the effect on share prices in particular.

16.2 The main effect on share prices is the law of supply and demand. If demand exceeds supply, the price rises; if supply exceeds demand, the price decreases.

16.3 There are three main groups of factors which affect supply and demand, as follows:

- General market factors

- Factors affecting particular sectors

- Factors affecting individual companies

General market factors

16.4 The four main general market factors which affect share prices are:

(a) **Interest rates**
An increase in interest rates will decrease both the demand for shares and their price because companies will be under pressure to meet the increased cost of borrowing.

(b) **Inflation rates**
A decrease in inflation will increase demand for shares and increase the price. This effect is due to investors seeing the decrease in inflation as a sign that economic growth is likely.

(c) **Exchange rates**

A decrease in exchange rates will decrease demand for shares and their price. Investors view the decrease in exchange rates as a negative sign which may be followed by rising interest rates.

(d) **Tax rates**

An increase in the rate of tax will decrease both the demand for shares and their price because investors will have less disposable income. In addition, dividends received may be affected due to an increased tax liability.

16.5 It should be noted that a reverse movement in each of these general market factors will have the opposite effects to those described above.

Factors affecting a particular market sector

16.6 Changes in the supply and demand of a product can have an influence across a particular market sector. For example, the house building industry is sensitive to the costs and availability of mortgages. Because this industry traditionally has high levels of borrowings to purchase building materials and land, etc., a downturn in the demand for houses can be costly to the individual construction companies. This can, of course, lead to a fall in the average share price across this sector, with the payment of lower dividends to shareholders.

Factors affecting individual companies

16.7 The success of a company can vary enormously and investors can look at financial information about a company in order to get an indication of how it has performed to date. More importantly, investors will want to evaluate the future potential of a company, which can be determined by considering three specific areas:

- Trading outlook

- Management ability

- Quality of earnings

Trading outlook

16.8 An individual company's trading outlook will be influenced by both the prevailing economic climate and the market sector within which it operates. The current trading position of a company will be reflected in its annual report and accounts. For example: How high are the company's borrowings? Does it have sufficient funds to expand its premises or invest in new materials or machinery? Does it export its products making it vulnerable to the fluctuations in currency exchange?

16.9 In addition, an investor can compare the dividend yield and P/E ratio for a company with the FT-Actuaries 500 Share Index for that industry. A lower than average yield may suggest the company's prospects are not particularly good.

Management ability

16.10 The quality of a company's management will not be found in the company's balance sheet and is a difficult factor to assess. The ability of management to recognise changing circumstances, and to amend the company's policies to adapt to these changes will be seen as positive factors by investment analysts. Similarly, companies which have high standards of business practice and nurture good relations with employees can be expected to produce high returns. Major changes within a company's management structure, for example the appointment of a new chairman, may give rise to an immediate change in the company's share price.

Quality of earnings

16.11 The quality of a company's earnings is generally reflected by their steady increase. Analysts will often forecast the profits of a company and the accuracy of their forecasts can be an indication of the stability and security of the company. Analysts will also be concerned with the nature and prospects of demand for a company's products, the diversification of the product range, and they will pay particular attention to a company's research and development plans. The investment rating of a company will take all these factors into account and a company with fluctuating success will not enjoy a high rating.

Student Activity 3

You should complete this student activity before reading the next section of the text. Answer the questions, then check your answers against the paragraph(s) indicated.

1. What information can be obtained from the bar chart given in example 11.8? (12.5)

2. How can share price changes be tracked from a point and figure chart? (12.7)

3. What significance do the three types of share price movement have for chartists? (13.2-13.4)

If you are unable to answer any of the questions satisfactorily, you should read the relevant paragraphs again. Your understanding of the text will be further tested in the self-assessment section at the end of this unit.

17 Sources of Information

17.1 There is a variety of published information available to investors and potential investors to enable them to keep up-to-date with the value of their investment holdings. The most easily accessible information is published in the financial papers and covers two areas; general market and sector performances and the performance of individual companies.

17.2 Useful publications include the following:

- Financial Times and other quality newspapers

- Investors Chronicle

- The Economist

- Money Management

- Stock Exchange Fact Book (free on request from the London Stock Exchange)

- Hambro Company Guide

General market and sector performance

17.3 There are a number of stock market indices published in the financial papers that follow movements in share prices. A full description of these indices and their uses can be found in Unit 10. Another useful index is the retail prices index which was introduced in 1974. The index, although not primarily a securities index, gives an indication of the prevailing economic climate in the UK and measures the movement of inflation.

Individual companies

17.4 Information about individual companies is published daily in the financial papers and extracts from the Financial Times are given below. Two sets of figures are given as different information is published on a Tuesday to Friday, than on a Monday.

Example 11.14: UK share prices - published information Tuesday - Friday

(1)	(2)	(3)	(4) 52 week		(5) Mkt	(6) Yld	(7)
	Price	+or-	high	low	Cap £m	Gr's	P/E
Regent Inns	920xd	+35	922½	327	149.0	1.1	28.9
Pizza Express	271xd	......	275	127	151.8	1.1	28.1
Tom Cobleigh	239	+2	258	173	95.2	1.4	38.8
Whitbread	708	+3	732	528	3,419	3.6	17.5

Source : Financial Times (6 March 1996)

(a) For Tuesday to Friday, the first column shows the name of the company and the nominal value per share. If no figure is shown, the nominal value is 25p. Where a company has more than one class of share in issue, for example ordinary shares and preference shares, both will be clearly listed.

(b) Column 2 shows the middle price of the share at the close of business, not the official price which can be found in the Stock Exchange Daily Official List. The middle price is the average of the selling and buying prices for that day. The letters 'xd' printed next to the share price indicate that the share is quoted ex dividend.

(c) Column 3 shows the increase or reduction in the closing price of the share compared to the closing price of the day before.

(d) Column 4 shows the highest and lowest prices of the share during the year.

(e) Column 5 gives an indication of the capital value of the company and is arrived at by multiplying the share price by the number of shares issued.

(f) Columns 6 and 7 indicate the gross dividend yield and the P/E ratio, both of which have been described in full earlier in this chapter.

Example 11.15: UK share prices - published information - Mondays only

	(1) Price	(2) Weekly% Change	(3) Dividend (Net)	(4) Dividend Cover	(5) Dividends Paid	(6) Last xd	(7) City Line
Regent Inns	883xd	1.5	7.9	4.0	Apr Oct	26.2	2190
Pizza Express	269xd	-.1	2.3	4.2	Apr Nov	26.2	4099
Tom Cobleigh	235	2.2	2.7	2.2	-	-	1944
Whitbread	718	0.4	20.6	2.0	Jan Jul	13.11	4488

Source : Financial Times (4 March 1996)

(g) Columns 1 and 2 remain the same.

(a) Column 3 shows the percentage change in the share price over the previous week's figure and gives an indication of the share's most recent performance.

(b) Column 4 shows the total net interim and final dividends that have been paid for the year.

(c) Column 5 shows the dividend cover which has been described in full earlier in this chapter.

(d) Column 6 shows the months in which the company will make interim and final dividend payments.

(e) Finally, column 7 shows the date when the shares last went ex dividend.

17.5 In addition to the information that is available in the financial papers, there are other sources of information available to investors.

18 Company Reports

18.1 As well as the financial information contained in a company's annual report and accounts, there is an abundance of other information included that may be useful to an investor. Such information may be included in the chairman's statement, the directors' report, the company's review of its activities or in the notes attaching to the accounts. Most companies will supply a copy of their accounts to anyone who is interested or, alternatively, an individual can apply to Companies House for a copy, for a small payment.

19 Extel Cards

19.1 The information published in a company's accounts is also published in the card services of Extel Financial Services Ltd. Unlike a company's accounts which will usually only detail two years' figures, the Extel cards will include several years' figures. These cards and fact sheets are produced for every company with a stock exchange listing. The companies themselves are required by the stock exchange to make the information available to Extel. Most brokers and analysts subscribe to Extel and will make the cards available to their clients. Most of the large banks will subscribe to Extel, and because the cards are expensive to purchase, an investor can always ask his bank to obtain a particular company's cards for him.

19.2 Three different types of card are published for quoted companies:

(a) **Annual Card**

The large amount of information that is included on an annual card is summarised as follows:

- The main business of the company

- The names of the directors

- The company's registered office, and registrars

- The company's broker

- The company's capital history

- Major shareholdings

And a five-year record of:

- Profit and loss accounts

- Balance sheets

- Earnings per share

- Dividend payments

- Dividend cover

- Net asset value per share

- Share price highs and lows

- Cash flow

plus:

- Income priority percentages for the current year

- A summary of the chairperson's last statement

(b) **News Card**

The news card provides updating information and contains details, for the last ten years, of all the company's key events, in particular those events that have had an effect on the capital structure of the company.

(c) **Analysts Card**

As its name suggests, this card includes information, for the last ten years, that is of use to an investment analyst, for example, key accounting ratios and dividend and earnings yields.

Datastream

19.3 Datastream is a database service that provides detailed graphs and charts from financial data. The company is constantly updating its on-line database containing over 300 million items, including UK and international equities, bonds, futures, options, company accounts and economic statistics. Its services are widely used by analysts, stockbrokers, fund managers and the financial papers.

Stock Exchange Yearbook

19.4 The Stock Exchange Yearbook is published annually and can be found in the reference section of most public libraries. It is particularly useful to investors who do not have access to the other specialised sources of information, such as Extel and Datastream. It summarises information about a company that is normally recorded at Companies House, although it provides less detailed financial information.

19.5   In addition, the Yearbook contains details of stock exchange practices that will be of particular interest to an investor, such as dealing, settlement and listings.

Stock Exchange Daily Official List

19.6   The Stock Exchange Daily Official List (SEDOL) is published by the stock exchange each working day. It provides a fuller list of all stocks and shares quoted on the stock exchange than is published in the Financial Times. It gives details of the last dividend paid, the date the share last went ex dividend, the dates of dividend payments and the business transacted each day, together with the prices used in the transactions, although it does not differentiate between a sale or a purchase transaction.

19.7   The stock exchange also publishes weekly information known as the Stock Exchange Weekly Official Intelligence, detailing forthcoming company meetings and capital reconstructions etc.

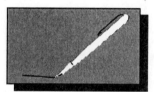

Student Activity 4

You should complete this student activity before attempting the self-assessment. Answer the questions, then check your answers against the paragraph(s) indicated.

1.   Compile a list of all the sources of information available to you   (17.2)
      to develop your knowledge of investments and the financial
      market. Are there any areas for which you need to find
      additional resources?

2.   What different information is given in a Financial Times   (17.4)
      published on a Monday that is not given in the rest of the
      week?

3.   What different Extel cards are there available?   (19.2)

4.   A private investor who does not have access to Datastream or   (18.1, 19.4)
      Extel requires some information on a company and its shares.
      Where could he obtain this information?

If you are unable to answer any of the questions satisfactorily, you should read the relevant paragraphs again. Your understanding of the text will be further tested in the following self-assessment.

Summary

Now that you have completed this unit, you should be able to:

❑ **Understand the basic principles of fundamental analysis**

❑ **Know the meaning of the terms net asset value and gearing in relation to shares**

❑ **Understand how the earnings of a share are calculated and what this means for investors**

❑ **Understand the types of investment ratio and what they indicate**

❑ **Understand the basic principles of technical analysis**

❑ **Know how the types of chart are compiled, the classic chart patterns and the information they provide**

❑ **Know what is meant by the term efficient market hypothesis**

❑ **Know the sources of information available to analysts and private investors**

If you can tick all the above boxes with confidence, you are ready to answer the questions which follow.

Self-Assessment Questions

1. What is the basic difference between fundamental analysis and technical analysis?

2. What does the level of gearing of a company indicate and how does it affect the shareholders?

3. How is the cash flow of a company calculated?

4. What are defined as the full earnings of a company's shareholders?

5. (a) A financial institution has a large holding of debentures in a company. Why would it be interested in the company's income gearing?

   (b) The shares offered by two different companies offer the same dividend rate. What does the income cover of each show?

6. What is the basic principle behind chartism?

7. When an analyst is looking at the performance of a particular company, what considerations will he take into account in predicting future share performance and dividend income?

8. When a share price quoted in the Financial Times has the letters 'xd' next to it, what does this indicate?

9. A customer asks you what the P/E ratio quoted in the press for his shareholding means. What would you reply?

10. What information is provided by SEDOL?

Unit 12

Cash Investments in Banks, Building Societies and National Savings

---

Objectives

Students are required to study the following topics:

- **Bank savings and investment products**
- **Building society accounts**
- **Tessas**
- **National Savings Bank products**
- **Finance houses**
- **Money market**

---

1 Introduction

1.1 The range of services and products available from banks and building societies has developed dramatically in recent years beyond the historical base of current accounts, loans and low-risk savings.

1.2 Banks and building societies are increasingly seeking to maximise business opportunities from their existing customer bases. To do this, they are selling a wider variety of products and services through differing distribution channels. In addition to their own traditional services, banks and building societies are committed to the sale of life assurance, pensions and other investment products, whether as appointed representatives, independent advisers or as product providers themselves.

1.3 Competition between banks and building societies is increasing as the number of services on offer rises. Special interest rates and mortgage offers are used to attract business and encourage customers to move their accounts from one provider to another. Building societies are also now able to provide similar services to banks including credit cards and loans, and can change from being a mutual association to a public company.

1.4 Although these institutions are regarded as secure and investors can assume that their money is safe, the recent collapses of BCCI and Barings indicate that no investment provider can be regarded as totally secure.

2 Bank Savings and Investment Products

2.1 The savings and investment products offered by banks range from traditional savings accounts, to unit trusts and personal equity plans (Peps). These are in addition to their current accounts.

Savings accounts

2.2   There is a variety of savings accounts designed for different needs. They range from those suitable for small investors, typically with a minimum deposit of £1, to those with a minimum deposit of say £10,000. Children's savings accounts can be opened by a parent, grandparent or other adult for the benefit of the child, or by the child him/herself. Interest can be paid gross if the adult certifies that the child is a non taxpayer. They are usually opened to provide savings for a child and to encourage a child to save as he grows older. Some customers fund these accounts with their child benefit payment.

2.3   Income of children that comes from their parents is generally taxed as the income of the parent. However, children can receive a capital sum from each parent that produces no more than £100 income per year (i.e. £200 in total from both parents), without a tax liability for either the parent or the child.

2.4   So, for example, a parent can deposit money in a child's bank or building society account, and the child may receive interest of up to £100 per year, tax-free. If the income exceeds the £100 limit, the whole amount is then taxed as the income of the parent.

2.5   National Savings children's bonus bonds and premiums to tax exempt children's friendly society policies may also be funded by parents in addition, without any tax liability.

2.6   Retired persons and those near retirement may be offered accounts which provide a regular income with interest payable monthly or yearly. Alternatively, the account can be used to save for a holiday or other requirements on reaching retirement.

2.7   Some savings accounts provide a cheque book and/or a cash card to make withdrawals via an automated till (ATM).

2.8   Tessas are another savings account offered by banks. Details are given later in this unit.

Deposit accounts

2.9   These are usually differentiated from savings accounts as they are used to hold lump sums rather than regular savings. Interest can be paid after a fixed period (time deposits) or at regular intervals (e.g. twice yearly), either back into the account or to the investor. Interest rates will depend on the current money market rates.

2.10   Accounts requiring larger deposits usually attract higher rates of interest. Interest rates may be tiered depending on the balance held, and may also depend on the period of notice required for withdrawals. Accounts with, for example, three months' notice as opposed to immediate access, can invest in different types of investment and receive a better rate of return. Investors in notice accounts will be able to withdraw money immediately in an emergency but may lose interest. Some accounts have a minimum amount which must be left in the account following withdrawals. Non taxpayers can apply to have interest paid gross.

2.11　Higher interest accounts are often referred to as premium accounts and usually require a minimum deposit of £500 - £1,000.

2.12　Time deposits tend to attract higher interest rates as money is tied up for a specified period. Typical periods range from three months to five years. There may be a penalty on early withdrawal.

2.13　Deposit accounts allow investment of a lump sum but there is no risk that the initial investment will be lost. The ability to withdraw interest means the account can be used to provide an income if required, or it can be reinvested in the account to give higher growth. Non taxpayers can receive interest gross.

2.14　Some banks also offer fixed-interest accounts for short periods, usually up to a year. They also offer offshore accounts for both UK resident and non-resident customers.

Personal equity plans and unit trusts

2.15　Banks can arrange for customers to invest in Peps and unit trusts and manage these investments. These are covered in later units.

Money market accounts

2.16　The money market is concerned with helping the cash flow problem of the wholesale market, i.e. the large banks, institutions and companies, who require short-term deposits or loans of very large amounts. A typical money market transaction will involve several million pounds and so individual investors are not normally involved. However, competition has meant that most banks now offer customers with large amounts to deposit e.g. over £25,000, access to money market rates through money market accounts.

2.17　These accounts are usually for a fixed period ranging from a week to 12 months although longer term and indefinite terms are also available. The investor is guaranteed the return of his initial deposit and may gain from the favourable interest rates on offer. The rate of interest will be fixed for the period of deposit whilst rates on indefinite term accounts are usually variable. Interest rates rise and fall frequently because they are determined by the supply and demand for money on the money market.

2.18　Overnight deposits are also available for very large sums, usually a minimum of £100,000, and interest for all these types of accounts is payable gross although it is taxable. Because of this the accounts are often used by organisations such as charitable associations which are exempt from tax and so do not have to reclaim tax deducted at source.

2.19　As deposits are usually made for a fixed period the investor will not have access to his cash during that time. Indefinite term accounts will usually have a period of notice for withdrawals.

2.20　These types of account offer investors a guaranteed return over the short-term. Returns are sizeable because of the size of the deposit which is made and can allow individuals who have a substantial sum of money which needs to be held on short-term deposit a way of making their money increase in value without having to tie it up in long-term investments or take any risk.

2.21　More recent developments in money market accounts include high-interest cheque accounts which will require a minimum initial deposit of around £2,500 and provide cheque books, debit cards and instant access. Interest rates normally vary depending on the account balance. For example, 5.5% gross on deposits over £250,000 reducing to 3.5% gross on balances between £2,500 and £25,000.

Deposit Protection Scheme

2.22　The Deposit Protection Scheme was introduced by the Banking Act 1979, amended by the Banking Act 1987 and the EU Directive 1995 on Deposit Guarantee Schemes.

2.23　The scheme set up a fund to which authorised banks must subscribe. In the event of a bank becoming insolvent depositors will receive 90% of the deposit, including accrued interest. The maximum protected deposit is £20,000, therefore the maximum an investor can receive is £18,000, or ECU 20,000 if greater.

2.24　The scheme applies to deposits in UK authorised banks, made in any branch in the European Economic Area.

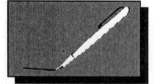

Student Activity 1

You should complete this student activity before reading the next section of the text. Answer the questions, then check your answers against the paragraph(s) indicated.

1.	Why do larger deposit accounts often attract higher interest rates?	(2.10)
2.	Describe two particular uses of a savings account for:	(2.2-2.6)
	(a) a man with young children	
	(b) a widower nearing retirement	
3	What level of risk do bank accounts present to a customer?	(2.13)

If you are unable to answer any of the questions satisfactorily, you should read the relevant paragraphs again. Your understanding of the text will be further tested in the self-assessment section at the end of this unit.

3　Building Society Accounts

3.1　The main difference to an account holder of having a building society account is that he is a part owner in the society as it is a mutual organisation. This gives him the voting rights and some times other benefits e.g. extra shares from a merger (such as the Leeds/Halifax merger). A bank account holder's rights are restricted to what is in his account.

3.2　The basic type of building society account is an ordinary share or paid-up account.

3.3 Various other accounts similar to those offered by banks are now also available from building societies, structured to give higher rates of interest for larger amounts of cash with different periods needed for repayment without penalties. These vary in name and structure with availability based on current market conditions.

3.4 Building society accounts are protected in a similar way to banks by the Investor Protection Scheme. In the event of collapse, a building society's deposit account holders will receive 100% of their deposit while other account holders will receive 90%, subject to a maximum deposit of £20,000.

Permanent interest bearing shares (Pibs)

3.5 Pibs are a type of share issued by building societies. They are quoted and traded on the stock exchange and offer a higher than average fixed interest rate. Unlike all other building society investments, Pibs are not covered by the statutory Investor Protection Scheme. In the event of a society being wound up, Pibs rank behind depositors and creditors. Pibs are irredeemable, and to reclaim the capital the investor must sell the shares. How much capital is repaid is not guaranteed and will depend on the price of the shares at that time.

3.6 Interest on the Pibs is paid half-yearly, net of basic rate tax which can be reclaimed by non taxpayers. From 6 April 1996 the tax charge was reduced to the lower rate of 20%. There is no liability to CGT on the profits from the sale of the shares.

3.7 Initially Pibs were aimed at large investors, with the minimum investment set at around £50,000. Recently however, issues with much lower investment limits, for example a minimum of £1,000, have made these shares more accessible to smaller investors. Their risk profile is similar to that of undated gilts, but they may achieve a higher return.

The Building Societies Association

3.8 This association represents the interests of its member building societies and as such acts as a liaison point with government departments and other important organisations. The building societies themselves are supervised by the Building Societies Commission which was set up in 1987.

4 Taxation of Bank and Building Society Accounts

4.1 Prior to 6 April 1996 all bank and building society accounts had tax deducted at source at the basic rate. People who were liable to tax at the lower rate of 20% could claim a repayment of the difference between lower and basic rates. Higher rate taxpayers had to account for the marginal rate tax i.e. 15% in their annual tax return.

4.2 From 6 April 1996 the liability to income tax on such accounts was reduced to the lower rate of 20%, except for higher rate taxpayers who continue to be liable at 40%. Basic rate tax payers have no further liability. Non taxpayers can complete Inland Revenue form IR85 to have interest paid gross. If this is not completed the tax can be reclaimed by non taxpayers by using form IR95.

4.3 Where an account is held jointly and each person has a different tax liability, interest can be paid separately. For example, if a husband and wife have a joint account and the wife is a non taxpayer, she can have half the interest paid gross.

4.4   All income from banks and building societies is subject to income tax, except for tax exempt special savings accounts, or Tessas. There is no capital gains tax liability on any bank or building society account.

5   Tax Exempt Special Savings Accounts (Tessas)

5.1   Tessas were introduced from 1 January 1991 as a five-year scheme that would be tax exempt as long as certain conditions were met. Tessas are available from banks and building societies that have decided to issue them. The facility to offer Tessas was extended to certain authorised credit institutions of other EU States from 2 January 1996.

5.2   A Tessa will last for five years and, as long as the capital remains untouched, any interest earned during that period will be entirely tax-free. The rate of interest payable is determined by the bank or building society issuing the Tessa and will generally be based on interest rates currently available, although a minority are fixed for the period of the Tessa.

5.3   Tessas are only available to United Kingdom residents aged 18 or over and are limited to one per person. The maximum saving for a Tessa is £9,000 over five years, which breaks down as a maximum of £3,000 in year one and a maximum of £1,800 each year following, up to £9,000.

5.4   This means that if an investor puts the maximum amount in his Tessa each year, the maximum in year five is £600. However, if the investor had not invested the maximum amount in any previous year then up to £1,800 can be invested. Some banks and building societies offer Tessa feeder accounts, giving the option of depositing a full £9,000 limit that will be fed into a Tessa on a regular basis within agreed limits. The feeder account will be subject to tax on the interest accruing, as for other deposit accounts.

5.5   Interest from the Tessa may be withdrawn annually, subject to a deduction for tax. Interest paid or credited on or after 6 April 1996 has a 20% tax deduction. For interest paid or credited prior to that date the amount that may be withdrawn is less tax at 25%. Any interest withdrawals can be fed back into the account as part of the investor's annual contribution. The tax deducted remains in the account and can be withdrawn at the end of the five-year period.

Example 12.1: Withdrawal from a Tessa

£3,000 was deposited (the first year maximum) at an agreed rate of 8%. The interest for year one would be £240. This could be withdrawn as follows:

Gross interest	£240
Tax @ 20%	£48
Withdrawal allowed	£192

The £48 would remain in the account and could be withdrawn at the end of the five years.

5.6   If too much is withdrawn from the Tessa, i.e. the capital or the tax element of the interest is used, the account ceases to be tax exempt. After five years the account will automatically cease to be exempt. If death occurs within five years the account will keep its tax-free status up to the date of death.

5.7   An investor who has held a Tessa for the full five-year term is now able to open a new Tessa with the full amount of capital, but not accumulated interest, held in the old account (maximum £9,000). The new account must be opened within six months of the old account maturing and may be held with the same institution as the previous Tessa or with a different one.

5.8   Those who invest less than £9,000 in the first year of the new account will be able to add to the account up to the existing limit of £1,800 per year. The new Tessa will continue to have an overall £9,000 limit and must be held for a full five years if interest is to remain tax-free.

5.9   Tessas were very successful initially because of their simplicity and their tax efficiency. They provide a level of interest that is tax-free, but it should be noted that the tax benefits will not be felt until the end of the five-year period.

5.10   Non taxpayers may be better advised to open a higher-interest bank or building society account rather than a Tessa because of the inflexibility of a Tessa, but this can be a good alternative for taxpayers who want a tax-efficient short-term saving with no risk and guaranteed results.

5.11   It is worth noting that the interest rates quoted are annual rates; most Tessas accept monthly payments but the actual interest received on these accounts will, of course, be less than the annual percentage quoted.

5.12   Competition between Tessa providers means that interest rates vary. Special offers may be made to attract business and only be available for limited periods. However, investors should note that if they decide to switch their Tessa to another provider there may be a penalty e.g. a flat fee plus loss of one month's interest.

5.13   Some Tessas offer a loyalty bonus paid at the end of the five years to encourage investors to keep their Tessa with the same provider. This should be taken into account when comparing interest rates as the amount of bonus may be worth more or less than an extra 1% in interest. The top current rates and offers are published in the national newspapers.

Student Activity 2

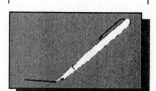

You should complete this student activity before reading the next section of the text. Answer the questions, then check your answers against the paragraph(s) indicated.

1.   What are permanent interest bearing shares and what type of   (3.5-3.7) investors are they suited to?

2.   How will the following customers be taxed on their building   (4.2) society savings account?

       (a) Jim is a higher rate taxpayer

(b) Sonia is a basic rate taxpayer

(c) Tom and Margaret are a retired couple living on Tom's occupational pension

3   Joan has a Tessa which will mature next month. What options   (5.7)
     does she have?

If you are unable to answer any of the questions satisfactorily, you should read the relevant paragraphs again. Your understanding of the text will be further tested in the self-assessment section at the end of this unit.

6   The National Savings Bank

6.1   The National Savings Bank was part of the Post Office until 1969, since then it has become an independent operation as a Treasury offshoot used to raise money from private investors for the government. It sells its services over the counter at post offices with various savings vehicles available that normally enjoy tax-free inducements.

6.2   The National Savings Bank also provides a service for personal investors for buying and selling gilts. These will be covered in a later unit. The products available from the NSB change from time to time and full details can be found at most post offices or via their telephone enquiry service (0645 645000).

6.3   The products available are listed below, with up-to-date interest rates.

Table 12.1: National Savings Bank summary

Interest Rates as at August 1996

Account	Interest	Conditions
Ordinary account	1.50% under £500 2.50% over £500	Maximum holding £10,000
Investment account	4.75% under £500 5.25% over £500 + up to £25,000 5.50% over £25,000	Maximum holding £100,000
Yearly plan (discontinued 31/1/95)	5.85% Tax-free	Hold for five years
Fixed-interest savings certificate (43rd Issue)	5.35% Tax-free	Hold for five years
Index-linked savings certificate (9th Issue)	2.5% plus RPI Tax-free	Hold for five years
Income bonds	6% under £25,000 6.25% over £25,000	Three months' notice for repayment
Capital bonds (Series J)	6.65%	Maximum holding £250,000
Childrens bonus bonds	6.75%	Maximum £1,000,

(H Series)	Tax-free	have to be held for five years
First option bond	4.8% net (6% gross)	Maximum £250,000
Pensioners guaranteed income bonds (Series 3)	7.0% p.a. gross fixed for first five years	Maximum holding £50,000 (or £100,000 if jointly owned)
General extension rate	3.51% Tax-free	(On matured 7th-34th issue savings certificates and yearly plan certificates)

Note that interest rates quoted are the compounded rate if the account or bond is held for the full term.

For up-to-date rates telephone the interest rate checkline on 0171-605-9483/4 (London) or 0141-631-2766 (Glasgow).

Ordinary account

6.4 This is a simple bank account where interest is paid gross but which is taxable, although the first £70 of interest of each account per person is tax-free. Joint accounts therefore receive the first £140 tax-free. The minimum deposit is £10, the maximum is £10,000 and up to £100 a day can be withdrawn on demand. There are two rates of interest, standard and higher. To qualify for the higher rate the account must be held for a full calendar year and have a minimum balance of £500.

Investment account

6.5 This is similar to the ordinary account but attracts higher interest and needs one month's notice for withdrawals. The entire interest is taxable but is paid gross. The minimum holding is £20, maximum £100,000. Interest rates can vary but will reflect current market rates.

Yearly plan

6.6 The yearly plan is a five-year savings contract that will earn a guaranteed rate of interest that is totally tax-free. The investor makes monthly payments by standing order for the first year, and these payments buy a four-year yearly plan certificate. The full guaranteed rate of interest is earned if the plan is held for the whole term. The minimum monthly investment is £20 and the maximum £400. When the certificate matures, the general extension rate is paid on the investment until it is withdrawn from the scheme.

6.7 This plan was withdrawn for new investors on 31 January 1995, but may still be held by investors until January 2000.

Savings certificate

6.8 There are two types of savings certificate, a fixed-interest certificate and an index-linked certificate. Both give a rate of interest guaranteed at issue if the certificates are held for five years. The index-linked certificate gives a lower rate but will add an inflation-proofed percentage to match changes in the retail prices index. Both these certificates have the benefit of tax-free returns, so are ideal for all taxpayers.

6.9   The minimum purchase in both cases is £100, with purchases above the minimum in units of £25. The maximum holding in each new issue of certificates is £10,000, plus a further £20,000 if reinvesting matured savings certificates and yearly plan certificates.

6.10   After five years the proceeds can be taken in cash, or reinvested in another certificate. Alternatively the matured certificate can be kept in force, although the interest rate will be reduced to the general extension rate.

6.11   Certificates can be cashed in before the fifth anniversary but they will earn a lower rate of interest. Nothing is earned on certificates repaid during the first year of investment, except for reinvestment certificates.

Income bonds

6.12   Income bonds give a variable interest rate paid monthly. Interest is paid gross but is taxable. The interest can be varied at six weeks' notice and the minimum purchase is £2,000 with a maximum holding of £250,000. The bonds can be cashed in at any time subject to three months' notice, although the amount of interest is reduced if the bonds are held for less than one year.

Capital bonds

6.13   Capital bonds must be held for a full five years to give a guaranteed rate of interest that is paid gross annually. The interest is not actually paid to the investor but is reinvested. However, interest is subject to income tax and must be declared annually on the investor's tax return. The maximum holding is £250,000, with a minimum holding of £100 and multiples thereof. At the end of the five years the investor receives a return of capital plus the gross interest accrued. If the bond is encashed earlier the interest rate will be lower than if held for the full five years. Interest is not paid on bonds cashed in before the first anniversary of purchase.

Children's bonus bonds

6.14   These bonds were introduced in June 1991 and are designed to give tax-free savings for under 16s. The bonds offer a guaranteed return when held for five years. No interest is earned if a bond is repaid in the first year, otherwise a flat rate of 5% p.a. is paid on repayment before the fifth anniversary.

6.15   The bond can be bought by anyone over age 16 for a child e.g. parent, grandparent, friend. The minimum purchase is £25. Larger purchases are in units of £25. The maximum holding is £1,000, this is in addition to holdings of all other issues of children's bonus bonds. After five years the bond can be continued for a further five years. It must cease at age 21 or earlier.

First option bonds

6.16   First stands for fixed-interest rate savings tax-paid. These bonds offer a fixed rate of interest for one year for savers aged 16 and over. A new rate is then fixed for the next year. The minimum investment is £1,000, and the maximum £250,000. Bonds of £20,000 or more earn an additional guaranteed bonus of 0.25% gross (0.2% net).

6.17   After the end of one year the bond holder has the option to continue the bond or encash it.

6.18   Interest is calculated daily but paid annually. Prior to 6 April 1996 interest was paid net of basic rate tax making the bonds particularly appealing to basic rate taxpayers. Since 6 April 1996 interest has been paid net of lower rate tax increasing the bond's appeal to lower rate taxpayers. Higher rate taxpayers need to pay the additional tax due. If the bond is encashed before the end of the first year no interest will be paid. Encashments made between subsequent anniversaries will receive the full value of the investment at the most recent anniversary, plus interest at half the current fixed rate for the period since then.

Pensioners guaranteed income bonds

6.19   These bonds were introduced on 21 January 1994 and are designed to help elderly savers who need a monthly income to meet regular bills. The bonds are available to those aged 60 and over and will pay a guaranteed rate of interest for the first five years. The interest is taxable but is paid gross making them particularly attractive to non taxpayers.

6.20   The minimum initial purchase is £500 with a maximum holding of £50,000 (or £100,000 for a joint holding).

6.21   Withdrawals, in whole or part, can be made at any fifth anniversary without penalty. At any other time, 60 days' notice is required and no interest will be paid during this time.

Premium bonds

6.22   It may be said that premium bonds are not an investment in that the £100 minimum purchase will only ever guarantee a return of capital. This, in real terms, would lead to losses due to inflation, however the gamble taken is that one of the major prizes will be won.

6.23   Although they are very much a gamble, it should be noted that a maximum bondholder (£20,000), given statistically average luck, should win a minimum of four prizes in a year. Of course, these prizes could be anything from £50 to the top prize of £1 million, but nothing is guaranteed.

6.24   Premium bonds are really a form of gambling but can be a fun way of gaining excellent returns if the bondholder is very lucky!

7   Finance Houses

7.1   Finance houses, commonly called hire-purchase companies, are generally known for the credit service they provide to the general public to assist with the purchase of consumer goods, for example, electrical equipment, furniture and cars. Unlike loans arranged through a bank or building society, credit is normally given at the point of sale, for example the garage where a car is bought.

7.2   The banks have increased their personal loan business in recent years which has meant a reduced market for hire-purchase finance. This means that only the less credit-worthy consumers are likely to require hire-purchase finance and so interest rates will be higher to reflect the increased risk for the creditor.

7.3   Many finance houses will accept cash deposits from investors for a fixed period and offer attractive interest rates. Rates are normally quoted for one, three and six months' notice although other longer or shorter periods can be arranged. Investors should beware that high interest rates generally mean that correspondingly high rates are being charged to borrowers indicating that they represent an above average risk for the lender. However, the higher risk means that the reward is greater than for deposits made in a more conventional type of deposit account. Small investors will normally choose a finance house which is partly or fully owned by one of the major banks which reduces the risk.

7.4   In addition the deposit will be covered by the Deposit Protection Scheme established under the Banking Act 1979.

Student Activity 3

You should complete this student activity before reading the next section of the text. Answer the questions then check your answers against the paragraph(s) indicated.

1.   Which National Savings products are: (6.3)

      a) Tax-free?

      b) Taxable but paid gross?

2.   Andrew has invested £1,000 in National Savings certificates   (6.8-6.11)
      (43rd issue). What will he receive after five years? What could
      he expect to receive if he cashed the certificates early?

3.   What National Savings product might you recommend to a   (6.15)
      grandparent wishing to invest some money for his 12 year old
      grand-daughter?

4.   Why should an investor be wary of very high interest rates   (7.3)
      offered by finance houses?

If you are unable to answer any of the questions satisfactorily, you should read the relevant paragraphs again. Your understanding of the text will be further tested in the self-assessment section at the end of this unit.

8   Risk and Accessibility

8.1   Investors who choose bank, building society or National Savings accounts are looking for capital security. They can be assured that the amount of capital they deposit or save cannot be reduced. Interest added to the capital will increase the value of the savings or deposit. However, because of this security investors should not expect high returns on their investment. Interest rates will vary depending on the type of account but will never offer the potentially high rates of return available from more speculative investments which carry the risk of capital loss.

Value of capital

8.2   It is also important for an investor to realise that while their capital is secure, if held over a number of years its value in real terms will be reduced due to inflation. Ten thousand pounds will buy less in five years' time than it can now. Investors who are concerned with this should look for index-linked products which offer some protection against the effects of inflation.

Interest rates

8.3   A fixed-interest rate allows an investor to know what return he will get on his money. Where interest is withdrawn as income this helps with budgeting. However fixed-interest rates are offered over a set term, and the risk to the investor is that higher interest may become available on alternative investments whilst his investment is tied into the fixed rate.

8.4   Variable rates of interest carry more risks, as a rate can fall and make other investments more attractive. The penalties for changing between different accounts may mean the investor has to keep his money where it is and hope that interest rates will rise again. The degree of risk this presents to the investor depends on how reliant he is on a minimum rate of return.

8.5   Very high rates of interest are normally only available to persons able to deposit large amounts. This may be of use to individuals requiring a short-term deposit account for sums of money acquired due to redundancy or on taking pension commutation at retirement.

Accessibility

8.6   Money can be withdrawn from any of the accounts described here at any time. However, depending on the purpose of the account the investor may lose some of the interest his money has, or would have, earned. Early encashment of capital from a Tessa will result in the loss of tax-free status and so have a longer-term effect.

8.7   The effect of the loss of interest will be greater on larger deposits, but again, the degree of risk to an investor depends on the individual circumstances. The main appeal of these types of accounts is that whilst the investor is prepared to tie money up for a specified term, or to wait for a particular time period before making withdrawals, money can be withdrawn immediately (within a few days) if necessary.

8.8   Certain accounts such as overnight money market accounts are designed for the short-term and are used by individuals who need the safe keeping of a large sum of money. This may arise, for example, on the sale of property where the money will be used to make another purchase in a few days. The investor can benefit from earning interest on the money while it is being held by the bank.

9   Choice of Product

9.1   The choice of product will depend on a number of features, both between products from the same provider, and similar products from different providers.

Interest rates

9.2 While National Savings interest rates are fixed for a current issue, banks and building societies can change interest rates at any time. Competition between providers means that an investor has to 'shop around' to find the best rates at a particular time. Where rates are not fixed, there is always the risk that they will change. Other features such as bonuses, or increases in interest rate after a given period should also be taken into account.

9.3 The way in which interest is credited can also make a difference to the returns the investor receives. If interest is credited to the account more frequently than annually, then interest will accrue faster. This will have more effect on larger deposits.

Tax

9.4 Interest is either taxable or tax-free. Only certain National Savings products and Tessas are tax-free accounts. Where interest is taxable it is either paid gross or net of lower rate tax.

9.5 In comparing interest rates it is important to remember that the same rate can have a different value to different taxpayers.

9.6 Where interest is paid gross a non taxpayer will not need to recover tax deducted. A higher rate taxpayer will benefit from deferring the tax liability for up to a year. This is more important where large sums are involved.

Example 12.2: Comparing effect of tax position on return

Interest paid at 6% tax-free

Non taxpayer

This would compare to an account paying 4.8% net of lower rate tax. Any account paying more than 4.8% net will give a better return.

Basic rate taxpayer

6% tax-free is the same as 7.5% gross. Anything higher than 7.5% gross will offer a better return.

Higher rate taxpayer

6% tax-free is the same as 10% gross.

9.7 It is important to remember that savings and deposit accounts, and National Savings products are often attractive to retired persons who may have a lower attitude to risk. They should be aware of the possible effect of investment income on the age allowance (refer back to Unit 3).

10 Summary

10.1 It is important to be aware of the different options available from the banks, building societies and National Savings since they will all have a part to play in the make-up of a customer's investment portfolio. In every case, the customer will need a no-risk, readily accessible form of cash for an emergency fund. In some cases, attitudes to risk may be so low that these will be the only vehicles that satisfy this criteria for the customer.

10.2 However, this will be an unusual position since most customers will have to make their money work harder in order to achieve their stated aims.

10.3 Bank and building society accounts and National Savings are excellent in the service they provide for savers but they are not designed as vehicles for long-term, high return results. When customers need such results they will have to turn to other investment vehicles and increasingly they will turn to investments that utilise the stock market for superior long-term results.

Student Activity 4

You should complete this student activity before attempting the self-assessment. Answer the questions, then check your answers against the paragraph(s) indicated.

1. An investor wants capital security from his investments. What effect does security have on capital value?   (8.2)

2. If an investor is considering switching his savings account to another provider who is offering a better interest rate what should he be made aware of?   (8.4)

3. Compare an account which credits interest annually with one which credits interest quarterly. Which one offers a better return for the customer, and why?   (9.3)

If you are unable to answer any of the questions satisfactorily, you should read the relevant paragraphs again. Your understanding of the text will be further tested in the following self-assessment.

Summary

Now that you have completed this unit, you should be able to:

☐ **Describe the different types of bank and building society savings and deposit accounts**

☐ **Describe the range of National Savings products**

☐ **Explain the taxation of cash investments**

☐ **Describe the risk profile and accessibility of cash investments**

If you can tick all the above boxes with confidence, you are ready to answer the questions which follow.

Self-Assessment

1. Tim Smith has just sold his newsagent shop and is about to complete the purchase of another business in a week's time. He needs to deposit the sale proceeds in his bank. What type of account would be suitable and why?

2. Jessica Bowman took out a Tessa four years ago. She deposited £2,000 in the first year and £1,000 in years two, three and four. She is a basic rate taxpayer.

    (a) What is the maximum amount she can pay into the account in year five?

    (b) If she withdrew more than the accumulated interest in year four what would be the effect?

    (c) Jessica intends to reinvest her Tessa at maturity. What are the restrictions on reinvesting in another Tessa and what should she consider before choosing which provider to use?

3. A retired couple are receiving pension income of £10,000 a year and wish to invest a lump sum of £15,000 in a National Savings product to produce income. The wife is a non taxpayer. Which product would be most suitable and why?

4. Explain the types of National Savings certificates available and their suitability for different types of investors.

5. What protection is given to investors in the event of a bank becoming insolvent?

6. Tom, Dick and Harry are a non taxpayer, a basic rate taxpayer and a higher rate taxpayer respectively. They all invest £100 in a building society account offering a fixed interest rate of 4.85% net. What does this mean in real terms for each of them?

7. What factors need to be considered when comparing interest rates offered by bank and building society accounts?

8. A customer asks if the value of the capital he has deposited in a building society account will increase over time. What would you reply?

9. What are the risks involved for a customer who chooses a deposit account with a variable interest rate?

10. What security does a depositor in a deposit account with a finance house have?

Unit 13

Gilts and Non Corporate Fixed-Interest Securities

Objectives

Students are required to study the following topics:

* **Introduction to gilts**

* **Classification of gilts**

* **Pricing of gilts**

* **Gilt yields**

* **Gilt issues**

* **Tax treatment of gilts**

* **Risk profile of gilts**

* **Local authority investments**

1   Introduction

1.1   Gilts are a form of security traded on the stock market. The income from gilts is guaranteed, and the capital value of an investment in gilts is totally secure if the stocks are held to maturity. Gilts may be sold at any time but a full return of capital is not guaranteed if the stocks are sold early.

2   What are Gilts?

2.1   Gilts is the name given to British government securities. The full name is gilt-edged securities, and they are so called because they are a very safe form of investment. Gilts are as guaranteed as the status of the British government and a gilt has never failed to pay interest or repay its capital value at maturity.

2.2   Gilts are issued by the government as a method of raising money. Where the government has insufficient income to meet its expenditure, it will need to borrow to make up the difference. This is known as the Public Sector Borrowing Requirement or PSBR. (The reverse, known as Public Sector Debt Repayment or PSDR occurs when the government has a surplus of funds and is able to repay some of its debts). Gilts are a way of borrowing money from the investing public to provide government finance. In return, the holder of the gilt will receive a fixed rate of interest and a return of the capital value at the end of a predetermined period.

303

Names of gilts

2.3 Gilts carry many different types of names: Exchequer, Conversion, Treasury, Funding, War Stock. These names no longer carry the importance they used to and are merely a way of differentiating different issues.

3 How Do They Work?

3.1 Gilts are denominated in lots of £100, which is referred to as the 'nominal value' or 'par value'. For £100, the investor is guaranteed to receive the 'coupon' or interest annually and, at the end of a predetermined period, a return of the nominal value, or £100. However, when an investor buys gilts he may actually pay more or less than £100 for a gilt with a nominal value of £100. Whether he makes a capital gain or not depends on how much he originally paid for the gilt.

The coupon

3.2 The 'coupon' is the fixed annual rate of interest calculated on the nominal value. The coupon is fixed at the time of issue, depending on market forces at that time, and coupons for different gilts issues vary widely. A glance at the financial pages of any broad sheet newspaper will give an idea of those available.

3.3 So, if the coupon was 5%, for example, an investor would receive interest of £5 per annum for the par value of £100.

3.4 The coupon is always quoted in the name of the gilt. The interest is now normally paid twice a year but obviously only half of the quoted coupon.

3.5 On certain stock and all variable rate gilts, the interest is paid quarterly. This can make these gilts slightly more attractive to certain types of investor, for example, those in retirement who are using the interest to supplement income.

Redemption date

3.6 Gilts will run for a different number of years, dependent upon date of issue and immediate needs. Most start their life with a redemption date of 15 years in the future or more. The redemption date is also known as the maturity date.

3.7 The redemption date can be seen in the name of the gilt. For example, a gilt issued with a fixed redemption date may be shown as Treasury 8% 2000. This means that the gilt will be redeemed by the government sometime during 2000. The exact date of repayment is usually known. A gilt issued with a flexible redemption date, i.e. Treasury $11\frac{1}{2}$% 2001-04 will be redeemed sometime between 1 January 2001 and 31 December 2004.

4 Classification of Gilts

4.1 Gilts are divided into a number of categories:

• Shorts

• Mediums

- Longs

- Variables

- Undated

4.2   The financial press lists shorts as having a life span of five years or less. The London Stock Exchange, however, classifies all gilts within seven years of maturity as shorts. Mediums last for between five and fifteen years or seven and fifteen years under the London Stock Exchange classification. Longs will mature in more than fifteen years.

4.3   Undated gilts have, as the name suggests, no redemption date and the government does not have any obligation to pay back the debt, only to keep on paying the coupon. Such stock was issued mostly during wars and times of national crisis and these gilts are also known as irredeemable. A large amount of War Loan Stock is held by the large institutional investors such as pension funds who acquired the gilts at a low price.

4.4   Variables will have two dates, for example 1999-2004, and the government will decide when redemption will be between these two dates, but definitely by the final date. If interest rates are above the coupon attaching to the gilt, then the government may delay redemption as they are effectively borrowing money at a rate that is cheaper than current interest rates. If interest rates are below the coupon, they may well redeem the stock at the earliest opportunity to save paying out higher interest.

Convertible rate gilts

4.5   Convertible rate gilts were introduced in 1973. The gilts are issued with an option to convert short-dated stock into longer-dated stock on a specified date. Convertible gilts do not carry the risk that longer-dated gilts carry. If interest rates are improving and an investor feels that the price of gilts is likely to rise in the near future, then he may wish to exercise the option and convert his holding into the longer-dated gilts in the hope of increasing the size of his holding when interest rates fall.

Example 13.1: How conversion can increase the value of an investor's holding

Mr Dickson holds 3,000 units of stock A. The current price of stock A is £95. He exercises his option to convert the stock to 5,000 units of stock B, current price £57.

After one year which has seen improved economic activity, the prices of stocks A and B have increased to £100 and £62 respectively.

Mr Dickson now holds £310,000 of stock B. If he had not exercised the conversion option, then the value of his holding in stock A would only have been £300,000.

Index-linked gilts

4.6   Index-linked gilts were introduced in 1982 to counteract the effects of inflation. The coupon and the par value both increase in line with the retail prices index, and so these gilts can be an excellent deal in inflationary times. The gilts carry a guaranteed coupon at issue, and this tends to be low, for example 2% or 2½%, as the investor can expect the amount of interest he receives to increase over the time he holds the gilts. Prices also tend to be higher than conventional gilts, again because the index-linking makes them a more attractive investment.

4.7   The coupon is increased by the movement in the RPI from the date eight months before issue to eight months before the interest payment date. As the interest is paid half-yearly the actual calculation looks like this:

Half yearly interest =
½ of <u>RPI eight months before interest payment</u> x coupon
        RPI eight months before issue

4.8   Similarly, the redemption value of the gilts is calculated by increasing the nominal value by movement in the RPI between the date eight months before issue and eight months before redemption. The method of indexation means that interest and redemption values of index-linked gilts do not take account of any changes in inflation in the eight month period immediately before payment or maturity.

Floating rate gilts

4.9   Floating rate gilts were introduced on 30 March 1994. Interest is paid on a quarterly basis at the three month London Interbank Bid Rate (LIBID) minus ½%. Although interest is paid gross, a UK taxpayer must declare the interest received on his annual tax return and pay the tax due either through PAYE or on the issue of an assessment.

Size of the market

4.10   On 29 December 1995, the total market value of gilt-edged stock issued was almost £259.5 billion. This is broken down as follows:

Shorts	28.48%
Mediums	40.97%
Longs	15.72%
Index-Linked	11.02%
Undated and Floating Rate	3.81%

4.11   Daily transactions of gilts average £6.7 billion, representing over 50% of the London Stock Exchange's business.

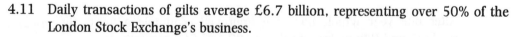

Student Activity 1

You should complete this student activity before reading the next section of the text. Answer the questions, then check your answers against the paragraph(s) indicated.

1.   An investor buys £1,000 worth of redeemable gilts for £1,200   (3.1, 3.3, 3.7, on 1 October 1995. The issue is the 'Treasury 9% 2004'.   4.1)

        (a) What is the coupon?

(b) When is the redemption date?

(c) What category would you put this gilt into?

(d) What is:

(i) The nominal amount bought?

(ii) The amount invested?

2. Explain why the coupon for index-linked gilts tends to be lower (4.6)
   at issue that conventional gilts, and why the price is often
   higher in comparison.

If you are unable to answer any of the questions satisfactorily, you should read the relevant paragraphs again. Your understanding of the text will be further tested in the self-assessment section at the end of this unit.

5   The Price of Gilts

5.1   Supply and demand are the main determining factors in the price of gilts. If investors are selling, prices will fall; if they are buying, then prices will rise.

5.2   There are four main objectives that will motivate investors to buy or sell gilts.

Interest rates

5.3   Shorter-dated gilts are in direct competition with banks and building societies for investors' funds and therefore are more sensitive to deposit interest rates. If interest rates are moving up, gilt yields must move up to remain competitive. As the interest rate, or coupon, of the gilt remains unaltered, it is the price of the gilt that must fall.

5.4   Interest rates rise and fall with the state of the economy. In buoyant conditions, people are willing to borrow money to spend, thereby increasing the demand for money. Lenders will charge more for lending and interest rates rise. Conversely, when the economy is slowing down and the demand for money is falling, interest rates will fall.

Exchange rates

5.5   The movement in international interest rates has an effect on sterling and, in turn, the price of gilts. Gilts basically represent the return on sterling and if that return is lower than the demand of foreign investors then the value of sterling falls - and vice versa. When sterling is weak, inflation is higher and the government is likely to increase interest rates to prop up sterling. Weak sterling generally means weak gilt prices.

Inflation

5.6   When an economy is booming, people are prepared to pay more for goods and services, which pushes up prices, generating inflation and higher interest rates. Investors in gilts demand higher yields to compete, so gilt prices will normally fall.

Market anticipations

5.7   An investor will analyse markets and economies and form conclusions about movements of interest, inflation and exchange rates in the future. If one investor's views are the same as other major investors in the market, there may be enough activity created to move prices substantially.

6 Gilt Yields

6.1 All gilts bear a nominal rate of interest, the coupon, which relates to the rate of interest on £100 nominal value of the stock.

6.2 The following interest yields can all be considered by an investor who is assessing whether to purchase or sell gilts at a given time.

Gross interest yield

6.3 This is also known as interim, flat or running yield. Yield is the genuine interest the investor would be receiving at today's market price.

6.4 For example, if the coupon was 5% and today's market price was £100 the actual interest the investor would receive would be 5%, since the gilt is at 'nominal' value. It therefore follows that if the gilt is below 'nominal' value on the stock exchange that the actual return would be above the coupon quoted. In the example given above, if the investor bought the gilt at £90 he would still receive £5 interest per annum but the yield would be 5.55%, as it would be £5 interest on £90, not on the nominal value of £100.

6.5 Similarly, if the gilt is above 'nominal' value on the stock exchange then the real return on the gilt would be less than the coupon quoted. In other words, if the price was £110 the investor would still receive £5 but the yield would be 4.5%.

6.6 The gross interest yield is quoted in the financial papers as 'Int' and can be calculated as follows:

$$\frac{\text{Coupon x 100}}{\text{Today's price}}$$

So, a gilt with an 8% coupon would have the following gross interest yields at the following prices:

Price £100 price - gross interest yield 8%

Price £88 price - gross interest yield 9.09%

Price £110 price - gross interest yield 7.27%

6.7 As you will see, the market price dictates the actual rate of interest the investor will receive from the gilt since, in this case, the £8 received for every nominal £100 the investor owns will be above or below 8% dependent upon the purchase price.

6.8 It is important to be aware of this because if gilts are purchased on the stock exchange the investor will very seldom realise the coupon quoted because the market price of the gilt will be above or below the 'nominal' value.

6.9 For example, if buying a gilt with a coupon of 15% expecting annual interest of £15 for every £100 purchased, the gross annual income rate would be only 10.7% if the current price was £140.

Gross redemption yield

6.10 The financial pages and specialist gilts lists will also quote the gross redemption yield, which is the yield that will be realised if the gilt is held to its redemption date. Note that gilts tend to return to their 'nominal' value the closer they get to their redemption date.

6.11 This is a complex calculation since it takes in capital profit on redemption as well as the interest earned. It is particularly important to be aware of this yield as it gives a realistic idea of the interest to be earned based on current market prices. The formula for calculating the gross redemption yield is illustrated below, although resort to the formula is rarely necessary.

Formula for calculating gross redemption yield

Market price of a gilt =

$$\frac{I}{(I+R)} + \frac{I}{(I+R)^2} + \frac{I}{(I+R)^3} + \frac{I}{(I+R)^n} + £100$$

Where I = Interest payment per period

N = Number of periods to redemption

R = Semi-annual yield to redemption

(i.e. the value you are seeking to find)

6.12 In the absence of a gilts list and a financial paper, an approximation of the gross redemption yield can be calculated by the following simplified formula:

Gross redemption = Interest yield + (-) $\frac{\text{Gain(loss) to maturity}}{\text{Period to maturity}}$
yield

6.13 When calculating the period to maturity in gilts with a variable redemption date, an assumption should be made as to the likely date of redemption (i.e. first date or last date) given the coupon rate and the current interest rates.

Example 13.2: Approximation of gross redemption yield

The following calculation illustrates how the approximation compares with the published gross redemption yield.

Treasury $8\frac{1}{2}$% 2005 being sold in 1996 at $107^{17}/_{32}$ (107.53) - published gross redemption yield 7.40%.

Interest yield	7.90%
Period to maturity	9 years
Current market price	£107.53
Average gain to maturity =	$\frac{(100 - 107.53)}{9}$ = -0.84
Gross redemption yield =	7.90 - 0.84 = 7.06%

Using the simplified method only produces an approximate figure for the gross redemption yield, in this case 7.06% compared with the published gross redemption yield of 7.40%. The simplified method becomes less accurate the nearer a stock comes to its redemption date.

6.14 The gross redemption yield is studied closely by analysts and investors deciding which gilts to buy and sell at a given time. If the gross redemption yield of one gilt far exceeds that of other comparable gilts this may lead to anomaly switching. The following example illustrates how heavy switching by the large institutional investors can have an impact on the price of a gilt and, in turn, on its gross redemption yield.

Example 13.3: Anomaly switching

Gilt	Gross Redemption Yield
1	8.00%
2	6.40%
3	6.30%

Investors who discover that gilt 1 is giving a far higher gross redemption yield than gilts 2 and 3 may well switch to gilt 1 by selling some of their stock in gilts 2 and 3.

The effect of this will be that the price of gilts 2 and 3 will fall due to a fall in demand which in turn will lead to an increase in their gross redemption yields. The price of gilt 1 will rise, leading to a fall in its gross redemption yield.

The price movements between the three gilts will produce gross redemption yields for each of approximately the same.

Net redemption yield

6.15 Although interest rates are quoted gross, interest will, in most instances be paid net of lower rate tax at 20%. Higher rate taxpayers will have an additional tax liability of 20%. Prior to 6 April 1996 interest was paid net of basic rate tax at 25%. Since the majority of private investors will be taxpayers, it is important to be able to calculate the net redemption yield. This is calculated as follows:

Net redemption = Net interest yield + (Gross redemption yield - Gross yield   interest yield)

Example 13.4: Net redemption yield

For the purposes of this calculation the following gilt is considered - Treasury $8^1/_2$% 2005 with a gross interest yield of 7.9% and a gross redemption yield of 7.40%.

	Lower and Basic rate taxpayers - 20%	Higher rate taxpayers - 40%
Gross interest yield	7.90	7.90

Tax liability	1.58	3.16
Net interest yield	6.32	4.74
Capital Loss Element	-0.50	-0.50
Net redemption yield	5.82%	4.24%

Grossed-up net redemption yield

6.16 Where an investor wishes to compare gilts with products that do not have redemption elements, for example cash investments, the most suitable method is to calculate the grossed-up net redemption yield for the gilt. This involves simply grossing-up the net redemption yield at the investor's highest marginal rate of tax for investment income, i.e. 20% or 40%.

Example 13.5: Grossed-up net redemption yield

Using the example in 13.4 - Treasury $8^{1}/_{2}$ % 2005 - the net redemption yields were 5.82% (20%) and 4.24% (40%). The gross net redemption yields therefore become:

$$5.82 \times \frac{100}{80} = 7.27\% \ (20\% \ \text{tax}) \ \text{or}$$

$$4.24 \times \frac{100}{60} = 7.07\% \ (40\% \ \text{tax})$$

Yield curves

6.17 Risk increases with time and it can generally be expected that longer-dated gilts will yield more to redemption date than shorter-dated gilts. However, the relationship between time and yield is not constant. Gilt analysts plot the yield of a gilt against years to redemption and produce three interest rate profiles, normal, flat and inverted.

6.18 The normal yield curve can be expected to decrease as redemption gets nearer. The level of risk anticipated by the investor is indicated by the steepness of the curve. If it is thought that inflation will be high in the future, investors will want to ensure they are getting a higher yield to compensate, i.e. they will want to pay less for their gilts.

6.19 A flat yield indicates greater investor confidence. Investors are prepared to accept a lower yield and pay more for longer-dated stock. It is possible to switch from longer-dated stocks to shorter, lower-risk stocks without sacrificing the yield.

6.20 An inverted yield indicates a high level of confidence in the future. Investors may be able to switch to shorter-dated stocks without reducing yield.

Reverse yield gap

6.21 The reverse yield gap occurs when comparing the returns on gilts and equities. Since gilts are government backed, they are seen by the investor to be a secure investment. Equities on the other hand are more risky and an investor could be expected to look for a higher return than on gilts. In the last

35-40 years this has not been so and has created what has become known as the reverse yield gap.

6.22 Investors, it would appear, are prepared to accept a lower initial yield from equities than from gilts in the knowledge that, over time, the dividend and capital value of equities can increase. The fixed-interest and redemption value of gilts leaves them open to the effects of inflation.

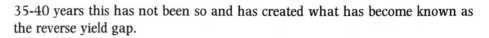

Student Activity 2

You should complete this student activity before reading the next section of the text. Answer the questions, then check your answers against the paragraph(s) indicated.

1.   How are gilt prices affected by changes in interest rates?   (5.3)

2.   An investor buys a gilt at £85 for which the coupon is 7.5%.   (6.6)
     How much will he receive in interest each year and what is
     the gross interest yield?

3.   Briefly explain the different types of yield which can be   (6.1-6.22)
     calculated, why they differ and what information they give to
     the investor.

If you are unable to answer any of the questions satisfactorily, you should read the relevant paragraphs again. Your understanding of the text will be further tested in the self-assessment section at the end of this unit.

7   New Gilts Issues

7.1   New gilts issues are purchased directly from the Bank of England. The public are invited to subscribe to a new issue of gilts by completing an application form published in the financial press with the prospectus advertising the issue.

7.2   Up until 1979, gilts were advertised with a fixed purchase price reflecting current market trends. However, following the issue of Treasury Stock $13^3/_4$% 2000-2003 in 1979 there was a significant rise in the price of gilts on the market between the price being advertised and the deadline for applications. This gilt became particularly attractive and was so over-subscribed that it was the object of much publicity.

7.3   To overcome this problem, the Bank of England now uses two alternative methods for fixing the price of a new issue:

• Tender issue

• Auction issue

Tender issue

7.4   The government sets a minimum tender price for the gilt and investors are invited to apply specifying the highest price they are prepared to pay. If the issue is under-subscribed at the minimum tender price, then all investors will get stock at this price. The remaining stock is held by the Bank of England Issue Department for issue at a later date via the tap mechanism which is described later in this unit. If the issue is over-subscribed, the whole of the issue is sold at the highest price at which the issue is fully taken up. This is known as the common issue price or common striking price.

Example 13.6: Tender issue

200 units of stock are issued with a minimum tender price of £94. The following applications are received.

Price	Units applied for	Cumulative total
£97	20	20
£96	80	100
£95	200	300
£94	60	360

The issue becomes fully subscribed at a price of £95, this then becomes the common issue price. The investors who applied for stock at £96 and £97 will be allocated the number of units of stock they requested at £95 each. The investors who applied at £95 will each get 50% of the amount they requested since their allocation is restricted. Those who applied at £94 will get nothing.

Auction issue

7.5 Large issues of gilts are often conducted through auctions. The new issue will be advertised in the financial press with application forms available in the press or from the Bank of England. The large scale investors, such as the financial institutions, can make competitive bids for the stock. The Bank of England conducts a 'Dutch Auction', accepting the highest bids first, and then lower bids until it has sold sufficient stock. The successful investors receive the gilts at the price bid.

7.6 The less experienced private investor can apply for gilts at the 'non competitive' bid price. This means that they do not have to specify a bid price; instead they are guaranteed stock up to a limit of £100,000 at the weighted average accepted price of the institutional competitive bids.

Tap mechanism

7.7 Gilt issues are rarely taken up in full, so part of the issue is taken up by the Bank of England. The stock is then sold to investors 'on tap' over a period, at a middle market price of the stock on the day of issue, i.e. the midpoint between the buying price and selling price. The 'tranches' are sold through the normal stock market dealing mechanism and rank equally to the existing issue of stock. Small issues of tap stock with a value of less than £100m are known as taplets.

7.8 Not all stock that is issued under the tap mechanism is new stock. Stock purchased originally by the Bank of England as part of the government's monetary policy can be reissued this way.

8 The Secondary Gilt Market

8.1 Gilts that have already been issued can be bought or sold in the secondary market in two main ways:

- Through a stockbroker/dealer - either directly or indirectly through an agent like a bank

- Through larger post offices on the National Savings Stock Register

Stock market

8.2 Most private investors hold only small portfolios and therefore do not deal direct with a stockbroker. Their transactions will be undertaken by an agent of the broker, e.g. a bank. The investor will give instructions to the agent who in turn will pass on the instructions to the broker for execution. The transaction is executed through the International Stock Exchange and settlement will be on the next business day.

8.3 It is important that an agent fully understands the instructions being given to him by the customer and he should have a clear understanding of the following:

- Does the customer wish to purchase or sell the gilts?

- The price instructions

- The name of the stock for purchase or sale

- The amount of stock to be traded, i.e. nominal or actual value

National Savings Stock Register (NSSR)

8.4 Most British government stocks can be purchased and sold through larger post offices who act as agents for the Stocks and Bonds Office. Commission charges are much lower than those of stockbrokers/dealers. For purchases, the minimum charge is £1, increasing by 50p for every £125 consideration (or part thereof) over £250. For sales, the scale is the same, except that small sales, less than £100, are charged at 10p for every £10 or part thereof.

8.5 It is very simple for an investor to make a purchase or sale. An application form, available from the Post Office, is completed and sent to the Stocks and Bonds Office.

8.6 The disadvantages of buying and selling gilts on the NSSR are briefly summarised as follows:

(a) Although a wide selection of gilts is available, it is not possible to purchase every gilt issued on the NSSR.

(b) Purchases are limited to £25,000 market value in any one stock on any one day; there is no limit on sales or total holdings or on the number of stocks that can be purchased in a day.

(c) Price limits cannot be set on a sale or purchase. Postal delays may lead to a delay between the decision to purchase or sell and the execution of that instruction. Market conditions and prices could change substantially in that time.

(d) Gilts purchased through the NSSR can only be sold through the register and cannot be sold through a broker. Similarly gilts purchased through a broker cannot be sold on the NSSR.

(e) The Stocks and Bonds Office acts solely as a buying/selling agent and does not offer any professional advice.

8.7   A leaflet entitled 'Government Stock', issued by National Savings, details the operation of the NSSR and is available from most post offices.

Accrued Interest Scheme

8.8   The Accrued Interest Scheme or AIS applies to the gilts market only. Accrued interest is the interest that builds up in the price of stock between interest dates. 37 days before an interest payment is due, a gilt becomes ex dividend (xd). This means that anyone who sells an ex dividend stock will still be entitled to the interest due. The portion which relates to the period from the date of settlement of the sale and the interest payment date will be deducted from the sale proceeds. If an investor buys an ex dividend stock, this portion of interest will be deducted from the cost in compensation.

8.9   For gilts sold cum dividend, the purchaser will receive all of the next interest payment. Interest for the period from the last interest date to the settlement date (normally the business day after purchase) is added to the purchase price to compensate the seller.

8.10   The scheme was introduced in the 1985 Finance Act and is designed to prevent investors avoiding their income tax liability on interest payments by selling stock cum dividend shortly before it is due to go ex dividend, thereby capitalising interest payments into tax exempt capital gains through the purchase price. All gilt-edged stock prices are quoted 'clean' which means that gross accrued interest is separated out of the price of stock and must be added or subtracted to arrive at the total purchase price.

Example 13.7: The effects of AIS where the purchase price is cum dividend

Investor A purchases £10,000 nominal of Exchequer 15% 1997 on 16 November - price £120 cum dividend. Interest on this stock is payable on 27 April and 27 October. Investor A will have to pay the seller, Investor B, the price for the stock plus the interest that has accrued from 28 October to 17 November (settlement date). Accrued interest is calculated as follows:

$$\frac{21 \text{ (28 October - 17 November)}}{182 \text{ (half year interest period)}} \times \frac{15\%}{2} \times £10,000 = £86.54$$

Therefore, excluding dealing costs, Investor A will have to pay Investor B £12,086.54.

Investor A will receive full interest of £750 on 27 April following the sale; Investor B will receive nothing on this date.

The interest on which the tax liability arises is as follows:

Investor A   £663.46 (£750 less £86.54)

Investor B   £86.54

Example 13.8: The effect of AIS where the purchase price is ex dividend

Investor C purchases £10,000 of nominal Exchequer 12% 2012 - 2017 on 16 November - price £95 ex dividend.

The next interest payment is due on 12 December. Investor C will have to pay Investor D, the seller, the purchase price less the interest that will accrue between the settlement date and December 12, i.e.

$$\frac{26}{183} \text{ (17 November - 12 December)} \times \frac{12}{2} \text{ per cent} \times £10,000 = £85.25$$

(half year interest period in days)

Therefore, excluding dealing costs, Investor C must pay Investor D £9,500 - £85.25 = £9,414.75.

Investor C will receive no interest on 12 December. Investor D will receive full interest of £600.

The interest on which a tax liability arises is as follows:

Investor C £85.25

Investor D £514.75 (£600 less £85.25)

9   How to Read the Financial Pages

9.1   The prices of government securities are shown in the UK Gilts Prices section of the financial press each day.

9.2   An extract from the Financial Times is illustrated below. As previously discussed, gilts are divided into categories and for simplicity one example from each category is illustrated.

Example 13.9: UK gilt prices as shown in the Financial Times

(1)	(2) Yield		(3)	(4)	(5) 52 week	
	Int	Red	Price £	+/-	High	Low
Shorts						
Exchequer $13\frac{1}{4}$ % 1996	14.85	6.20	$102^{11}/_{16}$	-	$109^{13}/_{52}$	$102^{11}/_{16}$
Mediums						
Treasury 8% 2000	7.63	6.79	$104^{27}/_{32}$	$+^{1}/_{6}$	$105^{5}/_{8}$	$96^{9}/_{16}$
Longs						
Conversion $6\frac{1}{4}$ % 2010	7.16	7.68	$87^{5}/_{16}$	$+^{3}/_{16}$	$87^{27}/_{32}$	$79^{9}/_{32}$
Undated						
Consols $2\frac{1}{2}$ %	7.77	-	$32^{3}/_{16}$	$+^{1}/_{8}$	$32^{15}/_{32}$	$28^{7}/_{8}$
Index-Linked						
Treasury $2\frac{1}{2}$ % 2001	2.86	3.32	$178^{19}/_{32}$	$+^{1}/_{16}$	$179^{1}/_{32}$	$165^{25}/_{32}$

Source: Financial Times (16 January 1996)

(a)   The first column shows the name of each gilt, the figure, e.g. 8%, is the coupon which is the dividend yield of the investment based on a price of £100.

(b)   Column two shows the gross interest yield and the gross redemption yield, both of which have been described fully earlier in this unit.

(c) Column three shows the mid market price at the close of the previous day's business. If two prices are printed, the lower price indicates the price at which an investor could have sold the gilt, and the higher price is the price that would have to be paid by an investor purchasing the gilt. Note the strange method of pricing gilts; they are still measured in $^1/_{32}$ and $^1/_2$ and similar, e.g. $125^1/_{32}$. This is merely a reflection of tradition and, as a rule of thumb, $^1/_{32}$ of a pound is about 3p; if it were decimalised $^1/_{32}$ would equal 3.125p.

(d) Column four shows the increase or reduction in the price compared to the closing price of the previous day. In Mondays' papers this column is replaced with details of when the gilt last went ex dividend.

(e) Column five shows the highest and lowest prices for the year so far. In Mondays' listings this column is replaced with details of the dates on which interest payments are made.

10 Taxation

10.1 Gilts normally pay interest half-yearly. Prior to 6 April 1996 interest was paid net of basic rate income tax. From this date interest is paid net of lower rate tax at 20%. Non taxpayers can reclaim the tax deducted at source, and higher rate taxpayers have an additional tax liability. Basic rate taxpayers have no further tax to pay.

10.2 There are six cases where interest is paid gross:

(a) War Loan $3^1/_2$%.

(b) Stocks purchased through the National Savings Stock Register.

(c) Where gross interest payable is not more than £2.50 per half year.

(d) Stock purchased by non-residents; these are known as FOTRA stocks (Free of Tax to Residents Abroad) and are marked # in the Financial Times. In addition, the stock certificates are marked: "Held on 'E' arrangement" .Such stock was issued to encourage overseas investors to purchase gilts and interest is paid gross to overseas residents. If held by UK residents, interest is paid net of tax.

(e) Interest from floating rate gilts.

(f) Charities and pension funds, on application, can receive interest gross.

10.3 If a UK taxpayer receives interest gross, he or she is still liable to pay tax and the interest received must be included in their tax return.

10.4 There is no capital gains tax liability for gains made at redemption or in the sale of gilts so this can be a very attractive proposition for higher rate taxpayers and anyone who has already incurred chargeable capital gains elsewhere.

11 Using Gilts in a Portfolio

11.1 Although a large bulk of gilts are bought by institutionalised investors e.g. pension funds and insurance companies, a number of private investors also invest directly in gilts.

11.2 The wide range of coupons and redemption dates means that investors can choose which are most suitable for their needs. For example, a higher rate taxpayer may require a gilt with a low coupon to reduce tax liability on the interest, but with a higher capital profit at redemption. This will, of course, depend on the price he pays for the gilt. There is also choice in the term of the investment depending on the redemption date.

Risk

11.3 The main advantage of investing in gilts is that the return is known and guaranteed over a fixed period (unless irredeemable). The investor will know what his capital gain, or loss, will be at a certain date. Where income is more important, the investor may be prepared to make a loss, although losses cannot be offset against capital gains made from other sources. The only risk that an investor will have to accept is the effects of changes in interest rates which may reduce the value of interest being received in comparison with other forms of investment. Prices are also likely to have fallen and so selling gilts at this time would produce a capital loss.

11.4 The effects of inflation on the real value of a capital gain also need to be considered, and if this is important the investor should buy index-linked gilts.

Spreading investment

11.5 Where a regular income from gilts is required an investor can buy a number of gilts with different payment dates.

11.6 If an investor does not want to hold all his gilts until redemption, a spread of investment in gilts with different coupons and redemption dates may mean profits can be made by selling gilts when prices rise.

Student Activity 3

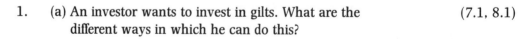

You should complete this student activity before reading the next section of the text. Answer the questions, then check your answers against the paragraph(s) indicated.

1. (a) An investor wants to invest in gilts. What are the different ways in which he can do this? (7.1, 8.1)

   (b) If a new gilt issue is not taken up in full what happens to the unsold stock? (7.7)

   (c) Suggest two advantages and two disadvantages to a small investor of buying and selling gilts through the NSSR. (8.6)

2. Investor A is buying a gilt which Investor B is selling. Explain the difference it will make to the price Investor A pays if the purchase price is cum dividend and not ex dividend. (8.8, 8.9)

3. A basic rate taxpayer receives interest from his gilt.

   (a) How often will he receive his payments? (10.1)

(b) How will they be taxed? (10.1)

(c) If he becomes a higher rate taxpayer next year what (10.1)
difference will this make to the amount of tax payable
and how is it paid?

If you are unable to answer any of the questions satisfactorily, you should read the relevant paragraphs again. Your understanding of the text will be further tested in the self-assessment section at the end of this unit.

12 Local Authority Investments

12.1 Some local authorities raise finance when it is required from the issue of fixed rate investments to the public. The capital is guaranteed by the issuing authority, and so the schemes carry a higher risk than similar schemes that are backed by central government. The rate of return on the investment may be slightly higher than a government-issued security on account of the increased risk.

12.2 Local authority investments may be in the form of marketable securities or non-marketable cash deposits. Not all local authorities choose to raise money in this way, and the details of schemes on offer are advertised in newspapers or may be obtained from stockbrokers. Investors are not restricted to buying from their own local authority.

12.3 Local authority investments are suitable for those seeking capital security and a fixed income, but who are prepared to take a slightly higher risk than that presented by bank and building society products in order to secure a higher return. Where security of income is a high priority, the longer-term schemes will be attractive.

Local authority deposits and mortgage bonds

12.4 Local authorities may seek to overcome a short-term cash crisis by paying an attractive rate of interest on large sums deposited for a short term, subject to a minimum period of seven days. The minimum investment is generally in the region of £25,000.

12.5 Longer-term mortgage bonds, for fixed periods of between one and ten years, may also be available. These are effectively loans to the local authority. The minimum investment will be around £500, and the rate of interest is fixed throughout the term. There is no facility to make withdrawals, and so the money is locked into the investment until the end of the term, although the local authority may be prepared to make an earlier repayment if interest rates fall and cheaper loans become available.

12.6 At the end of the term, the investor will receive a return of his capital, or may be able to reinvest at current rates.

Local authority marketable bonds and stocks

12.7 There are two types of quoted stocks that can be bought and sold on the stock exchange. They carry interest at a fixed rate and are redeemed at their nominal capital value after a fixed term. The advantage of the marketable securities is that whilst the term is fixed, the investor may be able to realise his investment by selling it to another investor.

12.8 The most common type are negotiable bonds, also known as yearling bonds. They have a fixed term of one year, and are often bought at a small discount to their nominal value.

12.9 The other type are local authority stocks. These are issued for a longer term and have a fixed redemption date.

Tax position

12.10 Prior to 6 April 1996 interest was paid net of basic rate tax. From this date interest is paid net of lower rate tax at 20%. Higher rate taxpayers will be liable for the additional higher rate tax i.e. 20% whereas non taxpayers may claim a refund of the overdeducted amount. Basic rate taxpayers have no further tax to pay. Alternatively, non taxpayers may register to receive interest payments gross by completing Inland Revenue Form R85.

13 Public Boards

13.1 Another sector of the loan market is that of the public boards, such as port authorities and the Agricultural Mortgage Corporation. The stock of some of these may resemble local authority stock in the degree of risk involved but there are others in which an investor should exercise caution. It is important for an investor to ascertain the exact terms of the stock and the nature of the security, before purchasing, so that it may be compared with other loans. Any gains made on the sale of public board stock are free from capital gains tax.

14 Commonwealth Government Stock

14.1 A number of stocks quoted on the London Stock Exchange have been issued by the governments of Commonwealth countries to raise finance, in sterling, as part of their monetary plans. Commonwealth stock accounts for only a tiny percentage of the market. The confidence placed in the governments of say, Australia and New Zealand, allows their stock to be quoted at prices comparable to United Kingdom local authority stocks. The political stability of a country can, of course, affect their risk. This was highlighted to the holders of Rhodesian Stocks, due for redemption in 1965, who did not receive repayment until 1980 due to Rhodesia's Unilateral Declaration of Independence in 1965. An investor should consider the risks involved and the political stability of the issuing government. In addition it should be realised that Commonwealth stocks do not carry the guarantee of the British government.

14.2 Commonwealth stocks are exempted from capital gains tax when denominated in sterling. In addition they are free of all UK taxes for residents abroad.

15 Foreign Government Stocks and Bonds

15.1 Some foreign governments have issued stocks and bonds that are quoted on the UK stock exchange. The foreign market is highly speculative and does not represent a good risk for the private investor. Many of the stocks quoted are effectively 'dead stock'. When a government has defaulted on a stock a subsequent government may propose a scheme under which some form of repayment may be made and which all investors are obliged to accept. It is not uncommon to find the same issue of stock listed twice; the unredeemed stock from which no payment can be expected and the stock with revised terms, probably less favourable than the original terms, that promises repayment.

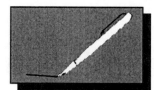

Student Activity 4

You should complete this student activity before attempting the self-assessment. Answer the questions, then check your answers against the paragraph(s) indicated.

1. Why do local authority investments carry a higher risk than similar government securities? (12.1)

2. An investor buys a negotiable bond. What return will this give him and within what timescales? ((12.7, 12.8)

If you are unable to answer any of the questions satisfactorily, you should read the relevant paragraphs again. Your understanding of the text will be further tested in the following self-assessment section.

Summary

Now that you have read this unit, you should be able to:

❑ **Understand the features of a gilt**

❑ **Describe how gilts are bought and sold**

❑ **Explain the different types of gilt on the market**

❑ **Understand the factors which affect gilt prices**

❑ **Explain the different interest yields**

❑ **Interpret published information on gilts**

❑ **Understand the tax treatment of gilts**

❑ **Understand the risk profile of gilts**

❑ **Apply the use of gilts to investor's objectives**

❑ **Explain the types of local authority stocks and bonds**

If you can tick all the above boxes with confidence, you are ready to answer the questions which follow.

Self-Assessment Questions

1. How would you explain how a gilt works in simple terms to a layman?

2. What is a convertible rate gilt?

3. Tom Smith is a basic rate taxpayer and buys £5,000 worth of Exch 12pc 1998 at £5,550.

   (a) Calculate the gross interest yield. What relevance does this figure have for Tom?

   (b) Calculate the net redemption yield. Assume the current gross redemption yield is 6.93. What does this figure tell Tom?

   (c) Tom wants to compare the return on his gilts with other investments which quote gross interest. How can he do this?

4. A new gilt issue is made using the tender issue method for fixing a price. What happens if the issue is over-subscribed?

5. How can an investor buy a gilt which is not sold through the National Savings Stock register?

6. Explain the differences in the tax treatment and method of payment between a non taxpayer, a basic rate taxpayer and a higher rate taxpayer on the interest they receive from their gilt holdings. How would this differ if the gilts had been bought through the NSSR?

7. George Smith is a higher rate taxpayer who has already made capital gains this year of £5,000. What is the advantage to him of a gilt?

8. Why may a higher rate taxpayer be more interested in the profit he can make at redemption than buying a gilt with a high coupon?

9. Julia Redmond wishes to expand her investment portfolio. Describe the level of risk of investing in fixed-interest securities and their position in a balanced portfolio.

10. What are the main types of local authority fixed rate investments available to the public?

Unit 14

Equities and Company Fixed-Interest Securities

Objectives

Students are required to study the following topics:

- Types of share

- Types of company

- Rights and duties of shareholders

- New issues

- Increasing company capital

- Taxation risk and accessibility of equities

- Types of company fixed-interest securities

1 Introduction

1.1 The capital of companies in the United Kingdom may be divided into two principal classes, share capital and loan capital, and this unit will consider both classes.

1.2 There has been an upsurge in private investment in shares in the 1980s and early 1990s mostly due to the government's privatisation issues and a realisation of the type of profits that can be made in owning and selling shares. The government has also been quick to give tax incentives for share ownership, mostly through the concept of personal equity plans, but also with incentives for employee share schemes.

2 What is an Equity?

2.1 An equity is an alternative name given to an ordinary share. A share is quite literally what it says it is, that is a share in the owners' capital of a company. They are referred to as equities because they give the holder a right to a proportion of the equity capital in a company.

2.2 Shares in a company are purchased because they are expected to produce an income in the form of a dividend and achieve capital growth. It is hoped that rising profits of a company will lead to increasing dividends and growth in the capital value of the shares.

2.3 Shares can be purchased by the investor through a stockbroker or acquired in ready made portfolios in the form of collective investments such as unit trusts, investment trusts or single premium life assurance policies.

Share dividends

2.4　A dividend is a payment made by a company to shareholders. It is broadly linked to the company's current and anticipated profits and is therefore not guaranteed since the amount paid is at the discretion of the directors of the company. The company is under no obligation to pay dividends, and the amount will fluctuate dependent on the performance of that company. The dividend paid to shareholders in a public company is a number of pence per share. The amount of profit distributed as dividends in relation to total profits can indicate the financial strength of a company.

2.5　For example, a company which makes profits of £1,200,000 can decide to distribute £300,000 as dividends and put the rest into reserves. The dividend is 'covered' four times which is regarded as 'well covered' .Where a company distributes more than its profits as dividends, i.e. by using reserves as well, this indicates that it may be in financial difficulty.

2.6　The dividend is normally paid twice a year on a specified due date in the form of a cheque to the shareholder. The income tax charge will have been deducted and the cheque will be accompanied by a tax voucher. Non taxpayers can use this to reclaim tax; higher rate taxpayers will have a further tax liability.

2.7　Shareholders may sometimes be offered a scrip dividend as an alternative to a cash dividend. A scrip dividend is paid in the form of additional shares and is similarly taxed as a cash dividend. A shareholder benefits by receiving additional shares free of charges and stamp duty.

2.8　Share prices are normally quoted as 'cum dividend' or 'ex dividend' .The 'cum dividend' price is that which carries the right to the next dividend. The 'ex dividend' price is that which does not carry the right to the dividend, which is to be paid shortly.

Nominal values

2.9　UK law requires shares of companies to have a nominal, or par, value. Investors may find it confusing that some companies have ordinary shares with nominal values of £1 each whilst others have values of 50p, 25p or 5p. The nominal value does not represent the current share price, merely the value of the share entered as share capital in the company's balance sheet. The difference between the share price on issue and the nominal value is entered as share premium in the balance sheet.

Example 14.1: Nominal values

The figures below illustrate that the denomination of shares can have little significance to the investor.

XYZ company has net assets of £10,000,000.

Shares issued could be 10,000,000 £1 shares or 20,000,000 50p shares or 40,000,000 25p shares.

The only significance this would hold for the investor is that the quoted price of the nominal £1 shares would be four times that of the 25p shares and twice that of the 50p shares.

3 Types of Share

3.1 Most equities will give a dividend and growth, but neither will be guaranteed as they depend totally on the performance of the company. So, if the company performs well there should be both a dividend and some growth. However, if the company performs badly there may be no dividend and a decrease in the value of the share. There are different types of securities available, though, that may give certain guarantees to the investor.

4 Ordinary Shares

4.1 The most typical share is the ordinary share. Ordinary shareholders have the right to all profits after payment of such items as salaries, taxes and other overheads, and after preference shareholder dividends have been paid.

4.2 Ordinary shares usually account for the bulk of the company's capital and will normally carry voting rights for the shareholder. The number of votes equals the number of shares held. Shareholders with a high percentage of shares in the company will therefore have some control over it.

4.3 However, the fact that they rank behind the holders of fixed-interest stock and preference shareholders means that they run the greatest risk as they may receive nothing if the company does not perform well. Conversely they will receive the greatest reward if the company does well.

4.4 Other types of ordinary share are issued by companies and these are discussed below.

Non-voting ordinary shares

4.5 The issue of this category of share is frowned upon by the stock exchange and, in consequence, they will not admit new non-voting shares to their listings. Non-voting shares, usually called 'A' ordinary shares, were originally devised to keep the voting control of the company in the hands of a few shareholders, while generating income from general investors. Where such shares still exist, they usually attract a lower market value than the ordinary voting shares. The price difference will usually become significant in a takeover situation. The non-voting shares will hold no attraction to an investor as acceptance or rejection of a takeover bid will rest with the voting shares.

Preferred ordinary shares

4.6 Preferred ordinary shareholders will receive restricted dividend rights and limited repayment if the company is wound up. The shares carry less risk than an ordinary share as they are repaid before an ordinary share in the event of liquidation. Such shares generally combine the fixed dividend of a preference share and the voting rights of an ordinary share.

Deferred ordinary shares

4.7 Deferred ordinary shareholders usually do not qualify for a dividend payment until the company's profits reach a predetermined level or until a particular date, or until the ordinary shareholders have received a certain level of dividend. To compensate for this deferral, the shareholder will usually receive more favourable voting rights. The shares are often held by the founder members of the company who wish to retain some degree of control when establishing a public company. For this reason, the shares are also known as founder shares.

Deferred dividend shares

4.8 Deferred dividend shares are very like deferred ordinary shares. The payment of a dividend is deferred until a certain date in the future, after which the shareholder enjoys full dividend rights on a par with an ordinary shareholder. The shares are generally issued at a lower price than other shares, making them particularly attractive to higher rate taxpayers who will benefit from capital appreciation as the date for the payment of the dividend approaches and the gap in the price of the shares moves closer to the ordinary share price.

Redeemable ordinary shares

4.9 The Companies Act 1981 has made it possible for a company to issue redeemable ordinary shares provided there is an element of non-redeemable equity in the company. Such shares carry all the rights of ordinary shares, e.g. voting rights, dividend rights, etc. and will be redeemed in accordance with their terms of issue. The issue of such shares is used as a way of raising medium-term finance for a company.

5 Preference Shares

5.1 Preference shareholders have a right to a fixed rate of dividend out of net profits before any dividend is paid on ordinary shares. Preference shareholders will also have priority after creditors to any distribution of assets if the company goes into liquidation. As a result of this reduced risk and fixed dividend, preference shareholders will not benefit to the same extent as ordinary shareholders in times when the company is doing well. Preference shares generally carry no voting rights.

5.2 There are variants on the type of preference share available and these are briefly summarised below. It is important that an investor is familiar with the terms attaching to a preference share holding before purchase so that he is aware of his repayment and dividend rights. Where a company has more than one issue of preference shares, it will state whether each issue ranks equally or in priority to another issue.

Cumulative preference shares

5.3 Most preference shares that are issued are cumulative preference shares. If a preference share is issued as non cumulative it must be clearly expressed as such. If a company has insufficient profits in a year to pay a cumulative preference share dividend, the shareholder's entitlement must be carried forward to the next year and be paid with the subsequent year's dividend before any payment is made to holders of a lower class of capital. Therefore, even if a cumulative preference share is many years in arrears, all such arrears must be settled before a dividend can be declared on lower ranking preference shares or ordinary shares.

5.4   Non cumulative preference shares forego the right to an unpaid dividend at the end of the financial year and no arrears are due when dividend payment is resumed.

Participating preference shares

5.5   A participating preference share is similar to a preferred ordinary share and entitles the shareholder to participate in the profits of the company beyond the fixed dividend. Such shares vary in their terms and will usually impose a maximum rate of extra participation in the company profits. In addition, the holders will enjoy a limited share in the company's surplus in the event of the company being wound up. As most participating preference shares were issued some years ago, an investor is unlikely to find such a share that still offers scope for increases in dividends.

Redeemable preference shares

5.6   Although most preference shares are undated, a number of redeemable preference shares have been issued with redemption set at either a fixed date in the future or at the company's option. Where the latter redemption method is set, this may be at any time or between two future dates. Of course, redemption can only be made if the company has sufficient profits to meet the repayments. An established successful company may be able to issue a new tranche of shares to finance the repayment but this will not be an option open to all companies. Redemption, therefore, is not guaranteed and an investor purchasing shares below par cannot be certain of a capital gain at maturity.

Convertible preference shares

5.7   These shares carry conversion rights which allow them, at the investor's option, to be changed into ordinary shares under the terms of the issue. The shares carry the right to a fixed dividend throughout the period the conversion option exists. Where the option is not taken up, the shares will be redeemed at par value. Before purchasing such shares, an investor must consider whether it is preferable to purchase convertible preference shares with a view to converting them into ordinary shares, or to purchase ordinary shares at the outset. Convertibles allow the shareholder to benefit from a guaranteed fixed income in the short term while monitoring the performance of the company with a view to converting into ordinary shares.

Zero dividend preference shares

5.8   This is a specialist type of preference share issued by investment trust companies. The shares will give the investor a fixed return at the end of the term, provided that the fund has sufficient assets to meet their repayment, but no income in the meantime.

5.9   Zeros are low-risk investments as only minimal growth is required from the investment trust to cover the final redemption price. They are suitable for investors who have a specified capital requirement at a future date. See Unit 18 for further details.

Stepped preference share

5.10   These shares are also issued by investment trusts, they combine a fixed capital return when the trust is wound up, with a regular income that will grow at a specified rate each year. They are suitable for investors who require a reasonably high and growing income and are prepared to accept some risk.

6 Warrants

6.1 A warrant is not a share, but a right to purchase a share in the company at a predetermined price (the exercise price) within a given time period. At the end of the time period, the right to purchase the share lapses and the warrant becomes worthless. Warrant holders are not entitled to vote.

6.2 A warrant provides no income and all the return is in the form of a capital gain. A warrant should ideally be converted when the share price is higher than the exercise price.

Example 14.2: Warrant issue

A warrant is issued by a company at a price of 20p per warrant. Each warrant entitles the holder to subscribe for one ordinary share at any time between 30 April 1994 to 31 October 2004 at a price of 100p per share.

If the holder decides to exercise his warrant he will have to pay 100p per share, this is known as the striking price.

After 31 October 2004 the warrant will lapse and become worthless.

If the share market price is 120p per share this is the break even price - 100p (exercise price) + 20p (warrant price) = 120p.

If the share market price is 150p per share a gain will be made of 30p per share.
150p - 100p (exercise price) - 20p (warrant price) = 30p.

However if the share market price dropped to less than 120p, the warrant may still have some value.

6.3 As the price of a warrant is a fraction of the ordinary share price, more shares can be controlled through investing say £1,000 in warrants than can be purchased outright. This is called gearing.

Example 14.3: Gearing

Warrant price 20p, ordinary price 80p

$$\text{Gearing} = \frac{80}{20} = 4$$

In this case four times the number of shares can be controlled through the warrant than can be bought outright with the same amount of money. If the shares are expected to exceed the break even price within the warrant period this is an attractive proposition.

6.4 However, warrants do carry high risk as they have no status in a liquidation and will be worthless if the share price fails to rise above the striking period before the warrant period ends.

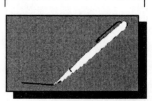

> ## Student Activity 1
>
> You should complete this student activity before reading the next section of the text. Answer the questions, then check your answers against the paragraph(s) indicated.

1. Doreen Hunt owns 5,000 ordinary shares in XYZ Company.   (4.2)
   What does this entitle her to?

2. Why is the price of an 'A' ordinary share usually lower than   (4.5)
   for an ordinary share?

3. Sally Graham has bought 1,000 warrants in Anyname   (6.2-6.4)
   Company. The warrant entitles her to buy ordinary shares at
   the price of 250p at any time between 1 July 1996 and 1 July
   2000. She paid a warrant price of 30p. The current price for
   the ordinary shares is 200p.

   (a) How much will Sally have to pay for each ordinary
   share if she converts the warrants?

   (b) When would it be worth her while to exercise the option?

   (c) What does the level of gearing indicate?

   (d) What is the premium?

If you are unable to answer any of the questions satisfactorily, you should read the relevant paragraphs again. Your understanding of the text will be further tested in the self-assessment section at the end of this unit.

7 Types of Company

7.1 Under the Companies Act 1985, provision is made for the formation of two kinds of company, a public limited company (plc) and a private company. It is important to note that not all public limited companies are quoted companies listed on the London Stock Exchange. However, to obtain a stock exchange listing, a company must be a public limited company and meet certain conditions.

7.2 A public limited company is a company limited by shares and whose memorandum or association states it to be a public company. The company must be registered as such and have the letters plc at the end of its name. In addition the company must have no fewer than two members and must have issued share capital of £50,000.

7.3 A private company, by definition, is a company that is not a public company. Although limited by shares in the same way as a public company, it cannot offer its shares or debentures for sale to the public.

8 Rights and Duties of Shareholders

8.1 When an investor buys a share in a public limited company, he becomes a part-owner of that company. The principal rights of the ordinary shareholders are listed and described below. In addition, shareholders are obliged to notify the company whenever a purchase or sale of their shares affects in any way a substantial interest in the company. The Companies Act 1989 requires any person acquiring a 3% interest in the voting capital of the company, or reducing or increasing such an interest by more than 1%, to notify the company with details of the transaction(s) within two days.

Principal rights of ordinary shareholders
- To receive the annual report and accounts
- To receive notice of the annual general meeting and other meetings of members
- To attend, vote, and speak at meetings
- To appoint a proxy to attend meetings, to request a poll, and to vote on a poll
- To share in the profits of the company - either in the form of dividends or by an increase in the reserves - and the residue on a winding up
- To subscribe for any new share capital or convertible loan stock in proportion to their existing holdings
- To transfer their shares freely unless restricted in the articles of association

Directors' report and audited accounts

8.2 All shareholders must be sent a copy of the directors' report and audited accounts prepared under standard accounting practices, not less than 21 days before the annual general meeting (AGM). Smaller investors may find the quantity of information included in the report overwhelming and for this reason the Companies Act 1989 allows listed companies to provide investors with a short form of the report and accounts unless a shareholder expresses a positive request for the fuller version.

8.3 The content of the report will be considered by the shareholders attending the AGM, who will have the opportunity to question the directors and comment on any aspect of the report.

Notification of meetings

8.4 The principal meeting of the shareholders each year is called the annual general meeting. One AGM must be held in every calendar year and the interval between such meetings must not exceed 15 months. The shareholders must be advised of the date, location and time of the meeting at least 21 days before it is due, together with details of the business it is proposed to discuss. The AGM generally provides the only regular opportunity for directors and shareholders to meet each other and shareholders are entitled to speak at this meeting if they wish to do so.

8.5 All other meetings of shareholders other than the AGM are called extraordinary general meetings. These can be called by the directors at any time with 14 days' notice, or 21 days' notice if a special resolution is to be passed.

8.6 All items of business at an AGM, other than routine business, and all issues presented to the shareholders at an extraordinary general meeting are termed special business. Certain types of special business require longer notice of 28 days, an example being the removal of a director or auditor before the end of their term of office.

Conduct of meetings

8.7 A minimum number of shareholders must be present at a meeting before business can be decided on at the meeting. This is known as a quorum and full details of how many members are needed to form a quorum can be found in the company's internal rules, the articles of association.

8.8 Voting on an issue at a meeting is normally by a show of hands and a shareholder will only have one vote regardless of the number of shares he owns. A poll can, however, be demanded by five or more members, or by members holding one-tenth of the voting capital. Where a poll is held, the usual procedure is to allow one vote for each share held.

8.9 A shareholder who is unable to attend a meeting can appoint a proxy to be present. A proxy cannot vote except on a poll, and can speak only to demand a poll. He cannot vote by a show of hands. Companies will issue proxy forms for shareholders unable to attend a meeting, suggesting the names of directors of the company who will act as proxies, voting as instructed by the shareholder, or, where no instruction is given, at their own discretion or by abstaining.

8.10 A corporate shareholder will appoint a representative of the company to attend a meeting. The representative will have full voting rights and is entitled to vote on a show of hands or a poll and may comment on any issue.

Resolutions

8.11 Business matters at meetings are determined by resolutions which are voted on. There are three types of resolution which can be passed:

- Ordinary resolution
- Special resolution
- Extraordinary resolution

8.12 An ordinary resolution is sufficient for most purposes, including all the routine business dealt with at an AGM, and is passed by a simple majority of those voting and requires at least 14 days' notice. Examples of other routine business dealt with in this way include increasing the authorised or issued share capital of the company or the appointment of a director.

8.13 A special resolution is required for fundamental business matters, for instance, to change the name of the company, to alter the clauses in the memorandum or any of the articles or to have the company wound up voluntarily when it is solvent. A special resolution is passed by a 75% majority of those voting and requires at least 21 days' notice.

8.14 An extraordinary resolution is less common and the most important matter requiring such a resolution to be passed is the winding up of the company where it cannot continue its business by reason of its liabilities. Such a resolution is passed by a 75% majority of those voting and requires at least 14 days' notice.

Electing directors

8.15 The control of a company is ultimately exercised by the shareholders of that company. However, the company is managed on a daily basis by its board of directors, and the company's articles of association will establish the directors' powers and duties. Directors are elected each year at the AGM and shareholders have the right to vote in the choice of a director. It is unlikely that a single shareholder will be able to influence the choice of director in a large company without the support of other shareholders or the institutional investors. Shareholders also have the power to remove a director although, without the support of others, an individual shareholder is unlikely to achieve this.

8.16 Directors will normally retire by rotation every three years and on reaching the age of 70, but in both circumstances they can offer themselves for re-election if the articles of association permit. Some companies' rules will not, in any event, allow persons over age 70 to act as directors.

Appointing auditors

8.17 The Companies Act 1985 requires that the auditors of a company must be re appointed by ordinary resolution at the AGM. This requirement provides a safeguard to shareholders who will have the opportunity to appoint new auditors if they are not satisfied with the way the existing auditors are carrying out their duties. If an auditor is being replaced or resigns, he must state whether or not there are any circumstances that should be reported to the shareholders and, if so, what these are. If an auditor is unable to make such a statement a full explanation stating the circumstances surrounding his departure must be given and the information made available to shareholders and major creditors.

Dividends

8.18 There are two types of dividend that may be paid by a company, interim and final. An interim dividend may be declared by the directors of the company but a final dividend can only be paid following approval by the ordinary shareholders at the AGM. An interim dividend will usually be paid during the second half of the company's year with a final dividend paid shortly after the AGM. Thus dividends are usually paid at about six-monthly intervals. The shareholders have the right, at the meeting, to reduce or even cancel a final dividend if they feel the directors have set the dividend too high. This right, however, does not extend to increasing a final dividend.

Shareholdings

8.19 Shareholders may purchase further shares in a company through a stockbroker, at any time, subject to the provisions of the substantial acquisition rules.

8.20 Shareholders are further automatically entitled to subscribe to any new share capital or convertible loan stock in proportion to their existing holdings. This entitlement, known as a pre-emptive right, enables a shareholder to protect his interest in the company from erosion as new shares are purchased by new investors.

8.21 Shareholders have the freedom to transfer their shares to whoever they wish. In most circumstances, this will be effected by a sale transaction through a stockbroker, without the original investor knowing the identity of the purchaser. Once again, the provisions of the substantial acquisition rules must be observed to prohibit an investor accumulating a controlling holding in a company and threatening a takeover bid without the knowledge of the company directors.

8.22 Where a company suspects that shares are being purchased by a nominee company for the purpose of an attempted takeover, they can ask the nominee company to disclose the identity of the holders of the shares.

8.23 Shareholders of a company have the right to remain so for as long as they wish. The only threat to their shareholding would occur if the company was the object of a takeover bid. Shareholders have the right to accept or reject a bid but must agree to abide by the decision of the majority. A bid may take the form of cash purchase of the existing shares, or maybe the offer of shares in the new company, or a combination of both.

Institutional investors

8.24 The term institutional investor is used to refer to insurance companies, pension funds, financial companies such as the merchant banks, unit trusts and investment trusts. All are providers of packaged investment products and as such will invest the funds they receive from individuals for the purpose of profit, primarily in gilts and equities.

8.25 Between the early 1960s and the early 1990s the proportion of ordinary shares in listed UK companies held directly by personal investors fell by approximately two-thirds, from almost 60% to less than 20%. The change in balance mirrors the growth of institutional and overseas involvement in company shares. The growth of financial institutions caused institutional ownership to rise from 48% in 1975 to 62% in 1993.

8.26 An institutional investor is able to fund a detailed ongoing analysis of a company and its shares, an option not feasible to the private individual, and share prices can be immediately affected by the sale or purchase of a large block of shares by an institutional investor. In addition, the institutional investors are able to secure competitive brokerage rates, given the size of their transactions.

8.27 Institutional investors are seen in financial markets as key shareholders and for this reason may be consulted, informally, by the companies they own shares in, more frequently than the ordinary shareholders. Legislation covering insider dealing is in place to protect the ordinary shareholders from the actions of the institutional investors who may acquire information which could prove beneficial to them, although it may not have been made available to the ordinary shareholder.

9　How New Issues are Made

9.1 There are a number of ways in which a company can offer its new share issue to the public.

Placing

9.2 With this method, the company allows its broker to offer the shares to its own customers. However, at least 25% of the shares being issued must be placed with another firm's private customers, or to the public to ensure that a market is made for these shares. Both listed shares and those on the AIM can be offered to investors this way.

9.3 Where the issue is over £50m, a maximum of 50% of shares may be placed with the issuing firm's own customers and the remainder offered to other firms.

9.4 There must be at least 30 shareholders per £1m shares placed, and a total of at least 100 private shareholders to ensure that this is still a form of public issue. A formal notice must be placed in at least two national papers.

Offer for sale

9.5 This method is used when shares are to be offered to the public at large and is most commonly used for listed companies. The issuing house buys all the shares that are to be sold, and then offers them to the public for a slightly higher price. The issuing house will use another merchant bank to underwrite the issue in case it is not fully subscribed.

9.6 The sequence of events is usually as follows:

(a) Pre-launch publicity.

(b) Pricing and underwriting.

(c) Issue of prospectus and application form.

(d) Advertisement in at least two newspapers.

(e) Deadline for completed applications.

(f) Basis of allocation announced - applications will need to be scaled down if over-subscribed. The issuing house will need to decide how to allocate if over-subscribed. Some investors may have preferential allocation, e.g. existing customers, etc.

(g) Letters of acceptance sent out (interim certificates).

(h) Dealing commences.

(i) Despatch of share certificates.

Offers for subscription

9.7 In this case, offers are made direct to the public and an issuing house is not used. This is most commonly used by the Bank of England and by investment trusts.

Introductions

9.8 This often applies to companies which are listed on other stock exchanges, e.g. overseas companies, and want to be listed in the UK to increase sources of capital. They will already have a large number of shareholders and may ask some of the major shareholders (usually the directors) to make some of their shares available on the market. The company will not raise capital in this way but will become listed on another stock exchange and so have access to a new range of potential shareholders, and another market, for future new issues.

9.9 Introductions are notified in the financial papers by advertisement.

10 Privatisation Issues

10.1 These generally work in the same way as other offers for sale. However, there are some particular characteristics which make them slightly different.

(a) Priority. Most privatisations have given their customers priority. When the shares are registered, these customers may receive loyalty bonuses such as free shares or discounts on bills.

(b) Payment in instalment. These shares are normally sold in instalments, i.e. part of the share price is paid immediately with the second instalment due after a specified period, e.g. six months later. Payment of the second and possible subsequent instalments is a legal liability. These shares are known as partly paid and can be sold as such, with the buyer liable for the second instalment. If the second instalment is not paid, the shareholder loses his right to the shares and they will be sold by the company to another investor.

(c) Prospectuses. Usually two are issued, with one a more simplified version for the inexperienced investor.

(d) Timing. Investors usually have a longer time to decide whether to apply for shares and the time between closing the offer and the commencement of dealing is longer.

10.2 Most privatisation issues have traded well above the offer price when dealing starts on the stock exchange.

10.3 The government usually has an entitlement to some of the shares in a company when it is privatised. This is known as a 'golden share' and allows the government a casting vote which it can use if necessary, e.g. in the possibility of a takeover. The golden share only lasts for a limited period, and its rights can be waived.

11 Share Options for Directors and Employees

11.1 There are a variety of share options available which enable directors and employees to buy shares in their employer's company, usually at a preferential price.

11.2 Once these shares have been allocated or bought by the individual, he can trade them in the same way as any other shares.

11.3 Full details of these schemes can be found in Unit 3.

12 Increasing the Capital of a Company

12.1 A company can make changes to its capital structure in various ways by both increasing or reducing its share capital. The following paragraphs will consider the different ways in which the capital structure of a company can be increased.

New issues

12.2 The principal purpose of a new issue of shares from a company that already has a quotation is to raise additional capital. In order to increase the issued share capital of the company, a meeting of shareholders will have to be arranged and an ordinary resolution passed.

Scrip issue

12.3 A scrip issue, also known as a capitalisation or bonus issue, represents only an adjustment to the share capital of a company and involves the distribution of part of the reserves in the form of additional shares to its existing shareholders.

12.4 The reserves of a company may increase in the course of its normal business activities for a number of reasons. As a result of retaining part of its profits it may have substantial revenue reserves which are distorting the share capital ratio on the company balance sheet. Alternatively, the value of its fixed assets, such as land or buildings, may be upwardly revalued, boosting reserves.

12.5 The effect of a scrip issue is to increase shareholders' holdings of ordinary shares in proportion to their existing holdings, at no cost to themselves. In addition, the market share price will reduce in exact proportion to the issue. Thus, if a company with 1,000,000 ordinary shares of £1 in issue decided to reduce its reserve account by £1,000,000 and to create £1,000,000 of new ordinary capital, shareholders would be issued with one new share of £1 for every share already held. In addition, it could be expected that the price of ordinary shares on the market would fall by one-half, thereby increasing their marketability. Private investors can be deterred by higher priced shares but may be attracted by lower priced shares.

12.6 The following examples illustrate the effect of a scrip issue on both the company balance sheet and the share price where the issue is on a 1 for 4 basis.

Example 14.4: Company balance sheet

Company ABC plc wishes to make a scrip issue on a 1 for 4 basis - ordinary shares are currently valued at £1 and number 1,000,000.

	Before scrip issue	After scrip issue
Ordinary share value (£1)	£1,000,000	£1,250,000
Revenue reserves	£ 500,000	£ 250,000
Balance	£1,500,000	£1,500,000

Example 14.5: Share price following scrip issue

Share price before scrip issue = £1

Using example 14.4:

1,000,000 ordinary shares @ £1   £1,000,000

250 ordinary shares @ no cost   Nil

1,250,000 ordinary shares   £1,000,000

Share price following scrip issue =

$$\frac{£1,000,000}{£1,250,000} = £0.80$$

12.7   It is not uncommon for the share price to be slightly more than that calculated, using the method illustrated, following a scrip issue. This can be for two reasons. A scrip issue is usually accompanied by either a profit statement, an increased dividend rate or an optimistic forecast of future profits, any of which could have the effect of increasing the price of the shares. The other reason is that the marketability of the share is increased following its overall price reduction.

12.8   A shareholder has no investment decision to make following a scrip issue. The shares are sent to the shareholder in the form of a renouncable share certificate, and no specific action has to be taken. On the expiry date, shown on the reverse of the certificate, the renouncable share certificate becomes an ordinary share certificate. If the holder wishes to sell or otherwise dispose of the shares he may complete the renunciation form on the reverse of the certificate and pass it to his broker or to the transferee.

12.9   The transfer of shares under such circumstances will not incur stamp duty, making them attractive to purchasers and, in general, renounced share certificates will trade at a price that is higher than that gained on the original shares.

12.10 A scrip issue must be distinguished from both a share split or consolidation. A share split involves the creation of a larger number of shares with a lower nominal value, for example, 1,000,000 x £1 shares may become 2,000,000 x 50p shares. The price of each individual share is thus reduced making them more marketable while retaining the company's reserves. A consolidation reduces the number of shares in issue and increases the nominal value of each share. The price of shares will increase making them more attractive to those investors who are unwilling to accept the impact small movements have on the returns of lower priced shares. A company will always cancel existing certificates and issue new certificates following a share split or consolidation. It is important that anyone selling shares for a shareholder checks the nominal value on the share certificate and compares it with the current published price. Any anomaly may suggest that a consolidation or share split may have taken place and it should be clearly established how many shares the holder actually owns.

13   Rights Issues

13.1   A rights issue is the issue of new shares to existing holders at a favourable price, in proportion to their existing holdings. A company may find it necessary to raise additional funds for expansion, particular projects, or for the repayment of short-term borrowing, and will take advice from their financial advisers as to whether a rights issue is the best way to achieve this. A rights issue is a two-stage process; the announcement to shareholders of the issue, and the period up to and including acceptance and payment of the purchase price.

The announcement

13.2 When a rights issue is announced, a provisional letter of allotment is sent to all shareholders, accompanied by a circular setting out the terms of the rights issue and the reasons why the company considers a rights issue to be appropriate. The provisional letter of allotment is a valuable document and acts as a receipt for the purchase price paid to the company by a shareholder, as well as being a negotiable document on the stock market.

13.3 Immediately following the despatch of provisional letters of allotment, existing shareholdings are dealt with on an 'ex rights' basis.

13.4 Following the announcement of a rights issue, a shareholder will effectively hold two types of share, old shares and new shares, and each will be traded separately and at different prices. From the example it can be seen that old shares prices will fall to the 'ex rights' price.

Example 14.6: Calculating the 'ex rights' price of old shares

Assume that company XYZ whose shares are quoted at £3.60 each makes a rights issue of one new ordinary share for every five held, at £2.40 per share. The position would be:

	£
Five old shares at £3.60 would cost	18.00
One new share will cost	2.40
The six shares would therefore cost	20.40
Each share is therefore worth ('ex rights' price)	3.40

13.5 Trading will not always take place at the 'ex rights' price as there are several factors that may cause this price to fluctuate. One is that, initially, many shareholders will not wish to subscribe for their rights and will sell them. Lack of confidence in the company's ability to maintain the dividend level on the new shares may be a determining factor for a shareholder considering whether to sell his rights. The fact that the supply of shares has been increased relative to demand is a depressing factor causing share prices to fall. If the announcement of the rights issue is accompanied by news of, say, a future highly profitable project then the demand for shares may increase, inflating the share price. External influences will, of course, have an impact on the share price, for example, a sudden crash in the stock market could be catastrophic.

13.6 A shareholder will also have new shares to trade and the value of his rights in the new shares can be considered in the following examples.

Example 14.7: Calculating the value of rights on new shares

Method 1

Value of rights = calculated 'ex rights' price - rights price

Using the example of company XYZ the calculation would be:

£3.40 - £2.40 = £1

Method 2

The value of rights may be considered on a nil paid basis in relation to the number of original shares as follows:

$$\frac{\text{Value of rights per new share}}{\text{Number of original shares per right}} = \frac{£1}{5} = 20p$$

Example 14.8: Partial sale of rights

Using the earlier example for company XYZ, assume a shareholder has been allocated 100 shares under the rights issue. He wishes to sell some of his rights to generate sufficient funds to take up the remainder of his rights. The formula is:

$$\frac{\text{Rights price}}{\text{Calculated 'ex rights' price}} \quad x \quad \text{Number of allocated shares}$$

$\frac{£2.40}{£3.40}$ x 100 = 70.58 (71 rights must be sold to purchase the remaining 29)

Acceptance and payment

13.7 Allotment letters follow a fairly standard form and, in addition to the name of the allottee and the details of issue, there is a timetable of dates that is relevant when considering the shareholder's options during a rights issue.

Example 14.9: Timetable for shareholder's options

Last date for splitting nil paid	Date 1
Last date for acceptance and payment	Date 2
Last date for splitting fully paid	Date 3
Last date for renunciation and registration	Date 4
Date for despatch of share certificate	Date 5

Taking up rights in full

- Shareholder to sent provisional allotment letter plus cheque to company registrar by date 2

- Shareholder will be sent back receipted provisional allotment letter

- Share certificate covering rights issue will be sent shortly after date 5; provisional allotment letter becomes valueless

Selling all rights through a bank/broker

- Shareholder must sign renunciation form on reverse of provisional allotment letter; document becomes fully negotiable as a bearer document with title to rights transferred by delivery

- CGT liability may arise if shareholder sells rights representing more than 5% of total post rights holding

- Settlement in cash will be immediate

- Purchaser must make payment in full to company registrar by date 2

- Purchaser of rights must complete details on registration form on reverse of provisional allotment letter and send to company registrar by date 4

Partial sale of rights through a bank/broker

- Banker/broker must request split letter for shares from company registrar by date 1

- Registrar must return two letters to banker/broker

- Letter for shares to be purchased must be returned to registrar accompanied by cheque by date 2

- Receipted letter to be returned to banker/broker; allotment letter then treated as if rights taken up in full

No action

- Shareholder's right to take up shares lapses if payment under the provisional allotment letter is not received by date 2

- Company will proceed to sell shares and will remit sale proceeds less the rights price and associated expenses to allottee

13.8 During the rights issue, an existing shareholder has the option to take up his rights in full, subject to payment by the due date; take up part of his rights and sell the remainder; sell his full rights or do nothing. A shareholder may wish to sell some of his rights to release sufficient funds to take up the remainder of his rights. A shareholder who elects to do nothing is in a worse position than if he sold the shares himself in full, incurring only broker's costs. This is because the company registrar will sell the shares on his behalf but will pass on the hidden costs of the rights issue to the shareholder.

13.9 Factors affecting a shareholder's choice of option are:

(a) Financing the purchase of shares - lack of finance may prompt a shareholder to consider realising existing assets to fund the purchase. The expected returns on both assets and rights must be considered. Similarly, where shares are being offered at a deep discount to their market value then the shareholder may consider borrowing the necessary funds to purchase the rights, and interest charges on borrowing must be compared with expected returns from the rights.

(b) View of the company - a shareholder may be encouraged to take up his rights issue if he feels the future of the company is promising; other shareholders may disagree with the reason for the rights issue and will not take up their rights.

(c) Increased shareholding - a shareholder looking to increase his holding in a company may find a rights issue attractive, particularly in view of the discounted share price and the absence of dealing costs. On the other hand, a shareholder may feel his holding in the company is sufficient and will not take up the rights.

(d) Market opinion - a shareholder may wish to take an informed opinion of the rights issue, from a stockbroker or analyst, before considering his options.

13.10 Once a shareholder has decided on the course of action he wishes to follow, the necessary documentation must be completed.

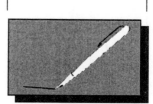

Student Activity 2

You should complete this student activity before reading the next section of the text. Answer the questions then check your answers against the paragraph(s) indicated.

1. (a) What is a scrip issue? (12.3)

   (b) What happens to the share price if there is a scrip issue? (12.5)

2. Sally has applied for some shares in a privatisation issue. The shares will be issued partly paid. Explain to Sally what this means and her obligations. (10.1)

3. Look through some recent issues of the Financial Times newspaper and find advertisements for new share issues (offers for sale). Make a note of the information they contain and the instructions for subscribers.

If you are unable to answer any of the questions satisfactorily you should read the relevant paragraphs again. Your understanding of the text will be further tested in the self-assessment section at the end of this unit.

14 Equities and Tax

Income tax

14.1 Any dividends that are paid to shareholders come in the form of a cheque that has had the income tax charge deducted, so the cheque will be accompanied by a tax voucher.

14.2 The income tax charged on dividends is 20% and the accompanying tax credit is also 20%. Both lower rate and basic rate taxpayers receive a tax credit that exactly matches the tax liability; higher rate taxpayers pay additional tax on the dividends at the difference between the higher rate and the value of the tax credit (currently an additional 20%). Shareholders who are non taxpayers may reclaim the tax credit from the Inland Revenue.

Capital gains tax

14.3 When an investor sells a share he will be liable to CGT on any gain. He can use his annual exemption (£6,300 1996-97), but any gains over that amount will be chargeable.

14.4 Any losses made can be offset against the gains. This means that if gains are above the exemption threshold, the investor could sell shares which are showing a loss to bring the gain below the threshold.

14.5 Another method of reducing or eliminating CGT on shares is 'bed and breakfasting' which involves selling shares one day and buying them back the next day. In this way profit is taken in smaller chunks and is kept within the exempt limit.

14.6 When a gain is made it can be indexed to take inflation into account. This was covered in Unit 6, but to recap, the formula is as follows:

Original cost multiplied by $\dfrac{RD - RI}{RI}$

RD - retail prices index in month of disposal.

RI - retail prices index in month of acquisition (or March 1982 if later).

Example 14.10: Calculating indexation allowance

An investor buys shares in May 1992 (RPI 139.3) for £2,000 and sells them for £8,500 in Dec 1995 (RPI 150.7):

$£2,000 \times \dfrac{150.7 - 139.3}{139.3} = £163.68$

This amount is then added to the original price of the shares to calculate the gain (or loss) made. So, as the original price was £2,000, this would be increased to £2,163.68 in order to calculate the gain i.e. £8,500 - £2,163.68 = £6,336.32.

Example 14.11: Bed and breakfasting

Bill White invests £10,000 in shares on 1 June 1993. The gain made on this initial investment each year is:

£2,000 in year 1
£2,500 in year 2
£5,500 in year 3

After three years he sells his shares.

The tax liability is calculated as follows:

Total value after three years	£20,000
Initial value	£10,000
The gain (total value less initial value)	£10,000
The indexation allowance (initial value multiplied by $\dfrac{RD - RI}{RI}$)	$£10,000 \times \dfrac{153.0-141.0}{141.0} = 851.06$

Adjusted gain	£9,148.94
Less annual allowance (1996-97)	£6,300.00
Gain to be taxed	£2,848.94
Tax at 24%	£ 683.75

Notes

- Assume Bill has no other capital gains and that he is a basic rate taxpayer
- RPI June 1993 - 141.0, June 1996 - 153.0

To reduce his tax liability, Bill could have decided to cash in his investment at the end of each year (making maximum use of his annual allowance) and immediately reinvest it.

Year 1

Initial value	£10,000
Gain this year	£ 2,000

Cash in and reinvest - no tax liability as gain is less than annual allowance

Year 2

New initial value	£12,000
Plus gain this year	£ 2,500

Cash in and reinvest - no tax liability as gain is less than annual allowance

Year 3

New initial value	£14,500
Plus gain this year	£ 5,500
Total value	£20,000

Cash in - no liability as gain is less than annual allowance.

Using bed and breakfasting has reduced Bill's tax liability to nil.

15 Risk and Accessibility

15.1 Investors who wish to invest directly in the stock market need to be aware of how volatile the market can be. Rumours of changes in interest rates, or currency exchange rates for example, can cause prices to rise or fall. A change in price of 1% may not seem much, but multiplied by an investment of tens or hundreds of thousands of shares indicates the potential loss which can be incurred by a slight fall in share price.

15.2 Of course, the main attraction is that large gains can also be made on the stock market. Any potential investor in shares needs to ensure that their equities are in the right place in their total portfolio. Someone who has insufficient easily accessible, secure funds may find they have to sell shares at a low price if cash is needed for an emergency. They also need to spread their investment to create a balanced portfolio. A spread of between 20 and 40 different companies means that shares producing poorer returns will be offset against those offering good returns.

15.3 The amount invested is also important. Apart from the privatisation types of share issue, the small investor will not have sufficient capital sums to make direct equity investment worthwhile. Investors need between £20,000 to £40,000 to invest in shares. Stockbrokers and bank or building society stockbroking services usually set a minimum level of investment under which they will not deal. The cost of the stockbroking service will also mean that smaller deals are relatively more expensive.

15.4   The stock market is not the place for the faint-hearted or the investor with a very conservative attitude to risk and it would be unwise to have all of any customer's investments totally in the stock market, despite the great benefits that can be gained. However, depending upon the customer's attitude to risk and his individual requirements, the stock market is an excellent place to realise long-term capital gains as a third part of a portfolio.

15.5   Of course, the problems of dealing with the stock market for an individual are vast, given lack of understanding, lack of time and accurate response methods to movements in the market and, for most people, direct dealing is out of the question. Luckily, there are now products available that allow people to invest indirectly on the stock markets and these will be examined in later units.

15.6   It is worth remembering at this point that legislation exists to protect shareholders against the fraudulent activities of a third party. The London Stock Exchange and the Securities and Futures Authority have compensation schemes that will compensate a shareholder who loses money through the fraudulent activities of a member firm. Shareholders are not so well protected where losses arise through the fraud or negligence of a company director. Although the companies acts contain provisions allowing a criminal prosecution to be raised against the director, the shareholders would have to sue the directors for their losses. It is unlikely that the directors would have sufficient funds to compensate the shareholders.

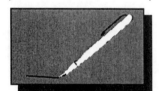

Student Activity 3

You should complete this student activity before reading the next section of the text. Answer the questions then check your answers against the paragraph(s) indicated.

1.   Malcolm receives dividend income of £12,000 in the current tax year (1996-97). His taxable earnings this year are £22,000.

   (a) Calculate his tax liability on the shares.   (14.2, 14.3)
   (b) How will he make his tax payments?
   (c) Assuming he has no other capital gains, what will his CGT liability be?

2.   How much would you suggest an investor needs to have   (15.3) available to invest in shares to make it worthwhile?

3.   Why is the risk of investing in shares so great?   (15.1)

If you are unable to answer any of the questions satisfactorily you should read the relevant paragraphs again. Your understanding of the text will be further tested in the self-assessment section at the end of this unit.

16   Company Fixed-Interest Securities

16.1   Companies will issue fixed-interest securities (sometimes referred to as corporate bonds) to raise loan capital to finance, for example, expansion or a new project. However, they will be wary of issuing fixed-interest stock when interest rates in the general economy are high and they will usually find other ways of financing their borrowing. When interest rates are low, a company will have no objection to being locked into paying a fixed rate of 'low' interest for a fixed term.

16.2　The holders of the loan capital are creditors of the company and have no rights in the company beyond the payment of interest on their loans and repayment in accordance with the terms of their issue. They cannot normally attend the annual general meeting. Loan capital may be secured or unsecured and companies will often issue both kinds of stock. The company's articles of association will specify how much may be borrowed by way of loan capital. Where the loan is secured, the capital is backed by assets which will be used to repay the loan stock if the company is wound up. Holders of unsecured loan stock will rank equally with the ordinary creditors of the company for repayment in the event of liquidation.

16.3　When a company is wound up because it is unable to meet its liabilities, the appointed liquidator will sell all the available assets and distribute them amongst the different classes of creditors. Each class of creditor must be fully repaid, in the following order, before payment can be made to the next class:

- Liquidator/receiver's expenses

- Preferential creditors

- Ordinary unsecured creditors

- Shareholders

A comparison with gilts

16.4　Company fixed-interest securities are similar to gilts, and several comparisons can be made.

16.5　Both types of security are issued with a fixed rate of interest and a specified redemption date, and although the investor will pay income tax on the interest he receives, any gains made will generally not be liable for capital gains tax.

16.6　The risk factor attaching to company fixed-interest securities is greater than that attaching to gilts. Gilts are securities of the British government and a gilt has never failed to pay interest or repay its capital value. Company fixed-interest securities, however, are ultimately dependent on the success or failure of the company.

16.7　Such fixed-interest securities are generally not as easy to buy and sell as gilts and it may not always be possible to buy exactly the stock selected. Although most loan stock of the largest companies can be bought and sold freely, the market value of UK corporate loan stock is approximately only one-tenth of that of gilts.

17　Types of Company Fixed-Interest Securities

17.1　A prospective investor wishing to invest in the company fixed-interest securities market can choose from an extensive range of stocks. The four most common types are:

- Debentures
- Unsecured loan stocks
- Subordinated loan stocks
- Convertible loan stocks

Debentures

17.2   A debenture is a fixed-interest security that is secured on all or part of a company's assets. Debentures are commonly secured on certain named assets, this is known as a fixed charge, with a floating charge over the remainder of the company's assets. Fixed charge assets may not be sold or altered in any way without permission from the debenture holder. A floating charge allows the company to deal with the remainder of its assets in the normal course of business, but if the company fails, the assets are available to be sold to repay the debenture holder.

17.3   It is usual for trustees to be appointed for the assets charged as debentures. In the event of the liquidation of the company, the trustees will arrange for the assets to be sold to repay the capital of the debenture and any arrears of interest. As debenture holders rank ahead of preferential creditors, ordinary shareholders and preference shareholders, the debenture holders can expect to see some form of repayment if the company fails. In addition, debenture interest must be paid before dividends on preference shares and ordinary shares.

17.4   In some cases, debenture holders will enjoy certain privileges. For example, Wimbledon has a large number of debenture holders who, instead of a fixed dividend, receive the right to certain centre court seats every year.

Unsecured loan stock

17.5   Unsecured loan stocks, also known as naked debentures, are fixed-interest securities which are not secured or charged on the company's assets. In the event of the company's failure, the holders rank equally with ordinary creditors, after preferential creditors but before shareholders. Certain unsecured loan stocks may carry some form of guarantee, for example, a parent company may guarantee the loan stock of a subsidiary company. Investors should pay particular attention to the terms of issue to establish the exact nature of the stock.

Subordinated loan stocks

17.6   These stocks are uncommon but may be issued by a small number of companies, notably the clearing banks. Repayment of the stock is subordinated to all the creditors, only ranking ahead of the shareholders. Because of the greater risk involved, the investor can expect to receive a better return than from other types of loan stock.

Convertible loan stocks

17.7   Convertible loan stocks are a hybrid of equities and fixed-interest securities. They give a guaranteed income through fixed-interest and carry rights to convert to a prearranged number of ordinary shares at agreed prices over a period of years.

17.8 There are many different convertible loan stocks available, each with its own conversion rights. Some have a short conversion, such as one month, during a number of consecutive years. Others have a specified date on which the conversion option may be exercised. If the option is not exercised at the agreed times, the stock becomes conventional loan stock.

17.9 A simplified example is given below so that the basic concepts can be grasped.

Example 14.12: Convertibles

Convertible stock is purchased in February 1996 at 290 pence, giving 9% per annum, with the option to convert to ordinary shares during the February of each of the subsequent three years.

Stock is normally quoted in £100 lots, so for every £100 this can be converted during February each year, as follows:

1997   34 shares
1998   33 shares
1999   32 shares

So, since the purchase price was 290 pence, the real price throughout the years can be calculated. For example, the conversion price in February 1998 would be:

$$\frac{£100}{33} \quad - \quad £3.03$$

A decision whether to convert at that time would need to be based on current market prices. So, if ordinary shares were available at £2.90 the conversion would not be attractive; however, if the current market value was £3.50 the conversion offers a good profit and the chance to continue to participate further in the profits of the company.

17.10 An investor will only be attracted by convertibles if he feels that the company is showing promise of success, the option is worthless if share prices are falling with no indication of recovery. A long conversion period will, of course, be more attractive to an investor where the success of the company can be expected, given time.

17.11 In certain circumstances, an investor who wishes to purchase ordinary shares in a company may find it more economic to purchase convertible shares. Although a rise in the price of ordinary shares tends to pull the price of convertibles up, a sudden rise may mean that the price of the convertibles will not rise immediately.

17.12 Convertibles may be particularly attractive to a higher rate taxpayer. The gain made on conversion need not be realised immediately and any capital gains tax liability may be deferred to suit the particular circumstances of the individual. The attractions to a company of issuing convertible loan stock to investors can be briefly summarised:

(a) Convertibles may be used as part of the consideration when a company is bidding to take over another company. The bidding company may offer convertible loan stock to the shareholders of the target company in exchange for their shares, thereby avoiding the need to issue large quantities of new share capital.

(b) Because of the attaching rights, a convertible will generally offer a lower rate of fixed-interest than a conventional loan stock. For this reason, a company is able to finance its borrowing at a cheaper rate. Similarly, where a company wishes to raise capital to finance a long-term project, the issue of convertible loan stock may be more attractive to investors than a rights issue could be to existing shareholders. The convertible loan stock guarantees the investors a fixed rate of income with the opportunity to participate further in the company's profits when the project starts to pay and they exercise their options. The existing shareholders, on the other hand, may not wish to gamble on the future profitability of the project by subscribing to a rights issue.

(c) A company that does well, following the issue of its convertible loan stock, can expect a large proportion of the options to be exercised. Thus, at redemption date the company will only have a small number of investors to repay.

18 Dealing in Company Fixed-Interest Securities

18.1 When issuing fixed-interest loan stock, most companies will appoint a trustee, generally a bank or insurance company, to act on behalf of the holders of the issue. Indeed, if the stock is to be quoted on the stock exchange, a trustee must be appointed. A trust deed is drawn up by the company and the trustee, setting out the terms of the issue.

18.2 New issues of fixed-interest securities are generally advertised in the financial papers, inviting subscriptions from the general public with the large institutions, for example banks and building societies, subscribing to a large proportion of the issue.

18.3 Existing loan stock that is quoted on the stock exchange can be bought and sold through a stockbroker, although it is not always immediately possible to match a buyer and a seller.

18.4 An investor wishing to buy company fixed-interest securities that are not quoted on the stock exchange would have to deal directly with the company. It is unlikely that such securities would hold any attraction for anyone other than a director or an employee of that company.

19 Redemption

19.1 The majority of stocks issued are redeemable at a specified date in the future. If a company is unable to redeem the stock and it is secured, the trustees are empowered to sell some or all of the assets charged to realise sufficient funds to redeem the stock. Most companies will anticipate redemption by setting aside a part of each year's profit to establish a sinking fund. The existence of a sinking fund improves the marketability of the stock and the terms of its operation will be detailed in the trust deed. A sinking fund can work in various ways and descriptions of the two most common follow.

Non-cumulative sinking fund

19.2 Sufficient profits are set aside each year and invested for growth to ensure that when the loan stock is due for redemption the necessary funds are available. Investment can be in another area of the company considered capable of producing the necessary growth or in any other suitable investment vehicle.

Cumulative sinking fund

19.3 The cash equivalent of the profit set aside can be used to meet the interest payments on the loan stock and to redeem a portion of the issued stock each year. There are two ways of redeeming issued stock, either by purchasing the stock itself in the open market or by selecting stockholders on the basis of a draw and redeeming their stock at par. Where drawn stock is redeemed when the market price is below par, then the investor is deemed to be lucky; however, the opposite applies when the market price of the stock is above par. By redeeming stock annually, the company reduces the annual interest payments it must make to stockholders, thus increasing the funds available for capital repayment.

20 Deep Discounted Securities

20.1 These company fixed-interest securities are issued at a discount to their redemption value, thus providing an investor with a specified capital gain at redemption date. A company will benefit from paying the lower interest rate that traditionally attaches to this type of security. Loan stock that is issued at a discount of more than ½% per year, based on the term from issue to redemption, or below 85% of its redemption value, attracts certain tax concessions. The gain at redemption is treated as annual interest that has accrued from issue to redemption, with the income tax liability being deferred until redemption. Stockholders will be liable to income tax at their highest marginal rate. The following example illustrates how to compare the value of a deep discounted security with a conventional fixed-interest security.

Example 14.13: Deep discounted securities

Company X issues loan stock 6.8% at a discounted price of £85 with a redemption value of £100.

To calculate the equivalent value of a conventional fixed-interest security, the following formula should be applied:

$$\frac{\text{par redemption value x coupon rate}}{\text{issue price}}$$

$$\text{i.e. } \frac{100 \times 6.8}{85} = 8\%$$

Therefore, the investor would require a fixed-interest rate of 8% on stock issued without a deep discount.

21 Risk and Company Fixed-Interest Securities

21.1 Taxation of fixed-interest securities is the same as for non fixed-interest income from company shares with basic rate tax liability already deducted

(20%). However, because of the fixed-interest element, risk is lower than for ordinary shares because income is guaranteed. Investors need to be aware though that if securities are offering a high yield in relation to the market average, this may represent an above average risk as the company may not be able to maintain the quoted rate.

21.2 Where securities are backed by specific assets of the company, i.e. debentures, the risk is lower than for other unsecured loan stocks.

21.3 Some corporate fixed-interest securities have failed to pay and so are more risky than gilts where the government has never failed. However, the government can offer lower interest rates because of the security it offers, so in terms of reward, corporate fixed-interest securities may offer more potential.

21.4 In summary, the main types of company shares and securities can be ranked in terms of risk as follows:

HIGH   Ordinary shares

                        Preference shares

                        Subordinated loan stock

                        Unsecured loan stock

                        Debentures with floating charge

LOW   Gilts

21.5 It should be noted that investment in equities or corporate fixed-interest securities is possible through a Pep, in which case the tax considerations are different. See Unit 17 for further details.

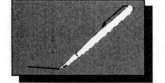

Student Activity 4

You should complete this student activity before attempting the self-assessment. Answer the questions, then check your answers against the paragraph(s) indicated.

1.   Why do companies usually issue fixed-interest securities?   (16.1)

2.   Jim Watson owns £10,000 worth of convertible loan stock   (17.8, 17.9)
      which has a conversion date of July 1998.

      (a) What factors will Jim need to take into consideration
          when he decides whether to exercise the option at
          the conversion date?
      (b) What will happen to the stock if he does not exercise
          the option?

3.   How can an investor compare the value of a deep discounted   (20.1)
      security with a conventional fixed-interest security?

If you are unable to answer any of the questions satisfactorily, you should read the relevant paragraphs again. Your understanding of the text will be further tested in the following self-assessment.

Summary

Now that you have completed this unit, you should be able to:

☐ **Describe the different types of shares**

☐ **Explain the rights and benefits of shareholders**

☐ **Know how dividend income is taxed**

☐ **Know how new share issues are made**

☐ **Explain how and why scrip issues and rights issues are made**

☐ **Explain why companies issue fixed-interest securities**

☐ **Describe the different types of corporate fixed-interest securities**

☐ **Understand the risk and accessibility of equities and fixed-interest securities**

If you can tick all the above boxes with confidence, you are ready to answer the questions which follow.

Self-Assessment Questions

1. Angela Turner has inherited some shares from her father. She has never owned shares before. Explain what type of return she can expect from the shares.

2. What is the difference between a preferred ordinary share and a preference share?

3. Why are preference shares less risky than ordinary shares?

4. An investor has purchased warrants in a company at a price of 25p. If the ordinary share price is 125p calculate the level of gearing. What does this mean for the investor?

5. A company decides to make a scrip issue of £1 shares on a one for one basis. What effect would this have on a shareholder with an existing holding of 5,000 shares?

6. Mark Prince has received a letter explaining that the ABC Company in which he has shares is making a rights issue.

   (a) What should he do with the letter?

   (b) Why are ABC likely to be making a rights issue?

   (c) Why may the price of shares in ABC fall after a rights issue?

7. An investor bought shares in 1990 and sells them in 1996. He is a higher rate taxpayer and will have a capital gains tax liability. How is this reduced by indexation?

8. How could a higher rate taxpayer avoid tax on his corporate fixed-interest securities?

9. In terms of risk, which types of corporate fixed-interest security would you rank as comparatively low and why?

10. An investor who is prepared to take some investment risk but requires a fixed income is comparing gilts and corporate fixed-interest securities. How would you compare them?

Unit 15

Derivatives

1 Introduction

1.1 A derivative is a financial instrument whose price is derived from the value of the underlying investments. Originally the underlying investments were commodities, which are basic substances such as oil, cocoa and tea. In recent years, the underlying investments have increasingly consisted of bonds, currencies, individual shares or share groups or stock market indices e.g. FT-SE 100. Options and futures are types of derivatives which are described in detail in this unit.

1.2 Both options and financial futures can now be traded on the London International Financial Futures and Options Exchange (Liffe). Liffe is currently the third largest exchange of its type in the world. Originally, options were traded on the London Traded Options Market (LTOM) which was formed in 1936 and futures were traded on the London International Financial Futures Exchange which was also known as 'Liffe'. Transactions are channelled through a centralised clearing system and members are regulated by the Securities and Futures Authority (SFA).

1.3 Derivatives are usually used by professional investors and institutions as 'hedging' vehicles to manage price risk either by increasing or reducing risk (or in Nick Leeson's case to sink Barings Bank). They can be a cautious way of enhancing portfolio returns, a convenient way of taking a position for little capital outlay or extremely dangerous if mishandled. They can be used by the private investor both profitably and safely if treated with caution and skill.

2 Options

2.1 An option represents the right to buy or sell an asset at a fixed price on a fixed date in the future, or before a fixed expiry date (American style option), which is restricted to a maximum of nine months in the case of Liffe's equity options. The person who buys the option pays a premium to the seller or 'writer' at the outset and money only changes hands for the asset if the option is exercised. The fixed price is called either the 'striking price' or 'exercise price'.

2.2   The option will either be a call or put option depending on whether the individual is buying the right to buy from or sell the asset to the writer. Call and put options in individual ordinary shares in UK and overseas companies, the FT-SE 100 Index and currency contracts can all be traded on Liffe.

2.3   Double options also exist which give the right to both buy and sell the option.

Call options

2.4   A call option involves the buyer paying a premium to the writer for the right to buy a share at a fixed price before the expiry date. If the option is exercised, the writer is obliged to sell the share to the option holder. An investor will buy a call option if he expects the share price to rise.

Example 15.1: Call option

A buyer pays 50p premium each for 12,000, £3.50 call options. The share is currently trading at £3.50.

If the share price rises to £5.50 and the option is exercised:

$$\text{Profit} = £5.50 - (£3.50 + £0.50)$$
$$= £1.50 \text{ per share}$$

$$\text{Total} = £1.50 \times 12,000$$
$$= £18,000$$

$$\text{Return on original premium} = \frac{£18,000}{£6,000} \times 100$$

$$= 300\%$$

If the share price falls below £3.50 the option will not be exercised and the loss will be:

$$£0.50 \times 12,000$$
$$= £6,000$$

If the investor had purchased shares immediately and the share price rises to £5.50:

$$\text{Number of shares purchased} = \frac{£6,000}{£3.50} = 1,714$$

$$\text{Profit} = 1,714 \times (£5.50 - £3.50) = £3,428$$

$$\text{Return on original investment} = \frac{£3,428}{£6,000} \times 100$$

$$= 57\%$$

2.5 As can be seen from the example, the option will only be exercised if the share price rises above the striking price; the investor makes a profit, taking into account the premium already paid.

2.6 If the share price falls below the striking price, and the option is exercised, the buyer would be paying above market value if the shares are bought from the writer, so this is when the option would not be exercised and only the premium paid would be the loss incurred.

2.7 The example also demonstrates that if the share price rises above the striking price, more profit is made if a call option has been purchased and subsequently exercised than if the shares were purchased immediately; this effect is called 'gearing'. However, if the share price falls below the striking price, and the investor has purchased a call option, he loses the premium paid and will have no shares, whereas the investor who has purchased the shares immediately does at least have an asset.

2.8 If the share price rises the option holder may consider exercising the option once the break even point has been exceeded. The writer will then miss out on any rise which exceeds the share price plus the premium.

Put options

2.9 A put option involves the buyer of the option paying a premium to the writer in return for the right to sell a share at a fixed price before the expiry date. If the buyer decides to exercise the option, the writer is obliged to buy the share from the option holder at the fixed price. An investor will purchase a put option if the share price is expected to fall. The writer of a put option receives premium income and speculates that there will not be a fall in the share price.

Example 15.2: Put option

A buyer has a holding of 10,000 shares which currently trade at £2.80. Due to fear of falling share prices, a put option at £3 per share is purchased at a premium of 20p.

If the share price falls to £2.50 and the option is exercised:

Profit = £3.00 - (£2.50 + £0.20)
= £0.30 per share

Total = £0.30 x 10,000
= £3,000

Return on original premium = $\frac{£3,000}{£2,000}$ x 100

= 150%

If the share price remains above £3 for the option period, the option will not be exercised and the buyer will lose £2,000 unless he is able to sell the shares elsewhere in the market for an amount which covers the premium paid.

2.10 As can be seen from the example, a put option will only be exercised if the share price falls below the striking price. The profit made takes into account the premium paid to the writer at the outset.

2.11 The buyer will not exercise the option if the share price is higher than the striking price because more profit can be made selling the share elsewhere in the market rather than to the writer. If the buyer cannot sell the share, the loss will be equal to the premium paid.

2.12 If the option holder is unsure as to whether the share price will rise or fall, the option could be sold to a third party as a traded option.

The option premium

2.13 The premium of an option has two component parts: intrinsic value and time value. A call option will have an intrinsic value if the current share price is higher than the option's strike price. A put option will have an intrinsic value if the current share price is lower than the option's strike price. Options with intrinsic value are referred to as 'in the money', those without any are 'out of the money' and those on the border line are 'at the money'.

2.14 The time value represents the unexpired time of the option. In that time the share price could fluctuate to any level and this is the gamble the holder has of whether to keep the option until expiry or if at expiry the time elapsed will see an advantageous change in the share price. Time value is the reason why comparatively few options are actually ever exercised much before expiry. Early exercise of an option will release its intrinsic value; the time value will be wasted. It will also incur higher dealing costs (commission and stamp duty) than simply selling the option on in the market-place. The volatility of the underlying share is a major component of time value - the higher a share's volatility, the higher the time value although it decreases sharply in the last few weeks of the option's life.

Traded equity options

2.15 Exercise prices quoted in the Financial Times always give one exercise price below the value of the underlying share and at least one above it. They will also give a number of expiry dates depending on the expiry cycle of the shares e.g. January, April, July, October, or February, May, August, November or March, June, September, December. These permutations of expiry date and exercise price for calls and puts are known as six series of the same class of option. When the share price closes outside the range of exercise prices for at least two days a new series will be introduced. Series will also be replaced when they expire.

Example 15.3: Traded options - ASDA

Share price	Exercise price	Calls Oct	Jan	Apr	Puts Oct	Jan	Apr
113.5	110	6.5	9.5	11.5	3.5	6.5	8
113.5	120	2.5	5.5	7.5	10	12	13

Source: Financial Times (July 1996)

2.16 In this example the current underlying price of the share is 113.5p. The exercise price of 110p means the option is in the money and has intrinsic value of 113.5p - 110p = 3.5p. The call option premium for October is 6.5p.

The difference between the premium and the intrinsic value is 3p which represents the time value and this will gradually depreciate over the life of the option.

2.17 If an option is bought at 120p it is out of the money and has no intrinsic value. The premiums quoted represent time value. These carry a greater risk as they will be worthless if the share price does not move from its present value. However, they also carry a greater reward because the premiums are low in relation to the underlying share price.

2.18 If the buyer expects the share price to fall below the exercise price he will buy a put option. If he bought an October put option for 3.5p the share price would have to fall below 110p to make the option worth exercising.

Index options

2.19 There are two types of FT-SE 100 Index options which are traded on Liffe. These are the Euro FT-SE 100 Index where options can only be exercised at the expiry date, 'European style' and the FT-SE 100 Index where options can be exercised at virtually any time up to the expiry date 'American style'. Expiry is the third Friday of the expiry month.

2.20 Details of these options are quoted in the Financial Times, as shown in the following extract.

FT-SE 100 Index option (Liffe) (*3666) £10 per full index point

	3500		3550		3600		3650		3700		3750		3800		3850	
	C	P	C	P	C	P	C	P	C	P	C	P	C	P	C	P
Aug	169	7½	125	13	84	22	49	40½	25½	66½	11	103½	4	146	1	193
Sep	192	24½	153½	35½	116½	48½	87	69	60	92½	38½	122	24	158	13½	199
Oct	207½	38½	170	50½	136½	66½	105½	85½	80	109½	57½	137	41	171	26	207½
Nov	226	49½	189	62	157	80½	126½	99	100½	123	77	149½	56½	178	40½	212½
Dec†	242	61			177	95			122½	139½			78	195½		

Calls 2,042 Puts 4,611

Euro style FT-SE 100 Index option (Liffe) £10 per full index point

	3475		3525		3575		3625		3675		3725		3775		3825	
	C	P	C	P	C	P	C	P	C	P	C	P	C	P	C	P
Aug	189	5½	143½	10½	101½	18	65	31	36½	52½	17½	83	7	122½	2½	167½
Sep	209½	19½	169	28½	132	40½	99	57½	70½	78½	47½	105	29½	136½	16½	173
Oct	227	32½	188	43	152½	57	120	73½	92	94½	68	120	48½	150½	33½	184½
Dec			230½	72½			166	105½			112	149			69	204
Mar†			270	102½			209½	138			154	179			110½	231½

Calls 1,091 Puts 7,608 * Underlying index value. Premiums shown are based on settlement prices.

† Long dated expiry months.

Source: Financial Times (July 1996)

2.21 The contract size quoted is £10 per index. In this example an investor could buy an out of the money November 1996 3750 call for 77 x £10. This means the cost of the option premium would be £10 x 77 = £770.

2.22　If the index had risen to 3850 by November 1996 then the profit would be £10 x (3850 - 3750) - £770 = £230. If the index had not reached 3750 by November 1996 then the £770 would be lost.

2.23　The Euro style index has exercise prices at 25 and 75 points whereas the other style index has exercise prices at 50 and 100 points. There are also differences in the expiry dates available.

3　The Trading Process

3.1　Trading in options is done through a stockbroker. Most stockbrokers now offer some form of option dealing service. Commissions tend to vary widely according to the service used e.g. full service or just execution-only. A full service would typically be charged at 2.25% to open a trade and 1.5% to close it, although discount firms would typically charge 1.5% and 1% respectively.

Liffe

3.2　The member firms of Liffe include most of the world's leading financial institutions. Users of Liffe include banks, bond dealers, corporate treasurers, equity market makers, swap traders, institutional investors, syndication managers, money market dealers and private investors. Its trading hours bridge the gap between the trading hours in the major international financial centres and real-time price information is available.

3.3　Trading on Liffe is carried out by an auction of bids and offers made in open competition on the trading floor. Prices are governed by supply and demand so they depend on the balance between buyers and sellers. Only Liffe members, of which there are currently approximately 200, are allowed to trade on the exchange floor. Anyone else who wishes to trade must get a Liffe member to trade on his behalf.

3.4　Most of the business is carried out by shouting and hand signals. The trading floor is arranged with central pits for each contract. These are surrounded by telephone booths which act as entry points for orders from outside. The stockbroker passes the deal to the representative on Liffe and a time stamp is printed to show when the order was received. Members send orders from the booths to the pit by hand signals or runners.

3.5　The trader stands in the pit which is associated with the contract which he is buying or selling and shouts his intended trade to the other traders. He uses hand signals to convey whether he wishes to buy or sell, the price at which he is willing to trade and the number of contracts he wishes to trade. The first trader to respond becomes the counterparty to the deal. Trader cards show the details of each trade executed by a trader.

3.6　Liffe officials watching the trading relay quotes and prices to displays within the exchange via the Price Distribution System (PDS). The PDS also relays the prices to vendors around the world. Open outcry trading is supplemented by screen-based trading on the Automated Pit Trading System (APT) which replicates the methods of open outcry trading on a computer screen. Members which use this system are linked by a network.

3.7　Following execution, confirmation of the trade is passed from the trading pit to the telephone booth, to the broker and back to the customer. The trades and their current bid and offer prices are relayed to a computer workstation. Details of the trade are also entered into Liffe's Trade Registration System (TRS) for matching and, once matched, the trade is registered with the London Clearing House (LCH) which acts as a guarantor. Settlement is the following business day for the premium payment and the exercise of the option. Writers will have deposited a margin with LCH as security for performing their obligations.

3.8   The Clearing Processing System (CPS) provides position maintenance and clearing functions which allow members to co-ordinate their trading, settlement, margining and risk management within one system. Once trading has ceased for the day, settlement prices are fed into this system and end of day processing is carried out. The results of its processing are then transmitted electronically to LCH.

Ofex

3.9   Options can also be traded off-exchange. For instance, Ofex is a facility which is managed by broker firm J.P. Jenkins Limited to allow trading in the shares of unquoted companies. It was created in October 1995 following a change to the rules of the stock exchange which allowed member firms to deal off-market.

3.10   Ofex companies are often those which were no longer able to trade on the stock exchange after the establishment of the Alternative Investments Market (AIM). The companies are often too small to have their shares traded on the senior markets. Ofex allows companies to prepare themselves for entry to the AIM or for application for a full stock exchange listing. Companies apply to J.P. Jenkins Limited for a facility to have trades matched in the shares of their company off-exchange.

3.11   Ofex is not a market in its own right; it is a mechanism by which stock exchange member firms can deal between each other off-exchange to effect matched business in the shares of unquoted companies. J.P. Jenkins Limited will make a market in any Ofex security and will accept buy and sell orders placed by stock exchange member firms on behalf of investors. Ofex's main aim is to match buyers and sellers and J.P. Jenkins Limited will act as market maker if there are sufficient shares available.

3.12   Private individuals have access to the Ofex facilities through the stock exchange member firms. Investment in Ofex companies has inherent risks because it is an unregulated trading facility. Dealings can be restricted because it may be difficult to find a buyer for the shares. However, liquidity is increased if J.P. Jenkins Limited acts as a market maker, making the current value of the shareholding more readily realisable. Furthermore, the vetting procedures for entry to Ofex are strict.

3.13   Newstrack provides a screen-based source of company news and financial data on the unquoted securities which are traded on Ofex. Information on Ofex companies is published on a weekly basis in the Financial Times.

4   The Risk Position

4.1   There are more risks involved for the writer of an option than for the buyer.

4.2 In return for the premium received, the writer runs the risk of having to buy or sell the share at a price which is less advantageous than the price which could have be obtained in the market. Particular risk is attached to writing call options on shares which the writer does not possess, known as a 'naked' writer. If the market price rises above the striking price and the buyer exercises the option, the writer will have to buy the shares in the market to meet his obligation. It is very unlikely that a private investor will be involved in writing the options, particularly as a 'naked' writer, due to the high level of risk attached. The only possible exception to this is writing puts on a stock that the investor is happy to buy anyway. The investor writing 140 puts for 5p will either keep the premium if the stock rises or acquire it for an effective price of 135p if it falls and the option is exercised.

4.3 Risks are also attached to buying options and, before a stockbroker executes a customer's instructions, the customer must sign and return one copy of a derivatives risk warning letter. The most risky call options to buy are ones which are out of the money because they consist only of time value which effectively decreases as the option nears expiry date. Most buyers of options are institutional investors, rather than private investors, because of risks already mentioned.

5 Use of Options

5.1 Options can be used either to take or protect against risky speculations. Call options can be used to achieve high gearing and make large profits for relatively small investments.

5.2 The options market is often used as an insurance against potential losses in the buying and selling of shares, normally referred to as 'hedging' .It is a way of minimising losses which can be potentially large in the amounts that are dealt with in this market-place. The trade-off is that the hedger will make a smaller but more stable gain while the speculator is willing to bear the large amounts of risk necessary to make large profits. Put options are often bought by institutional investors in declining markets when they do not wish to sell their holding of shares immediately but think that the share price is likely to fall; this is referred to as limiting their 'downside risk' by fixing a striking price below which the price of their shares cannot fall.

5.3 Options are often used as part of the life assurance bond's portfolio. Often investors are given a choice about the level of the capital guarantee; the lower the level of guarantee, the more derivatives can be used to achieve gearing to produce a potentially higher return to either capital or income. While guaranteed capital bonds are dominant in the market, high income bonds have emerged that use derivatives to gain a specific income level.

Student Activity 1

You should complete this student activity before reading the next section of the text. Answer the questions, then check your answers against the paragraph(s) indicated.

1. John Brown buys an option for 10p which he can exercise in six months' time at 80p. On the fixed option date the shares are priced at 120p.

(a) What is the striking price? (2.1)

(b) When would the option be described as in the money? (2.13)

(c) What profit will he make if he exercises the option? (2.4)

(d) What would happen if the share price was 750 at the option date? (2.6)

2. Look in a recent copy of the Financial Times for the traded options and index options sections.

(a) For the traded options compare the figures given in the example in this unit for ASDA and see what has changed. (2.15)

(b) For the index options compare how the FT-SE 100 Index has changed since the example quoted in this unit. Do you think the example quoted will have been worth exercising? (2.20)

If you are unable to answer any of the question satisfactorily, you should read the relevant paragraphs again. Your understanding of the text will be further tested in the self-assessment section at the end of this unit.

6 Futures

6.1 A future is a legally binding agreement to pay a specified price for a given quantity of an asset on a specified date in the future. On that date, the seller must make delivery and the buyer must take delivery and pay the seller the price agreed. The profits or losses are very much determined by the market prices at the time of purchase.

6.2 These types of contract have been in existence for centuries in one form or another in order to fund certain ventures such as crop farming, to finance fishing or whaling voyages or exportation of livestock. They were certainly present in Roman times. Because products take time to reach maturity or to be delivered it was difficult to anticipate what price they would get for the commodities. To resolve this a futures market for commodities was established and in 1811 a number of commodity markets joined together to become the London Commodity Exchange, now known as London FOX. In the US a group of Chicago merchants formed the Chicago Board of Trade in 1848. Farmers agreed to deliver their produce on a certain day for a fixed price - simple futures contracts.

6.3 Farmers had guaranteed sales at specified prices. Importers knew exactly what they would have to pay. Speculative traders would put up a small percentage, the 'margin', and agree a contract price. It could work as in the following example:

Example 15.4: Simple commodity futures

Contract to buy £10,000 of commodities in six months

Future contract price paid, a 10% margin = £1,000

If after four months the commodity price rises by 50% the investor can sell the future and close out the deal. That could net a profit of up to £5,000, a 500% return on his £1,000 investment.

6.4 The buyer of a futures contract is said to have taken a 'long' position and will make a gain if the value of the contract rises. The seller is said to have taken a 'short' position and will gain if the value of the futures contract falls.

6.5 For small investors the futures market now includes financial instruments, as well as commodities. Dealing in financial futures means entering into a financial futures contract on Liffe. This includes bonds, currencies, indices and certificates on Liffe, but not individual equities. It is very expensive and risky. One gilt future, for example, covers £50,000 worth of gilts. Margin trading enables investors to buy that future for much less, but the relatively small price magnifies losses as well as the profits. If the price drops the losses would keep growing. In practice Liffe, the market on which financial futures are traded, will not allow investors to run up indefinite losses. Liffe calculates investors' profits and losses at the end of each day and will ask for cash (extra margin) if the losses get too high.

6.6 Companies which use commodities need to know what the supply and demand will be and they should have the resources and experience to make a better judgement than most individuals. Despite the risks on futures, the concept of gearing up profits is attractive.

6.7 The examples below give a simplified illustration of how both a commodities future and a financial future work.

Example 15.5: Futures in commodities

Mr Jones has 100 head of pigs which Mr Smith offers £1 per head for in three months' time.

In three months' time it could be that supply is plentiful and therefore the price of pigs has dropped to only 50p per head, meaning a loss for Mr Smith.

However, if supply is limited, it could be that the price of pigs has increased to £1.50 per head, leading to a healthy profit for Mr Smith.

Example 15.6: Financial futures

An investor deposits £2,000 to buy a FT-SE 100 futures contract at 2530, priced at £25 per index point.

If the index rises to 2545, his gain will be:
(2545 - 2530) x £25
15 x £25 = £375

If the index falls to 2525, his loss will be:
(2530 - 2525) x £25
5 x £25 = £125

7 The Trading Process

7.1 Following the amalgamation of the exchanges for futures and options, they are both now traded on Liffe. Dealing in futures is through a stockbroker and a representative on Liffe, using the auction system of bids and offers made on the trading floor. A combination of open outcry trading and screen-based trading is again used and the processes involved are similar to the trading processes for options.

8 Risk Position

8.1 By entering into a futures contract, investors irrevocably commit themselves to whether they think the price of the index or financial instrument will rise or fall. For this reason, futures are more risky than options and will very rarely be entered into by private investors. Gains or losses can be very large. However, it should also be noted that an investor is only risking a proportion of the worth of the underlying shares rather than the whole value of the shares. So, for example, if an investor invests £5,000 into a futures contract the underlying shares may actually be worth £50,000. If he makes a loss because the value of the shares did not rise as expected, this loss will only be proportionate to the loss he would have incurred if he bought the shares outright.

8.2 Because a future is a legally binding agreement, the only way in which the buyer or seller can avoid taking or making delivery, is by entering into a second contract which reverses the position, however, a cash adjustment may still have to be made.

9 Use of Futures

9.1 Financial futures can be used to hedge portfolios, usually by using index futures which are linked to indices such as the FT-SE 100. When considering whether to buy shares or to buy futures and keep the cash on deposit in the meantime, the investor will consider the interest rates offered by a deposit account in comparison with the yield on the investment. Where equity yields are lower than bank interest rates it makes sense to buy FT-SE 100 futures and deposit cash in the bank to pay for the shares at the delivery date. However, the market adjusts for this fact and so the FT-SE 100 futures are usually quoted at about 10 points higher than the index itself if bank base rates are high. For example, if the FT-SE 100 Index was 3560 the FT-SE 100 futures for delivery in three months may well be quoted at 3660.

9.2 The main advantage of index futures is that they give investors the chance to benefit from movements in the market as reflected by the index rather than having to invest in the underlying assets themselves. The main difference in this type of future is that payment at delivery is made in cash rather than by delivery of goods. The FT-SE 100 Futures Index is quoted at £25 per index point so, for example, if an investor sold a future with a settlement price of 3667 this would have a cash value of 3667 x £25 = £91,675.

9.3 If an investor expects the market to fall, selling an index future will give protection because at the end of the period the buyer will have to buy the asset at the agreed price. If an investor expects the market to rise, buying a future will offer protection because the asset can be purchased at the end of the agreed period for the agreed price.

9.4 As mentioned previously, futures are not often used by private investors mainly because of the size of investment involved as well as the risk, but will be used by institutionalised investors such as fund managers and unit trust managers to hedge their portfolios or to manage cash flows.

10 Swaps

10.1 There are two main types of swap - currency swaps and interest rate swaps.

Interest rate swaps

10.2 An interest rate swap involves fixed rate interest payments being swapped for variable rates. Large companies are usually able to borrow over the long term at a fixed rate of interest because they tend to be a good credit risk. Smaller companies often have to borrow at a variable rate because they are usually higher risk; however, it is the smaller companies which often need to borrow at a fixed rate because they cannot withstand large increases in interest rates and they need to know the cost of expansion in advance.

10.3 If a large company and a smaller company decide to effect an interest rate swap, the smaller company takes over the fixed rate and the larger company takes over the variable rate at a slightly lower level with the smaller company paying the balance on the variable rate interest payment. The smaller company benefits from a fixed rate and the larger company benefits from being able to borrow at a lower variable rate than if it had borrowed from a bank.

10.4 The swaps market has expanded due to the fact that it is often cheaper for companies to deal directly with each other than through a bank. In addition, there is no great risk for either company because they are not actually lending to each other.

Currency swaps

10.5 A currency swap involves companies from different countries swapping interest payments in local currencies. A company can usually borrow funds in its local currency at a better rate than a company from another country which needed to borrow funds in the same currency, for instance if it needed to build a factory in that country. This is because banks often offer better rates to companies with which they are familiar. To counteract this fact, each company may borrow funds in its local currency and then swap the interest payments on the borrowing.

Student Activity 2

You should complete this student activity before attempting the self-assessment. Answer the questions, then check your answers against the paragraph(s) indicated.

1. If an investor enters into a futures contract, what is the position if the price falls below that specified at the agreed date for:

    (a) The buyer?   (6.7)
    (b) The seller?   (6.7)

2. A fund manager uses commodity futures as part of the fund's investment portfolio. What expertise do you think the manager will require? (6.6)

3. Why is the FT-SE 100 Futures Index usually higher than the ordinary FT-SE 100 Index? (9.1)

If you are unable to answer any of the questions satisfactorily, you should read the relevant paragraphs again. Your understanding of the text will be further tested in the following self-assessment.

Summary

Now that you have completed this unit, you should be able to:

☐ **Explain the difference between options and futures**

☐ **Know how options are priced**

☐ **Understand the types of options**

☐ **Know the risks of investing in options**

☐ **Explain how futures operate**

☐ **Know the different types of futures**

☐ **Know the risks of investing in futures**

☐ **Know how options and futures are traded**

If you can tick all the above boxes with confidence, you are ready to answer the questions which follow.

Self-Assessment Questions

1. What is an option?

2. What is the difference between a put option and a call option?

3. What is meant by time value?

4. Why may an investor who buys a call option when the exercise price is higher than the underlying share price have a potential for high returns?

5. Why does the writer of an option face more risk than the buyer?

6. What is meant by hedging?

7. What is a future?

8. An investor buys a FT-SE 100 futures contract at 3750 priced at £25 per index point for £3,000.

    (a) If the index rises to 3900 what will his gain be?

    (b) If the index falls to 3700 what will his loss be?

9. Why are futures more risky than options?

10. An investor asks why, if share prices are expected to rise, it would be advantageous to invest in financial futures. What would you reply?

Unit 16

Unit Trusts

Objectives

Students are required to study the following topics:

- The composition of a unit trust

- Authorisation

- Control

- Types of unit trust

- Investing in a unit trust

- Pricing

- The dealing process

- Taxation

- Uses

- Risk and accessibility

1 Introduction

1.1 A unit trust is a way of investing in a 'collective or packaged' investment scheme, allowing investment in worldwide stock markets without having to deal with the stock markets direct and by utilising the skills and experience of the company's trust managers.

1.2 A unit trust is a fund formed to manage investments collectively on behalf of a number of investors. This fund is governed by certain terms and conditions laid down by a trust deed. It is the responsibility of the trustee to ensure these are complied with.

1.3 They are promoted and sold by unit trust management companies, some of which are subsidiaries of life assurance marketing groups. They can be bought directly from the provider, through a representative or independent financial adviser.

1.4 Unit trusts fall into the packaged investment category as they invest in a spread of investments.

2 How Does a Unit Trust Work?

2.1 By combining the resources of numerous investors, the fund can buy holdings in a large number of companies in order to spread the risk of the fall in value of individual companies. This allows individuals to invest in markets which may otherwise be unsuitable due to the size of investment required to obtain the desired rate of return. The size of the trust also helps cut management charges and dealing commission when compared to those of an individual dealing directly in the markets. The individuals gain the benefit of the knowledge and actions of the experienced fund managers.

2.2 The value of the shares bought is divided up into units of equal worth and allocated to the individual investors, based on the amount of investment they have made.

2.3 Profit or loss is therefore based on the change in the value of the units. This is calculated by taking into account the current market price of the underlying securities held by the fund and deducting costs and charges.

3 Authorisation of a Unit Trust

3.1 If a trust wishes to advertise to the UK public it must be authorised by the Securities and Investments Board (SIB) under the Financial Services Act 1986 and must follow the rules laid down in the Financial Services (Regulated Schemes) Regulations 1991 regarding the markets and types of securities it can invest in. The general limits for an individual unit trust are laid out in the trust deed. A unit trust is prevented from advertising for investors if it is not authorised. Authorised unit trusts may be marketed in any of the EU member states provided they have applied for a UCITS (Undertaking for Collective Investment in Transferable Securities) certificate from the SIB.

Unregulated collective investment schemes

3.2 These unregulated schemes, which cannot be marketed to the general public, are funds which do not meet the detailed criteria laid down by the SIB regarding the size and structure of their holdings.

3.3 The schemes are controlled under the Financial Services (Promotion of Unregulated Schemes) Regulations 1991 which lay down detailed provisions as to when an authorised person can promote such schemes to customers.

3.4 An example of an unregulated scheme would be a specialist property based trust.

4 Who Controls the Trust?

4.1 The shares bought by the trust are the assets and are held by especially appointed independent trustees who control the issue or cancellation of units in line with the increase or decrease in the amount of money invested in the trust. A unit trust is an open-ended fund and the size of the trust can vary, dependent on the demand for the units. The trustees are the legal owners of the assets, holding them in trust for all unitholders.

4.2 The trustees of the fund are also responsible for ensuring that the fund managers act in accordance with the terms and conditions laid down in the trust deed. They also ensure all securities are properly entered in their name and ensure that any periodic distribution of income is made. Should the manager go into liquidation, receivership or become insolvent, the ultimate power to replace him lies with the trustees. Subject to a majority of unitholders voting for the removal of the manager the trustees would be able to act as authorised.

The trust deed

4.3 Trust deeds have to be approved by the SIB. With the DTI the SIB is also responsible for regulating authorised unit trusts, including the manager's investment and borrowing powers and pricing, issue and redemption of units. Any changes to the trust deed must be approved at a meeting of the unitholders.

Investment powers

4.4 Authorised unit trusts must invest only in specified securities, the greater part of which must be securities listed on recognised stock exchanges. Usually the trust deed will allow up to 5% of the funds to be invested in unquoted securities. An equity unit trust is prohibited from holding more than 10% of the total value of the fund in the shares of any one quoted company. Only four shares can be held up to this 10% limit. All other shares held must not exceed 5% of the fund. This means that a unit trust must have a minimum of 16 holdings. The trust deed may only alter the minimum and maximum limits set out by the SIB providing these limits in the regulations are not exceeded.

4.5 The trust deed will also limit the amount of capital of one company which can be purchased to around 10% of the issued share capital of the company. These limitations are intended to ensure that a unit trust has a broad spread of investments.

4.6 A unit trust investing in gilts must invest in at least six different issues of stock and no single stock holding can exceed 30%.

4.7 Unit trusts hold interest-bearing cash deposits for liquidity and cash flow purposes and may hold cash without limit during the initial offer period. Most fund managers maintain around 5% of a fund's assets in cash, although it is possible to invest in a trust of cash deposits. This enables investors to obtain higher interest rates, due to the pooling of funds in the trust, allowing the managers to obtain improved rates.

4.8 There are many different stock markets to deal in throughout the world. Most unit trusts limit themselves to specific areas of the globe, e.g. Japan, Asia, Germany, etc., and this is laid down in the trust deed. In effect, the deed gives the objectives of the trust, specifying which markets it is allowed to deal in. This may reflect certain world markets or may limit itself to certain sectors of the market. It can be that the unit trust is a global one that gives itself no limitations whatsoever. If there are limitations put on the trust by the trust deed, it will normally be reflected in its name.

4.9 The trust deed will require the unit trust to publish an annual report to unitholders together with a half yearly review listing the trust's holdings at that date and detailing both the capital and income funds.

Who manages the unit trust?

4.10 The unit trust itself can be managed by many different sources, including specialist unit trust groups, banks and large insurance companies. A fund manager will be appointed to promote the trust and oversee the investment policy and decide the best investments.

4.11 At the end of November 1995 there were 1,631 trusts in operation managing assets of £109.2 billion. The PIA regulates the marketing of unit trusts by its members and IMRO regulates the investment management activities of fund managers.

5 Types of Unit Trust

5.1 There are, broadly speaking, three types of unit trust, one with the objective of income, one with the objective of growth and one aiming for a steady income and capital growth. It will obviously depend on the customer's circumstances as to which is best for them, based on their need for either income or capital growth or both.

5.2 The three types of funds which currently account for over 50% of the unit trust market are:

- UK Growth Trusts

- UK Equity Income Trusts

- UK General Trust aiming for steady income and capital growth

5.3 Income producing unit trusts provide distribution units to the investor and growth producing unit trusts give accumulation units to the investor.

5.4 Distribution units usually pay income twice a year, net of tax and deduction of the manager's annual management charge of approximately 1-1½% p.a. Alternatively, where an investor does not wish to take a distribution, it can be reinvested in further units, subject of course to any initial charges. Where accumulation units are bought income is automatically reinvested without charge.

5.5 To be defined as an income fund the trust must aim to produce a yield in excess of 110% of the general market yield. For example, a UK Equity Income Fund should have a yield in excess of 110% of the yield of the FT Actuaries All-Share Index.

Categories of unit trusts

5.6 There is a wide variety of unit trusts available to investors, covering various investments and investment objectives. In order to attempt to simplify matters, the Association of Unit Trusts and Investment Funds (AUTIF) has categorised these. Each fund must be at least 80% invested in the particular sector, e.g. a UK fund must be at least 80% invested in the UK.

5.7 A fund will be reasonably diversified within its sector, although general or balanced funds will provide diversification across a wider area. For example, an international trust will spread risk across countries as well as securities.

5.8 The different categories are:

(a) **UK General Trusts** - a broadly based investment in mainly UK shares across a range of industries, aiming to provide steady income and capital growth.

(b) **UK Growth Trusts** - investment in mainly UK shares, either across a range of industries or in specialist areas such as small companies or recovery stocks, aiming to provide maximum capital growth.

(c) **UK Equity Income Trusts** - investment in ordinary shares of UK companies, aiming to produce high income.

(d) **UK Mixed Income Trusts** - investment in ordinary shares and fixed-interest securities, aiming to produce high income.

(e) **Gilt and Fixed Income Trusts** - investment in government securities and corporate bonds, either to produce high, secure income or for capital appreciation.

(f) **International Growth Trusts** - investment in a spread of world stock markets, either across a range of industries or in specialised situations, to produce maximum capital growth.

(g) **International Income Trusts** - investments in either a spread of world stock markets or one geographical area to provide above-average income.

(h) **Overseas Growth Trusts** - investment in a specific geographical area, e.g. North America, Europe, Far East (which in itself may be concentrated on one country e.g. France, Japan etc.). The unit trust may concentrate on specialised situations, e.g. smaller companies, technology, or reflect a general spread of shares. The aim is maximum growth.

(i) **Financial Trusts** - investment in shares of financial institutions either for income or growth, or a general fund (income and growth).

(j) **Property Trusts** - investment in property company shares, for income, growth or general.

(k) **Commodity Trusts** - investment in shares of companies producing energy, metals or 'soft' commodities such as cocoa, sugar etc.

(l) **Investment Trust Unit Trusts** - investment in investment trust shares. The underlying investment trust may invest in a wide range of companies.

(m) **Convertible Trusts** - investment in at least 60% convertible stock for income.

(n) **Bond Unit Trusts** - investment in government or international blue chip company bonds.

(o) **Deposit Unit Trusts** - investment in money market instruments.

Tracker funds

5.9 There has been a growth in the number of index or tracker funds aiming to replicate the growth of a chosen stock market index, the most common being the FT-SE 100, Dow Jones and Nikkei Dow. A unit trust set up for investment in this way will have certain advantages, namely:

(a) Costs may be lower as there is less management of the fund required.

(b) The fund cannot perform much worse than the market in general as the performance of the fund is linked to the index which is itself an indication of trends in the market.

Fund of funds

5.10 A number of unit trust management groups offer a fund of funds. This is a fund which invests in the other unit trust funds of a group, and is a managed fund. Its main advantage is that small investors can have some exposure to the more specialist funds, but can spread the risk more widely. As such, this is generally regarded as one of the lesser-risk funds and is often recommended to small investors.

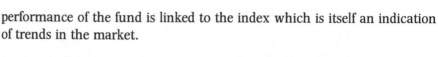

Student Activity 1

You should complete this student activity before reading the next section of the text. Answer the questions, then check your answers against the paragraph(s) indicated.

1. What are the main functions and requirements of:

   (a) The trustee of a unit trust?   (4.1, 4.2)

   (b) The manager of a unit trust?   (4.10)

2. What restriction is there on the amount an equity-based unit   (4.4)
   trust can invest in shares?

3. Obtain information about your own company's range of unit   (5.8)
   trust funds and state which of the unit trust categories each
   falls into.

If you are unable to answer any of the questions satisfactorily, you should read the relevant paragraphs again. Your understanding of the text will be further tested in the self-assessment section at the end of this unit.

6 Investment in a Unit Trust

6.1 Investment into a unit trust may be on a lump sum or regular savings basis and the individual unit trust will have its own specified limits. The minimum lump sum investment into a unit trust is usually between £500-£1,000. Regular savings plans will have a minimum monthly contribution of £25 upwards, although most have a minimum of £50.

6.2 Where a regular savings plan is used, the investor selects how much he wishes to invest each month. The investment can be stopped at any time and left to grow within the trust or cashed. The number of units purchased for the selected monthly investment will vary with the unit price; when the price is high fewer units will be bought than when the price is low. The average cost of units secured in this way tends to be less than the average of the unit prices, and this effect is known as pound cost averaging. The advantage to the investor is that he does not need to plan the timing of his investment in the same way as he would do if investing a lump sum. He does, of course, need to take care over the timing of the encashment.

Example 16.1: Pound cost averaging

Investment of £40 in a unit trust per month for 10 months:

Month	Unit Price (£)	Number Purchased (= £40 ÷ price)
1	5	8
2	4	10
3	5	8
4	6	6.67
5	8	5
6	7	5.71
7	7	5.71
8	6	6.67
9	5	8
10	5	8

Total units purchased	71.76
Total cost of units	£400 (= total invested per month x 10)
Average cost per unit	£5.57 (i.e. total cost of units / number of units)
Average unit price	£5.80 (i.e. total unit costs for 10 months / 10)

This example shows that the average cost to the investor, over the ten months, is less than the average unit price.

Regular income plan

6.3 Investors who wish to use their unit trusts to generate a regular income can do so by selecting a mix of several trusts from a manager's portfolio, typically six to eight, which distribute income on different dates. In this way the investor will receive a regular monthly or near monthly income. Of course the minimum level of investment is likely to be high to enable a spread of the investment over the selected funds.

7 The Pricing of a Unit Trust

7.1 The value of the units in a unit trust will vary according to whether they are being bought or sold. The terminology used, however, is not 'bought' and 'sold' but:

- Offer price (bought)

- Bid price (sold)

7.2 The difference between the two prices is known as the 'bid-offer spread'. The investor buys units at the offer price which is the maximum price at which units are sold by fund managers. In principle the offer price should reflect the cost of establishing a portfolio of shares equivalent to the existing portfolio.

7.3 Managers have to create new units when demand for units exceeds those on offer. To create new units, the fund manager will select an offer price at or near the quoted offer price, to include charges, and the trust will be deemed to be priced on an offer basis. The income from the sale of new units will be invested in more securities thereby increasing the size of the trust's portfolio.

7.4 The bid price is the minimum price at which the fund manager will repurchase units from an investor. In principle the bid price should not be less than the realisation value of the portfolio.

7.5 Where the demand for new units is less than the volume of units being encashed, the fund managers will have to realise some of the underlying investments from the fund to finance the repurchase of units. If the demand for units is low and encashments are exceeding purchase then the fund manager will select a price at or near the current bid price and the trust will be deemed to be priced on a bid basis.

7.6 The offer price will always exceed the bid price. The bid-offer spread includes the initial charge for creating units, and some dealing costs such as stamp duty. The initial charge will normally be between 1-6%.

7.7 To avoid the need to cancel or create units the manager can run a 'box' of units repurchased from unitholders which can be used to supply new investors. This procedure is known as a box arrangement.

7.8 Unit trust managers have to calculate the prices of units according to a formula laid down by the SIB, thereby creating a regulated maximum size to the bid-offer spread. Within this there will be variants dependent upon the need to buy or sell. This is normally fixed between 5-8% although it can be as high as 12%. Pricing within the industry is reasonably standard, however, management companies do cut charges from time to time to increase sales.

7.9 The following examples illustrate how bid and offer prices are calculated.

Example 16.2: Offer price calculation

Number of issued units	100,000
Lowest replacement price of the underlying investment	40.000 pence
Add stamp duty @ 0.5%	00.200
Add commission @ 0.25%	00.100
Add assumed accrued income per unit (£60,000 / 100,000)	<u>00.600</u> 40.900
Add initial charge @ 6%	<u>2.454</u> 43.354

Round to two decimal places to arrive at the maximum offer price per unit i.e. 43.35 pence.

Example 16.3: Bid price calculation

Number of issued units	100,000

Highest market dealing price of the
underlying investment per unit   39.0000 pence

Subtract commission @ 0.25%   00.0975

Add assumed accrued income per
unit (£60,000 / 100,000)   00.6000
                                              39.5025

Round to two decimal places to arrive at the maximum bid price per unit i.e.
39.50 pence.

7.10 There is also a cancellation price indicating the maximum spread between the
offer and bid prices, which is the minimum permissible price at which the
value of the units can be quoted. This is normally lower than the current bid
price and is determined by a formula laid down by the SIB. Unit trusts no
longer have to publish this price.

7.11 As well as the bid-offer spread, there will normally be an annual charge of
between 0.5%-2% taken directly from the fund. This can vary but is a
reflection of the cost of managing the unit trust. There is currently no
restriction on the level of administration charges a trust can make, but they
must be specified in the trust deed.

Historic or forward pricing

7.12 Unit trusts can be priced on either a historic or a forward pricing basis. Trust
managers are required to state a precise time during the day when valuations
will be carried out. Prices of unit trusts quoted in the financial papers will
carry the code 'H' or 'F' after the valuation time. For example, 1200H
indicates that the funds are revalued every day at 12 noon and dealt with on
a historic basis, that is, any deal done after 12 noon is at the price fixed at 12
noon. If the time is followed by an F this would indicate a forward pricing
basis. In this case, the investor would not know the precise price at which he
had dealt until the next 12 noon revaluation.

7.13 The fund manager can choose the valuation time, with the only proviso being
that it is set a minimum of two hours prior to any market opening in which it
has more than 40% of its investments.

Understanding published prices in the financial papers

7.14 An extract taken from the authorised unit trusts section of the Financial
Times is given below.

Example 16.4: Understanding published prices

AIB Unit Trust Managers Limited (1000) F
51 Belmont Rd, Uxbridge, Middx, UB8 1RZ 01895 259783

AIB Grofund American	5	200.1	211.7	+0.50	0.41
AIB Grofund Asia Pacific	5	109.4	116.3	+0.30	0.88
AIB Grofund Equity	5	278.1	295.8	+0.50	1.96
AIB Grofund Euro	5	253.9	268.7	+1.00	1.14
AIB Grofund Expt Balanced	3	128.3	132.9	....	5.14
AIB Grofund Gilt	3	77.99	80.40	+0.12	4.72

AIB Grofund Japan	5	178.5	188.9	-0.50	0.00

AXA Equity and Law Unit Trust Managers (1200)H
Equity & Law Hse, Corpn St, Coventry 01203 553231

General Inc	5	545.2	580.1	+0.8	2.50
General Acc	5	634.6	675.2	+0.8	2.50
UK Growth Acc	6	429.9	457.4	+0.6	2.70
UK Growth Inc	6	286.5	304.8	+0.5	2.70
Higher Inc Acc	6	786.6	836.9	+0.3	4.05

Source: Financial Times (26 January 1996)

7.15　For each unit trust the management name is shown, whether the trust is priced on a historic or forward basis and the time at which the price of the units is valued and set.

7.16　From the example, AIB Unit Trust Managers price their trusts on a forward basis at 10.00 a.m. each day. In addition, reading from left to right, the columns indicate:

AIB Grofund American	-	Fund name
5	-	Initial charge
200.1	-	Bid price
211.7	-	Offer price
+ 0.50	-	+ or - movement on the previous day's price
0.41	-	Gross yield

7.17　This means that an investor wishing to buy units will pay a price of 211.70p per unit. The initial charge will have already been included in that price and will be deducted from the money paid by the investor before units are purchased on his behalf. If he had bought the units yesterday, he would have paid a lower price as the movement on the previous day's price is shown as plus 0.50.

7.18　The gross yield indicates the potential for income of the investment. However, as it expresses the last declared annual dividend as a percentage of the offer price, it can only present a historic picture and not a reliable indication of future yield.

Student Activity 2

You should complete this student activity before reading the next section of the text. Answer the questions, then check your answers against the paragraph(s) indicated.

1.　Choose one fund from your company's range and note the current offer and bid prices. Explain the reasons for the difference between the two.　(7.2-7.6))

2.　What is the purpose of the valuation point, and at what time must it take place?　(7.12, 7.13)

3.　What difference does it make to an investor wishing to buy　(7.12)

units whether historic or forward pricing is used?

4.   What costs do the following charges pay for?   (7.6, 7.11)

(a) Initial charge

(b) Annual management charge

If you are unable to answer any of the questions satisfactorily, you should read the relevant paragraphs again. Your understanding of the text will be further tested in the self-assessment section at the end of this unit.

8   The Dealing Process

8.1   There are several ways in which an investor can buy or sell units in a unit trust i.e. by contacting the fund manager by telephone, by replying to an advertisement in a newspaper or other publication or through his bank, broker/dealer, financial adviser or other authorised person.

Buying units

8.2   On receipt of the application to purchase units the manager will issue a contract note showing the number of units, the price and the total amount payable. Following receipt of payment the manager may issue a certificate within 21 days giving the investor proof of ownership. The issue of a certificate is not mandatory however and the manager may issue non-certificated units. In such circumstances the contract note is proof of purchase.

8.3   An investor who purchases a unit trust as a result of a 'cold call' normally has the right to cancel the contract within 14 days of receipt of a cancellation notice and recoup either the original sum invested or the current offer price at the time of cancellation, whichever is less. This cancellation right does not extend to execution-only business by post or telephone or where the investor dealt through an authorised person with whom a client agreement existed.

8.4   It should be noted that if an investor cancels within the cancellation period, he is not guaranteed the full return of his original investment as the trust managers will have invested the money immediately on purchase and the price of units may then have fallen.

Share exchange scheme

8.5   A small holding of shares acquired through a privatisation issue or inheritance may prove expensive and time-consuming to realise through a stockbroker. Under a share exchange scheme, the unit trust manager offers advantageous terms to swap small quantities of shares, perhaps as little as £1,000 worth, for units. If the shares the investor has to offer can be absorbed into the manager's existing portfolio he may pay the current offer price giving the investor a potential saving of up to 3% if sold through a stockbroker. In some circumstances the manager may also pay the dealing costs. On the other hand some of the shares acquired this way may hold little appeal for the manager and terms offered may not be so good.

Selling units

8.6 When an investor is selling units it is the unit trust manager who buys them. On receipt of a sell order a contract note is issued showing the price and total proceeds. The investor must sign the renunciation form on the reverse of the certificate, giving up his rights to ownership of the units and send this to the manager, who will then send the investor a cheque for the proceeds. This amount is based on the bid price at which they are sold, which will depend on whether the price is quoted on a historic or forward basis, less appropriate charges. The time the sell order is received will determine which day's price should be used. Different companies will have different procedures for determining when an order to sell is defined as received. For example, if a signed form is taken into the branch before 12 noon, the price will be that day's price; if after 12 noon, the next day's price will apply. Settlement should normally be within five working days. Where the investor only wishes to sell part of his holding the renunciation form must indicate how many units are for sale and a balance certificate will be issued with the sale proceeds.

9 Taxation of Unit Trusts

9.1 Authorised unit trusts receive income that falls into two categories:

(a) Franked investment income is income in the form of dividends from UK companies. It has already borne tax at 20% and no further tax liability exists.

(b) Unfranked investment income is income from cash, fixed-interest securities, overseas shares and all other sources. It is received gross and is subject to advance corporation tax at the basic rate, currently 20% for the financial year 1996.

9.2 Prior to 1 April 1996, the rate of corporation tax paid by an authorised unit trust depended on the proportion of interest-bearing investments to equities held within the unit trust. If the trust's interest-bearing investments did not exceed 60% of the market value of its total investments during an accounting period, then the rate of tax for that period was 20%. Otherwise, a rate of 25% applied.

9.3 The unit trust fund is exempt from CGT on internal transactions so fund managers can buy or sell shares without facing a CGT bill.

Tax position of the investor

9.4 When income is distributed to investors, it is paid net of tax. From 6 April 1996, income is paid net of a 20% tax charge; both lower rate and basic rate taxpayers are deemed to have met their tax liability in full and have no further tax to pay. Non taxpayers may claim a refund of the tax deducted. Higher rate taxpayers will have an additional tax liability of the difference between lower and higher rate tax, i.e. 20%.

9.5 Prior to 6 April 1996, the rules depended on whether the unit trust was an equity-based or an interest-based fund. Individuals investing in interest-based funds received distributions net of 25% tax accompanied by a tax credit. Non taxpayers and lower rate taxpayers had to reclaim the appropriate amount of over-deducted tax. Higher rate taxpayers had an additional 15% liability. Individuals investing in equity-based funds received income net of a 20% tax charge, and higher rate taxpayers had an additional 20% liability. Basic rate taxpayers had no further tax to pay; non taxpayers could reclaim the over-deducted tax.

9.6 Where the unit trust income is reinvested, as in the case of a growth unit trust, the unit trust holder must declare this income on his tax return, even though he has not directly received the income. He will be given a tax credit for the appropriate amount of tax deducted and a higher rate taxpayer will have an extra tax liability.

9.7 Any gains made by individual investors on the sale of their units are liable to capital gains tax. Indexation can be applied, in the same way as for shares, to increase the acquisition price, and so reduce the size of the gain.

Example 16.5: Taxation of a unit trust gain by an investor

Jenny invests £4,000 in unit trusts in April 1990. On 10 November 1995, she sells her holding for £12,000. She is a higher rate taxpayer.

The gain is calculated by taking indexation into account as follows:

$$£4,000 \times \frac{149.8 - 125.1}{125.1} \qquad = £789.77$$

Add to original investment	= £4,789.77
Gain = £12,000 - £4,789.77	= £7,210.23
Less annual exemption (1995-96)	£6,000.00
Taxable gain	£1,210.23
Capital gains tax at 40%	£ 484.09

Note: RPI April 1990 = 125.1 November 1995 = 149.8

Bed and breakfasting

9.8 It is possible for a unitholder to limit exposure to CGT by bed and breakfasting. The unitholder would sell and then repurchase immediately to create a gain which can be covered by the CGT annual exemption limit. There is the risk of the price moving substantially during the time of the deals but fund managers may reduce charges for unitholders switching in this way.

Student Activity 3

You should complete this student activity before reading the next section of the text. Answer the questions, then check your answers against the paragraph(s) indicated.

Mike Townsend has invested in a UK Equity Income Fund Unit Trust from the Brightstar Investment Management Group. He is a higher rate taxpayer and receives an annual income from his unit trust which was £220 plus a tax credit of £55 in May 1996.

(a) What additional tax liability will he have? (9.4)

(b) If he makes a capital gain when he sells his units, how is (9.7)
any chargeable gain calculated?

(c) Describe the advantages of bed and breakfasting (9.8)

If you are unable to answer any of the questions satisfactorily, you should read the relevant paragraphs again. Your understanding of the text will be further tested in the self-assessment section at the end of this unit.

10 Uses of a Unit Trust

10.1 A unit trust may be an appropriate vehicle for first time investors in shares, investors wishing to concentrate on one specific investment area and long-term investors. The following describe some of the specific uses for unit trust investment.

Unit trusts and house purchase

10.2 As a long-term investment, a unit trust or selection of unit trusts could be used to accumulate capital to repay an interest-only mortgage. This method is only suitable for individuals who understand the possible fluctuations attached to stock market investments. Investments to build up the fund could be made regularly, perhaps topped up by lump sums when these are available, or on a lump sum basis only.

10.3 This type of repayment is accepted by most major mortgage lenders and allows the investor some flexibility. The mortgage can be repaid early if investment growth is better than expected, or if the mortgage is repaid by another method then the unit trust investment can be used for another purpose.

Unit trusts and school fees

10.4 School fees or further education costs could be funded by a programme of regular and/or lump sum investments to a range of unit trusts across a spread of investment areas. When money is required to meet fees, the investor sells an appropriate number of units in the trust of his choice. Again, this provides flexibility of use if circumstances change.

Unit trusts and retirement planning

10.5 A unit trust could be used to supplement the benefits on retirement payable from a pension plan. Where the investor is making maximum contributions to the pension, or requires greater flexibility on the spread of investment, timing of benefits or type of benefits, e.g. all as cash, a unit trust may be appropriate. Again, the fund may be built up from regular and/or lump sum investments.

10.6 Taxation considerations should be made here, i.e. ensure that the investor is making full use of all the tax advantages of investing in pension arrangements first. Also, when the investor is in receipt of the unit trust income, his age allowance may be lost depending on the amount of income received. Alternatively, he could reinvest the capital in another investment vehicle such as an annuity where part of the income is not taxed.

Unit trust Peps

10.7 Many people invest in unit trusts through a personal equity plan and it is advisable that anyone investing in unit trusts puts the full amount in a Pep first to gain the tax advantages. This is covered in more detail later in Unit 17.

11 Risk and Accessibility

11.1 As with all equity-based investments no one should invest in unit trusts if they are not able to accept that values can fall as well as rise. Unit trusts should be regarded as medium to long-term investments to enable fluctuations in unit values to be ironed out.

11.2 They offer access to equity investment to smaller investors, i.e. lump sum investment can usually start at £500 with regular savings starting from £25-£50 a month. The level of risk can be chosen by the investor by his selection of funds. Switching between funds is also available, and usually at a discount. However, this may incur a CGT charge as it involves selling units in one fund and buying them in another. The investor's annual exemption should be taken into account when calculating this liability.

11.3 Investors need to ensure that they have suitable emergency funds to avoid the need to sell units at a time of low prices if cash is needed. Unit trusts fall between the no-risk/low-risk investments e.g. deposit accounts and unit-linked investment plans, and the higher-risk direct equity investments.

11.4 Units can be sold at any time giving investors almost immediate access to funds. Administration means that it may take a minimum of a week before a cheque arrives. However, the procedure for encashing unit trust holdings, in full or in part, is simple for anyone.

11.5 The choice of type of units bought depends on the investor and his requirements. He may want capital growth, income or a combination of both. Where income is required the investor needs to consider what level of income is required. Where a high income is produced this may be detrimental to the capital value over the long term. If the capital reduces it will not be able to produce such a high income. An income-producing fund which offers a relatively high yield may not be as productive over the long term as one with a lower yield. This should be borne in mind when comparing with income provided by a bank or building society deposit account. The interest rate from a bank or building society may be similar to or higher than the unit trust yield, but over the longer term, the capital held in the account will not increase in value and so income will simply be based on the current interest rate. With the unit trust the underlying capital value should grow and so produce an increasing level of income.

11.6 Where investors do not have a lump sum to invest there are a number of regular savings plans available. As investment is spread, these benefit from pound cost averaging where units bought when prices are high are balanced by those bought when prices are low. When a lump sum investment is made all units are bought at the price prevailing at the time, and therefore the timing of the investment is more critical.

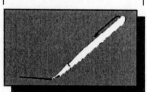

Student Activity 4

You should complete this student activity before attempting the self-assessment. Answer the questions, then check your answers against the paragraph(s) indicated.

Explain why a unit trust might be suitable for each of the following customers and highlight the advantages involved in each set of circumstances.

(a) Katie and Danny have an interest-only mortgage and understand the possible risks of stock market investment. (10.2, 10.3)

(b) Peter and Fiona have two young children and hope they will benefit from a good education. (10.4)

(c) Yvonne is making maximum contributions to a pension plan and wishes to supplement her pension income when she eventually retires. (10.5)

If you are unable to answer any of the questions satisfactorily, you should read the relevant paragraphs again. Your understanding of the text will be further tested in the following self-assessment.

Summary

Now that you have completed this unit, you should be able to:

☐ **Understand the composition of a unit trust**

☐ **Know the requirements for authorisation and control of a unit trust**

☐ **Know the different types of unit trust**

☐ **Understand how to invest in a unit trust**

☐ **Be able to explain the pricing of a unit trust and the charges involved**

☐ **Know the dealing process involved when buying and selling units**

☐ **Understand the taxation of a unit trust and the tax position of the investor**

☐ **Know the purpose and the main uses of a unit trust and how it meets investment objectives and needs**

☐ **Understand the risk position of a unit trust and its accessibility and flexibility**

If you can tick all the above boxes with confidence, you are ready to answer the questions which follow.

Self-Assessment Questions

1. Francis asks you to explain the benefits of investing in a unit trust as compared to dealing in the markets directly as an individual. What would you tell her?

2. Name two advantages of a unit trust which invests in tracker funds.

3. Andrea Clarke wants to invest in a unit trust. In what alternative ways can she purchase units?

4. What cancellation rights exist under a unit trust?

5. Timothy has purchased a unit trust. How could he sell some units if the need arose in the future?

6. What is the taxation treatment of franked investment income received by an authorised unit trust?

7. Define unfranked investment income and explain its taxation treatment.

8. Rebecca has a very low attitude to risk. Explain whether a unit trust would be a suitable investment for her and briefly give reasons for your answer.

9. Sebastian is considering purchasing a unit trust but is concerned about the access he would have to his funds. What could you tell him?

10. What factors should an investor consider when comparing the yield from a unit trust with the income provided by a building society deposit account?

Unit 17

Personal Equity Plans

Objectives

Students are required to study the following topics:

- **Clarification and restriction**

- **Investment areas**

- **Methods of contributing and limits**

- **Risk profile**

- **Encashments**

- **Uses**

1 Introduction

1.1 Personal equity plans (Peps) became available in January 1987 after being introduced in the 1986 Budget. At the time the government was involved in raising funds through a growing number of privatisation share issues. They were aiming to raise the level of share ownership amongst individuals and heighten both public awareness and involvement in the stock market.

1.2 Unfortunately, a rather complex set of rules did not initially lead to a massive take up of Peps despite their tax advantages, so successive finance acts have modified rules to make investment easier for the private individual.

2 What is a Pep?

2.1 A personal equity plan is a scheme to enable an individual to invest lump sums, or regular savings, up to set limits in UK shares, companies on the unlisted securities market, unit trusts and investment trusts. Peps are managed by various financial institutions on behalf of individuals with their particular attraction being that any income or gains made by the plan are completely tax-free.

Pep management

2.2 Personal equity plans are managed by plan managers from the controlling company. Companies that offer Peps include unit trust companies, clearing banks, stockbrokers, building societies and life assurance marketing groups. All Peps have to be Inland Revenue approved.

2.3 A number of providers also offer Peps which allow a more experienced investor more of the management of his plan. These include advisory Peps where managers offer advice on what to buy and sell, and when, and self-select Peps where the investor chooses his own holdings. Some of these may restrict the range of investments allowed. The penalty for greater self-selection is increased charges as dealing costs cannot so easily be spread between a number of investors.

Pep performance

2.4 The performance of Peps is very much dependent on the ability of the plan managers and, of course, movements in the stock market. Since they only started in 1987 there is not a great track record to judge them by but as a medium to long-term investment they should reflect movements in the stock market. Of course, nothing is guaranteed and investors should be aware that values can fall as well as rise.

2.5 Performance may be measured by the return on the capital invested (known as money weighted), or by comparison against the performance of another fund (time weighted). In either case it is based on the improvement in capital value plus income produced. As the value of the capital can decrease it is possible to produce a negative performance figure.

3 Pep Rules

3.1 The tax-free status of Peps means that they are a highly attractive proposition especially considering the potential gains that can be made over a period of time on the stock market. Their attractiveness leads to certain limitations and rules:

(a) Holders of Peps must be 18 or over, and resident in the UK for tax purposes.

(b) Trustees, minors, companies, clubs, societies etc. cannot invest in a Pep.

(c) An individual may only subscribe to one general Pep and/or one single company Pep in any tax year.

(d) Maximum investment is £6,000 for a general Pep plus a further £3,000 in a single company Pep in a tax year. Once the tax year has finished another Pep can be started.

(e) A Pep cannot be held jointly, although a husband and wife can each take out a plan.

(f) The ownership of the Pep must remain with the investor; a Pep cannot be assigned or written under trust.

3.2 There are other limitations, which will be covered shortly, but it should be noted that there is no minimum investment period for a Pep. As with any stock market investment it should be viewed as a medium to long-term investment but a Pep can be continued for as long as is required. A charge may be levied if a Pep is encashed in the first five years or so.

3.3 A seven day cancellation period applies to investments into a Pep. To avoid the complication of reversing a transaction, investment will only take place once the cancellation period has expired.

4 Pep Investment

4.1 The limits on investment ensure that Peps do the job their tax-free status was intended to do, that is encourage investment in UK companies. Since the commencement of the single European market in 1993, the UK had to broaden the scope of a Pep's investments to include shares in companies of the EU member states. Different restrictions apply to the different investment areas as follows.

Permitted investments for general Peps

4.2 A general Pep may invest directly in UK and EU shares, in qualifying unit trusts or investment trusts or in specified corporate bonds and convertibles of UK non-financial companies and preference shares in UK and EU companies.

4.3 A qualifying trust is one where at least 50% of the investment is in UK or EU quoted shares. These do not have to include any UK shares, so it is possible to invest in a Pep which has no element of UK based investment which may seem to contradict the stated aim of the government in introducing Peps.

4.4 Up to £1,500 can be invested in trusts which do not meet this requirement provided at least 50% of the investment is in equities. Such trusts will invest primarily in overseas equities.

Permitted investments for single company Peps

4.5 Single company Peps can invest in the shares of any single UK or other EU quoted company at any one time. The choice of share can sometimes be changed at the manager's or investor's discretion.

Excluded investments

4.6 Currently excluded from Pep funds are property and cash together with option based funds. Unit trusts and investment trusts investing in gilts are also excluded.

Regular savings/lump sum investment

4.7 An investor can choose to open a Pep with a lump sum or by paying regular contributions, depending on the rules of the individual plan. As with investments already discussed regular savings will benefit from pound cost averaging.

4.8 Additional lump sum payments can be made, or lump sums added to regular contribution plans, provided they do not exceed the maximum limit for the tax year.

Income or growth

4.9 Depending on the investor's requirement a Pep can be chosen to provide income, growth or a balance. As with unit trusts a high yield may indicate good performance, but caution should be used before deciding to invest in a high yielding Pep as this may be at the expense of capital growth and income in the future.

Cash deposits

4.10 Where a Pep fund is held on deposit, any interest paid out that exceeds £180 will be liable to income tax.

Buying and selling

4.11 When investing in a Pep it is a requirement that the funds used are those of the intended Pep holder. To assist in monitoring this when settling a purchase it is essential that any cheques are drawn on an account of the purchaser, e.g. a husband cannot write a cheque on his sole account to invest in a Pep in the name of his wife. Encashments will also be paid to the named person holding the Pep.

Student Activity 1

You should complete this student activity before reading the next section of the text. Answer the questions, then check your answers against the paragraph(s) indicated.

1. Name the limitations and rules which apply to investing in a PEP. (3.1)

2. Mrs Lourd has decided to purchase a Pep which invests in unit trusts. She asks you to explain what is meant by a qualifying trust. What would you tell her? (4.3)

3. Mr Godwin wants to purchase a Pep. What requirements apply to the cheque which he writes and to encashments made? (4.11)

If you are unable to answer any of the questions satisfactorily, you should read the relevant paragraphs again. Your understanding of the text will be further tested in the self-assessment section at the end of this unit.

5 Types of Pep

5.1 There are really only two types of Pep:

- General Pep

- Single company Pep

5.2 General Peps are the most common type. An individual may invest up to £6,000 per tax year in a general Pep, which may invest directly in shares or in collective investments such as unit trusts and investment trusts. There are several different categories of general Pep, some depending on the degree of investment advice and management provided by the plan manager and others relating to the type of investment used by the Pep.

Managed Peps

5.3 With a managed Pep all the investment decisions are made for the customer. This is after the customer has decided what his overall investment objective is and what he thinks will be best to achieve these objectives. It is not the responsibility of the Pep manager to advise customers when and if to cash in their holdings. As mentioned above the managed Peps can be further split up into various types depending on the underlying investment, i.e. into shares, unit trusts, investment trusts or a combination.

Self-select Peps

5.4   For these types of Peps the Pep provider creates the framework for the customer's own Pep, manages the plan and carries out the administration. The responsibility for selecting the shares or pooled investments to be included remains with the customer. If the plan manager gives advice on which shares the customer is to choose, then this is known as an 'advisory' Pep. The annual charge for this type of Pep should be in the region of 1%. To this must be added commission charges for buying and selling the chosen shares and the standard charges for operating the Pep on the customer's behalf. Again these types of Pep are most suitable for experienced investors who are prepared to take more of a risk.

Unit trust Peps

5.5   These are the most common form of Pep with more than two-thirds of Pep moneys available so far being allocated to this type of investment. The money available is invested in the unit trust fund, or funds, or may be limited to investing the full Pep allowance into a single fund, depending on how the fund manager runs the scheme. The unit trusts may be selected by the plan manager (managed) or more usually by the investor.

5.6   All schemes will have a minimum amount which can be invested in a single fund. However, in the majority of Peps the minimum lump sum will be around £500 or regular savings of £50 per month. Most unit trusts do not carry any additional charges for investing through a Pep. The typical rates for an annual charge are between 1% and 1.5%. Due to competition some managers do not apply the annual management charge, but instead will apply a charge if the investment is cashed in within a five-year period.

Investment trust Peps

5.7   Investment trust Peps, are also popular and widely marketed. As with a unit trust Pep the customer will be limited to either a single fund or the splitting of the allowance between funds. Even though investment trusts are a different type of pooled investment product to that of the unit trust the way the actual Pep operates and the choices the customer is given are very similar.

5.8   Again all schemes stipulate minimum levels of investment and sometimes the amount of moneys required for investment are higher than those of the unit trust Pep. The charges associated with an investment trust are normally lower than those of unit trusts so some operators impose an additional fee for Peps to cover administration fees and also have an annual charge.

Share Peps

5.9   The customer can invest directly into stocks and shares. As with other Peps, the fund manager will impose a charge at the outset of either a lump sum or a percentage of the initial investment, and an annual charge to cover administration costs.

5.10   A managed share Pep is one where the plan manager chooses the shares in which to invest the money and makes decisions about when to buy and sell the individual shares. All the investment decisions are made by the plan manager on the customer's behalf.

5.11 Share Peps may also be on a self-select basis. The investor chooses the shares in which to invest, perhaps from a limited list of those offered by the plan manager, and makes the buying and selling decisions. Under an advisory share Pep, the plan manager provides guidance on the selection, buying and selling of shares.

Mixed Peps

5.12 Some plan managers offer a mix of investments. For example a share based Pep may allow the investor to place part of the investment into unit trusts and part into shares. The investor usually chooses the percentage of the total invested which should be placed in unit trusts. Similarly a mix between shares and investment trusts, investment trusts and unit trusts, or shares, unit trusts and investment trusts may be offered. Where both unit trusts and investment trusts are included in the choice, the trusts may or may not be restricted to those from one investment group.

Corporate Peps

5.13 These are a specialised form of Pep set up by companies to encourage ownership of their shares, either by employees of the company or by outside investors. Corporate Peps are usually arranged by the company issuing the shares by means of a partnership agreement with a Pep plan manager, and some plan managers run hundreds of schemes of this type. There is not normally an initial charge for the Pep and the annual charge is normally set in the region of 0.5%. Once again the investor will still have to pay dealing charges. Although corporate Peps are generally used to offer a tax efficient method of share purchase for the employees of the company, they are also suited to the more specialist investor who is prepared to take the higher risk of exposure to only one share. It should be remembered that they may be more difficult to switch if market conditions change. Although a corporate Pep only invests in the shares of one company it may be either a general plan (accepting up to £6,000 p.a. investment) or a single company plan.

Corporate bond Peps

5.14 These types of Peps are relatively new to the investment market-place, the first being launched in July 1995. A corporate bond Pep allows the entire portfolio in investments other than shares. The bond Pep includes a variety but not the whole range of securities, corporate bonds, convertibles of UK companies, and preference shares in UK and European companies. This means that fixed-interest securities can be held in Peps thus providing some security, but reducing growth potential. Investors can invest in the fixed-interest securities themselves through a stockbroker, or indirectly through a unit trust Pep which invests in corporate bonds. Their use as a long-term investment has yet to be proven.

Single company Peps

5.15 A single company Pep permits an investment level of £3,000 in the shares of only one company, hence its marketing name. The minimum lump sum that can be invested in a single company Pep in the main tends to be around £500 to £1,000. Some plan managers will allow customers to invest on a monthly basis. As with other Peps there are annual charges which are typically between 0.5% and 1% a year.

5.16 Single company Peps can be subdivided into managed, self-select and corporate Peps, all of which have been discussed above. There is no necessity for an investor to hold a general Pep before effecting a single company Pep, nor for a general Pep holder to take out his single company Pep with the same plan manager, although in some cases plan managers may restrict the single company Pep to those also investing in their general Pep, or perhaps offer enhanced terms to investors effecting both general and single company plans.

5.17 If an investor wishes to build up a substantial holding within one company, he could use both his general Pep and single company Pep allowances to invest in corporate Peps of the same company.

Comparison of the types of Pep

5.18 The popularity of Peps since they were introduced in 1986 has increased substantially and so has the market-place they are sold within. The restrictions placed on them and the charges levied by them also reflect the variety of plans and with this comes the degree of complexity of operating the plans by the fund managers. The most popular Peps are based on unit trusts and the increased popularity can be linked to those investors who had previously had Tessas and now require a more tax-efficient home for their money.

5.19 For the ease of management, Peps investing in managed unit trusts are far easier for the inexperienced investor than say a self-select Pep which is at the other end of the scale. When comparing one Pep against another the risk factor must be taken into consideration and will depend on the scheme and the shares selected. Most Peps are equity investments and as such there is a risk as the investment may fall in value as well as increase in value.

5.20 New types of Pep are regularly being developed. An example of this is the index-tracker Pep which provides a return based on the rise (or fall) of the chosen index, commonly the FT-SE 100 index. This may be regarded as a lower risk because fluctuations of individual share prices tend to be smoothed out over the index as a whole, and the value of the index has tended to rise over the long term. However, the investor should be aware that as with all types of Pep, there are no guarantees.

Transferring existing shares

5.21 Investors with existing shares, unit trust or investment trust holdings can transfer these into most Peps. Up to the maximum limit can be transferred each tax year to avoid taxation. However, a CGT liability may arise as holdings must be sold first and then bought back by the Pep manager. Some managers will offer bed and breakfasting as a means of reducing liability. The amount invested in the Pep will be dependent on the share dealing price. Where transfer is within the same company, e.g. a unit trust holding transferred to a unit trust Pep, charges are usually lower than for outsiders.

5.22 There are two ways of avoiding a CGT liability. First new issues can be transferred into a Pep within 42 days of allocation to the investor. This has been commonly used for privatisation issues. Secondly, where an investor acquires shares through an employee SAYE linked share option scheme or a profit sharing scheme, then these shares can be transferred to a Pep within 90

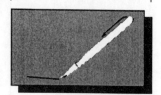

days of being allocated to or bought by the employee. This transfer will be exempt from CGT.

Student Activity 2

You should complete this student activity before reading the next section of the text. Answer the questions, then check your answers against the paragraph(s) indicated.

Jill Simms wants to invest in a Pep but is unsure about which   (5.4, 5.5, 5.13) type of Pep to purchase. She asks you specifically about unit trust Peps, corporate Peps and self-select Peps. What could you tell her about these types of Peps in the following areas:

(a) Investment funds

(b) Charges

(c) Risk

If you are unable to answer any of the questions satisfactorily, you should read the relevant paragraphs again. Your understanding of the text will be further tested in the self-assessment section at the end of this unit.

6   Pep Charges

6.1   Each Pep will have different charges, as described above, and these should be noted since they can be significant on the return if there are no great gains made.

6.2   The two major charges are the initial fee (normally between 1-5%) and the annual fee (normally between 1-2%). There are normally also dealing charges and exit charges. Unit trust Peps generally have the charges applicable to the particular unit trust they are investing in, and although charges vary between different providers in the market, most do not make any further charges for investing in the unit trust through a Pep.

Exit charge

6.3   Most Peps do not make a charge when the plan is encashed. However, unit trust Peps may levy a charge if encashment is within the first three to five years, usually on a sliding scale. It may be a cash value or on a percentage basis.

6.4   If the Pep has performed well these charges should be well outweighed by the tax benefits, particularly for individuals who can invest at or near the maximum levels and for higher rate taxpayers. It should also be remembered that performance is more important than charges, and choosing a Pep with lower charges does not mean the return will necessarily be any better than one with higher charges. As with any product bought, the investor may need to be prepared to pay more for a better quality of fund management.

7   Encashing a Pep

7.1   Tax-free withdrawals can be made at any time, although most plans will have a minimum amount which must be left in the plan e.g. £1,000 to keep it in force. However, Peps are intended to be medium to long-term investments and early encashments may inhibit future growth and may even reduce capital. A Pep can be fully encashed at any time, and, as stated above, some Peps will include an exit charge.

Death of an investor

7.2   A Pep is automatically terminated on the death of an investor. The underlying investments then become an asset of the deceased's estate. The plan managers may transfer either the cash value or the investments to the personal representatives. This may mean an IHT liability.

8   Risk and Accessibility

8.1   Peps carry a risk, which investors should be prepared to take, that they could lose some or all of their investment. Whilst the tax advantages are very attractive, investors who require capital security should not be advised to put their money into a Pep. The risk attached to a managed Pep tends to be lower than that attached to an equity Pep investing in a small range of shares. Peps which invest in international markets tend to involve increased risk but can also provide increased capital growth. The risk involved can be lessened by using collective funds such as unit trusts. If an investor chooses a corporate bond Pep, income can be maximised without a high level of risk to his investment; however, inflation must be considered because it is a fixed-interest investment. The level of risk attached to a corporate bond Pep is considered to be less than that attached to an equivalent equity Pep. Furthermore, single company Peps are usually more volatile than general Peps.

8.2   Risk should be borne in mind when considering the uses of a Pep. For instance, if a Pep is to be used for repaying a mortgage, it must be monitored to ensure that it is on target to repay the mortgage. Care should also be taken if a Pep is used to pay school fees because school fees have fixed payment dates and certain types of Pep are more volatile than others.

8.3   Where investors are prepared to take the risk they should be willing to leave their capital in the Pep over the longer term to ensure a good return. If investors require access to their funds, partial withdrawals can be made at any time without any tax liability. As mentioned earlier, however, the effects of early withdrawals may be detrimental to future performance.

8.4   Peps mostly offer only good news to investors, as long as the threats of the investment are understood, and there are very few bad points about them as investment vehicles. The rules governing Peps can and do alter with each finance act and it could be that a different government may cancel the Pep concept completely. This should not affect current Peps, but can still be a concern to an individual.

9   Uses of a Pep

9.1   A Pep is an excellent method of building up capital via the use of equity investments for the provision of a lump sum over a period of years, or a series of lump sums. If a customer invests regularly in Peps over the years they can build up a very substantial sum of tax-free money. This is attractive to all taxpayers but especially to those on higher rates as the gains will not be eaten into by higher rate tax. It must be borne in mind, however, that the value of the investment can fall in value as well as increase subject to the conditions of the stock market. The dividends available from the investments can be reinvested thus raising the value of the customer's investment.

9.2   The market place for Peps is large and the main differences between one provider and another is that of the charges for managing the fund and the setting up of the fund. These charges do vary and some contain early termination charges and some dealing charges. A customer should take all of these into consideration when choosing their provider.

9.3   It is not necessary for a potential Pep investor to save up and then invest a lump sum in a Pep as both unit trusts and investment trusts offer regular savings options. The minimum amount that a customer may wish to invest on a monthly basis may differ from one provider to another but the maximum a customer can invest each month is £500. Investing on a monthly basis rather than by a lump sum benefits from pound cost averaging. The customer does not have to watch the movement in share prices before parting with their money. Indeed, when share prices are falling the investor who invests on a monthly basis will be buying more units or shares so this is a particularly good way of building up capital investment.

9.4   Some customers use a Pep as a means of saving without earmarking the funds for future expenditure. Others will use a Pep for specific expenditure such as a mortgage repayment, school fees or provision for retirement.

9.5   As a Pep can be cashed in at any time or partial withdrawals taken, this provides a particularly useful vehicle for the payment of any large expenditure item such as a mortgage. Using a Pep to repay a mortgage offers flexibility because by increasing contributions, the mortgage could be repaid earlier. It is a relatively cheap method of repaying a mortgage, though life assurance needs to be effected separately.

9.6   A regular savings Pep is an effective method of building capital to pay for a child's private education in the future. The flexibility of a Pep allows parents to cash in the necessary sums when the fees become due.

9.7   Because of their flexibility, Peps can be particularly useful for retirement planning if an individual intends to take a career break i.e. the individual does not need to have an income, and contributions can be stopped and started at any time. A Pep offers an ideal alternative to an AVC in retirement planning as all the Pep can be taken in cash which is not allowed under AVC rules. Though contributions to a Pep do not attract tax relief, the income produced will be tax-free, unlike income from a pension. Another advantage is that the whole of the fund can be taken as tax-free cash whereas under a pension plan this amount is limited.

9.8   If the customer wishes to use his Pep to meet a major item of expenditure then he should concentrate on mainstream, low-risk investment such as utilities, blue chip companies and perhaps unit trusts that have some gilts in their portfolio. If there is no specific objective then the customer can be more adventurous and look towards smaller companies, overseas and emerging markets.

Student Activity 3

You should complete this student activity before attempting the self-assessment. Answer the questions, then check your answers against the paragraph(s) indicated.

1. Helena works as a marketing assistant. Her company does not (9.1, 9.3, 9.7) offer a pension scheme and she wishes to save for retirement. However, she intends to start a family shortly and take advantage of the five-year career break which her company offers. Explain the advantages a Pep could offer her.

2. Describe the other two common uses of a Pep, highlighting (8.1-8.4, 9.5, any particular factors which the investor should consider in 9.6) terms of risk.

If you are unable to answer any of the questions satisfactorily, you should read the relevant paragraphs again. Your understanding of the text will be further tested in the following self-assessment.

Summary

Now that you have completed this unit, you should be able to:

❑ **Know the various rules which apply to Peps**

❑ **Know the different areas of investment available to Peps**

❑ **Understand the different types of Pep**

❑ **Explain the charges which apply to Peps**

❑ **Understand the risks attached to Peps and their accessibility**

❑ **Understand the main uses of Peps**

If you can tick all the above boxes with confidence, you are ready to answer the questions which follow.

Self-Assessment Questions

1. Why should caution be exercised before deciding to invest in a high yielding Pep?

2. How do the minimum levels of investment and the charges associated with an investment trust Pep compare with a unit trust Pep?

3. Describe the possible investment areas for a corporate bond Pep.

4. Why might the index-tracker Pep be regarded as a lower risk than certain other types of Pep?

5. Karen has an existing shareholding and asks you whether she would be able to transfer this into a Pep. What would you tell her, particularly regarding taxation?

6. Explain how a mixed Pep works.

7. For whom might a corporate Pep be suitable?

8. How does an advisory share Pep operate?

9. Briefly describe the charges which may be associated with Peps.

10. Briefly describe the risk position of a managed Pep, a Pep investing overseas, a corporate bond Pep and a single company Pep.

Unit 18

Investment Trusts

1   Introduction to Investment Trusts

1.1   An investment trust is totally different to a unit trust and the two should not be confused, despite the similarity in name.

1.2   An investment trust is not, in fact, a trust but a limited company, subject to the same provisions of the Companies Act as other limited companies. The first one was set up in 1868. They can have an infinite life span or may be set up for a specific term, e.g. ten years. They are termed 'closed-ended' as they issue a fixed number of shares to their investors, although the share issue may be extended. The company buys shares in other companies or makes investments by using investors' or borrowed moneys, with the objective of making profits for its shareholders. An investment in an investment trust is very similar to an investment in an equity as the investor is buying a share in that particular company. Like unit trusts, investment companies provide a way in which small investors can obtain a spread of their investments with professional management.

1.3   Since investment trusts are companies in their own right, they can deal in any sectors they want, subject to their own memorandum and articles, and can even, like any other company, borrow money to fund investments. Shares are quoted on the stock exchange and may be bought and sold through a stockbroker, like any other equities.

1.4   There are currently around 300 investment trusts, run by members of the Association of Investment Trust Companies, managing around 5% of stock market capital.

2 Regulatory Controls

2.1 An investment trust must conform with regulations laid down by the companies acts, stock exchange rules and its own company memorandum and articles of association. In addition, to qualify for exemption from tax on capital gains, the company must be approved by the Inland Revenue as conforming with the definition of an investment trust company contained in the Income and Corporation Taxes Act 1988.

2.2 The chief requirements are that:

- The investment trust is resident in the UK and is not a 'close' company

- The company's income is derived wholly or mainly from securities (this is interpreted as about 70% or more)

- No holding (other than in another approved investment trust) must represent more than 15% of the investment trust company's investments

- Its own shares are quoted on the London Stock Exchange

- The company is debarred by its own memorandum and articles of association from distributing as dividends profits arising from the sale of investments

- It does not retain more than 15% (i.e. it must distribute at least 85%) of the income it receives from securities

2.3 Investment trusts are not covered by the provisions of the Financial Services Act as they do not deal directly with members of the public. A management company is, however, subject to authorisation requirements if it wishes to market the trust to the public. Investment trust managers are usually members of the Investment Management Regulatory Organisation (IMRO).

3 How an Investment Trust Works

3.1 An investment trust needs to be viewed as a public limited company as, whilst dealing in investments, its legal status is that of a quoted company. Its main objects are to deal in quoted, unquoted or private company shares to make a profit for its investors.

3.2 It is normally run by a minimum of five directors who, whilst they may make investment decisions themselves (a self-managed trust), would normally employ a management company to undertake this on their behalf reviewing investment policy with the board of directors on a regular basis. This may also include registration, administration and accountancy. A management company would also advise when setting up a new trust.

3.3 Unlike a unit trust, an investment trust is a 'closed-end' fund. This means that investment in it is limited to the number of shares issued, so the price of the investment trust shares will depend on market demand as well as the underlying assets held.

3.4 Issues of new capital can be made as in any other company, but the process is more complex.

Discount and premium

3.5   The price of investment trust shares may stand at a discount or premium to their net asset value. Net asset value (NAV) is calculated as the value of holdings in the investment trust, less its liabilities, divided by the number of shares held. The value of holdings is calculated as the mid market value of the trust's investments in quoted shares together with the directors' valuation of any unlisted shares and the value of any other assets held, including cash. This may differ from the share price on the market. Where share prices are higher than the net asset value they are at a premium; if lower then they are at a discount. So if the share price is 440p and the NAV is 400p, the premium is 10%. If the share price is 200p and the NAV is 220p, the discount is 10%.

3.6   If the shares are in demand the discount will narrow or even move to a premium. If they are bought at a discount the investor is buying a stake in more shares than he is paying for. So if a discount stands at 10%, every £90 invested effectively represents £100 worth of shares. If the discount narrows when the investor sells the shares, he will make a profit.

3.7   Where an investment trust has a wide discount it may encourage a takeover bid, particularly from institutions who may find it cheaper to buy the investment trust than to buy the same shares in the market place.

Gearing

3.8   Investment trusts are able to borrow long-term money at a fixed rate of interest for investment by issuing preference shares, debentures and other loan stock.

3.9   They may wish to do this if they have insufficient moneys to take advantage of a good investment which is available. They can also borrow short-term by raising an overdraft or loan from the banks in sterling or foreign currency. This is known as gearing.

3.10   If the investment produces a higher return than the rate of interest on the borrowings, the return to investors will be enhanced. The opposite is true if investment returns fall below the fixed interest rate, however the extra costs of borrowing will exaggerate a loss or reduced income. Gearing works best when in a rising market.

3.11   Gearing, therefore, carries a certain amount of risk for the investor, and shares quoted at a discount to their net asset value will partly compensate for this.

3.12   Interest on borrowings for gearing is allowed as an expense for tax purposes.

Example 18.1: Gearing

If an investment trust collects £1m in investors' money, it may choose to borrow a further £1 million so it has £2 million to invest.

If gains are, say, 20% the fund will have grown from £2 million to £2.4 million, meaning a profit of £0.4 million for the fund and its investors once the loan has been repaid.

Without such gearing, the 20% growth would produce a profit of only £0.2 million.

Such 'gearing' can, of course, have a similar negative effect if a loss is made!

Investment performance

3.13 As with other equity-based investments past performance is not a guarantee of future performance. With investment trusts it is especially difficult to spot a trust which is performing well due to the different ways of spreading risk and extent of gearing.

3.14 To assist, trusts are categorised and a snapshot of the performance of a trust is recorded in a performance table. This will tend to show if a trust has had a good performance over a long period.

3.15 The tables are based on net asset values and share price. The most basic performance table is shown in the Financial Times (see Example 18.2) but this does not give sufficient information on which to base an investment decision.

3.16 Statistical measurement is available normally over three, five and ten years ranking, for example, the top 30 and bottom 30 trusts and calculating the current worth of an original investment of £1,000. Trust managers however prefer to be ranked on their 'quartile performance', obviously wanting to be in the top quartile. Another measure of performance is often calculated on an indexed basis showing the current value of £100 invested at the start of a specified period. Tables can also show a trust's volatility. This is the smoothness of net asset performance over a period. Volatility can be affected by holding a smaller number of stocks, gearing or involvement in volatile markets or sectors.

3.17 The Association of Investment Trust Companies produces detailed monthly tables of investment trust performance which are available to investors.

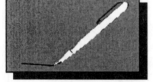

Student Activity 1

You should complete this student activity before reading the next section of the text. Answer the questions, then check your answers against the paragraph(s) indicated.

1. In what can an investment trust invest?   (1.2, 1.3)

2. Why are investment trusts described as 'closed-end'?   (1.2, 3.3)

3. How does an investor buy investment in an investment trust?   (1.3)

4. What is the net asset value (NAV)?   (3.5)

5. What is meant by the share price trading at: (3.5)

(a) A discount?

(b) A premium?

6. Calculate the discount or premium in the following examples: (3.5)

Share price £	NAV
100	120
185	200
220	230
120	100
96	90

If you are unable to answer any of the questions satisfactorily, you should read the relevant paragraphs again. Your understanding of the text will be further tested in the self-assessment section at the end of this unit.

4   Types of Investment Trusts

4.1   Investment trusts generally fall into two types, conventional and split-capital, reflecting the nature of their capital structures. They further divide into two broad areas of providing income or capital growth, but they can also provide a balance between the two. Investment trusts can operate in any part of the world or any sectors to make the most profit for shareholders. For each of the above types of trust, they deal in the same basic form of shares but split-capital trusts usually deal in highly geared ordinary shares to provide income, and zero-dividend preference shares to provide growth.

Conventional trusts

4.2   A conventional trust will issue ordinary shares, preference shares and, in some circumstances, loan stock. They may be established for an indefinite term, the oldest is currently over 100 years old, or for a limited term of say five or ten years.

4.3   A trust with a limited term means that any discount will narrow at the end of the term and investors can gain the full value of the investment trust's assets. However, shorter-term trusts may lose out on the benefits of long-term investment returns.

Split-capital investment trusts

4.4   As with other investment trusts the split-capital trust (sometimes referred to as split-level) should be viewed as a public limited company. Legal status is that of a quoted company, but they have a finite life, with a winding up date agreed at outset.

4.5   Somewhat sophisticated in structure they are extremely useful in investing for a special purpose or tailoring investments to individual needs. Having appeared in the 1960s, they were designed to take advantage of low tax rates on capital gains at a time when income tax rates were extremely high, 98% at its peak including the investment income surcharge.

4.6   Originally there were two classes of shares, one being the 'income shares', the second class being the 'capital shares'. Income shares will receive all the income generated by the whole portfolio whilst the capital shares will receive no income but at the time the trust is wound up, at the pre-set date, the remains of the funds or assets will be distributed between the capital shares creating the capital growth.

4.7 It can be seen therefore that there is a potential for growth or income. In recent years split-capital trusts have additionally issued zero-dividend and stepped preference shares, loan stock and warrants. The investor is therefore offered a wide range of shares to match his investment needs.

5 Types of Shares Issued by Investment Trusts

5.1 The main classes of share in the investment trust sector are summarised below. The type of shares selected by the investor will depend on his requirements for income and capital growth.

Ordinary shares

5.2 This type of share is entitled to all of the income and capital of the investment trust after the repayment of any of the trust's borrowings. Such shares are considered to be low-risk.

Highly geared ordinary shares

5.3 Designed to offer a high income, they also have an entitlement to assets at the date of winding up but only after the zeros and other fixed redemption prices have been paid.

5.4 However, there is a capital risk as there will need to be a substantial investment performance within the trust to meet the high income and provide capital growth.

Preference shares

5.5 Preference shares usually receive a fixed or predetermined rate of dividend, however some pay no dividend at all. Preference shares have a low-risk investment profile since on the winding up of the trust these shares rank ahead of ordinary shares for repayment. There are two types of preference shares to consider:

5.6 **Stepped preference shares** will combine a fixed capital return when the trust is wound up, with a regular income that will grow at a specified rate each year.

5.7 **Zero-divided preference shares (zeros)** are redeemed at a pre-determined fixed price, on a specified date, and although not guaranteed the trusts are designed to produce at least this level of capital at the specified date. These shares have no entitlement to income and therefore there is no income tax to pay.

5.8 They are suitable for cautious investors who require a fixed capital sum at a specific time. As the issue price, redemption price and years to maturity are known it is possible to calculate the gross yield to maturity. As the trust moves to its redemption date, the share price will usually rise to the redemption price and the gross yield to redemption will decline.

Income shares

5.9 As one would expect these are designed to provide a high income. However, there can be considerable variations. Some may have a predetermined redemption price when the trust is wound up, others may have this plus an additional entitlement to any surplus capital, after other share requirements have been met.

5.10 Some may only repay a small capital sum at the winding up of the trust, suitable for an investor who requires a high income over a fixed period but can stand a capital loss.

Capital shares

5.11 As previously stated these produce no income but have the potential of high capital growth although, of course, there is no guarantee of this. At the winding up of the trust, after all the requirements of the fixed capital entitlements have been met, the remaining assets are distributed to these capital shares.

Warrants

5.12 Warrants are not really shares at all but a certificate which gives the holder a right to purchase shares within the trust at a predetermined price on a specified date or dates in the future. This price is called the 'strike price' (also known as the 'exercise price').

5.13 There is only a real value if at the specified date the share price on the open market is higher than that of the strike price.

5.14 Warrants offer high risk/reward opportunities to an investor, particularly where the strike price is close to the share price. For example, if the share price is £2 and the exercise price is £1.80, then the minimum value of the warrant is 20p. A 10% rise in the share price would lead to a 100% increase in the value of the warrant.

Student Activity 2

You should complete this student activity before reading the next section of the text. Answer the questions, then check your answers against the paragraph(s) indicated.

1. What is the main difference between a conventional investment trust and a split-capital trust? (4.2, 4.4)

2. How does the winding up date affect the shares in a conventional investment trust? (4.3)

3. Briefly explain the shareholder's entitlement in each of the following classes of shares:

   (a) Ordinary shares (5.2)

   (b) Stepped preference shares (5.6)

   (c) Zero-dividend preference shares (5.7)

(d) Income shares   (5.9, 5.10)

(e) Capital shares   (5.11)

(f) Warrants   (5.12)

If you are unable to answer any of the questions satisfactorily, you should read the relevant paragraphs again. Your understanding of the text will be further tested in the self-assessment section at the end of this unit.

6   Savings and Investment Schemes

6.1   As previously mentioned, shares in an investment trust can be bought or sold via a stockbroker or directly from the managers through an approved savings and investment scheme. Investment may be on a lump sum basis from as little as £250 or on a regular saving basis so that investors can put £25 upwards per month into their selected investment trust. Shareholders can reinvest dividends from their shares to purchase additional shares. A number of investment trusts offer personal equity plans (Peps), often making no additional charge for investing this way, other than a nominal charge to cover the extra administration costs involved.

6.2   Share exchange schemes are usually available, and will involve selling existing shares and using the cash to buy investment trust shares. This may lead to a CGT liability.

6.3   Unlike a unit trust, an investment trust cannot advertise its own shares for sale but it can publicise both its results and its savings schemes in an effort to attract investors.

6.4   Shares bought direct from an investment trust manager will tend to be held in a nominee account so no share certificate will be issued to the investor.

7   Investment Trust Charges

7.1   Costs of investment vary considerably from company to company but tend to be lower than unit trust charges. Stockbrokers' commission is payable of up to 1% and stamp duty of 0.5% on each purchase and sale with a minimum commission of approximately £20 per execution-only deal. If a self-administered trust requires advice, fees will be greater. Some investment trust companies are now paying commission of up to 3% to introducers of lump sum investments to investment trusts, although commission is not always available on monthly savings schemes. Although there will be a dealing fee on eventual sale of shares, this tends to be less than the bid-offer spread of the unit trust. There may also be an annual management charge of up to 1% which may be renegotiated every two or three years. Newer trusts have also seen performance fees introduced subject to outperforming an agreed stock market index.

7.2   Other costs which may be levied but which are often borne by the trust include such items as auditors' fees, costs of publishing annual reports and directors' fees. This could be expected to add 0.02-0.05% to costs. If the investment is cashed in early then the investor is selling a number of shares in a quoted company and costs reflect this.

8 Understanding Published Prices in the Financial Papers

8.1 The following extract was taken from the London Share Service in the Financial Times:

Example 18.2: Understanding published prices

	Price	+or-	52 week high	low	Yld Gr's	NAV	Dis or Pm(-)
Approved by the Inland Revenue							
Govett High Inc	76	.....	86	70	9.2	88.1	13.7
Warrants	3½	.....	9	3	-	-	-
Govett Oriental	**426**	**+3**	**426**	**322**	**0.4**	**428.3**	**0.5**
Govett Strategic	297	+1	298	223	2.8	337.2	11.9
Greenfriar	463	.....	463	361	1.9	529	12.5
Gresham House	6	.....	19	6	-	-	-
Group Dev	46	.....	50	40	0.7	57.2	19.6
Warrants	14	.....	19	13	-	-	-
HTR Japanese	98	.....	100	67¾	-	98.7	0.07
Smlr Warrants	41	.....	45	26	-	-	-

Source: Financial Times (1 February 1996)

Reading from left to right, the columns indicate:

Govett Oriental	Name of investment trust
426 of the shares yesterday	Average of the sell and buy prices, i.e. the 'mid price'
+3	Change + or - on the previous day's price
426/322	Highest and lowest prices for the current year
0.4	Gross yield
428.3	Net asset value per share
0.5	Whether the share is trading at a discount or a premium to the net asset value per share

9 Taxation

The investment trust

9.1 Investment trusts enjoy similar tax treatment to unit trusts, in that neither will pay capital gains tax on their own portfolio dealings. In order to be exempt from CGT, an investment trust has to meet the criteria imposed by, and be approved by, the Inland Revenue. Dividends from other sources received as unfranked income, such as foreign shares, will have to be declared and corporation tax will be payable. The trust can reduce its tax liability by setting off expenses against the unfranked income, i.e. interest paid on fees and borrowing against dividend income such as foreign share dividends.

The investor

9.2 For the investor the position on any income is the same as for dividends on other shares. Dividends are paid net of tax and accompanied by a 20% tax credit. Lower rate and basic rate taxpayers have no further tax to pay, but higher rate taxpayers will be liable for the additional 20% marginal rate tax. Non taxpayers may reclaim the tax that has been deducted. When the investor sells shares in the trust, any gains are chargeable to CGT in the same way as gains on other shares in UK companies. Similarly, it should be remembered that gains can be indexed and each investor has an annual CGT exemption. Zeros are taxed as capital rather than income and will be attractive to investors not subject to CGT.

10 Risk and Accessibility

10.1 As with all forms of pooled investment the wider spread avoids some of the fluctuations in price compared with investing in the shares of a single company.

10.2 However, there are two levels of risk when buying investment trust shares. Firstly, the value of the underlying shares may rise or fall and secondly the discount may narrow or widen, so enhancing both the risk and possible gain.

10.3 Changes in the market will have more of an impact than on packaged investments, but the risk will be lower than for direct equity investment.

10.4 Investors who need to cash in their holdings can do so easily by selling their shares in the company, the only penalty being dealing costs.

11 Uses of an Investment Trust

11.1 An investment trust is a risky investment, based as it is on the stock markets and the ability of the managers. However, investment trusts offer a wide variety of equity investments, for income, growth or a combination of the two. The investor is able to take advantage of a broader spread of investment than he would otherwise be able to achieve by direct investment in shares and also utilise the management expertise of the trust managers. The type of investor most suited to investment trusts will be one prepared to take a medium to high risk, and is likely to have some knowledge and experience of the investment market.

11.2 An investment trust can be used to build capital for any purpose, such as retirement planning or educational funding. Alternatively, as seen earlier, a split-capital trust or income trust may be used to provide income from regular or lump sum investment.

11.3 An investment trust may also form a Pep investment, so expanding the types of investment available to the Pep investor.

Student Activity 3

You should complete this student activity before attempting the self-assessment. Answer the questions, then check your answers against the paragraph(s) indicated.

> Greg Fairchild asks you to explain the main methods by which he can buy investment trust shares and the types of charges he would incur. What information would you give him? (6.1-6.4, 7.1, 7.2)

If you are unable to answer any of the questions satisfactorily, you should read the relevant paragraphs again. Your understanding of the text will be further tested in the following self-assessment.

Summary

Now that you have completed this unit, you should be able to:

☐ **Know the regulatory controls which apply to investment trusts**

☐ **Understand how an investment trust works including pricing and gearing**

☐ **Know the main types of investment trust**

☐ **Know the charges which apply to investment trusts**

☐ **Understand published prices of investment trusts in financial papers**

☐ **Explain the taxation of an investment trust and the investor**

☐ **Understand the risks attached to investment trusts and their accessibility**

☐ **Know the main uses of investment trusts**

If you can tick all the above boxes with confidence, you are ready to answer the questions which follow.

Self-Assessment Questions

1. Briefly describe the two main differences between an investment trust and a unit trust.

2. What regulatory requirements apply to an investment trust company's income, holdings and profits arising from the sale of investments?

3. Briefly explain who runs an investment trust company.

4. Describe the methods which an investment trust company could use to raise money for investment both on a long-term and short-term basis.

5. What is the tax position for the investor on the receipt of dividends from an investment trust?

6. What tax, if any, may the investor be liable for when he sells shares in the investment trust?

7. What is the tax position for the investment trust on the receipt of unfranked income?

8. What is the tax position for the investment trust on the sale of shares?

9. What are the two main risks involved with an investment trust?

10. Which type of investor is most likely to be suited to investment trusts?

Unit 19

Alternative Forms of Investment

Objectives

Students are required to study the following topics:

- **Property investment**

- **Chattels**

- **Enterprise investment schemes**

- **Venture capital trusts**

- **Commodities**

- **Lloyd's of London**

- **Foreign exchange market**

1   Introduction

1.1   This unit will look at some of the other types of investment which may form part of an investment portfolio.

1.2   For example, a customer's house can often be seen as an investment as well as a place to live and bring up a family. There are many other 'investments' in a house: antiques, paintings, coins, stamp collections, etc. All were purchased at one price and will realise another price on sale. Additional investments could include commercial properties, venture capital trusts and commodities.

1.3   It is part of the adviser's role to consider opportunities for alternative forms of investment that may be used in achieving the customer's ultimate aims.

2   Investing in Property

2.1   Property can play a particularly important part in a customer's investment portfolio, both as an investment in its own right and as security for various forms of lending. It is a secure form of investment that cannot become valueless, other than in the case of a disaster e.g. fire, earthquake or other natural disaster, all of which can be insured against. The price is affected by supply and demand but also by location and condition of the property or surrounding area and its facilities. The following paragraphs describe three different ways of investing in property.

Owner occupied property

2.2   For most customers, owning their own home will prove to be a profitable investment over the long term. House prices in general have risen faster than the general rate of inflation and they are normally more stable than equity prices. The major price increases in the 1980s were, however, an exception to this. This was followed by the price crash in the early 1990s leaving many homeowners with negative equity. Increases are usually roughly in line with increase in earnings or spending power.

2.3   Mortgages for home purchase enjoy tax relief at source and although the value of the tax relief has been eroded by inflation and the reduction in the rate of Miras they are one of the very few forms of personal borrowing where tax relief is available. In addition, on the sale of a property that is the owner's nominated principal private residence there is no liability to capital gains tax. The costs associated with purchasing a property i.e. stamp duty, estate agents' and solicitors' fees, indemnity and administration fees and the mortgage repayments will, over the long term, be less than an individual would have to pay in rent for the property.

Types of mortgage

2.4   The choice of mortgage type will depend on the individual's circumstances. The amount will be determined by the value of the property, the amount of money the borrower has available to put towards the purchase price and the restrictions imposed by the lender.

2.5   The two main types of mortgage are the capital repayment method and the interest-only method. With a repayment method the borrower makes both capital and interest payments to the lender each month over the term of the loan. At the end of the term the mortgage will be repaid.

2.6   The interest-only method involves the use of an investment vehicle to repay the loan at the end of the term with interest payments being made monthly to the lender. The types of investment used are constantly increasing and range from the traditional endowment policy, or more commonly the low cost endowment, to Peps, pension plans and unit trusts. The risks of using these non-guaranteed types of investment to repay a mortgage have already been discussed in earlier units. Borrowers are also advised to take out life assurance to ensure their mortgage is repaid in the event of their death. In some cases this will be a condition of the mortgage.

2.7   More adventurous borrowers may choose currency mortgages which involve transferring a loan into a foreign currency to take advantage of lower interest rates. There is also an Ecu mortgage. The risks involved in this type of mortgage include the problems of currency fluctuations and the fact that certain currencies such as the deutschmark and the yen, which are most commonly associated with currency mortgages, have tended to appreciate over the longer term against the pound. If sterling falls the interest payments and capital loan will rise and this could represent a considerable risk to the borrower.

2.8   While owning property which is mortgaged may, strictly speaking, not be regarded as true ownership until the mortgage has been repaid, the majority of home owners will have some degree of equity in their home which can be used to their advantage.

Equity release schemes

2.9   Borrowers who wish to borrow a substantial amount can take out a loan secured against the value of the equity in their home. The equity is the excess in value over the size of mortgage and, particularly for persons who bought their property before the house price boom of the eighties, can represent a very large sum. The loan will be arranged in a similar way to a mortgage and be repaid in the same way.

2.10 The main disadvantage is that unlike a mortgage there is no tax relief on this type of loan. However, it may be an economical way of raising money as the borrower can make relatively low payments spread over a long period compared with an ordinary type of personal loan which will typically be short-term. The interest rate is also likely to be lower than that charged on an unsecured loan.

Rental property

2.11 Property purchased for the purpose of letting involves a certain amount of management skill on the part of the investor. Certain advantages can be associated with this type of investment.

Advantages

2.12 The rent provides a secure income for the investor as it is usually paid in advance and is subject to a periodic review. Most leases contain 'upward only' rent review clauses. As with owner occupied properties the capital value of the property will tend to keep pace with inflation over the long term, despite short-term falls in property values. The property can be used as collateral if the owner wishes to borrow funds against it. The loan interest can be offset against rental income making it tax efficient. It is a tangible investment which, for some, is important.

2.13 Trends in housing indicate that more people are renting houses on a short-term basis while they look for a home to buy. This trend is likely to continue as jobs become less secure and individuals need to move more often to remain in employment. Therefore, this form of income can be regarded as fairly secure at present.

Disadvantages

2.14 Although a property will normally be saleable, time and money is needed to complete the selling process and so the capital in the property cannot be realised quickly and bears costs. The landlord will usually be responsible for the costs of repair and maintenance to the property, which in most circumstances must be carried out immediately. Such maintenance could prove expensive.

2.15 When the property cannot be rented out, there is a risk of loss of rent through lack of a tenant, for example when an existing tenant vacates the property at the end of the lease and no new tenant can be found. There is also the risk that a tenant can turn out to be unsatisfactory. Although a landlord is protected by property law the laws are complex and may involve the use of a solicitor incurring further costs.

2.16 Because of the size of most property investments it may mean lack of diversification for the investor who has to tie up most of his capital in the property and has little to invest elsewhere. Also when property is sold, only one CGT allowance may be utilised.

Indirect investment

2.17 There are a number of ways of investing in property indirectly. The two traditional methods have been to buy shares in a property company or to take out a property bond through an insurance company. Although investment in a property company is seen as a stable investment there was poor performance of these shares in the early 1990s, particularly due to declining property prices and high interest rates. Bond values are more stable than property share prices partly due to the fact liquid assets are also held. This evens out the fluctuations of property investment and the need to pay the bond redemptions.

2.18 Since 1990 authorised property unit trusts have become available to the public and for the small investor they are an attractive alternative to property bonds. The trust is allowed to hold up to 80% of its portfolio in land and buildings and up to 35% in gilts and liquid assets.

Property shares

2.19 By investing in the shares of a property company the investor can benefit from diversification which is not possible through direct property investment (other than for very wealthy investors). The investments are managed for the investor by people who are likely to have considerably more knowledge of the market than him. Of course, this means that charges will be levied for this service but this may well be outweighed by the returns.

2.20 Property shares are usually highly geared as the company borrows to purchase more property. This means the shares are likely to rise in relation to the underlying assets. However, because high rates of interest have to be paid on the borrowings the share will have low earnings and dividends. This means they are more suitable for investors willing to sacrifice income for greater capital growth in the future.

2.21 The high degree of gearing contributes to the volatile nature of the property share market as compared to other types of shares because the underlying assets are more variable in value. Also, as with investment trusts, share prices will rise and fall independently of the net asset value depending in the level of demand.

Property bonds

2.22 Insurance companies will use money invested in property bonds to invest in industrial, commercial and agricultural property. The performance of these funds will therefore reflect the ups and downs in the property markets concerned and it is long-term performance that will give a better indication of the likely returns from this type of investment.

2.23 The two main problems for investors in property bonds are liquidity and valuation. The fund managers must keep a certain amount of their funds liquid or easily realisable to meet the demands of investors requiring withdrawals. If demand was unusually high at any particular time this could cause problems for the fund and so it is important that investors choose bonds which are issued by the large insurance companies who can provide the financial backing for the funds if necessary. In addition, the funds will require considerable sums to invest in property due to the cost of purchase, and new funds are unlikely to attract any sort of return until the amounts invested are high. This level of investment needs to continue for the fund managers to maintain a good spread of investments within the fund.

2.24 As far as valuation is concerned the only time the true value of the property is known is when it is sold. However, a valuation is required at the time investments are made into the fund and when withdrawals are made. The fund will normally have an independent valuation completed of all its properties each year. This valuation can then be updated each month by using an appropriate index such as the cost of new construction.

2.25 Other risks for the investor include the level of charges which may be levied and the fact that the investments of the fund cannot be fully supervised. Therefore, an unscrupulous insurance company may use its property fund to hold its unsuccessful property investments and so reduce the chances of investors to make a good return.

2.26 It is likely to be the investors with a more adventurous attitude to risk who will be attracted to this type of investment. Taxation will be the same as for other insurance bonds (see Unit 21) but the risks will be higher. Anyone requiring a short-term return will not be suited to property bonds as it is the long-term, large scale investments that are more likely to produce good returns.

Enterprise zones

2.27 Investors are also able to invest indirectly in property through enterprise zone trusts. An enterprise zone is one where the expenditure incurred or contracted for within ten years after creation of the zone on any buildings, other than houses, qualifies for an initial tax allowance of 100% on expenditure.

2.28 These zones are designated by the Secretary of State and are areas in which the government particularly wants to stimulate investment, but investors should realise that disposing of an investment in an enterprise zone may mean a loss of the allowance. This includes leasing the property within seven years.

2.29 Enterprise zone trusts offer individual investors a stake in a portfolio of commercial properties in enterprise zones, which should produce a regular income from rents. Investments are normally available at a minimum of £5,000 with no maximum limit. Tax relief is available at the investor's highest rate but only applies to the proportion used to buy or build property and not to land. This proportion is decided by the Inland Revenue. Some trusts may have a proportion of around 10% disallowed for tax relief, others may be higher.

2.30 Apart from the tax relief investors will be attracted by the facility to borrow up to 70% of their gross investment, and interest can be set against the income earned for tax purposes. The income distributed to investors will come from rent on the properties held by the trust, with a deduction for costs. Some trusts will offer a guaranteed income for a specified period after which it will depend on the success of the property to attract tenants or the prevailing rates of rent charged. However, the investor should be aware that interest on any loans cannot be offset against guaranteed income and so these payments are fully taxable.

2.31 These investments are high-risk as there have been cases where schemes have

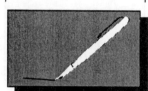

collapsed. This risk may be increased where a guaranteed return is offered as it is dependent on the financial strength of the provider. They should be regarded as long-term investments as tax relief is usually clawed back if investors withdraw their investment within 25 years. Administrative charges tend to be high and as many zones are now reaching the end of their ten-year life the shortage of new investment opportunities is causing prices to rise. However, for those prepared to take the risk current yields available are high compared with other forms of investment.

Student Activity 1

You should complete this student activity before reading the next section of the text. Answer the questions, then check your answers against the paragraph(s) indicated.

1.   What problems might be associated with a currency mortgage?   (2.7)

2.   Joe Smith wants to invest in property but is not sure whether   (2.17-2.26)
      property shares or property bonds would be safer. How would
      you compare the risk of the two investments?

3.   Why may an investor be attracted to investing in property to   (2.12, 2.13)
      let?

If you are unable to answer any of the questions satisfactorily, you should read the relevant paragraphs again. Your understanding of the text will be further tested in the self-assessment section at the end of this unit.

3   Investing in Chattels

3.1   An investor's personal possessions can provide diversification to a portfolio of investments. They provide no income but their value tends to rise at least in line with inflation and they may attract interest at times when other investment areas are depressed. Investments in this area which may appeal to the investor include jewellery, antique furniture, paintings, rare books and manuscripts, coins and stamps, vintage wines and cars. These types of investments will incur charges not normally associated with previously considered investments such as insurance premiums and specialist storage and security costs. In addition dealing charges tend to be higher than for other investments.

3.2   Investment in chattels for the small investor should perhaps be restricted to items which appeal to the owner for either their visual quality or their 'pastime' value.

3.3   For the large institutions, for example the pension funds, such alternative investments have proved popular. In the 1970s the British Rail pension fund held a wide ranging portfolio of assets including some valuable works of art and high quality antiques at a time when prices were relatively low. Some of these were later sold in the 1980s and 1990s at peak prices.

3.4   The risk can be high due to the following circumstances:

- Change in tastes by experts and investors

- Maintenance, rotation and storage costs

- Insurance premiums

- Subsequent discovery of the article not being genuine

- Flooding the market with similar items of quality

- Cost of purchase/sale

3.5   The main advantages are that gains may be made whilst other investments fall or through the sudden increase in value of assets due to increasing popularity and demand by experts or investors.

4   Commodities

4.1   Commodities can be bought and sold easily, in large quantities, on the specialist markets, usually based in London. Commodities are raw materials which fall into two broad areas, 'hard' and 'soft'. Hard commodities are most metals e.g. copper, lead, gold, silver etc. together with diamonds; soft commodities are mostly foodstuffs such as barley, wheat, coffee, cocoa. Commodities are either traded as "physicals" for immediate delivery and at on the spot prices, or for delivery in the future. Futures have been considered in more detail in Unit 15.

4.2   Dealing directly in commodities is not practical for most investors and trading is normally generated by the suppliers and major users of the items. Indirect investment in commodities, for example through unit trusts, may also be possible.

5   Enterprise Investment Schemes (EIS)

5.1   Enterprise investment schemes (EIS) were introduced in January 1994 to replace business expansion schemes with the aim of encouraging investment in small, unquoted companies. Tax relief is given to qualifying individuals who subscribe for qualifying shares in qualifying companies.

5.2   The definitions of these terms can be complex but is briefly summarised as follows:

(a)   A qualifying individual is not connected with the company (i.e. excludes directors and employees). Non UK residents are eligible but can only claim tax relief against UK tax liability.

(b)   Qualifying shares are new ordinary shares which cannot be redeemed for at least five years.

(c)   A qualifying company is an unquoted trading company carrying on business wholly or mainly in the UK. This can include companies whose shares are quoted on the AIM. Non-qualifying companies include those providing finance, legal and accountancy services.

Tax relief

5.3   Tax relief can be claimed on investments up to £100,000 per individual, so married couples can each claim relief on this amount. Relief is given at a rate of 20% in the tax year when the shares are bought. One-half of the amount subscribed before 6 October in any tax year can be carried back for relief in the previous year up to a maximum of £15,000. Under self-assessment the tax relief will relate to the previous year but will be given in the year the shares are subscribed for.

5.4   The minimum amount that can be subscribed is £500 except if the investment is made through an approved investment fund. If the shares are disposed of before five years the tax relief will be withdrawn. If the shares are held for the minimum five years and are then sold at a profit there will be no CGT charge. If a loss is made this can be offset against other chargeable gains.

EIS reinvestment relief

5.5   If a chargeable gain made on the sale of any asset is reinvested in EIS shares the gain may be deferred if the purchase is within one year before and three years after the disposal. The deferred gain will become chargeable on disposal of the shares other than to a spouse. It may then be deferred again by a further EIS investment.

Risk

5.6   These investments tend to be higher risk as they are funding new ventures with little or no track record, which may or may not be successful.

Business expansion schemes

5.7   These were phased out at the end of 1993 to be replaced by the EIS. They differ in that the types of investments available under the BES included private rented housing and tax relief was available up to 40%. However, the relief was only available on investments up to £40,000. BES were withdrawn because they were tending to drift away from their original aim of raising finance for new high-risk ventures. EIS projects have more restrictions to rectify some of these problems.

6   Venture Capital Trusts (VCTs)

6.1   Venture capital trusts were introduced from 6 April 1995 primarily to encourage investment in unquoted trading companies with growth potential but needing funds. The difference between a VCT and an EIS is that investment is not directly in the shares themselves but in a trust.

6.2   The investor buys shares in the trust, similar to an investment trust. The VCT must be quoted on the stock exchange and, as with investment trusts, is exempt from corporation tax and CGT. The investor must be 18 years or older to be eligible.

Taxation aspects

6.3   Income tax relief is given at 20% on investments in new ordinary shares not exceeding £100,000 in any one tax year, provided the shares are held for a minimum of five years. This being the case any gains are free from both income and capital gains taxes.

6.4   Dividends from ordinary shares in VCTs are also exempt from tax up to £100,000 total in shares acquired in one year.

Capital gains tax

6.5   In addition to the exemption from CGT by reinvesting any gains on disposal of VCTs back into a qualifying unlisted trading company, the investor can defer any liability to CGT on gains made from disposal of other assets. This is termed reinvestment relief, and is available within the period one year prior to and one year following the date of disposal. For higher rate taxpayers this could mean a deferment of 40%.

Example 19.1: Investment in VCTs

Mark Walker buys existing shares in a VCT on 1 May 1996 from an existing shareholder. He pays a purchase price of £50,000.

In September 1996 he subscribes for £80,000 worth of new shares in a VCT.

His total investment in the year is £130,000.

He will not get tax relief on the purchase of existing shares.

Tax relief of 20% will be given on the new shares i.e. £16,000.

The dividends on the purchased shares will be exempt from tax. The dividends on £50,000 of the new shares will also be exempt, as this brings the total up to £100,000. CGT exemptions will also apply to these amounts.

If Mark makes a chargeable gain for CGT on any disposals between 1 September 1996 and 1 September 1998 he can defer them against the £80,000 'reinvested' in new VCT shares.

Restrictions on VCTs

(a)   A minimum of 70% of the investment must be held in qualifying unlisted trading companies with a maximum of 15% being allowed in any one single company or group of companies.

(b)   Investment by the VCT in qualifying companies may be in equities, loans, or fixed-interest stocks but at least 30% of these investments must be in new ordinary shares. This limit was initially 50% imposed by the Chancellor but subsequently amended to allow greater investment flexibility in March 1995.

(c)   The VCT is prohibited from investing more than £1 million in any one company or group of companies whose gross assets exceed £10 million immediately preceding the investment or £11 million immediately after.

(d)   The VCT has up to three years to meet the 70% qualifying unlisted trading and 30% ordinary share requirements, and if investments are held by a VCT in an unquoted trading company when such a company becomes quoted, then the investment may be treated as in an unquoted company for a further five years.

6.6   VCTs are likely to appeal to investors requiring a higher degree of risk, with an objective of tax-free growth/income potential. There can be some diversification of risk as the trust can be spread over a number of companies. Higher rate taxpayers will be attracted by the potential initial 60% tax relief (20% income tax and 40% CGT deferral).

7 Lloyd's of London

7.1 Investors in the Lloyd's insurance market are known as 'Names'. To be eligible, a Name must:

(a) Have assets exceeding £250,000 excluding main residence of which at least 60% is in cash, quoted securities or guaranteed savings such as banks or building societies. No more than 40% may be in assets such as freehold property or leasehold property with no less than 50 years unexpired.

(b) Be supported by two existing members.

(c) Satisfy the committee of suitability.

(d) Exceed the solvency test on 31 December each year.

7.2 Investors benefit from the premium income from insurance underwriting and investment income from the syndicates' deposit reserve and other funds. But the risk level is high especially as there is unlimited liability which could and has led to bankruptcy. Underwriting profits and losses are not finally assessed for three years after the year in question, thereby producing dividends or losses in the fourth year.

7.3 It is now possible for limited companies to invest, thereby allowing investment trusts to qualify. They may underwrite Lloyd's syndicates to a limit of twice the capital involved. This therefore allows private investors to gain access to the investment trust with an investment as low as £1,000. These trusts may also qualify as a Pep. Another distinct advantage is the limited liability which will not exceed the amount invested.

7.4 Costs and charges are considerable and include fees and commission to:

- Lloyd's

- Lloyd's members' agents

- Trust manager

7.5 Assessment for taxation has been on a current year basis. From 1997-98 underwriting profits are assessed by reference to the underwriting year where profits are declared in the year of assessment (i.e. underwriting year 1994, profits declared 1997 is assessed in 1997-98).

8 The Foreign Exchange Market

8.1 Foreign exchange (Forex) dealing happens in all the world markets but is focused on the three main centres of London, New York and Tokyo. The main types of investors in the Forex market are large institutional investors, and companies who require foreign currency to invest abroad. The Forex market operates in a similar way to the gilts market with competing market makers offering to buy and sell from their dealing rooms. There is no physical building where the Forex is based. The dealers mainly consist of the major international banks and have teams of dealers around the world. The market makers also deal with each other and through Forex brokers. The brokers have access on VDUs to the latest currency prices which change constantly and investors also have access to this information so they can know the market price of most currencies at any time.

8.2 Currencies are priced against the dollar and the difference between the price at which currency is bought and sold is very small due to the large volume of currency being traded. The dealers make their profits by dealing in very large sums of money. More profit can be made from dealing in less popular currencies than in exchanging pounds sterling for US dollars.

8.3 Because the market makers make their profit from the bid-offer spread, they may also try to make money by holding on to a currency if they think the price is likely to rise. This could be in a matter of hours. In this way, a profit of several hundred thousand dollars can be made by buying £100m worth of a particular currency and selling it a few hours later.

The spot market

8.4 Where transactions are for immediate delivery of foreign currency they take place on the spot market. Transactions must be settled within two days. The spot prices quoted in the Financial Times are the best buy/sell rates quoted towards the end of trading in London on the previous day.

Using derivatives

8.5 Companies can use currency derivatives to hedge against Forex movements. This can be in any of the following ways:

(a) Using a forward - a customised agreement between a market maker and a company to buy or sell a specific amount of currency on a fixed date in the future at a fixed price. If the forward price of the currency is higher than the spot price (i.e. the current price on the market) the currency is said to be trading at a premium. If the spot price is higher than the forward price, it is said to be trading at a discount. Forward prices are quoted in the Financial Times.

(b) Using futures - these mirror the spot price but mean that the company will not have to pay out in full for several months. Unlike forwards they are not custom-made arrangements, but they are more liquid because they will be attractive to more investors.

(c) Using options - options can be customised by a market maker, or a traded option on a future.

8.6 Of course, there is a risk that the hedging will not achieve its aim but the investor must be prepared to take this risk.

Private investors

8.7 In addition to large institutional investors and companies, individuals who are travelling abroad may also invest directly in the Forex market by purchasing an amount of the chosen currency. However, usually an individual will arrange this through his bank. The investor may open a current or deposit account designated in a foreign currency, either at a UK bank or in a foreign country, or in a UK branch of an overseas bank. A foreign currency bank account may be useful if substantial travelling is undertaken, although it is likely to be subject to higher administrative charges and is exposed to exchange rate fluctuations.

Suitability and risk

8.8 Dealing in the currency markets is a very complex area and presents a high degree of risk for investors without expert knowledge. Exchange rates fluctuate for a variety of reasons, primarily economic or political, either in the UK or foreign country. The main principle for investors is that UK buyers will benefit from a strong pound whereas sellers will benefit from a weak pound. The effect of fluctuations in exchange rates is shown in the following example.

Example 19.2: Fluctuations in exchange rates

Suppose 150 American shares were purchased at $30 when the £ stood at $2.00. The cost would be:

$$\frac{150 \times \$30}{\$2.00} = £2,250$$

Again suppose that the share price does not move but the £ falls to $1.50, the sterling value would become:

$$\frac{150 \times \$30}{\$1.50} = £3,000$$

There has been a sterling gain of £750 without a movement in the local share price. Conversely if the shares had been purchased at the $1.50 rate and sold at the $2 rate, the loss would be £750.

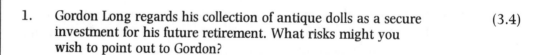

Student Activity 2

You should complete this student activity before attempting the self-assessment. Answer the questions, then check your answers against the paragraph(s) indicated.

1. Gordon Long regards his collection of antique dolls as a secure investment for his future retirement. What risks might you wish to point out to Gordon? (3.4)

2. (a) Who is eligible to invest in an enterprise investment scheme? (5.2)

   (b) A married couple both wish to invest in an EIS. What is the joint maximum amount they can invest? (5.3)

   (c) What tax relief is available? (5.3)

3. How is a higher rate taxpayer able to defer his CGT liability if he has an investment in a venture capital trust? (6.5)

4. A customer asks you about the risk involved in being a Name at Lloyd's of London. What would you say? (7.2)

If you are unable to answer any of the questions satisfactorily, you should read the relevant paragraphs again. Your understanding of the text will be further tested in the following self-assessment.

Summary

Now that you have completed this unit, you should be able to:

☐ **Describe the different ways of investing in property**

☐ **Explain the risks involved in property investment**

☐ **Know why investment in chattels carries high risk/reward potential**

☐ **Understand the advantages and disadvantages of enterprise investment schemes**

☐ **Understand the advantages and disadvantages of venture capital trusts**

☐ **Know the risk of being a Name at Lloyd's of London**

☐ **Know the risks of the foreign exchange market**

If you can tick all the above boxes with confidence, you are ready to answer the questions which follow.

Self-Assessment Questions

1. What factors affect the price of property?

2. What risk does a borrower who has a Pep mortgage carry?

3. Why do insurance companies need to maintain a realistic valuation of the property investments held in their property funds?

4. What tax relief is available on investment in an enterprise zone trust?

5. What is the difference between commodities traded as physicals and those traded as futures?

6. Tom Watson has a large number of investments and is a higher rate taxpayer. He has made capital gains of £10,000 this year and is looking at ways to mitigate this liability. What facility does an enterprise investment scheme offer?

7. Jonathan Taylor has bought £40,000 worth of new shares in a venture capital trust.

   (a) What tax relief will he get on this purchase?

   (b) What tax will he pay on the dividends?

(c) Why do VCTs enjoy favourable tax treatment?

8. What is the tax treatment of a VCT?

9. (a) If an investor wants to become a Name at Lloyd's of London, what assets must he have?

   (b) What return does this type of investment provide?

10. For what type of investor would you recommend currency investment and why?

Unit 20

Offshore Deposits and Investments

Objectives

Students are required to study the following topics:

* **Reasons for investing offshore**

* **Deposits**

* **Indirect equity investment**

* **Investment holdings**

* **Taxation**

* **Offshore markets**

* **Disadvantages of investing offshore**

* **Trusts and offshore investments**

1 Introduction

1.1 Offshore investment is generally believed to be more complex and tax efficient than investing in the UK, while also being subject to greater levels of risk. Like all generalisations, this has some basis in fact, but is not a complete and accurate assessment of the situation. It is true to say that while this can be the case when investing outside the UK, there are circumstances when the individual's tax position could be worse as a result of the investment and other circumstances where a portfolio could benefit from exposure to offshore risks.

1.2 The term 'offshore fund' will be used throughout this text and includes a range of investment types, like investment trusts or unit trusts and similar products. Generally based in a foreign tax haven, such as the Channel Islands, the Isle of Man or Luxembourg, the variety of funds available can be confusing, covering as they do, equity-based funds in the UK or international markets, fixed-interest securities in the world's financial market-place, and highly specialised or general investment bases. Before considering the different types of investment medium available to the offshore investor, some of the reasons for such investments should be considered.

Schemes recognised under the Financial Services Act 1986 (FSA)

1.3 Some offshore funds are recognised by the Securities and Investments Board (SIB) under different sections of the FSA, to include Ucits (see later in this unit) which gain automatic recognition, and certain funds from 'designated territories' .The latter are those funds where SIB believes an investor would be afforded at least an equivalent amount of protection as they would receive had they been investing in a UK unit trust.

1.4   Those that are recognised can be sold in the same way as unit trusts, except for cold-calling where cancellation rules do not apply.

Unrecognised schemes

1.5   Funds without SIB recognition cannot be sold direct to the public, but must be marketed to intermediaries and professional investment advisers. They would then normally be used for those clients with whom the intermediary has a well established, and discretionary management, relationship.

2   Why Invest Offshore?

Diversification

2.1   Investing in one geographic sector tends to restrict the opportunities for growth in an investor's portfolio, as the factors that dictate movement will affect that sector as a single entity, to a large extent. In order to increase the positive factors, and the potential returns that can be made, diversifying into other markets can offer the investor far more opportunity to benefit from a larger number of successful, or growing, markets. Each separate economy has its own influences, although they may be based upon the same types of conditions such as inflation, industrial output and interest rates. By combining investments across a portfolio the investor is allowed the benefits of experiencing different growth opportunities, while helping to reduce the risks associated with a narrow investment spread.

Risk

2.2   While most views of offshore investments must include a clear awareness of the nature of investment risk, by spreading the investor's portfolio across different areas they are allowed to reduce some of the risk by 'not having all their eggs in one basket' .Of course, some markets are by their very nature subject to more risk, and fluctuation, than others. Think of an economy like that of Argentina with its history of rampant inflation, compared to that of a more settled economy like Germany. It may be, though, that this risk, with its potential for higher returns, is just what the portfolio needs to include to give it a better balance and to allow the investor to achieve his objectives.

2.3   However, in addition to the economic risk associated with any investment, especially in fragile economies, should be added the political climate in the country, that may have a major impact on the economy. This can be particularly important when considering investment in those Third World economies with a particularly volatile political situation, for example.

2.4   The third feature that can be associated with foreign investment is that of exchange rates and currency fluctuations. While this can be an effective hedge against the risks of the investor's base currency depreciating, it also carries a risk of the investment having to be realised back into that currency just at the wrong time, with any currency gains thus being wiped out.

Dynamic growth

2.5   As mentioned above, the potential in some economies for rapid growth is one of the main attractions of offshore investment. The dynamic economies allow the portfolio to capitalise on, sometimes, spectacular growth, typically amongst those in the Far East and around the Pacific Rim. These are often known as 'Tiger' or 'Dragon' markets. Of course, they often tend to be subject to the widest fluctuations as well, sometimes crashing as spectacularly as they rose.

Specialised markets

2.6　In some cases it may be appropriate for the investor to contemplate investment into highly specialised markets or sectors. This may necessitate having to look offshore for the medium into which to place his money. For example, gold and mining shares are not as easily available to the UK investor as a sterling investment. While the shares may well be quoted in London, often they can only be purchased in another currency, and at a premium. If they were bought on their own listed exchange the price may be cheaper, even allowing for different sets of brokerage fees and currency exchange costs.

2.7　The benefits of investing into specialised markets include a further opportunity to spread the investment portfolio and a chance to invest in a sector in which the investor has some interest, such as a trading relationship with companies in that sector.

Taxation

2.8　Perhaps often seen as the major benefit is the potential to arrange investments in a more tax-efficient way by looking at the offshore market-place, and taxation is covered in detail later.

3　Deposits

3.1　Perhaps the most straightforward of offshore routes available to the individual investor is that of deposit-based investment. Typically offered by tax havens such as the Channel Islands or the Isle of Man, these investments are basically built around bank or building society accounts.

3.2　The investments may have varying levels of flexibility attached to them, in much the same way as UK accounts, ranging from instant access accounts through to timed deposit and deposit bond investments. These offer correspondingly increasing rates of interest dependent on the term, in the same way as UK accounts. The interest rates offered tend to be higher than the UK equivalent investment.

Taxation principles

3.3　One of the main advantages available to the UK investor is the gross payment of interest on offshore deposits. For a higher rate taxpayer, for example, this represents a considerable potential saving. The drawback is, however, that as soon as the interest is remitted (brought into) the UK it may be subject to income tax. This can be offset by allowing the interest to roll-up in a gross environment, to gain the best effect of compounding, until such time as the monies are required. Of course, this only defers the eventual liability on the interest, unless a way can be found to mitigate the tax in the future.

3.4　A further factor that will affect the tax-efficiency, or otherwise, of the investment will be the individual's residence status. It is the determination of the individual's country of residence, ordinarily resident or domiciled status that will decide what tax, if any, is due on the interest received from offshore deposits. This will also affect their UK liability to tax on the proceeds from any investments.

Risk

3.5 Risk is a further consideration in any form of investment planning, which needs to be taken into account when placing monies offshore. The deposit-based investment should, of course, help to minimise the effects of risk greatly, but some level of risk can never be entirely ruled out.

3.6 Unlike the UK market with its potential compensation payments covering some of a deposit balance in the event of the insolvency of the provider, there may be no such arrangements covering the proposed offshore investment.

3.7 A further aspect that relates to risks associated with offshore deposits is that of the rate of return offered by the institution with which the deposit is held. Any interest offered will depend on economic conditions as well as political considerations. These may cause rates to become less attractive to the UK investor, indeed if conditions were to change radically the imposition of some form of controls on foreign investment, or more importantly the realising of those investments, would also be a very real option to the authorities. This may be particularly relevant if the government wanted to stop a run on the currency, as nearly happened in Hong Kong after Chinese comments during the run up to the colony being handed back to China. This would certainly make the deposit medium less viable, if it did not go as far as to close it off completely.

4 Indirect Equity Investment

4.1 Investment into equity-based investments offshore can be effected in the same ways as in the UK, by either direct or indirect investment. The hazards of direct investment have already been alluded to, but will be covered in more detail later. The more commonly used routes are by indirect investment and this is described in the following paragraphs.

Ucits

4.2 Undertakings for Collective Investments in Transferable Securities (Ucits) were developed in an attempt to help foster collective investments across the European Union (EU). In effect, the 1989 EU Directive that established the rules governing Ucits allows investment funds that are established in one EU member state to be sold in others, and vice versa. They work in very similar ways to UK unit trusts, with restrictions on the investments they may hold. In fact, most unit trusts satisfy these requirements, although typically these are not common in Europe, apart from in the UK and Ireland.

4.3 The requirements that govern Ucits include the assets they may hold. They may not invest in property directly but in property company shares, for example. Nor can they invest in a fund of funds. Furthermore, like unit trusts they cannot invest in commodities.

4.4 One of the fundamental features of Ucits is that they must, again like unit trusts, be open-ended. This is the major reason why investment trusts cannot be Ucits, due to their closed nature.

Oeics

4.5 These are open-ended investment companies, and many offshore investments offered in the UK are likely to be of this type. They have a wide spectrum in which to invest, including commodities or futures, but this may mean they do not qualify as Ucits if they are too highly focused. This would be similar to a UK based unit trust being unable to buy the shares of certain investment trusts.

4.6 Their most attractive feature is the fact that the investments held within the Oeics can be switched internally between holdings, thus helping to reduce some of the costs this normally entails, and some of the possible risk of exchange rate fluctuations. The holdings are split into funds, each being denominated as a separate class of shares in the company, with each fund potentially covering a number of investment areas. Thus, if the investor wishes to move his holding he is, effectively, carrying out a share exchange.

SICAV and VCC

4.7 Societes d'Investissement a Capitale Variable (SICAV) and variable capital companies (VCC) are, essentially, a hybrid of unit and investment trust features. They have no fixed capital limits and can issue, or redeem, shares at any time. They are investment funds run as companies with the objective of returning a profit to their shareholders in much the same way as equity shareholders can expect dividends. Although they can hold a wide range of shares, they are closed funds, and tend, therefore, to carry more risk than unit trusts.

Offshore Bonds

4.8 These bonds are, basically, a version of the life assurance bond issued in the UK, through the companies' offshore subsidiaries. They are structured in the same way, although the main difference between them is the taxation that is applied to the offshore variants. Often investing in a range of the other offshore funds, bonds can be an effective way of obtaining a gross roll-up of interest, especially if the investment can be left for the longer-term. However, the fact that charges are often higher for offshore bonds than their onshore competitors can have a mitigating effect on this increase.

4.9 The effect of taxation will be felt on encashment when the full weight of any tax liability is levied. With the onshore bond having been taxed at the basic rate, within the fund, the higher rate taxpayer will only have a liability for the difference on the encashment value. The offshore investor will be liable to the higher rate of tax on the full gain:

Example 20.1: Taxation of bonds

	Onshore bond	Offshore bonds
Gross gain	£50,000	£50,000
Tax deducted at source 20%	£10,000	-
Net amount payable	£40,000	

Higher rate liability at 16%   £ 6,400 at 40% £20,000

Net gain   £33,600   £30,000

Because the basic rate tax liability on the onshore bond has been met by the insurance company, the higher rate taxpayer is only liable to an additional 16% tax on the bond proceeds.

4.10 A further point worth noting regarding offshore bonds is the taxation of fund switches. In an onshore bond the investor can switch between the different funds available with the only charge likely to be an administration charge of some nature. For the offshore investor a switch triggers a chargeable event which can cause the realisation of a gain, and a consequent tax liability may arise.

4.11 One way in which the investor may mitigate some of the potential tax liability is to use the tax deferred withdrawal facility of 5% of the initial capital investment. While this is available for offshore bondholders, it is only applied to bonds. Other forms of offshore investment, investment into the funds directly for example, cannot benefit.

Student Activity 1

You should complete this student activity before reading the next section of the text. Answer the questions, then check your answers against the paragraph(s) indicated.

1. List any advantages to an investor in considering investing offshore, opposed to any benefits of onshore investment.   (2.1-2.8)

2. What risks might an investor with an offshore deposit account have to consider?   (3.5-3.7)

If you are unable to answer any of the questions satisfactorily, you should read the relevant paragraphs again. Your understanding of the text will be further tested in the self-assessment section at the end of this unit.

5 Investment Holdings

Currencies

5.1 Currency investment takes a number of different forms, ranging from the deposit of currencies with institutions, like banks and UK building societies, for an interest return through to the foreign exchange (Forex) market. This latter form is, obviously, the most speculative and the shortest-term, with the investment generally being made to capitalise on swings in exchange rates in a highly volatile marketplace. (See Unit 19.)

5.2 The alternative available to the individual investor is the currency based fund. This may be divided into smaller funds, encompassing a range of different currencies, in an umbrella arrangement. Some of these funds will be managed funds, in an attempt to mirror the fluctuations in the Forex market. The other funds will allow the investor to switch between currencies, again to benefit from more advantageous exchange and interest rates.

5.3   Obviously by their very nature, currency investments in the short-term will be a high-risk strategy, with the risk tending to be smoothed into, perhaps, a more medium level as the investment term increases. However, the risk can never be fully eradicated, especially when one remembers that the UK investor will, in most cases, want to bring their investment monies back into the UK at some future date, at which time it will again be subject to the risk of an adverse exchange rate as it is converted back to sterling.

Equities

5.4   In order to give a portfolio a chance to benefit from 'real growth' and beat the effects of long-term inflation, it must include some form of equity investment. This is often available to the offshore investor through equity funds that are structured in the same way as the equity-based funds available to the onshore investor. Different funds cover the various investment sectors, either geographic sectors or market sectors. Also available will be funds specialising in particular companies, or specifically in 'emerging economies' .They all have the common feature of being comprised of equities in their particular chosen area, but also tend to aim to achieve growth rather than income. Of course, each market-place has its own set of risks attached, while many equity markets are now so closely related and linked by electronic trading and arbitrage. This can have major ramifications on the equities market-place as a whole, as so visibly happened in October 1987.

Fixed-interest securities

5.5   By contrast to the equity funds, fixed-interest funds often aim to achieve a high income return for the investor, due to their underlying assets being in government securities or other holdings that are not subject to income tax. For the same reasons as seen in Unit 13, offshore investors looking for income may be well suited to fixed-interest funds.

5.6   The funds are often based on a spread of different investments, although some may specialise in one type of security, or market, e.g. US Treasury Bonds (T-Bonds). Each of the major fixed-interest markets have a sector of their own, thus the sterling gilts market will consistently be one of the largest available when compared with the T-Bond or the Japanese Government yen bond.

Student Activity 2

You should complete this student activity before reading the next section of the text. Answer the questions, then check your answers against the paragraph(s) indicated.

Philip White wishes to invest offshore. Outline to him the main risks involved in:

(a) Currency investment.   (5.3)

(b) Equity investment   (5.4)

If you are unable to answer any of the questions satisfactorily, you should read the relevant paragraphs again. Your understanding of the text will be further tested in the self-assessment section at the end of this unit.

6 Taxation

6.1 For taxation purposes for UK investors, offshore funds are usually divided into two types, each of which can include versions of those already seen. It is important for the investor, and for his advisers, to ensure they are aware of the investment particulars before entering into a commitment, as the same type of basic investment could be either a distributor or a non-distributor fund.

Distributor funds

6.2 Distributor funds are those where at least 85% of the fund's net income is distributed to the investors, although they can also include those funds that make, and retain, less than 1% of the value of their assets in income. The rate is reduced to 42.5% for commodity funds. Their status is reviewed annually, with the fund supplying the Inland Revenue with acceptable information before the distributor status can be granted.

6.3 The major advantage of a distributor fund is that, although an offshore fund, normal CGT rules will be applied, with annual exemptions and indexation permitted. Any income received will be paid gross but subject to the investor's normal treatment for income tax.

Non-distributor funds

6.4 For non-distributor funds the investor's residence and domicile status are particularly important, with their main feature being a gross roll-up of interest.

6.5 The UK resident and domiciled investor will be liable for income and capital gains tax on the full proceeds of the fund, with no annual exemptions or indexation applied to the gains. A UK resident but non-domiciled investor will be subject to income tax under Schedule D Case VI on income receivable from non-distributor funds, despite the fact that income and gains are normally only taxed when brought into the UK. For the non-UK resident investor, the situation may be more favourable, with income and gains not being liable for UK taxes, although they may still be subject to their own country's tax regime.

Offshore bonds

6.6 When a higher rate taxpayer takes out a UK based bond investing in various different funds he may only be subject to tax at the difference between the basic and higher rates of tax, for example where gains within the fund are exempt from tax. In the offshore fund this would not be the case, the full higher rate of tax would be payable.

6.7 Alternatively, where the onshore investor may be able to benefit from the fact that the fund has been taxed at source and apply an indexation factor, the offshore fund investor cannot take the same route. There will also be a liability for the full higher rate of tax.

6.8 Offshore funds are, however, free of UK CGT on the sale of their assets, unlike onshore funds, and thus the investor can benefit from a more active management of the investment. This does not mean, though, that there will never be a liability to CGT, it is deferred to the end of the investment and due on final encashment.

6.9   While no UK income tax is due on any income distributed from the investment there may be a withholding tax deduction made if the investment is equity-based, with a consequent reduction in the overall returns provided. There will also be a liability on the income received by the UK investor which will be subject to his highest rate of tax. If the dividend has already been subject to withholding tax he may be liable to some double taxation. Where the fund is based on fixed-interest securities, the income received will normally provide a gross income to investors.

6.10   There may also be a tax levy made on funds by the country in which they are based, which would be charged irrespective of the nature of the fund, for instance, funds in Jersey have to pay a flat charge for corporation tax purposes.

Double taxation

6.11   Under agreements between the UK and other countries, arrangements exist which allow the investor to avoid having to pay tax in two separate countries on the income and gains from offshore investments, with the tax payable being due in either one country or the other. In some cases tax is due in both countries, and the tax in the foreign country can be offset against the UK tax. This foreign tax is usually known as 'withholding tax' .Where the foreign liability exceeds that in the UK, it is not possible to reclaim the excess against the UK liability. Where no such agreements exist, unilateral relief of the lower of the UK tax and the foreign tax may be claimed against UK tax.

Income tax

6.12   In addition to pure investments, the area of offshore rules also includes life policies that have an investment content. Any offshore policy issued since 18 November 1983 is non-qualifying, and thus may create a liability when a chargeable event occurs (see Unit 21). However, due to the policy being based offshore, there is a concession made to the investor who may not have been resident for the full term of the investment. This could reduce the gain to nil, depending on the time spent resident, by dividing the number of resident days by the number of policy days completed.

6.13   The calculation of a tax liability when a gain has arisen is different to that for UK life policies, with the taxpayer's full rate of tax being accounted for in a more overt way. For onshore policies the basic rate of tax has been deducted at source before the policyholder receives the proceeds, which is not the case with offshore policies. As seen in the case of the bonds, this taxation of the whole gain can be detrimental to the eventual amount received by the investor as shown in example 20.1 earlier in this unit.

6.14   Additionally, UK life policies are subject to a top-slicing calculation on the gains. This is also different for offshore investments. Unlike the UK, where any chargeable event effectively rebases the date of the policy for the purposes of calculating a gain, the offshore policy will always retain its inception date as the period from which a gain must be calculated. This can be reduced by deducting the years for which the policyholder was non-resident from the number of years over which the gain was made.

Example 20.2: Top slicing gains on offshore bonds

Janet Pearce invested £50,000 in an offshore bond in 1990.

Each year she withdrew £3,000 (i.e. 6% of the original investment), £500 of which was chargeable at the time as it was over the 5% withdrawal limit.

After 6 years she encashed the bond for £90,000.

Her final tax liability is calculated as follows:

£90,000 plus £18,000 =	£108,000
Less original investment =	£ 50,000
Less previous chargeable withdrawals =	£ 3,000
Taxable gain	£ 55,000
Divided by number of policy years (six) =	£ 9,167 - to be added to income (top-slicing)

If Janet had been non-resident for two years the gain would be reduced proportionately i.e. by a third and top-sliced by four. Gain £36,666, top-sliced = £9,167. When tax liability is established the slice would then be multiplied by four to establish taxable gain = £36,668 rather than by six.

6.15 Thus, gains made on offshore policies are generally subject to the investor's full rate of income tax. If the provider of the product is based in an EU or EEA country, is taxed at a rate of at least 20% on income and gains for UK policyholders, and has not reinsured the investment portion of the contract, the charge may be reduced to the difference between higher and basic rate tax.

Inheritance tax

6.16 The taxation aspects relating to offshore investments have focused on income and capital gains tax, without making mention of inheritance tax (IHT). This should not be taken to mean that IHT does not apply in the context of offshore investments. Indeed, it is a very real consideration, being geared more to the investor's domicile rather than his residence.

6.17 The two basic principles to remember are that all the assets of an individual who is UK domiciled are subject to IHT, irrespective of whether the assets are located outside the UK, and that any UK based assets are subject to IHT no matter where their owner is domiciled, (see Unit 7), although one should also bear in mind the IHT liability rules for those who have been ordinarily UK resident for seventeen of the previous twenty years, and for the three years subsequent to any change of domicile.

6.18 It is in the attempted mitigation of IHT that the investor may be well advised to consider transferring offshore assets into trusts.

Tax planning

6.19 The majority of tax planning routes available involve the setting up of various trusts, although there are a number of exercises that can be conducted to help reduce the likely effects of taxation of the investment's returns. The first is to carefully consider the type of investment that is required, whether a distributor or non-distributor fund is more suitable, for example.

6.20 For the non-resident, expatriate investor, there are also other considerations. While abroad their tax situation may mean they need do little else once they have made their investment decisions. But should they return to the UK, their tax position is likely to change dramatically. In these cases they could consider encashing most of the value of a life policy, say, while still outside the UK to benefit from its tax treatment, then continue the reduced policy when back in the UK to build up its value once again. They could then benefit from not having been resident all through the policy term as seen earlier.

6.21 An alternative could be for the returning investor to transfer ownership of the asset to his spouse, who remains non-resident, and thus avoid the taxation implications of having the asset brought into the UK.

6.22 Less viable as a tax planning medium, although one that appeals to the wealthy investor, is to contemplate moving abroad. If an asset has been held for a considerable time and is likely to realise a large gain, for example, changing residence well in advance of its being subject to a disposal may well save a CGT liability. Of course, this may not avoid IHT if the asset is still held in the UK, but may prove a workable solution for some offshore investments.

Student Activity 3

You should complete this student activity before reading the next section of the text. Answer the questions, then check your answers against the paragraph(s) indicated.

1. George Francis took out a bond in 1990 for an initial investment of £200,000, and encashed it early in 1996 for £320,000. The bond ran for six complete years, and George took a withdrawal each year of £12,000.
   (a) Calculate the chargeable gain to George on final encashment, but not the tax payable.   (6.14)

   (b) How would this change if George had been a non-resident for four complete years between 1991 and 1995?

2. Anita Jackson has invested in offshore equity funds which are   (6.2, 6.3) distributor funds for tax purposes. How will her investment income be taxed?

3. Summarise the taxation advantages of offshore investment for   (6.1-6.22) the different types of investor, including those who are non-UK resident and non-domiciled.

If you are unable to answer any of the questions satisfactorily, you should read the relevant paragraphs again. Your understanding of the text will be further tested in the self-assessment section at the end of this unit.

7 Offshore Markets

North America

7.1 Second only to the Japanese equity market in size, the USA boasts a number of major stock exchanges listing a huge variety of shares and stocks for the investor. As the world's biggest single influence on economic conditions, direct exposure to the North American market allows the investor to further diversify their portfolio into a wide choice of different sectors. The market itself is well developed, with sophisticated controls in place, and easy access to company information from which the potential investor can choose. The US investment market tends to perform in a similar way to the UK, with the UK often following the American lead, but with careful timing it may be possible for the investor to capitalise on local differences to make a substantial profit, either based on the market's movement, or on a positive exchange rate.

Japan

7.2 Although larger than the US Market, the difference is not now so marked as it was in the early to mid-1980s. The strength of the Japanese economy has, however, begun to re-establish itself since the beginning of the 1990s, when the economy started to show signs of sustainable growth. The Japanese economy, with its huge industrial base, like the US market, drives a significant number of other economies around the world, with its exports and with the companies that locate facilities to exploit local market conditions.

7.3 One attraction of the Japanese market to the offshore investor is the sheer range of opportunities available with sectors from industrial, and chemical, manufacturing based equities through to high technology companies, at the leading edge of research and development. This allows the diversification mentioned earlier, both within one market-place, and in addition to other investments already in the investor's portfolio, as well as access to a market with a history of some strong growth.

Europe

7.4 The European equity market has tended to be dominated by the UK market, despite the number of different exchanges that exist. For this reason, and the fact that European companies and investors use their stock markets less than other markets for raising finance, the European market has not been a major player in the investment market-place, when compared to the US, Japan and the UK. With the growing importance of global markets and trading agreements, however, this has begun to change, with the European Union now becoming one of the world's leading economic areas with which to trade.

7.5 For the investor this means that more and more companies seek listings on the local exchanges to finance their operations in the area, and opportunities are presented to speculators. With the number of different markets, and the different economic attitudes of the countries that make up Europe, the movement of equities is always likely to be difficult to predict. For the investor looking to perhaps have a more actively managed portfolio, moving between investments regularly, the opportunities to make profits on exchange rate and currency fluctuations are, therefore, more plentiful.

Far East

7.6 This area consists of a variety of different markets, subject to different economic influences. The Australian market is well established as is that of New Zealand, while the markets of Taiwan and Indonesia, for example, are still establishing themselves as regular havens for foreign investment.

7.7 Indeed, it is in the smaller markets that the greatest investment opportunities tend to be found, as noted earlier. A large amount of the trade conducted by these economies is with either the US market, or Japan, and as result the performances of the equity markets are very closely linked with those of the two big economies. The relative strength of the US dollar and Japanese yen also have a major impact on the trading conditions that affect the Far Eastern stock markets, as indeed do all the other equity markets around the world. Even with the rapid increase in tourism and manufacturing in the area, rather than a reliance on the export of commodities to the US and Japan, these economies are still likely to be very closely linked to the major markets, and their performances will similarly affected.

Emerging markets

7.8 This is a term used to define the countries where sound economies are developing, rather than those that are well established, and typically include South America, most of Asia, Africa and parts of Eastern Europe. As conditions have improved in these countries, so has the potential for economic growth, with many of them consistently outperforming the mature, established economies of the developed world.

7.9 With the countries often needing to attract foreign investment to help facilitate growth, investment rules and regulations are designed to encourage the foreign investor into the economy. This can have the consequent effect of creating a stability to the economy which further attracts foreign investment. In the meantime, the growth potential for the early investor can be particularly impressive. Of course, this carries an inherent risk as well.

7.10 The negative aspect of this type of rapid growth can be seen in a number of South American economies, where the level of investment leads to increased values, which in turn leads to further investment, and so on. Eventually the bubble bursts, with often disastrous consequences for the investors affected.

Financial indices

7.11 Some formal measure must be in place for any investor to keep track of their investment performance, usually by way of various indices. The Financial Times publishes market performance indicators for foreign markets. These can take two forms, one of which is the FT-Actuaries World Index, which measures the performance of a sample of typical shares in each market and then applies a weighting against the share to the whole market. The second is to list the index used in each country, such as the Dow Jones index in the US. Again most of these are weighted against the market, to account for company capitalisations, although this is not the case for all the indices used.

7.12 In addition the International Finance Corporation, which is a part of the World Bank, produces a number of indices which provide an indication of performance. However, these are calculated on a different basis to the other indices, and the investor must take care to ensure they are aware of the basis for calculating any of these measuring tools before relying on them for their investment decisions.

7.13 It should also be noted that an index can only give an indication of performance across a sector, or market, rather than specific detail about a particular stock or equity. It is against this performance 'benchmark' that the individual investment is measured, historically, and only provides an indication of the likely future performance that can be obtained. This is very similar to the risk warning given that should be given to investors in the UK market.

8 Disadvantages of Investing Offshore

8.1 While it can be seen from the above that there may a number of advantages available to the offshore investor, there may also be disadvantages of which they need to be made aware. Although some of these have already been discussed, a summary is provided here.

8.2 Risk has been described as including a number of different influences, including exchange and interest rates, and political as well as economic factors. Tax also has been covered in some depth, with the complexity of the situation proving a disadvantage all of its own, as does the fact that double taxation is not a universally available facility for the investor to use.

8.3 With any attempt to invest offshore may come delay in trying either to gather enough accurate information on which to base a reasoned buying decision, or in receiving acknowledgement that the transaction has been completed. This is particularly of relevance where the investment is in equities, with different settlement periods affecting the time taken for the receipt of certificates to verify the holding, essential in the event of wishing to sell the shares quickly. In some countries, Japan for example, share certificates cannot be taken out of the country, so a UK based investor has to leave them, usually with a nominee of some kind.

8.4 Regulation and market controls vary widely, with some countries having advanced regulatory structures in place to protect investors. Others have controls that limit the amount of foreign investment that can be made, causing, sometimes, unrealistic distortions in the price.

8.5 Costs may be higher than investing into the UK, with possible duplicate brokerage costs on the transaction, especially if a local broker has to retain share certificates. The cost of currency exchange, or the higher price noted above for foreign held investments, or even the fact that some equities will only be sold in standard amounts, called 'board lots', which are charged at a different rate from non-standard amounts, may also influence the costs of setting up the investment.

Section 739

8.6 The offshore investor taking out a life policy based investment may fall foul of Section 739 of the Income and Corporation Taxes Act, designed as an anti-avoidance tool for the Inland Revenue. If income becomes payable to somebody either resident or domiciled outside the UK following a transfer of assets, or as a result of that transfer someone not ordinarily a UK resident can benefit from the income, Section 739 allows the Inland Revenue to charge tax as if the recipient were ordinarily resident.

8.7 The Inland Revenue seem to apply this to individual investments placed in life policies, rather than where the investor takes a 'standard policy', openly available. However, in a Court of Appeal case, CIR vs. Willoughby (1995) STC143, the transfer was held to have had to be made while the investor was resident, and that if there were specified rules regarding the taxation of the policy's gains, the offshore policy could not be used as a tax avoidance tool. The Inland Revenue is in the process of an appeal to the House of Lords on the case, and until a decision is reached, it appears that there is no difference between the pooled investment funds open to any investor, and those taken out as a medium to receive the investor's existing assets.

9 Trusts and Offshore Investments

9.1 Trusts are covered in detail in Unit 9, but their uses to offshore investors are worth considering at this point. For the UK investor moving abroad (subject to the three-year period for IHT purposes) or for the foreign investor coming into the UK but not having income remitted to the UK from the trust, the uses of trusts can be fairly straightforward and beneficial. Again, though, it is the rules surrounding domicile that are of particular relevance to this area.

9.2 It should be remembered that a transfer to a trust by a UK domiciled individual will be treated as a transfer of value for IHT purposes, regardless of where the trust, and the asset, are subsequently situated. Likewise, gifting to a non-resident trust can create a CGT liability on non-exempt assets, which could have an adverse effect on a portfolio's value if the asset's value at the time of gift was higher than its original cost. This will, at least, crystallise the gain which will not then be held over until the eventual disposal of the asset, presumably at an even higher value and consequent liability.

9.3 If the settlor is non-UK domiciled before settling the property into the trust, that property will be excluded from IHT, and if the property passes to a spouse, his own domicile can be arranged to best suit his circumstances. They do not have to match those of the spouse. Where he is UK domiciled the property reverts to being chargeable property on the spouse's death, so careful consideration should be given to this planning area.

9.4 Where funds in an overseas trust make gains, these would be taxable for a UK resident, but will accumulate tax-free until distributed to UK beneficiaries. Thus if he is not resident, no CGT liability exists at the time the gain is made, or at any future date.

9.5 It should be noted that for income tax purposes, the presence of one UK resident trustee will make the trust resident for tax purposes, unless the settlor was not resident, ordinarily resident or domiciled when making the settlement.

9.6 There are many varieties of trust arrangement using offshore products but the main types are will trusts, discretionary trusts, gift trusts, loan trusts and split trust bonds.

Student Activity 4

You should complete this student activity before attempting the self-assessment. Answer the questions, then check your answers against the paragraph(s) indicated.

1. What place does investment in emerging markets have in an investor's portfolio?   (7.8-7.10)

2. What additional problems might an investor incur when investing in offshore equities rather than UK equities?   (8.3)

3. If an investor places an offshore bond under trust, what is the IHT treatment?   (9.2)

If you are unable to answer any of the questions satisfactorily, you should read the relevant paragraphs again. Your understanding of the text will be further tested in the following self-assessment.

Summary

Now that you have read this unit, you should be able to:

☐ **Establish the reasons for an investor to consider investing offshore**

☐ **Recognise the main taxation effects, and advantages, of offshore investment**

☐ **Identify the nature of risk, how it can affect investment made offshore, and how it may be mitigated**

☐ **Ascertain the factors that should be considered before making an investment offshore, and their potential disadvantages**

If you can tick all the above boxes with confidence, you are ready to answer the questions which follow.

Self-Assessment Questions

1. How does diversifying an investment portfolio to include offshore investments benefit the investor?

2. What type of risks may be associated with offshore investments?

3. Why may offshore deposits not be a secure investment medium to add to an investor's portfolio?

4. In what ways do Ucits resemble UK unit trusts?

5. How does switching within an offshore bond differ from that in the onshore life assurance investment bond?

6. What is usually the main aim of offshore fixed-interest security based funds, and why?

7. How are non-distributor offshore funds taxed for the investor who, although a resident, is not domiciled in the UK?

8. What is meant by the term 'double taxation'?

9. What are the principles to remember when considering the inheritance tax implications of offshore investments?

10. Which section of the Income and Corporation Taxes Act is particularly worth noting for offshore investment, and what effect does it have on the investment?

Unit 21

Insurance Related Products

Objectives

Students are required to study the following topics:

- **Investment basis of insurance products**

- **Uses of investment policies**

- **Insurance products for protection**

- **Taxation of insurance products**

- **Second-hand policies**

- **Annuities**

- **Pensions**

1 Insurance Products as an Investment

1.1 Many products offered by life assurance companies can be considered as investment products, and many investors will include products available from life offices as part of their investment portfolio. These are often referred to as indirect investments because the underlying investments are not held directly by the investor.

1.2 These products fall into two broad areas, life assurance and annuities. Life assurance products combine regular savings or lump sum investment with some element of protection in the event of death. Annuities are a form of lump sum investment to provide income.

1.3 The Inland Revenue constantly reviews the taxation of life assurance policies and it is likely that there may be changes in the near future to areas such as the taxation of single premium investment bonds. It should be remembered when considering this type of investment that any taxation changes may have a retroactive effect. Taxation will be covered more fully at the end of the unit.

1.4 Within the category of insurance products which have an investment element, the proportion of insurance cover compared with the investment element can vary greatly. Some products, such as low-cost endowments, have a substantial element of insurance which is important if protection is required when death occurs, generally to pay off a mortgage. However, other products have been developed where the insurance element is low and the product is primarily used as an investment e.g. single premium bonds.

1.5 The range of products available from life assurance marketing groups may also include personal equity plans and unit trusts, which have been covered in previous units.

2   Investment Basis

2.1   The success of a life assurance policy as an investment will depend on the performance of the underlying funds and on the charging structure. Both regular premium and single premium contracts are widely available on the following bases:

- With-profits

- Unit-linked (also known as investment-linked)

- Unitised with-profits

With-profits

2.2   The advantage to an investor who buys a with-profits policy is that he is guaranteed a return at the end of the term. In addition, once bonuses are added to the policy they also become guaranteed, provided the policy is kept in force until maturity.

2.3   The disadvantage is that this level of security means that the rewards will not be as high as they could be if the money was invested in a different investment product.

2.4   The investor has no choice over where his money is invested, and the performance of the with-profits fund is reflected in the bonus rates declared by the life company each year. The investor will have no other indications (other than the occasional press reports) on how well the company's investments are performing.

2.5   The standard with-profits endowment is a basic with-profits policy. Level, regular premiums are paid usually monthly, or annually to purchase a guaranteed sum assured payable on maturity or earlier death. Bonuses are added each year to the guaranteed sum assured at the life office's declared rate. An additional terminal bonus may be added on maturity or earlier death, based on a percentage of the total annual bonuses already allotted. The eventual return due to the investor will be the total of the guaranteed sum assured, annual bonuses and terminal bonus.

2.6   Estimates of benefits given to customers can only be based on PIA assumed rates of 5% and 10%. However, life offices can be judged by looking at past performance bearing in mind that there is no guarantee that future performance will match that of the past.

2.7   Bonuses are not directly linked to investment performance in the same way as unit-linked policies so it is possible for a life office to use its reserves to cushion the effect of sharp rises and falls which a unit-linked investment may suffer. Over the last ten years most with-profit policies have beaten inflation, however, many actuaries feel that bonus rates have been at unrealistic levels for some time and recently there have been widespread reductions particularly on terminal bonuses.

Unit-linked

2.8   The main advantages to an investor who buys a unit-linked policy are that he can choose which investment fund(s) his premiums are invested in, and he can switch between funds if performance is disappointing.

2.9 Sometimes switches are free, but often a small charge, perhaps 0.5% of the value of the units, is levied if more than one switch is made in a year. If required, policies can often be invested in more than one fund. The investor knows what charges will be deducted from his investments, and can follow investment performance in the financial sections of the major newspapers.

2.10 A policy will buy the units at the current offer price, and each time an investor pays a premium the number of units allocated to the policy will increase. The total value of the units will determine the value of the policy. The value of the units will depend on the performance of the investment fund.

2.11 The risk of investing in a unit-linked policy depends on the underlying investment performance of the funds to which it is linked, but this in turn often depends on the exact days on which the policy is effected and cashed in. If unit prices are low at times during the policy term, this can be to the saver's benefit, as when prices are low the premiums will buy more units than if prices were higher. There will be a better return if prices are low for a long period and then rise just before the policy is cashed in, than if the prices rise to the same level but at a consistent growth rate. This is because units have been bought at a lower cost in the years of low prices. The effects of pound cost averaging will balance some of the risk over the long-term.

2.12 Some companies offer a wider range of unit-linked funds than others, and some will be more speculative than others. The main funds offered are given below, together with a brief description of their main areas of investment. Obviously individual companies' funds may differ in the particular emphasis they will put on each area of investment.

　　(a) **Managed fund** - This fund is ideal for investors who want to leave the choice to experts, i.e. the fund managers. It will consist of a mix of UK and overseas equities, fixed-interest stocks, property and index-linked investments. The wide spread of investments reduces the element of risk, but returns may not be as high as with other funds.

　　(b) **Equity fund** - This is usually confined to shares in UK companies quoted on the stock exchange, and the fund manager will select those companies showing above average returns or potential.

　　(c) **Property fund** - Investments are mainly in commercial and industrial property, both freehold and leasehold. Property is regarded as a good hedge against extreme fluctuations in the market.

　　(d) **Fixed-interest fund** - This fund involves less risk as it invests in fixed-interest stocks with a guaranteed interest rate over the medium to long-term i.e. those sold by the government, local authorities, corporations and foreign governments. They may include gilts. The higher degree of security means a lower potential return.

　　(e) **Cash fund** - The fund is used in the short term to protect capital. It invests in deposits and short-term money instruments, and some companies encourage or automatically switch investments into the cash fund in the last few months of a plan to consolidate gains made and protect them against last minute fluctuations in the stock market. Some cash funds may guarantee that unit prices will not fall.

　　(f) **North American fund** - This is similar to the equity fund but investing in larger US companies, and sometimes in selected smaller companies showing good potential.

(g) **Japanese fund** - This fund invests in the shares of major Japanese companies. The risk may be higher, although performance of Japanese companies - particularly in manufacturing - has been high in recent years, and so the potential returns can be high too.

(h) **Far East fund** - Investment is mainly in Japan but also in other Far Eastern countries such as Korea and Taiwan. Fund managers tend to choose a mix of investments in what is regarded as a growth area. The risk is higher but the potential returns are also high.

(i) **SE Asia fund** - This is another growth area with a number of emerging economies, particularly in Malaysia and Singapore. Again this is a higher-risk fund but with potentially high returns.

(j) **European fund** - Investment is in a broad spectrum of equities in any European country and sector as chosen by the fund mangers. The fund usually excludes UK equities. The potential is good in this fund because of the spread of investments and the more detailed knowledge of European markets.

(k) **International fund** - This fund invests mostly in overseas equities but may also include UK equities, and also in fixed-interest stocks. The risk depends on the mix of investments chosen by the fund managers, but the spread should offer some security against wide fluctuations in performance.

Unitised with-profits

2.13 The main advantage of a unitised with-profit policy is that it offers the security of a conventional with-profits policy by guaranteeing a minimum death and maturity value, and the flexibility of a unit-linked policy. Units can be encashed if required and taken as a partial withdrawal. Bonuses are usually given as additional units therefore it is easy for an investor to see how the value of a policy is increasing. Charges can be deducted by cancelling units or by only using a proportion of premiums to buy units.

2.14 Where an investor has a choice of investing in a unitised with-profits fund and a number of unit-linked funds, a spread of investments will offer more stability than if all the contribution was put into the more risky funds. Therefore, there is a choice for the more risk averse investors.

2.15 The main disadvantage is that usually, once investments are directed into the unitised with-profits fund, they cannot be switched into another fund. Neither can investments in another fund be switched into the unitised fund.

3 Regular Savings Plans

3.1 Life assurance companies offer a wide variety of regular premium policies for savings and investment, issued on a conventional or unitised with-profits or unit-linked basis. Most regular premium life assurance contracts are qualifying endowment or whole life policies, so that the proceeds are generally free of income tax and capital gains tax provided the policy is not altered or surrendered early.

3.2   Regular savings plans may have a fixed term, which will be a minimum of ten years if the policy is a qualifying one. However, flexible policies are becoming increasingly popular, with options for example to cash in part of a policy, reinvest the maturity proceeds or to continue the investment at the end of the initial term.

3.3   These policies often come with a number of options which can be exercised if circumstances required it. Examples of these include policies with increasing premiums which allow the cover to keep pace with rises in income and inflation. Some unit-linked policies allow the policy to continue once the original maturity date has been reached, with the policyholder being able to encash the policy when it is required rather than on a specified date.

3.4   Regular savings policies are often used in connection with house purchase, and for saving for a variety of purposes. Examples of this are to pay for school fees, to save for a child's 18th or 21st birthday, or to provide additional capital on retirement, with some plans allowing for the maturity date to be on the 60th or 65th birthday. Many companies market endowment plans under a brand name which implies a specific use e.g. "School Fees Plan" or "Child's Plan".

3.5   However, these policies should be regarded as a long-term investment. Life assurance policies are not suitable for investors who need to have access to their savings at short notice as there are penalties for cashing the policies before the end of the term and higher rate taxpayers may be liable for marginal tax on the policy proceeds.

Children's plans

3.6   A policy which is designed to allow an adult to provide a lump sum for a child will usually be an endowment policy on the life of the adult who also pays the premiums. The maturity date is normally chosen as any date after the named (or nominated) child has reached 18. At maturity there is a choice for the adult to either take the lump sum which is free of tax and use it for the benefit of the child, or to use it as a single premium for an endowment policy on the life of the child. This gives the child guaranteed insurability as no underwriting will be required.

3.7   A friendly society is particularly well suited for children's policies because the investment is often fairly small and the underlying funds are tax-free.

Friendly society tax-exempt savings policies

3.8   Friendly societies are mutual organisations which offer a variety of savings and insurance products and services. Before the development of the welfare state, friendly societies provided cover for medical expenses as well as small savings plans for the general population. Membership of friendly societies reached a peak in 1945 when there were 2,740 active societies with 8.7m members. However by 1991 the number of societies still writing new business had dwindled to 350.

3.9   Although many friendly societies now offer a broader range of products, the main product for many is the tax-exempt savings policy. These are either whole life or endowment policies and may be on a with-profits or unit-linked basis.

3.10 The advantage of these policies is that the friendly society does not have to pay any income tax or capital gains tax on the investment returns achieved on its funds. The return to the saver is therefore potentially much greater than on a policy issued by an ordinary life office where the underlying funds are taxed. The amount which may be invested by an individual is currently limited to £25 per month or £270 per year, this limit applies to the total of all friendly society policies owned by an individual.

3.11 The Finance Act 1991 permitted children under 18 to effect tax-exempt friendly society policies, allowing parents to have their own policy for £270 and in addition one for each of their children.

3.12 Once again, these policies are only suitable for investors who are likely to be able to maintain them through the term, since there are statutory limitations on the benefits which can be paid on early surrender.

3.13 The Friendly Societies Act 1992 introduced important changes for friendly societies, enabling them to incorporate and set up subsidiaries to operate in new markets, for example lending to members, acting as agent for another lender, establishing and managing unit trusts and Peps. Societies are now able to sell general insurance, investment management services and become involved in projects such as sheltered housing and residential and nursing homes.

Maximum investment plans

3.14 As the name implies, maximum investment plans are designed to provide a higher level of investment than other types of endowment, by providing only the minimum level of life cover required to ensure the policy is qualifying.

3.15 The plan is a ten-year unit-linked endowment with a minimum death benefit of at least 75% of premiums payable over the term. On death the greater of this amount, or the bid value of units is normally payable. At the end of ten years the bid value of units is payable, with some plans having the option to continue or to reinvest some or all of the maturity proceeds. On surrender the bid value of the units is usually payable, although a surrender charge may be deducted, particularly in the early years.

3.16 As with other endowments surrender before three-quarters of the term (i.e. $7\frac{1}{2}$ years) may incur a tax liability if the gain takes the policyholder over the higher rate tax threshold. The main value of these plans is to higher rate taxpayers who benefit from growth of investment being taxed at 20% with no further liability on receipt at maturity, compared with other forms of investment which would be liable to 40% tax in the hands of the investor.

Student Activity 1

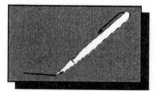

You should complete this student activity before reading the next section of the text. Answer the questions, then check your answers against the paragraph(s) indicated.

1. A customer asks you to explain what a unitised with-profits policy is and how it differs from an ordinary with-profits policy. Outline the main features and differences. (2.13)

2.   Define the accessibility of an insurance-based savings product.   (3.5)

3.   How can an investor in a unit-linked policy benefit from pound   (2.11)
        cost averaging?

If you are unable to answer any of the questions satisfactorily, you should read the relevant paragraphs again. Your understanding of the text will be further tested in the self-assessment section at the end of this unit.

4   Single Premium Investments

4.1   There are different types of single premium policies, also known as bonds, available from life offices, which are either single premium non-qualifying whole life or endowment policies. As with regular premium policies the contracts are available on a with-profits basis or unit-linked basis, and may offer withdrawal facilities to provide income. The policies usually allow the facility to make additional investments if the investor wishes. The bond may be split into a number of policies (segmentation or clustering) to allow ease of taking partial withdrawals.

4.2   Up to 5% of the original investment may be withdrawn each year without giving rise to a tax liability. Any unused portion of this allowance may be carried forward to allow extra income to be taken in future years.

4.3   Otherwise gains arising on death, maturity or surrender, including any withdrawals by partial surrenders over the 5% allowance, are chargeable to marginal rate tax for higher rate taxpayers. Top-slicing relief is given, which involves dividing the gain by the number of years that the bond has been held. The amount resulting is added as a top-slice of the bondholder's income to determine the rate of tax, which is then applied to the full gain. This is explained more fully at the end of this unit.

4.4   Investors whose income, including the profit from the bond, does not exceed the basic rate tax band will not be liable for any tax on the proceeds on maturity or surrender. Bonds may be useful for example for higher rate taxpayers who are able to defer encashing their policies until their income drops to the basic rate band, perhaps on retirement. Basic rate taxpayers whose earnings are near the higher rate tax threshold may find that in future gains may take them over the limit and they will be taxed when the bond is encashed.

4.5   The following example shows the potential benefits of taking withdrawals using the different methods available i.e. regular withdrawals, partial withdrawals or encashing individual policies. The benefits of taking partial withdrawals will depend on the bondholder's particular circumstances. Large withdrawals which exceed the rate of growth will reduce the capital value and thus reduce potential for growth in the future.

Example 21.1: Making withdrawals from an investment bond

Geoff invests £9,000 in an investment bond. He keeps it in force for 12 years. The following example compares his tax liability on the different methods of withdrawing lump sums from the bond.

In years one to nine Geoff is a higher rate taxpayer. He then retires and his taxable income is as follows Year 10 - £22,200, Year 11 - £23,200, Year 12 £24,000. Assume the 1996-97 tax rates and thresholds remain the same throughout the term of the bond:

Marginal rate tax	16%
Higher rate tax	40%
Higher rate tax threshold	£25,500

(a) Regular withdrawals

From year five until year 11, Geoff withdraws 8% each year. He then encashes the bond for £32,650 on the 12th anniversary of purchase.

Years 5-10 inclusive - No tax liability as 8% withdrawal falls within cumulative allowance

Year 11 - £90 liable to tax. No actual tax to pay as not over higher rate threshold (see table below)

Year 12 - Full encashment
£32,650 plus £5,040 (7x£720 (8%)) less £90 (previous taxable gain) less initial premium = £28,600
Slice = £2,383, add to income = £26,383
Excess over tax threshold = £883 x 16% = £141.28
Tax to pay £141.28 x 12 = £1,695.36

Cumulative allowance for regular withdrawals

Allowance each year = 5% of original premium (i.e. £450) plus any unused allowance from previous years.

Year	Withdrawals (£)	Total Allowance (£)	Excess to carry forward (£)
5	720	450 x 5 = 2250	1530
6	720	450 + 1530 = 1980	1260
7	720	450 + 1260 = 1710	990
8	720	450 + 990 = 1440	720
9	720	450 + 720 = 1170	450
10	720	450 + 450 = 900	180
11	720	450 + 180 = 630	-90

(b) Partial withdrawals

Geoff makes the following withdrawals from the bond

Year 5	£3,500
Year 8	£5,000
Year 10	£8,000
Year 12	Fully encashed for £21,190

Year 5 - Withdraws £3,500. Max. allowance up to year 5 = £2,250
Gain = £1,250. Slice = £250

Tax to pay £250 x 16% = £40 x 5 = £200

Year 8 - Withdraws £5,000. Max. allowance years 6-8 = £1,350
Gain = £3,650. Slice = £1,216 (Years 6-8)
Tax to pay £1,216 x 16% = £194.56 x 3 = £583.68

Year 10 - Withdraws £8,000. Max. allowance year 9 - year 10 = £900
Gain = £7,100. Slice = £3,550 (Years 9 - 10)
Slice plus taxable income = £25,750
Tax to pay £250 x 16% = £40 x 2 = £80

Year 12 - Full encashment
Gain = £21,190 + £16,500 (previous withdrawals) less
previous taxable gains less original premium = £16,690
Slice = £1,391
Add to income (£24,000 + £1,391) = £25,391
No tax to pay

(c) Encashment of policies. Initial premium £2,000 for each

Geoff splits the bond into four policies of £2,000 each. He encashes a policy in full in each of the following years.

Year 5 for £3,500

Year 8 for £5,000

Year 10 for £12,000

Year 12 for £17,190

Year 5 - Policy 1 fully encashed for £3,500
Gain = £1,500. Tax to pay £240

Year 8 - Policy 2 fully encashed for £5,000
Gain = £3,000. Tax to pay £480

Year 10 - Policy 3 fully encashed for £12,000
Gain = £10,000
Slice - £1,000. Added to income of £22,200
= £23,200. No tax to pay

Year 12 - Policy 4 fully encashed for £17,190
Gain = £15,190
Slice = £1,266 Added to income of £24,000
= £25,266. No tax to pay

Unit-linked bonds

4.6 These single premium whole life policies are typically written for a minimum investment of approximately £3,000. The bond has no fixed maturity date by which it must be encashed and on the death of the investor the benefit payable is expressed as a percentage of the units attaching to the bond at the date of death, typically 101%.

4.7 In terms of charges attaching to the product, the bid-offer spread means that units will be worth up to 5% less the day after purchase. Some life offices offer bonus units to offset this 'up front' cost in the form of an initial bonus, for example 2% for larger investments. Loyalty units may be given, either alternatively or in addition, typically after three or six years.

4.8   Any fund management charge is reflected in the unit price.

Automatic income

4.9   A customer may wish to receive regular income from the bond and this can be arranged by a regular encashment of units to the value of the income required. The payment of an income may start from the outset or may be requested by the investor when the bond has achieved some growth of capital.

4.10   Income may be expressed as a fixed percentage, e.g. 4% of the investment value per annum, or as a fixed amount e.g. £300 a quarter. The income may be taken monthly, quarterly, half-yearly or yearly. Where an investor establishes a bond to provide funds to meet a particular objective in the future, it is important that the investor understands that the withdrawal of income will detract from the full encashment value of the bond.

4.11   Partial encashments from the bond may generally be made at any time, subject to a minimum encashment, for example £250, provided the policy maintains a minimum value of say £1,000.

4.12   Policies may be arranged on a single life (own life or life of another) or joint life first death or last survivor basis. Joint life last survivor policies will remain in force until the death of the last of the lives assured.

Property bonds

4.13   Over the long term, property bonds are an attractive investment, their prices reflect the ups and downs in industrial, commercial and agricultural property and the timing of the purchase is of crucial importance.

4.14   As described in Unit 19 the main problems with a property fund are liquidity and valuation. Fund managers must maintain a degree of liquidity so that withdrawals can be met as they occur. It would be advisable to purchase bonds issued by leading companies that have the backing of a large insurance company.

4.15   Property is difficult to value as the only real value is its price at sale. However, a fund will have all its properties independently valued each year. The early performance of a new fund is not necessarily representative of its success, it is medium to long-term performance that counts.

Managed bonds

4.16   These are assurance contracts that are linked on the unit principle to a number of underlying funds. The typical managed bond consists of elements of equities, fixed-interest stock and property, but this is the managers' choice. Some bonds could contain only fixed-interest securities.

4.17   These bonds provide a degree of flexibility, as managers can invest new funds in those areas that appear to offer the best returns for investors at that time.

Tracker bonds

4.18 Tracker bonds may be offered by some life companies and are single premium whole life or endowment policies. They will generally offer a guaranteed return of capital at the end of the investment term, typically two, three or five years, together with a specified percentage, say 100%, of the rise in a particular stock market index e.g. the FT-SE 100 Index in the UK.

4.19 The bonds are designed for those who are attracted by the possibility of achieving the growth in the stock market, but with a guaranteed return of capital at the end of the term.

4.20 Investors should be prepared to leave their investment intact for the full term to benefit fully from the returns offered. However, if there is no rise in the index over the term, the investor will receive only a return of his original investment. The bond offers a link only to the capital growth in the stock market and does not pass back to the investor any dividend income arising from the shares of the companies included in the selected index.

With-profit bonds

4.21 Single premium with-profit endowment bonds, maturing after a specified term, e.g. 10 years, are offered by some life offices. Similar to a regular premium endowment, the bond guarantees a specific sum payable on maturity. Bonuses may be added to the guaranteed sum assured each year and the life office may pay a terminal bonus at maturity or on early encashment.

4.22 With-profits bonds may be encashed early, however, projected early encashment values cannot be guaranteed as they are based on two assumptions:

- The continuation of current reversionary bonus rates
- The continuation of the life office's surrender value basis

4.23 The benefit payable on the death of the investor within the term is typically the greater of the single premium invested or the encashment value at the date of death. However, where the investor is willing to be medically underwritten, the death benefit may be equal to the guaranteed sum plus bonuses on death.

4.24 Life offices generally restrict the amount of single premium endowment business they write to maintain the balance within the with-profit fund between single premium investors and annual premium policyholders.

Guaranteed income and guaranteed growth bonds

4.25 These are single premium investments that are packaged to provide a fixed rate of income or growth over a pre-selected term, usually five years, in addition to the return of the original capital sum at the end of the period or on earlier death. They are offered by some life companies and are often available for a limited period only. The income is usually paid yearly in arrears and is guaranteed. The rate offered varies according to market conditions but is currently around 6%.

4.26 The underlying contract may be a single premium endowment or whole life policy. The contract may be unit-linked or with-profits. The provider will usually invest in gilts to ensure the guaranteed return after five years. Some offer an additional return linked to the increase in FT-SE 100 or RPI over the term.

4.27 For a basic rate taxpayer, there is no liability to tax on the income or gains from the bond as tax will have been borne by the underlying life fund. The tax rules applying to other single premium policies apply, so for higher rate taxpayers and borderline basic rate taxpayers there may be a liability to tax at maturity. Where income is taken during the term it will normally be within the 5% limit.

4.28 The combination of security and good net returns make this an attractive investment for a basic rate taxpayer. However, there is a possibility of a tax liability on maturity if by then, the investor is a higher rate taxpayer. On maturity, there is a chargeable gain of the last year's income plus the first 5% of each previous year's income. This gain, top-sliced by the term of the bond is added to the investor's other income in the tax year when it matures. If this brings the investor into the higher rate band he will have to pay tax at his top rate minus the basic rate on the whole gain. These bonds would therefore be especially attractive to individuals who are sure that they will remain basic rate taxpayers for the term of the contract e.g. retired people.

4.29 Guaranteed growth bonds are similar to guaranteed income bonds but no income is paid. A single premium is paid by the investor and a capital sum is guaranteed in three, four or five years' time. The current market rate is around 6% per annum and so a five-year bond for £15,000 would pay out £20,073 at current rates on maturity. The investor is getting a guaranteed capital growth which is free of capital gains tax and basic rate income tax. Some bonds provide a guarantee of return at maturity plus an additional lump sum based on the rise in the FT-SE 100 Index over the set period.

4.30 Neither type of guaranteed bond should be used if the investor may need to cash in early. Surrender values are often not available and if they are given, they will usually result in a yield much lower than the guaranteed rate.

5 Annuities

5.1 An annuity is a regular income which is purchased by the payment of a lump sum known as the purchase price. The person to whom the annuity is paid is known as the annuitant. Where the annuitant buys an annuity out of his own capital it is known as a purchased life annuity, and can be for any purpose.

5.2 An annuity which has to be purchased under the terms of a pension scheme or pension plan on the retirement of a scheme member is known as a compulsory purchase annuity. The notes which follow relate to purchased life annuities.

5.3 An annuity may be paid for the remainder of the lifetime of the annuitant or may be a temporary annuity, payable for a fixed term only. An immediate annuity starts as soon as the purchase price has been paid; a deferred annuity commences at a fixed date in the future.

5.4   There are many other variations; for example the annuity may be level or increased by a fixed amount in the course of payment. It may cease on the death of the annuitant or be guaranteed to be paid for a minimum number of years. Joint life annuities are available and may continue in full or at a reduced rate on the first death. A full list of the types of annuity is given below.

Types of annuity

(a)   Immediate: Annuity payments commence as soon as the purchase price is invested. Payments continue until death.

(b)   Deferred: Payments begin at a selected date in the future, after a deferred period. The purchase price may be paid as a lump sum or regular payments.

(c)   Temporary: Annuity payments are made for a fixed term, but cease on death if earlier.

(d)   Certain: A form of temporary annuity where payments continue for a fixed term regardless of whether the annuitant dies within that period or not.

(e)   Life/joint life/last survivor: Payments continue throughout life, or in the case of joint annuities until the death of either the first to die or the last survivor. For last survivor annuities, the payments may remain the same on first death or reduce by a specified amount, for example 50%.

(f)   Guaranteed: Payments are made throughout life, but are guaranteed for a fixed period e.g. five or ten years. If the annuitant dies during the guaranteed period payments will continue for that time. If the annuitant dies after the guaranteed period payments will cease immediately.

(g)   Escalating: To give some protection against inflation escalating annuities offer payments which increase each year. Most increase at 3% or 5% per annum compound, but some increase in line with increases in RPI. Unit-linked annuities are also available where payments can fluctuate from year to year although the overall long-trend should be upwards.

       For a given purchase price the initial annuity payment for an escalating annuity will be lower than for a level annuity where payments remain the same throughout.

(h)   Capital protected: The total payments made are guaranteed to at least equal the purchase price. If an annuitant dies before this level has been reached, the balance will be repaid to his estate.

5.5   Some annuities may offer a surrender value if the investor wishes to cash in his investment.

5.6   Annuity rates are dependent upon the life expectancy of the annuitant and so will secure a lower income for a younger person than for an older person, since the life office has the prospect of paying the annuity to a younger annuitant for a longer term. Consequently, annuities provide a more attractive investment return for older lives. Impaired life annuities are becoming more popular for the same reason.

5.7   Annuity payments can be made monthly, quarterly, half-yearly or annually,

469

in advance or in arrears. Payments in arrears can be with or without proportion. If a payment is made with proportion, on death an amount relating to the period from last payment date to the date of death can be made.

5.8 Annuities are generally most suitable for investors whose need for income is more important than the need to preserve capital. This could include for example, an elderly couple who need to supplement income, have a capital sum to invest and have no dependants. Using their capital now is more relevant than the need to retain it to pass on to children or grandchildren.

5.9 The choice of annuity depends on circumstances. An escalating annuity will be useful for individuals who are concerned about the effects of inflation. An investor who wants to ensure that his capital is returned to his estate if he dies can choose a capital protected annuity. However, it should be remembered that the more guarantees there are in an annuity then the lower the level of payments will be.

Example 21.2: Top annuity rates

The top annuity rates for a purchase price of £10,000 for a male aged 65 in July 1996 were:

Immediate annuity   1195.10 p.a.

Escalating immediate   803.80 p.a.
annuity 5% p.a. compound

Payable half-yearly in arrears, without proportion or guarantee

Source: Planned Savings (August 1996)

5.10 Deferred annuities have a number of uses including pension provision and school fees planning, and once they are in payment they can be level or escalating.

5.11 The risk attaching to an annuity relates mainly to the effects of inflation and the loss of capital in the event of early death. There is no element of investment risk. However, as far as accessibility is concerned, once the capital has been invested it cannot be withdrawn by the annuitant other than as the agreed level of income. With a deferred annuity, where death occurs before the end of the deferred period, there may be a return of contributions. However, annuities are not suitable for investors who may need access to their investment.

Back-to-back arrangements

5.12 Life assurance companies offer investment plans which use annuities in conjunction with life policies. A lump sum investment is made and part of this is taken as the first premium under a life policy with the balance used as the purchase price of an immediate annuity. The annuity then funds the future premiums under the life policy. A wide variety of plans are available, either to provide income or maximum growth. The plan may be a combination of a temporary annuity and endowment running for a fixed term, or combine a lifetime annuity with a whole life policy. These have been discussed under arrangements for IHT planning.

5.13 Other variations include using temporary annuities to fund regular investments into unit trusts or personal equity plans.

Home income plans

5.14 These are available to retired people, generally aged 70 or over, who wish to increase their income. The plan combines a mortgage with an annuity and so is only applicable to home owners who do not have an existing mortgage.

5.15 The lender provides a mortgage of up to 80% of the value of the property, and the loan is used to buy a life annuity to provide income. Interest is payable on the loan, with tax relief of 24% (1996-97) available to everyone aged 65 or over, regardless of tax status. Tax relief is only given on loans up to £30,000 however, and this is often the maximum loan offered by lenders.

5.16 The loan remains outstanding on death unless it is repaid earlier, and will be repaid from the sale of the house or from the estate. There should be a reasonable equity in the property for the deceased annuitant's heirs, assuming house prices remain stable or increase over the mortgage period.

5.17 Providers of home income plans may be insurance companies or building societies. Life companies often offer a lower fixed interest rate, and can arrange for the net interest to be deducted from the annuity payment before it is paid to the annuitant.

5.18 Loans through a building society or bank may offer variable or fixed rates, and allow the borrower to choose an annuity from a number of providers. In this way a better annuity rate may be found.

6 Uses of Investment Policies

6.1 Life assurance contracts can form a very useful part of an investment portfolio, and offer an effective way of spreading risk for cautious investors. Life assurance provides access to a variety of investments that would not otherwise be available to small investors, and professional investment management for those who either do not have the necessary expertise or do not wish to actively manage their own investment portfolio.

School fees

6.2 Many life companies offer arrangements designed to meet school fees. The purpose of these arrangements is to secure a fund either by payment of a lump sum or a series of regular payments, and then use the fund to meet school fees when due.

6.3 Traditionally these will be provided by an endowment policy with the maturity value being used to buy an annuity, or by an annuity paid for by a single premium. Alternatively, a series of endowments with consecutive maturity dates can be used or a unit-linked policy which is issued as a series of clusters each being cashed in as required. In addition unit-linked endowments which offer a potentially higher return, and Peps and unit trusts are being marketed as possible methods of meeting school fees.

6.4 With the growth in interest in private education a number of charitable trusts have been set up. These benefit from certain tax advantages because of their charitable status, and usually offer a number of different plans for customers.

Second-hand policies

6.5   Recently there has been increasing interest in the buying and selling of existing life policies and endowment policies. Turnover has risen 25-fold in the last five or six years and could quadruple again in the next five.

6.6   The original policyholder who does not want or cannot afford the payments on a policy, will generally find that the selling price on the market will be better than the surrender value offered by the life company. This can be by a substantial margin of up to 25%, although 10-15% is a more realistic average.

6.7   Investors must expect to pay a premium or commission to buy a policy but in spite of future premiums needing to be paid, the yield on maturity should be good and there is the chance of an early profit if the life assured dies. Buyers of life policies may include private investors, trustees and investment companies.

6.8   The seller must execute a deed of assignment in favour of the buyer and hand the policy to him. The buyer must serve notice on the life office under the Policies of Assurance Act 1867 to protect his interest and to prevent payment on maturity to the original owner by mistake.

6.9   After the sale the buyer will be responsible for premiums falling due. He should also keep in touch with the life assured so as to be aware of any death claim. The main benefit to the buyer is that he has a guaranteed investment, probably short-term depending on the years already in force, and so is taking a low risk. The product will already have acquired guaranteed bonuses, and as current trends are for bonus rates to fall, these will be higher than could be obtained by taking out a new policy.

6.10   Any market maker, agent or auctioneer who participates in this market requires authorisation and most firms are members of the PIA. Each firm has its own business standards usually based on acceptable life offices, minimum surrender values and years of the policy left to run. The policies usually traded are with-profit endowments and some with-profit bonds; older with-profit policies with only a few years to run to maturity from old established offices are the most popular.

Viatical settlements

6.11   An alternative to selling an endowment policy on the second-hand market is the viatical settlement which is suitable for the terminally ill. These policyholders can sell their policies for a cash sum to use on nursing care or to make other provision for themselves or their dependants.

6.12   The policy is assigned to the buyer who will then make a claim from the life company when the life assured dies. There are a few companies who make up the major part of the viatical market and they usually set limits on the minimum sum assured that they will accept.

6.13   The lump sum paid to the policyholder will be around 60-80% of the death benefit and the payment will be larger the nearer to death the life assured is likely to be. There are usually no charges made by the buyer who will also meet any underwriting and administration costs. Each arrangement will vary depending on the individual circumstances, and timing of the payment is crucial to the life assured as he may need to meet a number of costs associated with his illness and have a limited period in which to spend the money.

6.14 The lump sum paid for the policy is tax-free for basic rate taxpayers but higher rate taxpayers will have an additional liability. The viatical company will receive the life policy benefits tax-free on the death of the life assured. The life assured must bear in mind that the lump sum may affect eligibility for state benefits. Other problems may arise if the policy was written in trust and the permission of the beneficiaries will be needed if the trust is to be revoked. This will not be possible if the beneficiaries are minors. It is important for the life assured to also consider the position of any dependants who would have benefited from the policy if it was not assigned. Are they still provided for when he dies?

6.15 Viatical settlements usually pay higher sums than could be obtained on the second-hand market. Some life companies are now writing terminal illness clauses into certain policies in which payment will be made on diagnosis of terminal illness depending of the life expectancy. Viatical companies make their profits on the policies which pay out on death only a short while after they have bought them. Where the seller lives for a longer than expected period the company will have to wait to recoup their money.

6.16 As the market for critical illness policies grows it is likely that the viatical settlement market will decrease. However, it currently provides a method of releasing cash for those who really need it.

Student Activity 2

You should complete this student activity before reading the next section of the text. Answer the questions, then check your answers against the paragraph(s) indicated.

1. What are the main considerations an investor needs to make when deciding whether to take withdrawals from his single premium bond? (4.2-4.5)

2. Graham West is currently a higher rate taxpayer and has just invested £7,000 in a five-year guaranteed growth bond with returns linked to the FT-SE 100 Index. He is due to retire in two years' time and so his income will fall.

   (a) Will he be able to cash in the bond early? (4.30)

   (b) How will his change in level of income be of benefit when the bond matures? (4.28)

3. A 59 year old female and a 65 year old male both invest the same amount in an annuity. Why would the female get a lower level of income? (5.6)

4. What advantages do you think an investor could gain from buying a second-hand endowment policy? (6.7, 6.9)

If you are unable to answer any of the questions satisfactorily, you should read the relevant paragraphs again. Your understanding of the text will be further tested in the self-assessment section at the end of this unit.

7   Insurance Products for Protection

7.1   The policies most suited to protection against death fall into two types - term assurance and whole life assurance. Protection against ill-health is provided by permanent health insurance, critical illness insurance and long term care insurance. There are also products designed specifically to protect loan payments against ill-health, death or redundancy.

7.2   Term assurance was the first type of life assurance to be offered to the public. Life cover is given for a specified term and the sum assured is payable only if death occurs within that time. These policies do not have a surrender value at any time. Premiums are low and are based on the sum assured and the life assured's age at entry and so this is the cheapest form of life cover.

7.3   Whole life assurance differs from term assurance in that cover is provided for the whole of the individual's life, provided the premiums are maintained. Conventional whole life policies can be written with or without-profits. Whole life policies are more expensive than term assurance but give greater long-term benefits.

7.4   Unit-linked whole life policies provide a minimum sum assured for the whole of the customer's life, as with conventional policies. Part of the premium is put into investment funds selected by the customer. The cash value of the policy reflects the investment performance of these funds. If this value exceeds the sum assured at the time of death the value of the fund will be paid instead as a death benefit. The policy will be reviewed from time to time and the premium adjusted (or the sum assured reduced) in the light of actual investment results.

8   Term Assurance Products

8.1   There are several types of term assurance policy available from insurance companies (life and composite), and friendly societies. The different types include:

- Level term assurance

- Convertible term assurance

- Personal pension term assurance

- Decreasing term assurance

- Mortgage protection assurance

- Family income benefit

- Increasing term assurance

- Convertible, increasing, renewable term assurance

- Additional voluntary contribution term assurance

8.2   All of the above types of policy are variations on the theme of term assurance and the following details compare their features and how they work.

Level term assurance

8.3   The sum assured under a level term assurance is payable only if the life assured dies within a given period of time. The term and sum assured of the contract are fixed at the outset and if the life assured survives the term nothing is payable.

8.4   This type of policy is widely used to provide family protection cover at minimum cost, especially if the cover is required for a limited period only, for example to age 21 of the youngest child. It may also be used to cover outstanding debts so that in the event of the borrower's death before the loan has been repaid the policy proceeds can be used to settle the debt.

Table 21.1: Level term assurance

Term of policy	Fixed
Amount payable on death	Fixed
Amount payable at end of terms	Nil
Premiums	Fixed throughout term

Convertible term assurance

8.5   This type of policy is similar to level term assurance but provides the customer with an opportunity to change the policy to something more permanent, such as whole life or endowment assurance at any time during the policy term. No further medical evidence is required.

8.6   If the option to convert is exercised, the premium will increase and will depend on the new type of policy selected and the customer's age at the time of exercising the option. If the option is not exercised the policy continues to the end of the original term. Generally, the policyholder may choose to convert all or part of the sum assured, and the terms of the policy will specify whether any unconverted portion may remain in force as a term assurance or is cancelled.

8.7   The advantage of convertible term assurance is that it enables a young person to obtain high life cover at a low premium, with the opportunity to convert to a different form of assurance at a later date, when a higher premium can be afforded.

8.8   Some companies, however, are no longer prepared to offer convertible terms on a long-term basis owing to the Aids problem. Convertible terms are more often offered on a short-term basis e.g. five years.

Table 21.2: Convertible term assurance

Term of policy	Fixed
Amount payable on death	Fixed

| Amount payable at end of term | Nil |
| Premiums | Fixed throughout term |

Decreasing term assurance

8.9 This is a term assurance policy where the amount of life cover reduces over the term of the policy.

8.10 The reduction can be made by regular or irregular amounts, or the sum assured may be level for a certain period and then decrease according to a scale, according to the requirements of the customer. Some policies include a conversion option so that the outstanding sum assured may be converted to a whole life or endowment policy.

8.11 Although the sum assured decreases over the term, the premium is usually level and may cease to be paid within the last three to four years of the policy term.

8.12 Uses of decreasing term assurance include protection of debt which is being paid off over a fixed period - they can be designed to suit the particular needs of a customer.

8.13 Certain types of policy have been designed to meet potential IHT liability of a Pet. The sum assured decreases in line with the reduction in potential liability after the first three years. The donee will effect the policy on the life of the donor.

Table 21.3: Decreasing term assurance

Term of policy	Fixed
Amount payable on death	Amount of cover remaining
Amount payable at end of term	Nil
Premiums	Fixed

Mortgage protection policy

8.14 This is a form of decreasing term assurance. The sum assured and term are selected to coincide with the outstanding balance and term of a repayment mortgage. The sum assured decreases in line with a given rate of interest and should be sufficient to repay the outstanding balance of the mortgage on premature death.

Table 21.4: Mortgage protection policy

Term of policy	Term of mortgage
Amount payable on death	Amount of mortgage remaining
Amount payable at end of term	Nil
Premiums	Fixed

Family income benefit

8.15 This is a decreasing term assurance with the sum assured payable in instalments from the date of death for the remainder of the selected term. The income benefit may also be taken as a lump sum which would be less than the sum of the instalments due to be paid. If the life assured dies within the term a guaranteed annual income is payable, monthly or quarterly in advance, from the date of death for the balance of the term. The policy is suitable for individuals with a young family particularly where they have little experience of handling lump sums. It could be set up with an expiry date which coincides with the youngest child's 18th or 21st birthday and the income benefit would replace the breadwinner's income in the event of early death.

8.16 Family income benefit policies may also be arranged so that the income benefit increases by a selected amount each year, for example 3% or 5% per annum compound, to keep pace with salary increases and inflation.

Table 21.5: Family income benefit

Term of policy	Fixed
Amount payable on death	Fixed at outset
Amount payable at end of term	Nil
Premiums	Fixed

Increasing term assurance

8.17 This is a term assurance where the sum assured increases each year by a given amount selected at the outset. The premiums may increase or remain level.

8.18 It is suitable for customers whose need for cover is expected to increase, perhaps because they have elderly dependent relatives, or to provide a measure of protection against the effects of inflation.

Convertible, increasable, renewable term assurance

8.19 This is flexible term assurance which includes one or more of the following options:

- Conversion option - the policy may be converted in part or in whole, to a more permanent policy at any time during the term of the policy

- Renewable option - the policy may be renewed at the end of the term

- Increased option - the sum assured may be increased within certain limits at fixed dates within the policy term

8.20 These options may be exercised without providing further medical evidence. The premium rates will be those applying to the age of the life assured and type of policy at that time.

8.21 This type of policy is not widely available because of medical underwriting considerations following the emergence of Aids.

Personal pension term assurance

8.22 This type of term assurance is available to the self-employed and to people in non-pensionable employment.

8.23 Premiums of up to 5% of net relevant earnings are eligible for tax relief at the highest rate of tax paid by the individual. This means that the actual cost to the customer can be reduced by between 20% and 40% depending on their tax rate.

8.24 Policies may be written as level term, decreasing term, increasing term or family income benefit to provide protection for dependants in the event of the early death of an income-earner.

Additional voluntary contribution term assurance

8.25 In a similar way to personal pension term assurance, term assurance with the added benefit of tax relief can be provided under an additional voluntary contribution (AVC) scheme through the employer's scheme, or from elsewhere under a free standing additional voluntary contribution (FSAVC) scheme.

8.26 AVCs are only available to an employee who is a member of a company pension scheme and the combined benefits available from the company scheme and AVC or FSAVC must not exceed Inland Revenue limits.

8.27 The maximum amounts of life cover permitted by the Inland Revenue are:

4 x salary lump sum

Widow(er)'s/Dependant's pension of $^4/_9$ths of the employee's salary

8.28 An employee can make up a shortfall in benefits provided by his employer using AVCs.

9 Whole Life Assurance Products

9.1 Whole life policies provide permanent cover and are used for family and estate protection. Whole life assurance may be on a non-profit, with-profit (including low cost versions) and unit-linked basis.

Non-profit whole life assurance

9.2 Under conventional non-profit policies the sum assured is selected by the customer at the outset and remains level throughout the policy. There is now little demand for this type of cover as there is no protection against the effects of inflation over a term which could be 30 years or more.

Whole life assurance with-profits

9.3 The sum assured will increase annually by the addition of reversionary bonuses. Once these bonuses have been declared they are guaranteed. The sum assured plus all attaching bonuses are paid on death, whenever this occurs.

9.4 Premiums may be paid throughout life or for a limited period selected at the outset of the policy, perhaps to coincide with retirement age. Life cover continues until death and the policy will continue to receive bonuses.

9.5 If the customer does not wish to withdraw the cash value of the policy and at the same time wishes to cease paying the premiums, he can leave the policy in force but with a reduced amount of life cover. This is known as a paid-up policy, which can be surrendered at a later date if required.

9.6 This type of cover is useful for cautious investors who require a guaranteed return plus some growth which protects against the effects of inflation. Whole life policies are often used in inheritance tax planning.

Table 21.6: Whole life with-profits

Term of policy	Life
Amount payable on death	Fixed amount, plus bonuses
Amount payable at end of term	End of term is death
Premiums	Fixed at outset of policy

Low cost whole life assurance

9.7 These policies are a combination of whole life with-profits and decreasing term assurance, to give a target sum assured on death for a lower premium than under a full with-profit policy. The whole life assurance sum assured will increase annually by the addition of bonuses and the decreasing term assurance will reduce annually by a pre-set amount which should be in line with the estimated bonuses.

9.8 This type of policy provides protection throughout life but is cheaper than a full with-profits policy. The disadvantage is that the sum assured will not achieve the same level of growth as a with-profits whole life assurance.

Table 21.7: Low cost whole life assurance

Term of policy	Life
Amount payable on death	Fixed amount, plus bonuses after the expiry of term assurance
Amount payable at end of term	End of term is death
Premiums	Fixed at outset of policy, reducing after expiry of term assurance

Unit-linked whole life assurance

9.9 Unit-linked whole life policies (also known as flexible whole life policies) combine life assurance protection with investment. The sum assured is set by the policyholder within certain maximum and minimum limits and, subject to satisfactory evidence of health can be increased to the maximum allowable for his current age at any time. There is usually also a 'standard' level of cover which can be supported by a regular, level premium throughout the premium payment term. The cost of the life assurance cover is calculated each month based on the current sum at risk and units are cancelled to cover cost.

9.10 Regular policy reviews, when the current fund value and premium levels are assessed, may mean that the policyholder has to increase premiums to maintain existing levels of cover, or reduce the sum assured. Reviews usually take place every five to ten years.

9.11 The amount payable on death is the greater of the chosen level of life cover and the value of the units held at that time.

9.12 These flexible policies allow the level of cover to be altered from time to time and offer other options which help the policyholder to change the policy to specific and changing needs throughout his lifetime. This may include the alteration of life cover on marriage or the birth of a child. Critical illness cover may also be included as an option.

9.13 Someone with a family to provide for might choose the maximum amount of life cover at the outset. In later years when high life cover is no longer required the sum assured can be reduced and more of the investment retained as units in the investment funds. Details on the range of investment funds for unit-linked policies were given earlier in this unit.

9.14 Policies which include a wide variety of options are sometimes known as universal policies and tend to be marketed under a specific brand name by different companies. It should be remembered that although a wide choice is provided the customer cannot afford to cover everything. High protection will be at the expense of investment return and vice versa. There may also be a number of restrictions on cover and the exercise of options.

Table 21.8: Unit-linked whole life assurance

Term of policy	Life
Amount payable on death	Value of the policy, with minimum of fixed amount
Amount payable at end of term	End of term is death
Premium	Fixed at outset for a number of years, subject to review

10   Health Insurance

10.1 Protection against ill-health is provided by policies that pay out a guaranteed income or capital sum in the event of ill-health or disability. Those offered by life companies tend to provide permanent cover, whereas general insurance companies offer renewable sickness and accident policies.

Permanent health insurance

10.2 Permanent health insurance (PHI) provides an income to an individual who is unable to work due to accident or sickness. Regardless of how many claims are made or how long they last the contract cannot be terminated by the insurer.

10.3   Generally, the maximum benefit payable cannot exceed 75% of salary less any state benefits which the policyholder could expect to receive. Some companies are reducing this maximum percentage since individual PHI benefits are no longer taxable. The upper limit on benefits is imposed by insurers, and exists to encourage claimants to return to work.

10.4   All PHI contracts have a deferred period which is the period of time which must elapse between becoming sick or disabled and the benefits being payable. Typical deferred periods are 4, 8, 13, 26, 52 or 104 weeks. Which deferred period a customer chooses will depend on his occupation, how long he would continue to receive any income in the event of illness and the cost of the policy. A customer who is self-employed may find that his income ceases immediately after falling ill, and that any state benefits due to him are very limited. On the other hand, an employee may continue to receive a salary from his employer for a given period, say 26 weeks.

10.5   Disablement will be defined in the policy in one of the following ways:

- Unable to follow normal occupation and not following any other

- Unable to follow normal occupation or any other reasonably suited to by training, education or experience, and not following any other

- Unable to follow any occupation

10.6   The policy will expire from age 50 to a maximum of age 65, generally to coincide with the insured's normal retirement date. The benefit, when payable, ceases either when:

- The insured dies

- The insured is no longer disabled as defined by the policy

- The policy expires

10.7   If a claimant recovers sufficiently to resume his normal occupation and then suffers a relapse the benefit would generally start again immediately. If the claimant has to take less well paid employment as a result of the illness or disablement, proportionate benefits may be payable. The policy will 'top-up' the reduced earnings to 75% of the original income protected. Some policies will provide for benefits to increase before and during a claim at a fixed rate, typically 3%, 5%, or 7% p.a.

10.8   Premium levels are affected by the proposer's occupation. The more hazardous the occupation the higher the premium. Typically, there are four categories of occupation:

- Administrative

- Supervisory

- Supervisory and manual

- Manual

10.9   Certain occupations are excluded for PHI cover. These may vary between life companies. Premiums for women are substantially higher than for men because of the statistically higher rates of morbidity for women. Existing illness or injuries may be excluded from the terms of the contract and no benefits paid for claims related to existing conditions. Similar terms may also apply to hazardous leisure pursuits.

10.10 Other exclusions include pregnancy and childbirth, self-inflicted injury, disability arising from alcohol or drugs and disability due to war or a criminal act. Housewives/husbands may also be covered for limited benefits under special PHI contracts.

Table 21.9: Permanent health insurance

Term of policy	Fixed
Amount payable on death	Nil
Amount payable at end of term	Nil
Amount payable on claim	Fixed
Premiums	Fixed at outset

Group PHI

10.11 Some employers provide group PHI schemes for their employees. Benefits will be the same as for individual PHI policies but the employer normally pays the premiums and the benefits will be paid by the insurance company directly to him. Benefits are then passed on to the employee in lieu of salary or wages.

10.12 Free cover is usually available. This means a specified level of cover is provided without medical evidence provided the employee is actively at work on the day cover commences. This enables employees with a poor health record still to be included. There are usually eligibility rules for joining a group scheme e.g. employed for three months.

Critical illness insurance

10.13 Critical illness insurance, also known as dread disease cover, provides a lump sum on diagnosis of certain illnesses or medical conditions and can be written on a single life or joint life first claim basis. It may be offered as a stand-alone contract, or as an optional benefit.

10.14 A key feature of critical illness insurance is that the sum insured is paid out as a lump sum on diagnosis, and that the illness need not be terminal. At a time when income is in jeopardy because work is impractical, money is thus made available by the insurance policy to ease any financial strains. It can also be used to meet any additional costs such as specialist care, nursing care or house alterations needed as a consequence.

10.15 The standard range of conditions covered by most critical illness policies is:

- Heart attack
- Stroke
- Cancer
- Coronary artery disease surgery
- Kidney failure
- Major organ transplant

- Permanent total disability

Other illnesses sometimes included are:

- Paralysis
- Multiple sclerosis
- Blindness
- Loss of limbs

10.16 The definition of each of the insured conditions varies between companies, although there is a move towards using standardised wordings to make it easier for customers.

10.17 A typical critical illness policy is a unit-linked, whole life policy, providing choice of investment funds, with switching facilities, waiver of premium options and variation of sum assured option. Alternatively the policy may be based on a term assurance, to provide benefits on diagnosis of a critical illness or on earlier death within a specified term. At the end of the selected term the policy expires if no valid claim has arisen. Some critical illness policies are written as a type of health insurance rather than life assurance and provide benefit on diagnosis of a critical illness only. The policy expires without value at the end of the term and no benefit is payable on death. Maximum age at entry is usually between 60 and 65 although it may be lower for term type contracts.

10.18 Benefits are normally paid after 28 days from diagnosis of a specified illness, and death benefits are payable only if a valid claim for critical illness has not been made. However where death benefits are payable under the terms of the contract, they are paid regardless of the cause of death. Early encashment is available, the surrender value normally being the bid value of the units.

10.19 Although it is easy to see why there is a need for permanent health insurance, the need for critical illness cover is not often obvious. However, the following needs or uses are easily identifiable:

- Provision of private care, e.g. long-term hospital treatment usually excluded from PHI
- Alterations to living accommodation, e.g. installation of extra bathroom facilities, chair lifts etc.
- Purchase of specialised mechanical equipment, e.g. kidney dialysis machine
- Repayment of mortgage

10.20 Group critical illness is also available with a fixed lump sum or a multiple of salary benefit. Premiums paid by the employer are an allowable business expense but are treated as a benefit in kind for employees. Benefits are tax-free.

Table 21.10 Critical illness insurance

Term of policy	Life
Amount payable on death or claim	Value of the policy, with minimum of fixed amount

Amount payable at end of term	End of term is death or claim
Premiums	Fixed at outset for a number of years, subject to review

Waiver of premium

10.21 Many investment and protection contracts, including those used in connection with interest-only mortgages and pension plans, include an option for regular contributions to be suspended if the policyholder is temporarily or permanently unable to work due to ill-health or disability. Although the premiums are waived during the period of incapacity, they are treated as having been paid by the life office and the benefits of the policy are maintained.

Long term care insurance (LTCI)

10.22 This is the newest form of protection cover to be introduced into the UK, although long term care insurance has been underwritten in the USA for over ten years and is also now established in other markets around the world.

10.23 LTCI provides the costs of home nursing or care in a nursing home if the policyholder suffers from a disabling condition which limits his ability to look after himself. The benefits under LTCI policies are typically payable when the policyholder is unable to perform two or three of a range of activities of daily living (ADLs). Although the definition of ADLs will vary according to the different products, the standard range covers the following activities:

- Washing and bathing

- Using the toilet

- Dressing

- Continence

- Mobility

- Feeding

10.24 Claims can also be triggered by the diagnosis of an organic mental impairment such as Alzheimer's Disease, senility or irreversible dementia.

10.25 There will usually be a deferred period from the diagnosis of the need for care until commencement of the benefit payments. The level of benefit will be set when the plan is taken out. The policy may also provide cash for special equipment or devices such as wheelchairs.

10.26 Premiums for LTCI may be paid regularly throughout the policyholder's lifetime or on a single premium basis with a lump sum being invested when the care is needed. In some cases the lump sum payment may come from the proceeds of the sale of a house. Benefits are tax-free because they are usually paid direct to the care provider and not the policyholder and so do not form part of his income.

10.27 As the proportion of elderly persons in the population increases this type of cover is likely to become more popular. The government is also encouraging this type of cover as state provision is reducing. Some people may perceive the need to fund for nursing care for their future as more important than other areas of planning. Obviously this will depend on individual circumstances, perception of the potential problem and family history.

Table 21.11: Long term care insurance

Term of policy	Life
Amount payable on death	Nil
Amount payable at end of term	End of term is death
Amount payable on claim	Fixed
Premiums	Fixed at outset or single

Private medical insurance (medical expenses)

10.28 Private medical insurance meets the costs of medical treatment for customers who require either in-patient, out-patient or day care privately. It is an annual renewable contract and premiums will be based on age, increasing as the insured gets older. It is available on a single, joint or family basis. It may be taken out in conjunction with a PHI policy or as a stand-alone policy.

10.29 Cover may vary, but will usually exclude medical conditions for which the insured has previously received treatment over a specified period, and conditions such as those related to pregnancy and childbirth.

10.30 Expenses covered include the cost of an operation including the specialists' and anaesthetists' fees, dressing etc., and nursing costs. A maximum sum insured will be given for each type of expense. There is usually an excess e.g. £50-£100.

10.31 The majority of people with private medical insurance have arranged it through their employer. It may be contributory or the employer may pay the premiums. If premiums are paid by an employer they will be taxable for the employee as a benefit in kind.

10.32 Premiums paid by, or on behalf of, those aged 60 or over receive basic rate tax relief. The relief is given to whoever pays the premiums, e.g. a son or daughter paying for elderly parents. Benefits are not taxed and are usually paid directly to the hospital or consultant.

10.33 The main advantage of private medical insurance is that consultations and operations can be arranged quickly without the need to wait for lengthy periods which may be necessary with the NHS. Conditions which may be inconvenient or painful, but not life-threatening, and which therefore do not receive priority with the NHS, can be dealt with at a time suitable for the customer.

10.34 Some schemes are available for lower premiums which offer private treatment if the NHS waiting list is longer than a specified period e.g. six weeks. This enables customers who cannot afford the full premium access to private care if they can wait for a short period.

Personal accident and sickness

10.35 This is an annual general insurance contract which pays benefits if the insured suffers an accident or is unable to work for a long period. The policy will pay a specified lump sum in the event of a number of conditions due to accident such as death, disability or loss of limbs.

10.36 It will also pay a specified income if the insured cannot work due to illness. The benefit will be payable after a short deferred period, but will only continue for a maximum period of one or two years.

10.37 Cover can be taken out by groups or individuals. Groups often take out a policy for a specified type of accident cover e.g. by a sports club, or even for a particular event e.g. a rally or tournament.

10.38 Cover is cheaper than for PHI, but the policy is renewable each year and therefore may be cancelled by the insurer if claims are too frequent. Also the level of income benefit is not related to actual income normally received. Benefits are normally tax-free.

11 Loan Payment Protection

11.1 Many customers taking unsecured personal loans or secured loans (including mortgages) depend on their continuing income to maintain the repayments. In all cases customers should be encouraged to protect the loan in the event of death, ill-health or redundancy. Loan payment protection plans are widely available and will pay loan instalments for 12-18 months if the customer is unable to work because of ill-health, or is made redundant. This helps the customer to maintain his lifestyle without running up debts until he is able to return to work. Some policies also repay the loan in full on death.

Redundancy

11.2 Redundancy protection is generally only available in connection with mortgage payments for an additional cost. It will meet the net mortgage interest payments in the event of the insured being made redundant, but not all policies cover the associated costs such as related life assurance premiums.

11.3 The risks of being made redundant have risen in the last few years making this type of cover more necessary for large numbers of new borrowers. Existing borrowers may be able to add the cover to an existing arrangement.

11.4 Following recent changes in income support rules (October 1995) there is an increased need for individuals to ensure they have some protection. New borrowers are not eligible to receive income support to meet their mortgage interest payments for the first nine months of unemployment. The same applies for the first two months for existing borrowers at this date, with limited assistance for the next four months. The cap on this support is £100,000 (formerly £150,000).

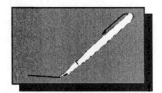

Student Activity 3

You should complete this student activity before reading the next section of the text. Answer the questions, then check your answers against the paragraph(s) indicated.

1. Tony is a member of his employer's occupational scheme and
    also has an AVC. He needs a basic protection policy. What
    different options are open to him and which would you
    recommend?   (8.1)

2. How can a flexible whole life policy be used to provide relevant
    protection for an individual throughout life?   (9.9, 9.12)

3. Linda Jenkins is a self-employed business consultant. She has
    adequate life assurance but needs some form of health
    insurance. Explain the differences between PHI and critical
    illness insurance to her.   (10.2-10.20)

If you are unable to answer any of the questions satisfactorily, you should read the
relevant paragraphs again. Your understanding of the text will be further tested in
the self-assessment section at the end of this unit.

12   Taxation of Life Assurance and Pension Policies

12.1   This part of the unit provides a description of the taxation of life assurance,
pension and health insurance products, both for the premiums and the
benefits.

12.2   It is important for an individual to be aware of the tax implications of any
policies he takes out. Product technical specifications should also highlight the
taxation implications of a particular product. However, the benefits of a
product and how it is taxed, or the tax-free benefits it offers, may vary
according to the individual's circumstances.

Taxation of life offices

12.3   The life office is responsible for paying any tax due on the investments made
with policyholders' money, therefore proceeds are passed on to the
policyholder free of basic rate income tax and capital gains tax. Certain
contracts may incur a liability to higher rate income tax. The life company
will be charged to corporation tax on its investment income and chargeable
gains at the reduced rate of 20% which applies to savings income for
individuals.

12.4   Pension funds are treated differently with investments being allowed to
accumulate free of income tax or capital gains tax. However, the policyholder
has to pay tax on the pension.

13   Life Policies

13.1   There are two main types of life policy for taxation purposes:

*   Qualifying

*   Non-qualifying

13.2   The distinction was introduced in 1968 by the Inland Revenue for income tax
purposes. Any pre 1968 policies still in force will be exempt from the
qualifying and non-qualifying provisions.

13.3 Qualifying policies are eligible for more favourable tax treatment i.e. the proceeds will be tax-free provided that the qualifying conditions are met and maintained throughout the policy term.

Qualifying life assurance policies

13.4 The definition of a qualifying policy is a complex one but, in broad terms a policy will be qualifying if it meets the following criteria:

- Must secure a capital sum on death, earlier disability or no earlier than ten years after the policy is taken out

- Premiums must be payable annually or more frequently

- The sum assured must not be less than 75% of the premiums payable during the term of the policy

- Premiums payable in any one year must not exceed twice the premiums payable in any other year

- Premiums payable in any one year must not be more than $1/8$th of total premiums payable over the policy term

13.5 The product information issued by the life company will give exact details as to which policies are qualifying or non-qualifying. In broad terms, most regular premium policies which are whole life, endowment and term assurance will be qualifying policies and therefore have no tax liability for the policyholder.

13.6 If the rules for qualifying policies are broken the policy can become non-qualifying and there could be a tax liability for the policyholder when any money is withdrawn (see Section 14 below).

Life assurance premium relief (LAPR)

13.7 For qualifying policies taken out on or before 13 March 1984 tax relief is allowable on premiums up to £1,500 p.a. (or one-sixth of total income if larger). The amount of relief is 12.5% and will normally be obtained by deducting the tax relief from the premium before it is paid to the life office. In order to be eligible for tax relief the policy must be issued on the life of the policyholder or policyholder's spouse, the premium must be paid by the policyholder or his spouse, and the payer must be resident in the UK when the premium is paid.

13.8 LAPR is not available on policies taken out or significantly amended on or after 14 March 1984.

Non-qualifying life assurance policies

13.9 Policies which do not meet the criteria outlined above are termed non-qualifying policies. The most important category of these is single premium policies - frequently described as single premium bonds. It also includes short-term (usually five-year) policies.

13.10 Qualifying policies may subsequently become non-qualifying if there are significant changes to premium levels or sums assured.

13.11 With non-qualifying policies there is the possibility of a tax liability for the policyholder when any money is withdrawn.

14   Chargeable Events

14.1   For both non-qualifying and qualifying policies tax is only payable on the policy proceeds if:

- A chargeable event occurs

- A gain arises from the chargeable event

- The gain, subject to top-slicing, added to the taxpayer's total income for the year takes it into the higher rate tax bracket

Chargeable events on qualifying policies

14.2   Chargeable events are:

- Death or maturity if the policy has been previously made paid-up within the first ten years (or three-quarters of the term if less)

- Surrender in the first ten years of the policy (or three-quarters of the term if less)

- Assignment of the policy for money or money's worth in the first ten years of the policy (or three quarters of the term if less)

Chargeable events on non-qualifying policies

14.3   Chargeable events can be summarised as:

- Death of the life assured

- Maturity of the policy

- Surrender of the policy

- Assignment of the policy for money or money's worth

- Excess occurring on partial surrenders over 5% allowance

Tax liability on chargeable events

14.4   There is no liability to basic rate income tax or capital gains tax on any policy proceeds. However, if the average capital appreciation comes within the higher rate tax band when added to income in the tax year of the chargeable event, it is chargeable to income tax at the marginal rate, i.e. the difference between basic rate tax and higher rate tax (currently 16%).

14.5   If a chargeable event occurs then a calculation must be made to see if any gain takes the policyholder into the higher rate tax bracket. Firstly the gain is calculated by deducting the total premium(s) paid from the policy proceeds. Where the chargeable event is death then the mortality element of any proceeds is not liable to tax and should be deducted.

14.6   Then a calculation known as 'top-slicing' is made. This is used to take account of the fact that the gain has occurred over the life of the policy and not just in that year. The gain is divided by the number of full years for which the policy has been held. This gives the 'slice' that is added to the policyholder's taxable income for that year to see if there is a higher rate tax liability.

14.7   The difference between basic rate and higher rate tax is charged on any part of the gain which exceeds the basic rate tax threshold for each year the policy has been in force. The following example shows how this works:

Example 21.3: Top-slicing

A five-year policy of £10,000 was cashed in for £15,000 having run its full five-year term, giving a gain of £5,000.

A top-slice, therefore, is £5,000 (the gain) divided by five (the number of years of the policy) giving a slice of £1,000.

If the policyholder had a taxable income of £25,000 the tax liability would be calculated as follows:

Top slice	£ 1,000
Taxable income	£25,000
Total taxable income	£26,000
Using 1996-97 rates	£26,000 less £25,500 = £500 to be charged at marginal rate

Tax at 16% on £500 for each year policy has been in force

16% x £500) x 5

Tax payable on gain = £400

(This example assumes no withdrawals or partial surrenders during the term of the policy.)

Partial surrenders or withdrawals

14.8 A withdrawal from a policy is normally regarded as a partial surrender. Withdrawals of up to 5% p.a. of the initial investment are allowed from non-qualifying policies. The withdrawal is not liable to tax at the time it is made, but will be added to the final value of the policy at the time it is fully encashed (i.e. at maturity, on death or at final encashment). The withdrawals made are cumulative so no more than 20 years partial withdrawals can be made without immediate tax liability.

14.9 For higher rate taxpayers, or basic rate taxpayers near the top of the band, the timing of withdrawals and final encashment is important. Those who are near to retirement may defer liability to higher rate tax and on retirement may find their income reduces below the higher rate threshold.

14.10 If a withdrawal in excess of 5% is made in a year, that excess will be liable to tax if it takes the policyholder into the higher rate tax bracket. At final encashment any tax already paid will be taken into account.

14.11 Some policies are issued as a 'cluster', i.e. a number of small policies usually identical to each other, to enable withdrawals to be made more easily. Each policy is treated separately for tax purposes. Refer back to Example 21.1 for a comparison of the tax treatment of the different methods of withdrawal.

Full surrenders and paid-up policies

14.12 A qualifying policy which is surrendered or made paid-up within ten years (or three-quarters of the term if less) from the commencement date may be liable to tax on the proceeds. Therefore, the decision to stop paying premiums to a policy must be considered carefully, particularly within this period.

14.13 A non-qualifying policy which is surrendered or made paid-up at any time during its term may be liable to tax on the proceeds.

Policy options

14.14 Where a non-qualifying policy has an option to use all the proceeds at maturity as a single premium (or as several premiums) to a new policy there will be no tax charge. This can be a useful way of deferring tax liability for higher rate taxpayers.

14.15 If part of the proceeds is used to buy a new policy then that part will not be liable to tax. Any gain withdrawn, however, will be subject to tax.

Amendments

14.16 It is important for a policyholder to understand the implications of any amendments made to a policy, for example, reducing the sum assured or extending the term of the policy. Any significant amendment to a qualifying policy where premiums enjoy LAPR will mean the tax relief is lost.

14.17 A reduction in sum assured may mean the policy becomes non-qualifying; often policies stipulate that the lower sum assured limit is above the qualifying limit.

Age allowance

14.18 An indirect tax charge may be incurred by policyholders who are aged 65 or over and receive the higher personal or higher married couple's allowance. Any excess of proceeds over premiums paid is added to the policyholder's total income. If this takes him over the limit for age allowance eligibility the benefit will be lost or reduced for that year.

Inheritance tax

14.19 Unless a life policy, whether qualifying or non-qualifying, has been written under trust, any lump sum payable on death will be counted as an asset of the estate of the life assured. Therefore, it may be subject to IHT if the nil rate threshold is exceeded. Certain policies, particularly protection policies, have a large sum assured which can considerably increase the size of an estate.

15 Second-Hand Policies

15.1 As an alternative to surrendering an endowment policy mid-term, the policyholder may have the option to sell the policy to a third party as discussed earlier in this unit.

Selling a qualifying policy

15.2 There is no tax liability to the vendor of a policy which is still qualifying at the time of sale (i.e. it has been in force for at least ten years or three-quarters of the term, if less than ten years).

Selling a non-qualifying policy

15.3 If a policy is sold before it has been in force for ten years or three-quarters of the policy term, if less than ten years, the sale will represent a chargeable event. In this case, basic rate tax will be deemed to have been paid by the life fund. A vendor who is a higher rate taxpayer may be liable to pay the difference between higher and basic rate tax (subject to top slicing) on the selling price less the premiums paid to the date of the sale.

Buying a qualifying policy

15.4 At maturity of a qualifying policy or on the death of the life assured within the policy term the new owner of the policy may be liable to CGT at his highest marginal rate of tax if his annual CGT allowance has already been used. The capital gain would be the maturity value or death benefit less the acquisition cost of the policy and the premiums paid since acquisition, subject to indexation relief.

15.5 If a qualifying policy is bought jointly (e.g. by a married couple), two CGT allowances are applied before CGT is payable. Qualifying policies are not subject to income tax.

Buying a non-qualifying policy

15.6 The maturity value or death benefit of a non-qualifying policy is liable to income tax and CGT at the higher rate for new owners who are higher rate taxpayers.

15.7 The difference between higher rate and basic rate income tax is charged on the maturity value or death benefit less the premiums paid to the policy from inception; there is no indexation relief.

15.8 Where both income tax and CGT are payable, the taxable gain is reduced by the amount that is subject to income tax. It is unlikely that CGT will be payable in addition to income tax.

On the death of the buyer

15.9 If the buyer of a policy dies before the maturity date the current surrender value of the policy or the selling price if the policy is re-sold in the second-hand market will form part of his estate. A second-hand policy may be placed in trust by the new owner to avoid an IHT liability.

16 Friendly Society Policies

16.1 The profits of friendly societies are normally exempt from income tax and corporation tax, where they arise from life or endowment business. Where the premiums of a policy do not exceed £270 p.a. (for yearly premiums) or £300 p.a. (for more frequent premiums) there is no tax liability on the investment of contributions. These policies therefore, have a potential for faster growth than other types of policy. A typical 'tax-exempt plan' as they are generally known, will be for ten years with a £25 monthly premium.

16.2 Policies are also now available to children under 18 and parents can pay the premiums to a child's tax-exempt policy without incurring a tax charge.

17 Children's Policies

17.1 A child (i.e. a person under 18) is liable to tax on income in his own right. Any policy proceeds payable to a child will be taxed in the same way as for an adult if the premiums have been paid by the child from his own income. However, where a parent has paid the premiums for the child then the proceeds are treated as the parent's income.

17.2 Some children's policies stipulate an age limit under which the death benefit is restricted to a return of premiums, thus avoiding any possible tax liability. Others impose a minimum maturity date often coinciding with the 18th or 21st birthday. This is to avoid any problems with legal responsibility and contractual obligations of minors.

18 Annuities

18.1 Purchased life annuities are used to provide a regular income. Part of the income is regarded as a return of the capital originally invested and so is not taxable. The remainder (the interest element) is liable to income tax and is normally paid net of tax at 20%. Higher rate taxpayers will be individually liable for the difference between the tax deducted and higher rate tax on their annuity income (i.e. an additional 20%).

18.2 Where income from an annuity is used to pay life policy premiums (under a back-to-back arrangement) with an expected lump sum at maturity at least equal to the initial investment, the income will include an interest element net of tax at 20% for lower and basic rate taxpayers and 40% tax for higher rate taxpayers.

18.3 If an annuity ceases on death there is no tax liability.

18.4 If an annuity is payable for a fixed period and continues after death it will be paid to the personal representatives. Income will be paid net of lower rate tax. The outstanding payments of the annuity will also form part of the deceased's estate and will therefore be chargeable to inheritance tax.

19 Offshore Policies

19.1 The United Kingdom tax rules for life policies include special provisions for policies issued by a life assurance company resident outside the UK. Such policies are commonly known as offshore or international policies and they are non-qualifying. These were discussed in Unit 20 but the tax treatment is summarised again below for reference.

19.2 The funds underlying an offshore policy are not subject to life fund taxation. Where funds invest in assets in countries where the income is taxed at source, this tax, known as withholding tax, may not always be recoverable.

19.3 The gross-roll up of funds provides an important boost to performance, since for any assumed return, an investment will build up faster than in an equivalent life fund which is subject to tax.

19.4 Offshore policies benefit from double taxation agreements between governments of different countries. The purpose of the agreement is to prevent tax being paid in both countries in respect of the same income.

19.5 For UK residents tax does not become payable under a policy until proceeds arise. Certain transactions create chargeable events which are liable to lower, basic and possible higher rate tax charges, or which may result in loss of age allowance, for those entitled to it. Transactions that create a chargeable event are:

- Death of the life assured

- Maturity of the policy

- Surrender of the policy

- Assignment of the policy for money or money's worth

- Excess occurring on partial surrenders over 5% allowance

19.6 For non-UK residents the tax laws appropriate to their country of residence will apply.

19.7 Time apportionment relief may be available in respect of a chargeable gain under an offshore policy so that where the policyholder has been resident for tax purposes outside the UK for part of the period since the policy commenced, the tax liability may be reduced, usually by the period of non-residency.

19.8 In an attempt to prevent the avoidance of income tax by the transfer of assets abroad by an individual ordinarily resident in the UK, the Inland Revenue introduced anti-avoidance provisions. Offshore policies may be affected by such provisions which apply to bonds linked to personalised funds.

20 Health Insurance

20.1 The different types of health or sickness cover provide different types of benefits and are therefore taxed differently.

Permanent heath insurance (PHI)

20.2 Prior to 6 April 1996, the benefits from a PHI policy were treated as income and subject to income tax. However, for the first 12 months from the time entitlement to benefit arose, benefits were exempt from income tax. From 6 April 1996, insurance benefits are no longer taxable where they become payable if the person entitled to them is sick or disabled. This includes benefits which are payable during convalescence or rehabilitation, or to top up earned income when it is reduced following sickness or disability.

20.3 Where an employer either receives the benefits from a PHI policy taken out in the name of an employee, or pays the premiums to a policy with the benefits paid to an employee, tax will be payable. If the employee has contributed to the premiums, the proportion of benefits attributable to his contributions will not be taxed. However, premiums paid by an employer may be treated as a trading expense and thus receive tax relief. Benefits received by an employer are usually treated as business receipts and therefore paid gross by the insurance company. The employee will be taxed on the benefits through

PAYE but they do not count as benefits in kind.

Critical illness cover

20.4 Benefits are free of income tax as payment on diagnosis of a critical illness is not a chargeable event. There is no capital gains tax liability either. Where the life insured dies not long after payment due to a critical illness any lump sum left will form part of the deceased's estate and so may be liable to IHT.

20.5 Policies which provide cover on death or earlier diagnosis can be written in trust but care must be taken to separate the rights of the policyholder to the critical illness benefit from those of the beneficiaries to the death benefit. If the trust wording is unclear an IHT liability may arise.

20.6 Some policies are non-qualifying, and although the lump sum payable on diagnosis of a critical illness is tax-free, if payment is made on death or surrender there may be a chargeable event.

Long term care

20.7 There are several different types of long term care cover. However, the benefits are generally paid either to the policyholder or directly to the care provider (e.g. a nursing home). Income benefits paid to the policyholder are not taxable in the event of accident, sickness, disability or infirmity, but only where the policy is taken out before the need for care becomes apparent. If the insurance company pays the benefit directly to the care provider there will be no tax liability for the policyholder in any event.

20.8 Where benefits are provided by payment of a lump sum this may be a form of annuity where taxation will be on the interest element only.

Private medical insurance

20.9 Tax relief at basic rate is available on premiums paid for private medical insurance for persons aged 60 and over.

21 Personal Pensions

21.1 Personal pensions have several tax advantages:

- Contributions build up in a fund which is not liable to income tax or capital gains tax on its investment returns

- Contributions are given tax relief at the highest rate paid by the policyholder

- Part of the benefits can be taken as a tax-free lump sum

- Any lump sum payable by the policy on death before retirement is normally tax-free

- Additional life assurance taken out in conjunction with a pension enjoys tax relief on premiums

Contributions

21.2 The maximum contributions which may be made in a tax year are as follows:

Age	Percentage of 'net relevant earnings'
35 or less	17.5
36 - 45	20.0
46 - 50	25.0
51 - 55	30.0
56 - 60	35.0
61 - 75	40.0

21.3   Where contributions are being made by both employee and employer the total contribution is subject to the above limits. There is also a maximum limit on 'net relevant earnings' of £82,200 (1996-97) known as the earnings cap.

Tax relief

21.4   Tax relief is available on contributions within the maximum contribution limits, at the highest rate of income tax paid by the individual. Self-employed contributions are payable gross. Tax relief is claimed through the annual tax return. Employees pay contributions net of basic rate tax which is 24% for 1996-97. Any higher rate relief due to the individual is claimed through his annual tax return.

21.5   If an employee who took out a plan before 1996 wishes to maintain his level of gross contributions to a pension scheme, net contributions will have to increase by 1% to reflect the change in basic rate tax. If tax rates change in the future, contribution levels may again need to be changed.

21.6   Employer's contributions are payable gross, but are normally allowable against the taxable profits of the business.

Life assurance

21.7   A maximum of 5% of net relevant earnings can be used to provide a lump sum death benefit in the form of term assurance expiring no later than age 75. Tax relief is given on the premiums comparing favourably with an ordinary term assurance policy where tax relief is not available. The 5% limit must be part of the overall limit for pension contributions given above.

21.8   These policies may be written under trust thereby avoiding any liability to inheritance tax. Most pension policies also provide a return of premiums paid plus interest or the value of the fund accumulated at time of death if the planholder dies before retirement. This may also be written under trust as above, but more usually will be paid at the discretion of the scheme administrator. This means liability to inheritance tax is avoided.

Lump sum benefits

21.9   Where part of the retirement benefit is taken as a lump sum (commutation) this must not exceed one-quarter of the fund. It is payable tax-free.

Pension

21.10 The pension is taxed as earned income with basic rate tax normally deducted at source. It is usually provided by a compulsory purchase annuity, which is fully taxable unlike a purchased life annuity. If the planholder takes part of his pension entitlement as cash, but needs income, he can buy a purchased life annuity and only pay tax on the interest element.

22 Occupational Pension Schemes

22.1 Occupational pensions i.e. employer related group schemes, executive pension plans, additional voluntary contributions (AVCs), including free-standing additional voluntary contributions (FSAVCs) enjoy similar tax advantages to personal pensions:

- Contributions build up in a fund which is not liable to income tax or capital gains tax on investment returns

- Contributions are given tax relief at the highest rate paid by the policyholder

- Any lump sum payable by the policy on death before retirement is normally tax-free

Contributions

22.2 The maximum amount that an employee may contribute is 15% of earnings each year including AVCs and FSAVCs. There is a maximum limit on earnings of £82,200 (1996-97) known as the earnings cap.

22.3 There is no limit to the maximum contribution that an employer may make. However, contributions are limited to providing maximum approvable benefits.

Tax relief

22.4 Tax relief is available on employees' contributions within the maximum limit, at the highest rate of income tax paid by the individual. Contributions including AVCs are deducted from gross pay before taxable income is calculated.

22.5 FSAVCs are paid net of basic rate tax, with the employee responsible for reclaiming any higher rate tax relief at the year end.

22.6 Employer's contributions are deductible from profits as an expense of management. There is no liability to National Insurance contributions on the amount of contribution paid by the employer and employee. (Note that if that amount was paid as salary instead there would be liability to NI contributions).

Life assurance

22.7 The maximum lump sum on death-in-service is four times salary. A refund of the employee's contributions, with interest, may also be paid. Provided this is paid at the discretion of the scheme trustees it is free of inheritance tax. In addition, a pension may be provided for a spouse or dependant on the death of the employee not exceeding two-thirds of the maximum pension which could have been provided for the employee. Such pensions are taxed as earned income.

Lump sum benefits

22.8 Part of the benefits can be taken as a tax-free lump sum (commutation). The maximum is equal to $^3/_{80}$ths of final salary (limited to the earnings cap) for each year of service up to 40 years. Alternatively, the lump sum can be calculated as 2.25 times the pension before commutation if this gives a higher figure.

22.9 The earnings cap applies to the definition of final salary. The lump sum is also subject to an overall limit of 1½ times the earnings cap (i.e. £123,300 for 1996-97).

22.10 Benefits secured by AVCs or FSAVCs cannot be commuted and must provide pension benefits.

Pension

22.11 The maximum pension at normal pension age is two-thirds of final salary, provided that the employee has completed 20 years' service with the employer. Those with less service are restricted to a maximum pension of $^1/_{30}$th of final salary for each year of service. The pensions are taxed as earned income. As with personal pensions, persons requiring income rather than cash could use their commutation entitlement to purchase an annuity and only pay tax on the interest element.

23 Life Assurance and Pension Products in the Portfolio

23.1 These products fall into two types, those providing protection and those used as an investment. Protection is a vital part of any individual's financial plan and should always be considered before any form of savings or investment. Individual circumstances will determine which types of protection are required e.g. does the customer have dependants, is he self-employed, does he have any loan commitments to protect and so on. These products are mostly treated for tax in the same way for all individuals so this need not be a consideration when making a choice.

23.2 Where a customer requires some type of investment, the main attraction of life assurance products is their degree of security. They can provide a guaranteed return on death, and with-profits policies will provide a guaranteed return at maturity. If a customer wants to take some risk then unit-linked products may be suitable provided the customer is willing to accept the risk that the value of his policy may fall.

23.3 As with all other types of investment discussed in this module, these products can play a part in an investment portfolio depending on the individual's circumstances, and should be balanced by other more risky products if the customer wants to ensure good returns. Where a customer has a limited budget they can be a good way of providing both protection and some investment element, and form the basis of a portfolio which can be developed in the future.

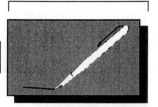

Student Activity 4

You should complete this student activity before attempting the self-assessment. Answer the questions, then check your answers against the paragraph(s) indicated.

1. Sheila Walsh invests £15,000 in a ten-year single premium (14.7, 14.8) investment bond. She is a higher rate taxpayer. During the ten years she withdraws £700 in year 3 and £5,000 in year 5. At maturity she receives £20,000. Calculate the chargeable gain at maturity.

2. What is the tax position of benefits received from the following?

   (a) Tom invests £10,000 in an annuity certain for 15 years. (18.1)

   (b) Sarah receives regular payments from a personal pension (21.10) annuity.

   (c) Laura and William (both aged 15) receive an income from (18.1) annuities bought by the trustees of a settlement made by their father.

   (d) Jo invests £15,000 in a joint life last survivor deferred (18.1) annuity.

3. Max Shepherd took out a ten-year with-profits endowment four years ago. He now needs the cash and has decided to sell the policy rather than surrender it.

   (a) How will his tax status affect any tax liability on the sale? (15.3)

   (b) If Max dies two years' later what tax liability will the (15.6-15.8) buyer have?

If you are unable to answer any of the questions satisfactorily, you should read the relevant paragraphs again. Your understanding of the text will be further tested in the following self-assessment.

Summary

Now that you have completed this unit, you should be able to:

☐ **Describe the different types of life assurance products available**

☐ **Describe the different types of health insurance products and annuities**

☐ **Define the circumstances when each type of product could be used**

☐ **Explain the tax treatment of each product**

☐ **Understand how these products fit into a balanced investment portfolio**

If you can tick all the above boxes with confidence, you are ready to answer the questions which follow.

Self-Assessment Questions

1. How much can an individual invest in tax-exempt savings plans issued by friendly societies in a tax year?

2. What is a viatical settlement?

3. A married couple with two young children and a repayment mortgage need some protection. What types of policy would be suitable?

4. When will the benefit under a critical illness insurance become payable?

5. Why do life assurance policies not carry a basic rate tax liability for policyholders?

6. Jim has taxable income of £24,000 and has made a gain of £9,000 on his single premium bond. He did not take any withdrawals during the five-year term. How much will he be taxed on his gain?

7. Alistair has a non-qualifying policy which has an option to use the maturity proceeds to buy another similar policy. What will the tax treatment of the proceeds of the original policy at maturity be?

8. Edward Black has lived and worked in Hong Kong for the last eight years. He is now living in the UK and is a higher rate taxpayer. He invested £20,000 in a ten-year offshore bond eight years ago.

   (a) How will the chargeable gain be calculated at maturity?

(b) Explain why Edward might not be any better off investing in another offshore policy when he is resident in the UK.

9. An employee is receiving PHI benefits from his employer's group PHI scheme. What is the tax position on these benefits?

10. A self-employed man is considering whether to use direct investments to save for his future retirement or to take out a personal pension. What would you say to him?

Appendix

Answers to Self-Assessment Questions

Unit 1

1. Direct taxation is imposed directly on the taxpayer. Indirect taxation is paid indirectly as part of the price of goods or services.

2. • Income tax
   • Capital gains tax
   • Inheritance tax
   • National Insurance

3. In the Finance Act in the following March.

4. (a) The status of an individual in any tax year.
   (b) The status of an individual on a regular basis.
   (c) The country which an individual regards as his natural home.

5. Because it affects liability to UK tax.

6. In her own right. It is not affected by the status of her husband.

7. As France is in the EEA she will probably be liable for French taxes on the sale and not to CGT in the UK. Normally the principle would be that she would be liable for gains made anywhere worldwide, although any foreign tax paid would be taken into account, but different arrangements apply to EEA countries. This would also be the case if there was a double taxation agreement with France.

8. Belgium, France, Germany, Italy, Luxembourg, Netherlands, UK, Denmark, Ireland, Greece, Portugal, Spain, Finland, Austria, Sweden, Iceland, Norway and Liechtenstein.

9. Yes, they will be liable to UK tax. He will be granted residence status from the date he arrives in the UK as he intends to stay for at least two years.

10. Yes, because he was domiciled in the UK less than three years before his death.

Unit 2

1. Employees.

2.   (a) Earned income - wages, bonuses, tips, commission, business profits of a partnership, occupational pension, etc..

   (b) Unearned income - building society interest, share dividends, trust income, income from gilts, certain rental income, etc..

3.   Employees and most directors earning over £8,500 a year. Named after the employer's form for benefits in kind. It affects taxation treatment of certain benefits.

4.   Tax relief is restricted to first £8,000.

5.   As the house is partly used for business, the mortgage cannot be in Miras and they will have to apply to the Inland Revenue for tax relief.

6.   £43 i.e. 43p per mile x 100 miles.

7.   £30 net is worth £39.48 gross, i.e. an extra £9.48 a month. The charity reclaims the tax relief from the Inland Revenue.

8.   Yes - at basic rate deducted from premiums.

9.   Monica - £4,910 personal allowance plus age allowance.

   Eddie - £4,901 plus £3,115 married couple's age allowance. This is then reduced because income exceeds £15,200 by £2,800. Reduction is £1,400.

   Personal allowance reduced by £1,145 to basic level of £3,765.
   Married couple's age allowance reduced by remaining £255 to £2,860.
   Eddie's reduced allowances are now £6,625.

10. Eligible for allowance in tax year, they get married but reduced by 5/12ths (i.e. April - August).

Unit 3

1.   Ben:

	Income	£21,000
	Less pension contribution	£850
		£20,150
	Less personal allowance	£3,765
	Less MCA	£1,790
	Plus allowance restriction	£670
		£4,885

Taxable income	£15,265
Tax on first £3,900 @ 20%	£780
Tax on £11,365 @ 24%	£2,727.60
Total tax liability	£3,507.60

Fliss:

Total income	£8,000
Personal allowance	£3,765
Taxable income	£4,235
Tax on first £3,900	£780
Tax on £335 @ 24%	£80.40
	£860.40

2. (a)

Personal allowance	- husband	£5,090
	- wife	£5,090
Married couple's allowance		£3,155
Total		£13,335
Basic state pension (couple)		£5,083
Unused allowances		£8,252

(b) • Share investments between them to utilise all allowances

• Use high yield investments

• Choose good income-producing investments

• Choose investments with tax-free income

• Remember that the first £3,900 each of income is taxed at 20%

3. (a) $\frac{1}{12}$th of £5,555 i.e. £462.91.

(b) Tax and NI contributions deducted from employee's, plus employer's NI contributions.

(c) Certificate given to an employee after the end of the tax year, to show pay, tax and NI contributions for the previous year.

4. • Yes

• Yes

• No

• Yes

5. (a) Yes

(b) Yes

(c) No

(d) No

(e) No

6. • Pay slips

    • Notes of expenses

    • Benefits paid by employer

    • Building society accounts

    • Other investments

    • Pensions not paid through employer

    • Payments to charities

7. Lump sum is tax-free. Pension taxed as earned income.

8. (a) Save £5 - £250 a month in an SAYE account.

    (b) Three, five or seven years.

    (c) He uses the SAYE contract proceeds to buy shares in his employer's company at a favourable price (i.e. not less than 80% of the market value of the shares at the time the option was originally granted).

9. No answer to this question.

10. As income through PAYE.

Unit 4

1. Cases I and II of Schedule D.

2. 1 January to 5 April 1997.

3. It will be based on the agreed partnership share decided between all the partners.

4. (a) 1997-98 taxed to end of tax year, i.e. 1 September 1997 to 5 April 1998
        1998-99 taxed on a/c year ending in tax year, i.e. 1 July 1997 to 30 June 1998.

    (b) Overlap of September 1997 - April 1998. Will be relieved either when he leaves or partnership changes a/c dates.

5. Because of the averaging of two years' accounts used as a basis for tax

liability in this year, businesses may try and increase their profits for these years to gain tax advantages. The Revenue may challenge certain business transactions to ensure they have a valid reason for the transaction. If not, then an additional tax charge may be levied.

6.   £5,000 on 31 January 1998 and £5,000 on 31 July.

7.   Based on period 1 January 1997 to 5 April 1998. May be able to offset overlap relief incurred when started trading.

8.   No, if from business profits.

9.   It is a way of reducing the value of assets in the accounts to take depreciation into account. For example, a business owns machinery with a limited life span. Each year it can reduce the value of this asset in the accounts by 25%.

10.   No, they can offset them against income in the previous year.

Unit 5

1.   See paragraph 2.2 for full list.

2.   To pay secondary Class 1 contributions.
     To deduct contributions from employees pay.

3.   He pays lower contributions and so does employer. Employee pays rates reduced by 1.8% on MBEs. Employer gets reduction of 3% on rates on MBEs. If using an APP, then NI contributions are not reduced as DSS pays rebate of difference between contracted-in and contracted-out contributions into the plan.

4.   Jenny:
     Salary = £22,500 + £2,500 = £25,000/52 = £480.77 a week
     LEL - £61   UEL - £455
     2% x £61 = £1.22
     8.2% x £394 (£455 - £61) = £32.31. Total = £33.53/week

     Employer:
     7.2% x (£455 - £61) - £28.37 plus 10.2% x £61 = £6.22 = £34.59
     10.2% x £25.77 = £2.63.   Total = £37.22/week

5.   He will normally continue to pay NI contributions for the first 52 weeks. If he

carried on working abroad after this time he will be liable to pay contributions in Belgium. However, if he is likely to return to the UK after say two years, he will probably be able to continue paying NI contributions in the UK to ensure his record is not broken. If not, he can pay voluntary contributions. His employer will also have to pay NI contributions when the employee does.

6.   (a) £15,000 profits
Class 2 £6.05
Class 4 £15,000 - £6,860 = £8,140 x 6% = £488.40/52 = £9.39
Total = £9.39

   (b) She will be liable for UK NI contributions once she is deemed resident for tax purposes. However, if she is intending to return for good she may want to start payments as soon as she is earning.

   (c) Class 2 can be paid by direct debit or quarterly following a bill from the DSS. Class 4 are due at the same time as the tax instalments, i.e. January and July, and will be based on the amount due the previous year for the transitional 1996-97 year. She can then reclaim a refund or be billed for any extra in the following January.

7.   (a) He will pay Class 1 NI contributions as normal on the teacher's pay but will not be liable for Class 2 or 4 contributions as his self-employed earnings are not high enough.

   (b) Simon is self-employed for both sets of earnings so all income will be added together to calculate NI contributions.

   (c) As each set of earnings is from a different employer, she will have separate Class 1 liabilities for each. The earnings from the cleaning job are below the LEL so will not be liable.

8. Basic pension, incapacity benefit, maternity allowance and widow's benefits based on husband's contributions.

9. Some contributory benefits are taxable, including unemployment benefit and pensions. Also statutory maternity pay is liable for NI contributions.

10.   (a) Relates to Class 1 contributions. Currently £61. If a person earns below this amount each week, then he will not be liable to pay NI contributions. If earning over this amount, the employee pays a set percentage of £61, i.e. 2%.

   (b) Relates to Class 1 earnings. Currently £455. If employee earns above this limit he will not pay NI contributions on the excess but the employer will.

   (c) Term used to describe earnings between LEL and UEL. Contracting-out reduction only applies to earnings in the MBE.

Unit 6

1. The asset should be insured if it is valuable. Persons may be tempted to destroy an asset to avoid CGT.

2. Half the annual exemption applies. Tax at 24% except for accumulations and discretionary trusts which are charged at 34%.

3. With the balancing payment for income tax due 31 January following the end of the tax year.

4. Losses can be carried forward indefinitely but when a claim for relief is made it must be within five years and ten months from the end of the tax year in which the loss was made.

5. (a) £900 at 20%
        £6,100 at 24% = £1,644

    (b) £7,000 at 24% = £1,680

    (c) £7,000 at 40% = £2,800

6. He will probably incur stockbroker's charges and so will lose a little bit in value between selling and rebuying. There is also the possibility that prices could increase between the two transactions.

7. Rollover - given where replacement asset has a life of more than 60 years. Used to reduce cost of replacement for CGT purposes.

    Holdover - given where replacement asset has life of less than 60 years (depreciating asset). Relief given by allowing gain to be held over for up to ten years.

8. (a) No tax to pay. Anyone who inherits an asset will be treated as having acquired it at the market value on the date of death.

    (b) These can be carried back for up to three previous tax years and set against gains. A tax refund will be made if applicable.

9. Husband and wife are taxed separately and each have their own exemption, i.e. £6,300 each in 1996-97. Tax is calculated on the net gain, i.e. all chargeable gains made in a year less all allowable losses.

    Cannot carry-forward any unused exemption but can carry-forward any losses. Cannot set one spouse's losses against another spouse's gain but can transfer ownership before the gain or loss is made.

10.   A personal chattel, i.e. a tangible, movable asset such as furniture is exempted from CGT if the gain on its disposal is less than £6,000.

Unit 7

1.   The unfinished property will be valued on the relevant date as if work had been completed and the cost of completing the work will then be deducted as a charge against Mr William's estate.

2.   Capital transfers for family maintenance are exempt transfers for IHT purposes.

3.   Transfer of £300,000 less £200,000 nil rate band = £100,000. Full IHT payable would be £40,000. Death is four to five years from the date of the transfer, therefore tapering relief decreases the tax liability to £24,000 (60% of the full scale).

4.   David must have used the land for agricultural purposes for two years prior to the transfer, or he must have owned the land for seven years prior to the transfer with the land being used by himself or another person for agricultural purposes.

5.   It is possible to use the death-in-service payment which is usually free from IHT when written under a discretionary trust. The sum, which is a maximum of four times salary, can be used to meet an IHT liability and tax relief is available on contributions to the scheme.

6.   The principal aim of a loan trust is to freeze liability. An interest-free loan is made to the trustees which forms part of the estate's assets. A single premium bond is purchased by the trustees using the loan. The bond falls outside the estate thus freezing the IHT liability to the amount of the outstanding loan. The trustees use the bond withdrawal facility to make loan repayments to the client.

7.   Adam and Teresa could equalise ownership of assets to reduce potential inheritance tax liability. Adam can gift assets to Teresa using the inter-spouse exemption and this would allow full use to be made of the nil rate band if she were to die first.

8.   Alan's wife will take the personal chattels, £125,000 absolutely and a life interest in half the residue i.e. £237,500. The four children take £59,375 each immediately and the half in which his wife had a life interest, shared between them, on her death.

9. A valid will must be in writing and it must be properly executed. Privileged wills are an exception to this rule and these can be made verbally by soldiers on active service.

10. Richard can disclaim the legacy at any time before he accepts it but it must be within two years of his father's death. He must not have taken any benefit from the legacy and there must have been no consideration in money or money's worth.

Unit 8

1. Companies estimate and pay their own tax within nine months of the end of the accounting period. Returns and accounts must be submitted for assessment within 12 months.

2. (a) 33%
   (b) 20%

3. Both receive dividend with a tax credit for basic rate tax. Basic rate taxpayer need take no further action. Higher rate taxpayer must pay further 20% on grossed up dividend via his tax assessment.

4. The payment of dividend plus ACT made by a company.

5. Can carry-forward the excess to the next tax year to be offset against further franked payments.

6. No tax credit although treated as tax paid at 20%. Higher rate taxpayer has further 20% liability.

7. Fixed or ad valorem.

8. To ensure that they can be used, e.g. for house purchase, need to register title to property, cannot do this unless document is stamped.

9. • Buying a house

   • Buying a leasehold property

   • On a tenancy agreement

   • On buying stocks and shares

10. Levied on share transactions which escape stamp duty at rate of 0.5%.

Unit 9

1. The three certainties which must exist are certainty of intention, certainty of subject matter and certainty of objects.

2. (a) A life interest provides the beneficiary with an income from the trust but the capital cannot be used by him.

   (b) A beneficiary who holds a life interest is referred to as a life tenant.

   (c) While the life tenant is alive, the remaindermen hold a reversionary interest in the trust. The property then passes to them on the death of the life tenant.

   (d) A contingent beneficiary is someone whose interest in the trust depends on a specified event occurring.

3. The trust investments must be of a 'suitable' nature. The trustee should aim to diversify the trust's investments if appropriate. The trust's investment portfolio should be regularly reviewed to take account of changing investment conditions and changing beneficiary needs.

4. Under the Variation of Trusts Act 1958 the court may alter a trust for the benefit of:

   • Beneficiaries who are incapable of consenting to the unanimous decision by beneficiaries requirement, due to incapacity or infancy

   • Beneficiaries with contingent interests

   • Unborn beneficiaries

   • Beneficiaries under a protective trust who hold a discretionary interest

5. An accumulation and maintenance trust is a type of discretionary trust which allows the settlor to transfer property to a minor without the minor having access to the property at too young an age. The beneficiaries become legally entitled to any income of the trust property on reaching a specified age, no later than 25. The income must be held by the trustees with the power to use it for maintenance, education or the benefit of the beneficiaries, or accumulated until one of them becomes entitled to the income. It must last no longer than 25 years.

6. The trustees will deduct tax at 24% from the £7,000 income which the trust receives i.e. £1,680. The £300 expenses will then be deducted from this and Julia will receive £5,020. This is equivalent to a grossed up income of £6,605. Because she is a higher rate taxpayer, she will have an additional liability of 16% of £6,605 i.e. £1,057.

7. An accumulation and maintenance trust is a type of discretionary trust and is taxed in the same way. The income is subject to tax at 24% plus an additional

rate of tax, currently 10%, making a total liability of 34% which the trustees must pay.

8. Trustees are eligible for half an individual's annual CGT exemption i.e. £3,150 (1996-97). This is split equally if the settlor has created more than one trust. Therefore, the CGT payable on Trust A will be £25,000 less half of £3,150, at a rate of 24% i.e. £5,622.

9. When an interest-in-possession trust is set up, it is treated as a Pet. If Martin dies within seven years of setting up the trust, it will become chargeable.

10. (a) An absolute trust should be used when the beneficiary is a known individual and the contract is for his benefit absolutely.

    (b) A flexible trust should be used when flexibility is needed regarding the beneficiary of the contract proceeds.

Unit 10

1. Ones with no risk to capital, e.g. National Savings, Tessas, deposit accounts, guaranteed bonds.

2. Purpose of investment, e.g. to fund for retirement, save for specific purpose, etc.. Customer's attitude to risk. Need for income, capital growth or both. Customer preferences. Timescales involved. Tax status of customer, e.g. potential CGT liability.

3. Market risk - emerging markets are more volatile and prone to fluctuations.

    Product risk - companies in developing countries are likely to be less secure and may fail. George is unlikely to receive any compensation if this happens. Any return will depend on how his shares rank under insolvency rules of the particular company(s) concerned.

    Tax risk - likely to be a higher rate taxpayer and so have income tax and CGT liability. If he makes a large profit, this means a large tax bill. Tax liability is also affected by tax treatment in the country concerned.

4. Gross dividend = £3,750. Net of 40% tax = £2,250 which means a further reduction of £750.

5. Income produced at the expense of capital growth, whether income is reinvested, inflation rates, falling interest rates, supply and demand for investment, e.g. share price at time of sale, exchange rates if foreign

investment.

6. Companies normally issue shares to raise capital. A listing on the LSE means access to a large number of potential buyers. Being quoted also raises the company profile and can increase investors' confidence in it. Overseas companies may want to attract UK business.

7. Market makers quote bid and offer prices for particular shares. Stockbrokers wishing to deal in those shares will use the relevant market makers to buy or sell the shares required and obtain the best price.

8. (a) Currently five, moving towards three in 1997
   (b) No
   (c) The nominee company
   (d) The stockbroker will pass them on to Alan

9. The information given in the Financial Times breaks down the index into sectors so the investor can compare the performance of his particular shares with the performance of the food retailing companies quoted in the index. Over a particular period, he will be able to judge whether the performance of his particular investment is matching the index or is better or worse. He may then decide to alter the balance of his portfolio.

10. There are so many securities listed on the LSE that it is impossible to track the fluctuations of each one and obtain an overall picture of market trends. So the indicators were introduced to give a representative picture of the general mood of the market.

Unit 11

1. Fundamental analysis looks forward at future earnings and dividends of a share. Technical analysis looks backward at past patterns in price movements.

2. Gearing is the ratio of the amount of funds a company has borrowed to its total capital assets. It affects shareholders in two ways. Firstly, they will gain more profit on shares if the return on the total assets, including the borrowed funds, is higher than the cost of borrowing. Secondly, it will affect the shareholder's claim on the company assets if it goes into liquidation.

3. By adding the retained profits of the company to the depreciation charge, as shown in the profit and loss account.

4. Net profit of the company after corporation tax has been paid plus the amount

of recoverable ACT.

5.   (a) This will indicate the ability of a company to pay the interest on its borrowed funds which includes debentures.

        (b) If the income cover of one is higher, this will indicate that it is more secure than the other as it shows how much of a company's assets are available to meet its obligations, such as loan interest and different types of dividends.

6.   That share price movements create a pattern over time which, if repeated, should create a similar result in the future. When patterns are identified, they can be used to estimate probability for the future.

7.   Trading outlook - economic climate and effect on the relevant sector and company. Current trading position of company, e.g. level of borrowing, etc.

        Management ability - high standards of business practice and management ability, likely changes in structure.

        Quality of earnings - forecast of future profits, potential demand for company's products/services, development plans.

8.   The share is quoted ex-dividend. Anyone buying the share will not have the right to the next dividend so the price quoted reflects this.

9.   The P/E ratio compares the share price with the earnings (i.e. dividends) per share. If the ratio is high, i.e. around 20 or more, this indicates the share is performing well and can be expected to increase in the future. A low ratio, e.g. four or less, indicates that the share is not doing well and is not highly regarded in the market.

10.   A list published daily by the LSE which gives more details than provided by the Financial Times. It includes details of the last dividend paid, dates of dividend payments and the business transacted each day.

Unit 12

1.   He should deposit the money in a money market account to take advantage of the higher interest rates available. He can open a short-term account, e.g. seven day and will be able to withdraw his money then. There is no risk to his capital and the interest will be paid gross and can be withdrawn at the same time.

2. (a) £1,800

    (b) The account would lose its tax-exempt status and she would have to pay on all the interest credited over the last four years. Any interest earned before 6 April 1996 would be taxed at 25% and after that date at 20%.

    (c) She can put the full amount of capital, but not interest, in a new Tessa, either with her current provider or another. It must be opened within six months of maturity. If she invests less than the £9,000 maximum, she can add up to the existing limit of £1,800 each year. Different providers offer different interest rates and bonuses so she needs to shop around to get the best offer. However, interest rates can vary so she should be aware that a good rate now may not continue in the future.

3. Pensioner's guaranteed income bond in wife's name only would provide regular monthly income. Can invest up to £50,000 and rate of interest, currently 7%, is guaranteed. Income is paid gross so no tax liability if paid to wife who is a non taxpayer. Can withdraw after five years or reinvest to continue income at the new rate if required.

4. Two types available - fixed-interest and index-linked. Both offer guaranteed interest rates if held for five years which is fixed at time of issue. Index-linked certificate has a lower interest rate but it is added to the RPI. Both are tax-free at maturity. Minimum investment is £100 so available to most people. Can be suitable for any taxpayers as tax-free. Must be able to tie money up for five years as lower interest rates are paid if cashed in early. Index-linked certificates keep returns in line with inflation so if RPI rises, so does interest on the certificate. The value at maturity may be closer to real value of capital after five years. Certificates can be encashed or reinvested after five years.

5. Deposit protection scheme provides compensation of 90% of deposit (max £18,000).

6. Dick is a basic rate taxpayer so he will get 4.85% as tax has already been deducted. However, Tom is a non taxpayer and will be able to receive interest gross. This will be at 5.82%. Harry will have a further 20% tax to pay making the interest he will actually receive equivalent to 3.49%.

7. • Size of deposit

    • When interest is credited

    • Whether interest rates exceed inflation

    • Rates indicate financial strength - how much do they need to attract business

    • Effects of taxation, exchange rates if in foreign currency

8. The capital will be secure, but its value will decrease over time due to inflation. It is only increased by the addition of interest which will add to its value if kept in the account.

9. • The rate may fall in comparison with other investments

   • Penalties may be too restrictive to allow him to move his account

   • Interest rates might not always keep pace with inflation

   • No guarantee of a certain level of return

10. • If with a finance house owned by a bank there is less risk of returns not being made

   • Covered by the Deposit Protection Scheme

Unit 13

1. The investor pays a price for a gilt and receives payments of interest twice a year. The amount he pays for the gilt will depend on current prices on the stock exchange. The amount of interest depends on the coupon which is expressed as a percentage of the original value of the gilt which is £100. If the coupon is 6% the interest received will be £6. This amount will always be the same regardless of the current price of the gilt. If the gilt is held to its redemption date, the investor will receive £100. If he sells it before then, he will get the current price which may be more or less than £100.

2. Gilts with an option to convert from short-date to longer-date on a specified date. If prices of gilts are likely to rise in the near future, the investor may be wise to exercise his option and hopefully increase the value of his holding.

3. (a) Coupon 12%, price £100

   $$\text{Yield} = \frac{\text{coupon} \times 100}{\text{today's price}}$$

   i.e. $\frac{12 \times 100}{111}$ = 10.8%

   This shows Tom what the interest he receives is actually worth in relation to the price he paid.

   (b) Net redemption yield = net interest yield + (gross redemption yield - gross interest yield)

   Gross interest yield   = 10.8
   Tax liability   = 2.16
   Net interest yield   = 8.64

   8.64 + (6.93 - 10.8) = 4.77

   This tells Tom what the yield will be at redemption date, taking tax deducted into account.

(c) By grossing up the net redemption yield. In this case it will be

$$4.77 \times \frac{100}{80} = 5.96\%$$

4. The whole of the issue will be sold at the price at which it becomes fully taken up, e.g. minimum price is £95 for 100 units of stock. 50 are applied for at £95 and 50 at £96. All units will be sold at the price of £96.

5. By using a stockbroker, usually through a bank. The investor will give instructions to the bank on what he wants to buy and the amount to invest, and the bank will pass these details on to the stockbroker who will execute the deal on the stock exchange.

6. Tax is deducted at 20% at source. Non taxpayers can reclaim tax. Basic rate taxpayers have no further liability and higher rate taxpayers have to declare the interest on their tax returns and pay the additional 20%.

    If the gilts were bought through the NSSR, the interest would be paid gross so the non taxpayer would not need to reclaim any tax paid. The basic rate taxpayer would have to declare the interest on his tax return.

7. There is no CGT liability on redemption or sale. This will save George tax at 40% compared with other types of investments which do have a CGT liability. It is also useful as he has nearly used up his CGT exemption limit.

8. As he would pay tax at 40% on any interest payments he may prefer to buy a gilt with a low coupon which is below par value so that he can take a larger tax-free profit at redemption.

9. Julia will know the return she will make on her investment and that is guaranteed for a fixed period. However, the effect of interest rates on the amount received each year means that its value in real terms can vary and may fall in comparison with other forms of investment. The degree of risk depends on how important the income is to Julia. There is no risk of losing all of the original investment so gilts are safer than other forms of investment such as equities and Peps. However, the potential returns are not as great.

    Other forms of fixed-interest security may be slightly riskier than gilts as they are backed by less permanent and stable issuers than the government. However, they also offer a fixed return and capital security.

    They provide security of capital in a portfolio but must be held until redemption to ensure this. However, reward may not be as great as investments which are not capital secure.

10. Deposits - where an investor can deposit a large sum for a short term for an attractive rate of interest.

    Mortgage bonds - investment for fixed period, i.e. one to ten years.

Fixed-interest rate and capital returned at end of period.

Negotiable bonds - One-year fixed term and fixed-interest rate. Can be sold and bought on the stock exchange.

Local authority stocks - longer-term and fixed redemption date.

Unit 14

1. She will receive dividends which are taxable but the amount is not guaranteed. This is because they are based on a company's profits. In some years the company may decide not to pay any dividends at all. She may also make a profit (or a loss) if she sells the shares. There are no guarantees on dividends or share prices so returns cannot be predicted or relied on. She will need expert advice in what to do with her shares.

2. The preferred ordinary share carries voting rights which the preference share does not.

3. There are two reasons. Firstly, preference shareholders receive a fixed rate of dividend which is paid before any dividends are paid to ordinary shareholders. Secondly, they also have preference in the event of the company becoming wound up.

4. Gearing is calculated as share price divided by the warrant price, i.e. 125/25 = 5. This means that the investor can buy five times the number of warrants for 125p than shares. If the shares exceed the break even price, then the warrant will be worth exercising and the investor will have invested well in buying warrants.

5. He will receive a further 5,000 shares but the value of his existing shares will be reduced by half on the stock market. However, these shares may be more easy to sell because of their lower price.

6. (a) Keep it as he must either return it with his cheque if he takes up the issue, or he can sell it to someone else to take up the issue.

    (b) To raise funds.

    (c) A number of shareholders may decide to sell their rights and this could have an effect on confidence in the company and reduce the demand. Therefore, there would be an increase in the number of shares on the market in relation to the demand for them.

7. The original cost is increased by indexation, i.e. to take inflation into account,

thus reducing the gain made and so the tax liability.

8. By investing via a Pep.

9. Those which are secured by company assets will carry a lower risk than unsecured stock, e.g. debentures which are secured on specified assets of the company.

10. Gilts are issued by the government and have never failed to deliver so are less risky. However, they tend to offer a lower interest rate because of this security. Company fixed-interest securities tend to carry more risk because a company can collapse or fail to deliver the returns. They tend to offer higher interest rates because they carry more risk. If an investor holds fixed-interest securities they may not be as easy to sell as gilts. He would be best advised to only invest in large, well-known companies to avoid this problem and hopefully reduce the risk.

Unit 15

1. The right to buy or sell an asset at a fixed price on a fixed expiry date or before the end of a fixed period if American style option.

2. Put is an option to sell, call is an option to buy.

3. It is the possibility that the option is still worth exercising. It depends on the time period to option date and how close the option is to being in the money. Time value reduces rapidly the nearer it gets to expiry as there is less time for the option to increase in value.

4. Because the premium will be relatively low in relation to the share price. If the share price rises to more than the exercise price before the option date, the investor could make a substantial profit. However, he also carries the risk that the share price might not rise.

5. The buyer can choose whether to exercise an option depending on market conditions at the time. The writer must buy or sell if the option is exercised and has no choice over this. Therefore, he could make a loss if he has to buy or sell a share at a less profitable price than it could be bought or sold on the market.

6. A method of minimising losses by using options or futures. Instead of buying the underlying assets, the investor can buy appropriate futures or options depending on the investment requirement. Index derivatives are particularly

useful in this as they minimise the losses that are made on the actual shares by making gains on the changes in stock market indices which will not rise and fall as sharply.

7. An agreement to buy or sell an investment at a future date at a fixed price. The buyer must buy and the seller must sell.

8. (a) 3900 - 3750 = 150 x £25 = £3750

    (b) 3750 - 3700 = 50 x £25 = £1250

9. The investor has to buy or sell and can only avoid this by selling the future before its exercise date.

10. The exercise price of the future will have to be decided at the time the future is purchased. If the market is likely to rise then the investor will be able to make a profit, if the index is higher than predicted.

Unit 16

1. By investing in a unit trust rather than directly in the markets as an individual, risk is spread as holdings can be bought in a larger number of companies. Investment can be made in markets in which an individual might not have been able to invest due to the size of holding required for a good rate of return. Management charges and dealing commissions are usually lower. Investors also benefit from the knowledge of the fund managers.

2. A unit trust which invests in tracker funds usually has lower costs because less management of the fund is required. Since the fund performance is linked to an index which reflects the trends in the market, the fund cannot usually perform worse than the market in general.

3. Investment can be made on either a lump sum or regular savings basis within the trust's specified limits.

4. If a unit trust is purchased as a result of a 'cold call', the investor usually has a 14-day cancellation period following receipt of the cancellation notice. The investor will receive the lower of the original investment or the offer price at the time of cancellation. Cancellation rights do not apply if the investment is made on an execution-only basis by post or telephone, or through an authorised person with whom a client agreement exists.

5. Timothy will sign the renunciation form on the back of the certificate which

shows the price and total proceeds. He will then send this to the unit trust manager who will issue him with a cheque.

6. Franked investment income has already borne tax at 20% so there is no further tax liability.

7. Unfranked investment income is derived from cash, fixed-interest securities, overseas shares and all other sources. It is received gross and is subject to advance corporation tax at the basic rate, currently 20%.

8. A unit trust would probably not be a suitable investment for her because there is the risk that unit values can fall as well as rise.

9. The units can be sold at any time, giving him almost immediate access to his funds. He would normally receive a cheque after a week to take account of the administration.

10. Though the interest on a building society deposit account may equal or exceed the yield on a unit trust, over the long term the capital held in the building society account will not increase. In the case of the unit trust, the underlying capital value should grow and will produce an increasing level of income.

Unit 17

1. A Pep which currently produces a high yield may be at the expense of capital growth and future income.

2. The minimum investment level for an investment trust Pep may be higher than for a unit trust Pep but the charges are normally lower.

3. A corporate bond Pep can invest in the whole range of securities, corporate bonds, convertibles of UK companies, and preference shares of European companies.

4. The return on an index-tracker Pep is based on the movement of an index, often the FT-SE 100. Fluctuations in individual share prices tend to be smoothed out over the index as a whole and the index usually rises over the long term.

5. The shareholding could be transferred into a Pep up to the limit for the tax year. A CGT liability may arise because the holding has to be sold and then bought back by the Pep manager. The Pep manager may offer bed and

breakfasting as a means of reducing this. If the shares are a new issue which is transferred within 42 days of allocation, or if they were acquired through a SAYE scheme or a profit sharing scheme and transferred within 90 days of allocation or purchase, CGT liability can be avoided.

6. The plan manager offers a mix of investments which could be, for instance, shares and unit trusts, shares and investment trusts or unit trusts and investment trusts. The investor chooses the percentage of the total invested which is placed in each investment.

7. Corporate Peps could be suitable for the employees of the company who want a tax-efficient method of share purchase. They could also be suitable for outside specialist investors who are prepared to take the risk of being exposed to only one share.

8. The investor chooses the shares in which to invest and makes the buying and selling decisions. The plan manager provides guidance on these decisions.

9. The two main charges are the initial fee, normally 1-5%, and the annual fee, normally 1-2%. Dealing charges will be applied and an exit charge is occasionally applied when the plan is encashed; this mostly occurs when a unit trust Pep is encashed within the first three to five years.

10. A managed Pep tends to be considered as a lower risk than an equity Pep investing in fewer shares. A Pep investing in international markets tends to be more risky than Peps which invest solely in the UK. A corporate bond Pep is viewed as a relatively low-risk type of Pep because it is a fixed-interest investment which offers a high level of income. Single company Peps tend to be a more risky investment than general Peps.

Unit 18

1. An investment trust is not a trust but a limited company, subject to the provisions of the Companies Act like any other limited company. Unlike a unit trust, an investment trust is 'closed-end' since it issues a fixed number of shares.

2. About 70% or more of the company's income must be derived wholly or mainly from securities. Other than holdings in another approved investment trust, no single holding must represent more than 15% of the investment trust company's investments. Profits from the sale of investments cannot be distributed as dividends.

3. A minimum of five directors usually run the company. They often employ a

management company to make investment decisions on their behalf, with regular reviews of these decisions. If a self-managed trust is involved, the directors make the investment decisions themselves. The type of areas in which the management company could become involved include accountancy, administration, registration and providing advice when a new trust is set up.

4. Long-term finance can be raised by issuing preference shares, debentures and other loan stock. Short-term finance can be raised by overdraft or loan from a bank in sterling or foreign currency.

5. Dividends are received net of 20% tax and accompanied by a tax credit. Non taxpayers may reclaim the tax deducted. Lower and basic rate taxpayers have no further liability. Higher rate taxpayers have an additional tax liability of 20%.

6. Gains made when the investor sells shares may be liable to CGT.

7. Unfranked income must be declared and corporation tax will become payable. This liability may be reduced by offsetting expenses such as loan interest against it.

8. There is no CGT liability on the sale of shares within the trust.

9. The value of the underlying shares might rise or fall and the discount may narrow or widen.

10. Investment trusts tend to be most suitable for investors who are prepared to take a medium to high risk and who have some knowledge and experience of the investment market.

Unit 19

1. Supply and demand, location and condition.

2. That the value of the Pep will be insufficient to repay the loan at the end of the mortgage term.

3. Because a valuation is needed at the time an investment is made into the fund to set unit prices and also at the time of withdrawal to determine how much the units are worth.

4.   Tax relief is available at the investor's highest rate on investment in buildings but not land.

5.   Physicals are bought and sold for immediate delivery whereas futures are bought or sold for delivery at a date in the future.

6.   If he reinvests the chargeable gain (which may be reduced to £3,700 after deducting the annual exemption) into an EIS he will not be liable for CGT until he disposes of his EIS shares. This may be at a time when he has no other chargeable gains or is a basic rate taxpayer.

7.   (a) 20%, i.e. £8,000.
      (b) None - they are exempt.
      (c) To encourage investment in them.

8.   It is exempt from corporation tax and CGT.

9.   (a) At least £250,000 excluding main residence. At least 60% of this must be in cash, quoted securities or in bank or building society accounts.

      (a) Premium income from insurance underwriting and investment income from syndicates' reserves.

10.   Speculative investors with knowledge of currency market. Currency changes and exchange rates make this a volatile market. For this reason, most investors are institutions, it is unlikely that individuals will invest in the Forex market.

Unit 20

1.   Diversifying the portfolio allows the investor access to other markets than that of the UK, for example, each with its own set of economic influences in addition to those present in a global marketplace. Inflation, interest rates and industrial output will all affect the local market in a different way to their effect on the investor's base market.

2.   Individual markets experience different levels of inflation, rampant inflation can lead to weakening of the market's value as the currency and economy depreciates. Political influences on the market also subject investments to risk, as different political parties may not have positive views of foreign investment and make the climate less attractive to investors. Likewise, currency exchange rates and controls may also pose an adverse risk to offshore investors.

3. Offshore deposit accounts do not provide the same compensatory arrangements to their onshore counterparts in the event of the provider's insolvency, nor do interest rates necessarily reflect the same influences as those in the UK. In the event of the reimposition of exchange controls the investor may not be able to gain easy access to his funds, thus perhaps typing them into less attractive accounts for the long term.

4. Ucits' assets are restricted, in that they may not invest directly into property or commodities, for example. The case is the same for UK unit trusts.

5. A switch within an offshore bond creates a chargeable event on which a gain may arise. The onshore bond is not subject to this situation, the switch is an internal transfer and may experience an administrative charge, with any chargeable event only occurring on a partial surrender, in excess of the cumulative annual 5% allowance.

6. Income. Due to most of the assets being held in government securities and exempt from income tax on their coupon distributions, the income paid out can be more tax-efficient, especially as these are distributor funds on which income tax may otherwise be payable.

7. Tax is due under Schedule D Case VI, regardless of whether it is remitted to the UK or not.

8. Under double taxation agreements between the UK government and those of other countries, where an investor investing offshore creates a tax liability, tax will usually only be paid in one of the two countries.

9. Any assets belonging to a UK domiciled investor are subject to IHT, no matter where the assets are situated, as are any assets located in the UK for any investor, regardless of their country of domicile.

10. Section 739 relates to offshore investments in that it concerns income paid to someone outside the UK from assets that have been transferred offshore. Where the individual was originally a UK resident, for example, moved offshore and subsequently transferred their assets, the Inland Revenue will view this as an attempt to avoid paying taxes due, and will subject the income to tax as if the individual in receipt of the income is ordinarily UK resident.

Unit 21

1. £25 a month or £270 a year.

2. A way of releasing the value of a life policy where someone is terminally ill.

Usually they sell the policy to a third party (a viatical company). When the life assured dies, the third party claims the sum assured from the insurance company.

3.   Family income benefit - provides an income on death of first to die.

Mortgage protection - will repay mortgage if one partner dies.

Convertible term may also be useful if circumstances likely to change in future.

Flexible whole life - cover can be adapted as circumstances change. Will be a more expensive option.

4.   Usually on diagnosis of an insured condition.

5.   Because the underlying investments have already been taxed at 20%.

6.   Gain will be top-sliced, i.e. £9,000 divided by 5 = £1,800.
This is added to income, i.e. £24,000 plus £1,800 = £25,800.
After deducting basic rate threshold, this leaves £300 to be taxed at marginal rate tax.
£300 x 5 = £1,500 @ 16% = £240 tax to pay.

7.   If all the proceeds are used as a single premium to a new policy, they will not be taxed. If part are taken as cash, that element will be liable to tax.

8.   (a) Gain x 2/10ths (1/5th).

(b) The gain will be taxed at 40% in his hands. An offshore policy will be taxed at 16% when paid to him (having had tax at 20% already deducted at source) so may produce a higher net gain.

9.   He will be taxed through PAYE on the payments.

10.   Tax advantages of personal pension include fund builds up free of income tax and CGT so rolls up quicker than other types of taxable investment. Contributions receive tax relief. Part of benefits can be taken tax-free (lump sum). Need to compare with tax treatment of alternative investments to decide which will give best return. Variety of investment choice available under pension plan but will incur charges.

Glossary

'A' shares: Ordinary shares where the holder does not normally have voting rights.

Accrued interest: Interest that is due but has not been paid or received.

Accumulation and maintenance trusts: These are a special kind of discretionary trust, giving flexibility to a parent or grandparent in providing funds for the benefit of children.

Accumulation units: In the majority of instances normally used for unit trusts or life assurance unit-linked funds where interest and dividends are added on or reinvested to increase the value of the unit.

Actuary: A person who is skilled in evaluating and assessing risks, principally those of life assurance companies and pension funds.

Additional voluntary contributions (AVCs): A method whereby an employee can make extra contributions to his employer's pension scheme in order to secure additional pension benefits on retirement. These contributions qualify for certain tax incentives.

Advance corporation tax (ACT): Companies have to pay ACT on their dividends and other qualifying distributions, which is taken into account when corporation tax is due.

Age allowance: An additional income tax allowance for a single person or married couple where one of the parties is over the age of 65 years. Increases at age 75.

Alternative investment market (AIM): Market for smaller, younger, unquoted companies. Generally higher risk because of the small size of the companies involved and the limited liquidity.

Annualised percentage rate (APR): Primarily used for borrowing rates. The total gross annual interest charges on capital outstanding over the period of the loan or investment.

Annuity: A guaranteed regular income payment that continues for life unless otherwise restricted.

Arbitrage: The practice of trading on two different markets in an attempt to profit from the difference in prices of the same type of contract, i.e. trading on Liffe in London and CBOT in Chicago on US T-Bonds.

Asset value: The value of a company after the liabilities have been deducted from the tangible assets.

Authorised unit trust: A unit trust that the Department of Trade and Industry has sanctioned under the terms of the Prevention of Fraud (Investments) Act 1958.

Back-to-back arrangement: An investment plan using an annuity in conjunction with a life assurance policy.

Balance sheet: A statement from a company showing its financial position on a given date. This is normally the last day of a company accounting period.

Bare trust: A trust in which the trustee has no obligation except to hand over the trust property to a person entitled to it, at the latter's request, normally when the beneficiary 'comes of age'.

Bear market: A weak or falling market.

Bed and breakfast: The selling of an asset on one day and buying it back the next day in order to establish the amount of capital gain or loss for tax purposes after utilising the annual CGT allowance.

Beneficiary: A person entitled to benefit from a trust.

Benefit in kind: The value of additional benefits from an employer, such as the availability of a car, which are taxable, generally by an alteration in PAYE tax code.

Best advice: The Financial Services Act 1986 deems it mandatory that a customer receives recommendations from an adviser that are based upon the customers needs.

Bid price: The price of shares or stock that a market maker will be prepared to buy at.

Bid-offer spread: The difference between the buying price and selling price of a share or unit.

Blue chip: An investment of stock or shares that is fundamentally solid.

Bonds: An alternative name for fixed-interest securities, principally those issued by governments.

Bonuses: Amounts issued to the policyholders of with-profits life assurance policies. They are dependent on the profitability of the life assurance company and are at the discretion of the company.

Broker: A person who acts as the middleman between the seller and buyer of stocks and shares.

Broker/dealer: A dealer in stocks and shares who buys them and holds them for resale. They are also involved in the marketing of stocks and shares on the behalf of customers.

Bull market: A rising market.

Call option: The right (but not obligation) to buy a stated amount of securities at a specified price during a specified period.

Capital gains tax (CGT): A tax on certain realised capital profits.

Certificate: A document that proves title in registered stock or shares. This document has, in the majority of circumstances, no monetary value.

Chargeable event: An action such as the selling of a share which is likely to give rise to income tax, capital gains tax or inheritance tax.

Chargeable transfers: Gifts which are not free or potentially exempt from inheritance tax. Tax may be due at the time of the gift. Chargeable transfers are largely gifts to companies and certain types of discretionary trust.

Chattels: Tangible, moveable property, i.e. coins, furniture, jewellery, works of art and motor vehicles.

Close company: A company that is under the control of not more than five people or its directors.

Commodities: This normally refers to raw materials and food stuffs, such as metals or corn, rice, coffee etc. that are traded in large quantities for immediate or future delivery.

Composite rate tax (CRT): An amount of tax deducted at source, at a fixed rate on most short-term deposits.

Controlling director (20% director): A director who, alone or together with one or more associates, owns or is able to control, directly or indirectly, 20% or more of the ordinary shares of the company.

Corporation tax: The level of tax that a company is charged on its profits.

Coupon (1): Voucher attached to a bearer security, entitling the holder to collect a dividend or interest payment.

Coupon (2): Rate of interest on a fixed-interest security e.g. 5% coupon pays interest of 5% p.a. on face value of the stock.

Crest: The Bank of England's paperless share settlement system.

Cum ('with'): Used to describe a security which entitles the purchaser to a forthcoming dividend or issue.

Debenture: A charge on an asset of a company normally buildings, plant, equipment and machinery.

Deed of covenant: A deed containing an undertaking to pay an agreed amount over an agreed period. Certain tax advantages can be obtained through the use of covenants, particularly in the case of four-year covenants in favour of charities.

Deferred annuity: An annuity which will issue income payments at a future date.

Derivative: A security with a price derived from, and dependent on the price of an underlying asset.

Dividend: The distribution of company profits to the shareholders. The profits are declared net of tax and the shareholder receives a tax credit.

Dividend yield: Annual grossed-up dividend per share, expressed as a percentage of the current share price.

Domicile: Domicile is the country regarded as an individual's permanent home. Can be changed from domicile of origin (birthplace) to domicile of choice.

Double taxation agreement: Agreement between two countries to prevent income earned in one country being taxed in both countries where a person lives in another country.

Earnings: The net profits of a company used for the ordinary shareholders which can be either declared as a dividend or kept within the company.

Earnings yield: Earnings per share divided by the price per share, reciprocal of the price-earnings ratio.

Emerging markets: Countries whose economies are developing. Present higher risk.

Endowment: A form of life assurance, with or without-profits, proceeds paid out at a pre agreed date, or on earlier death.

Equity: The value of the assets of a company after the deduction of all debts and other charges registered on the asset.

Equity-linked: Term that is used to describe a type of insurance policy that has its final worth linked to the performance of a fund or ordinary shares.

Estate: The property left by a person on death.

Ex ('without'): Used to describe a security which entitles the vendor to receive a forthcoming dividend or issue.

Execution-only: A term that is used to establish the relationship between a customer and a financial adviser. The adviser will only act on the instructions of the customer and will not provide any advice.

Financial adviser: An individual who provides financial advice on savings, pensions and investments who is regulated by his own self-regulating body.

Financial Services Act 1986 (FSA): Act regulating the provision of financial services to private investors.

Flat yield: Yield on a stock ignoring any profit or loss to redemption.

Flotation: A new company joining the stock market where its shares can be traded freely by members of the public.

Forex: Foreign exchange. Exchanging the money of one country for that of another.

Franked income: Relates to dividends received by one company from another that has paid corporation tax on its profits.

Free-standing additional voluntary contributions (FSAVC): A method whereby an employed person can make extra contributions to a pension scheme that is not operated by his employer. These extra contributions will help to secure additional pension benefits on retirement.

FT-SE All Share Index: The major UK capitalisation-weighted index consisting of over 900 shares.

FT-SE 100 Index: Index of the 100 largest London listed stock.

Fund manager: An appointed member of staff employed by a company whose day to day activity is involved with the management of investment funds.

Fund of funds: Investment fund (e.g. unit trust) which invests in other specialist funds within the group.

Futures: An operation which is often practised by speculators who buy and sell contracts for the delivery or purchase of assets at a future date. These contracts are often linked to the commodities markets.

Gearing: The relationship of loan capital and preference capital to the ordinary or total capital of a company. High gearing means debts are high in relation to equity capital.

Gilts: Fixed-interest securities issued by the UK government.

Gilt-edged market makers (Gemms): Dealers in gilts only, often subsidiaries of larger securities houses.

Gross: A figure that that normally relates to income where tax has not been deducted.

Gross redemption yield: The net redemption yield grossed up at the investor's marginal rate of tax to provide a comparison with any investments which declare interest before tax has been deducted.

Growth: A net increase sometimes referred to as capital gain on an asset.

Guaranteed income bond: Normally issued by life assurance companies which provide the investor with a fixed income and the return of his capital at the end of an agreed period of time.

Hedging: A method by which an investor can protect himself against possible loss by buying investments at a fixed price for delivery later.

Independent financial adviser (IFA): An adviser who acts as the agent of the customer and may offer the products of any provider.

Independent taxation: From 6 April 1990 married couples have been treated as separate individuals for tax purposes.

Index fund: A fund designed to replicate a stock market index in terms of constituents and performance.

Index-linked gilts: A special class of UK gilt which is indexed to the retail prices index.

Index option: An option based on a stock market index.

Indexation allowance: The term used for the revaluation of the original cost of an asset or item of expenditure to take account of the increase in the retail prices index between the month of acquisition or expenditure and the month of disposal when calculating a capital gain.

Indirect taxation: This is a tax on expenditure as opposed to personal taxation.

Inheritance tax (IHT): A capital tax applied to assets left at death, and gifts made within seven years of death.

Insider dealing: The buying or selling of any security or option on the basis of privileged price sensitive information. A criminal offence under the Companies Securities (Insider Dealing) Act 1985.

Inter-dealers: Brokers who act as intermediaries between dealers in government securities.

Intestacy: Applies in England and Wales when a person dies without making a will.

Investment Management Regulatory Authority (IMRO): A self-regulating organisation acting as the lead regulator for investment management and collective investment schemes.

Investment trust: A company investing in other companies as its principal business.

Irredeemable: A stock which, by its terms of issue, cannot be repaid. Used loosely to describe a stock with no final redemption date.

Joint life assurance: A life assurance which is paid out on the first or second death of the lives assured.

Key man assurance: A life assurance policy taken out by a company on an individual whose death would create a financial loss for his employer or partners.

Leasehold: Property including land which is subject to a lease from the freeholder.

Liffe: The London International Financial Futures and Options Exchange where almost all of the UK's equity and fixed-interest derivatives are traded.

Liquidity: The ease at which assets can be transferred into cash.

Long-dated: Describes a stock with generally more than 15 years to redemption.

Lower rate tax: 20%, payable on the first £3,900 of taxable income.

Managed bonds: These are life assurance policies that are linked to a fund that is made up of equity, property and fixed-interest elements.

Managed fund: A fund which is under the control of an investment manager.

Market maker: A stock exchange member firm which is obliged to buy and sell the securities in which it is registered.

Market value: The amount which an asset could be sold for on the open market. It is dependent on the supply and demand of that asset at the time of the proposed sale.

Maturity: The final redemption date of stock, or end of term of a bond or life assurance policy.

Medium-dated: Describes a stock with between five and 15 years to redemption.

Money market: This is the market where institutions can lodge or borrow money for a short period of time at various rates of interest.

Mortgage: A loan normally provided for the purchase of land or buildings. The loan is then secured on the land or buildings.

Mortgage interest relief at source (Miras): The system that allows for tax relief on mortgage interest to be deducted by the borrower from payments made to the lender.

Mutual company: A company with no shareholders that is owned by its members. Profits are distributed amongst members.

Mutual life assurance company: All profits from the company are distributed to the policyholders.

National Insurance: A fund that was set up to provide benefits on sickness or unemployment. The contributions fund the National Health Service and are paid by those earning above a certain minimum income level and by employers.

Net asset value: The value of a company after all debts have been paid.

Net profit: The profit of a company after all expenses, costs and depreciation have been taken into consideration. This is calculated prior to any dividends being made.

Net redemption yield: Yield to redemption after deducting income tax and capital gains tax (if any).

Net worth: The value of the share capital of a company.

Nominal price: A figure that is used where no trade price is available or the buyers and sellers prices are a long way apart.

Nominee: An individual or institution who has shares or investments registered in their name but they may not necessarily be the owners of those shares or investments.

Occupational pension: The name for a pension gained as a result of salaried employment.

Offer for sale: A company's shares being made available to the public by the sponsor of the issue.

Offer price: The price that an asset is being offered for sale and the price that a buyer will a deal on.

Offshore funds: These are funds that operate from tax havens outside the UK.

Open-ended investment companies (Oeics): Collective investment schemes investing in transferable securities - similar to unit trusts but with a corporate (rather than trust) form.

Options: The right to buy or sell the investment at a pre agreed price at some time in the future.

Ordinary residence: The country where a person is habitually resident.

Ordinary shares: The type of share that gives the holder an entitlement to the company's earnings.

P11D: The benefits and expenses payments for directors and employees earning £8,500 per annum or more. A P11D employee is charged to tax on all expenses, payments received and on the cash equivalent of virtually all benefits provided.

Paid-up: The term given to the situation when premiums to a life assurance policy or pension plan cease before the maturity date and the policy is not cashed in.

Par: The nominal value of stocks or shares.

PAYE: The system that employers use to deduct tax from an employee's earnings and pay the tax direct to the Inland Revenue.

Pension: An income paid to an individual at retirement. This income can be generated from the state, a company pension or a private pension plan.

Pension age: Pension age is normally the age at which the state pension commences. Also refers to the date a private arrangement will commence payment.

Permanent health insurance: A policy designed to replace income in the event of prolonged sickness of the policyholder.

Personal allowances: A part of a person's income which is not taxed. The amount depends on personal circumstances.

Personal equity plan (PEP): Allows investors tax-free investment in shares and a variety of collective investment schemes.

Personal Investment Authority (PIA): A self-regulating organisation acting as lead regulator for marketing of packaged products and other investment business done with or directly for private investors.

Portfolio: The total range of investments within an individual fund, or belonging to an individual investor.

Pound cost averaging: The practice whereby a fixed sum is allocated for the purchase of a particular investment on a monthly or other periodic basis, and so averages out the fluctuations in purchase prices.

Preference share: Type of share carrying a fixed-income return. Ranking in priority to ordinary shares for both earnings and assets.

Price/earnings ratio: The ratio of the price of a share to the last published (net) earnings per share for a trading period.

Profit and loss: A part of a set of company's accounts which shows the income and expenditure over a given period.

Put option: The right (but not obligation) to sell a stated amount of securities at a specified price during a specified period.

Qualifying policy: A policy that meets certain requirements, e.g. term of 10 years, and so produces tax-free benefits.

Redeemable: Describes a stock with a redemption date.

Redemption yield: Income return and annual profit or loss to redemption as a percentage of the cost of a dated stock.

Repayment mortgage: A mortgage where capital and interest are paid over a period of time.

Residence: The country where an individual is living in a particular tax year.

Retail prices index (RPI): The index measuring rises in the cost of goods and services over a period of time. Often used as the basis for level of increase in investment returns.

Reversionary bonus: This represents an amount added to a with-profits life assurance policy and is based on the profitability of the life assurance company.

Rights issue: An invitation to existing shareholders to purchase new shares, in a fixed ratio to those already held, at a price which is generally below the market price of the old shares.

Risk management: The removal or reduction of threats to assets, earnings and people, by identifying and assessing the risks and then controlling the risks, either financially (e.g. through insurance) or physically.

Risk profile: The degree of risk offered by an investment. Also used to describe an investor's particular attitude to risk.

Schedules: Classification of income for the calculation and payment of tax.

Scrip issue: An issue of shares, fully paid to existing holders, with no payments to be made, representing an increase in issued capital by converting reserves into shares and only arising from an accounting change. Also called bonus or capitalisation issue.

Securities and Futures Authority (SFA): A self-regulating organisation acting as the lead regulator for activities relating to dealings in financial and commodities futures, options and stock exchange securities.

Securities and Investments Board (SIB): The agency appointed by the government under the Financial Services Act 1986 to oversee the regulation of the investment industry.

Self-assessment: From 1996-97 taxpayers will be able to self-assess their own income and capital gains tax, or calculations may be conducted by the Revenue if returns are received by 3 September after the end of the tax year.

Self-regulating organisation (SRO): An organisation that is approved by the Securities and Investments Board, responsible for monitoring the conduct of investment business by its members.

Settlement: A disposition of land or other property made by deed, will or, very rarely, by statute.

Settlor: Person who creates a trust or settlement and transfers assets into it.

Share capital: The total amount of share and loan stock issued or to be issued by a limited company.

Short-dated: Stock that is redeemable within five years.

Societes d'Investissement a Capital Variable (SICAV): Closed-end collective investment funds run on a corporate basis, with no fixed capital limits.

Speculative risk: A risky purchase of an investment which may go up or down in value. Can produce high rewards or great losses.

Split-level trust: An investment trust with more than one type of share capital, each entitled to a different part of the profits of the trust.

Stamp duty: The tax on legal documents such as the sale or purchase of shares or the conveyance of a property to a new owner.

State earnings related pension (Serps): This is an earnings related top-up to the basic state pension and is paid for by an additional amount of National Insurance contributions.

Stock exchange: The place where stocks and shares are bought and sold.

Sum assured: A sum that is guaranteed to be paid out from a life assurance policy at maturity or on death of the policyholder.

Surrender value: The surrender value is the current value of life assurance policy investment less any penalties chargeable.

Tax credit: A dividend slip that confirms that the income has been paid less tax at the basic rate.

Tax exempt special savings account (Tessa): A deposit account available where the amount invested is exempt from tax if the capital is not withdrawn within a five-year period.

Tax schedules: The different types of earnings separated by the Inland Revenue by the use of letter codes.

Tax shelter: A form of investment that is legitimately sheltered from tax.

Term assurance: An insurance policy taken out for a fixed period. If death occurs during the period the sum assured is fully paid out. In the event of the policyholder surviving the fixed period nothing is payable by the insurers.

Terminal bonus: A bonus that is added to with-profits life assurance when a policy matures. The value of the bonus depends on the profits made by the life office or its investment funds and is not guaranteed.

Tied agent: An adviser who can only provide investment advice on his employer's range of products.

Top-slicing: A term used for assessing the rate of tax payable on a chargeable gain occurring within a life assurance policy.

Trust: A trust, sometimes called a settlement, arises when someone transfers assets to trustees who hold them, and the income from them, for the benefit of one or more persons.

Trust deed: Document defining powers of trustee and objects of a trust. May be a will or deed.

Trustee: An individual or company appointed to carry out the purposes of a trust, in accordance with the provisions of the trust and general principles of trust law.

Undated: No fixed date for redemption.

Undertakings for collective investments in transferable securities (Ucits): A collective fund which meets specified rules enabling it to be marketed in EC member states.

Unearned income: Money received from interest or dividends. Income that does not arise from employment.

Unfranked income: Interest paid out of moneys which have not borne corporation tax.

Unit trust: An indirect investment in stocks and shares managed on behalf of investors, who buy units in the trust and as a result of the performance of the unit trust the value of their units increases or decreases.

US Treasury bonds (US T-Bonds): The American equivalent of the UK's long-term gilt contract, typically dated around 30 years.

Variable Capital Company (VCC): Closed-end, collective investment funds run on a corporate basis, with no fixed capital limits.

Venture capital trusts (VCT): Invest in small, unquoted trading companies which can include companies on the alternative investment market, and operate like conventional investment trusts. Tax relief on the purchase of shares at 20%, free of income and capital gains tax.

Warrant: A negotiable right to subscribe for stock or shares at some time in the future.

Whole life: A life assurance contract where premiums are paid for life or up to a certain age with an assured benefit on death when it occurs.

Will: A legal document where someone states what should happen to their assets when they die.

Winding up: Liquidation of a company.

Working capital: The current assets of a company minus current liabilities.

Yield: Return on an investment shown as a percentage of the money invested.

Zero-coupon bond: A bond which carries no interest but is issued at discount which provides a capital gain when redeemed at face value.

Index